Cambridge Imperial and Post-Colonial Studies Series

Series Editors
Richard Drayton
Department of History
King's College London
London, UK

Saul Dubow
Magdalene College
University of Cambridge
Cambridge, UK

The Cambridge Imperial and Post-Colonial Studies series is a well-established collection of over 100 volumes focussing on empires in world history and on the societies and cultures that emerged from, and challenged, colonial rule. The collection includes transnational, comparative and connective studies, as well as works addressing the ways in which particular regions or nations interact with global forces. In its formative years, the series focused on the British Empire and Commonwealth, but there is now no imperial system, period of human history or part of the world that lies outside of its compass. While we particularly welcome the first monographs of young researchers, we also seek major studies by more senior scholars, and welcome collections of essays with a strong thematic focus that help to set new research agendas. As well as history, the series includes work on politics, economics, culture, archaeology, literature, science, art, medicine, and war. Our aim is to collect the most exciting new scholarship on world history and to make this available to a broad scholarly readership in a timely manner.

More information about this series at
http://www.palgrave.com/gp/series/13937

Véronique Dimier • Sarah Stockwell
Editors

The Business of Development in Post-Colonial Africa

palgrave
macmillan

Editors
Véronique Dimier
Faculty of Philosophy and
Social Science
Université Libre de Bruxelles
Bruxelles, Belgium

Sarah Stockwell
Department of History
King's College London
London, UK

ISSN 2635-1633   ISSN 2635-1641   (electronic)
Cambridge Imperial and Post-Colonial Studies Series
ISBN 978-3-030-51105-0   ISBN 978-3-030-51106-7   (eBook)
https://doi.org/10.1007/978-3-030-51106-7

Cover illustration: Peter Jordan / Alamy Stock Photo
Cover design by eStudio Calamar

This Palgrave Macmillan imprint is published by the registered company Springer Nature
Switzerland AG.
The registered company address is: Gewerbestrasse 11, 6330 Cham, Switzerland

ACKNOWLEDGEMENTS

This volume is the outcome of a conference which was organised by Véronique Dimier at the University of Strasbourg in October 2017 and financed through the Gutenberg Chair. We are most grateful to the local councils of the Alsace Region, which funded the chair, and to SAGE, the research Centre on Society, Stakeholders and Government in Europe, at the University of Strasbourg, which hosted the conference. We are especially grateful to Hélène Michel, whose support was invaluable, to the team of SAGE for their logistical help and to the REPI (Recherche et Etudes en Politique Internationale, ULB) for financial help relating to the use of the photo on the front cover. We are also grateful to Cormac McMahon, Jan Yves Bart and Antony Patrinos for their assistance with translating several chapters into English, as well as to Arthur Burns for all his support. We would also like to express our sincere thanks to the series editors, the anonymous readers and to our editors at Palgrave, and particularly to Molly Beck and Joseph Johnson.

CONTENTS

ABBREVIATIONS

AAMS	Associated African and Malagasy States.
ACP	African Caribbean Pacific Group of States.
AEF	Afrique Équatoriale Française.
AFD	Agence française de développement.
Ascoop	Association coopérative.
BAO	Banque de l'Afrique Occidentale.
BAP	Bureau algérien des pétroles.
BCEAC	Banque centrale des États d'Afrique Centrale.
BDI	Bundesverband der Deutschen Industrie.
BDPA	Bureau pour le développement de la production agricole.
BIDI	Banque ivoirienne de développement industriel.
BNDA	Banque nationale de développement agricole de Côte d'Ivoire.
BP	British Petroleum.
BRP	Bureau de recherche de pétrole.
CCCE	Caisse centrale de coopération économique.
CCFL	Caisse centrale de la France libre.
CCFOM	Caisse centrale de la France d'outre-mer.
CDA	Colonial Development Act.
CDC	Colonial/Commonwealth Development Corporation.
CDI	Centre de développement industriel/Centre for Industrial Development.
CEFBS/CEFEB	Center of Economic, Financial and Banking Studies.
CEP	Compagnie d'exploitation pétrolière.
CFAO	Compagnie française d'Afrique Occidentale.
CFCI	Compagnie française de Côte d'Ivoire.
CFP	Compagnie française de pétrole.

CIAN	Conseil des investisseurs en Afrique Noire.
CNPF	Conseil national du patronat français.
CRAN	Compagnie raffinage Afrique Nord.
CREDICODI	Credit of Côte d'Ivoire.
CRO	Commonwealth Relations Office (UK).
DAC/CAD	Development Assistance Committee.
DEC	Direction de l'énergie et des carburants.
DLR	Thomas De La Rue and Company Ltd.
DRC	Democratic Republic of Congo.
EAA	East Africa Association.
EAI	East African Industries Ltd.
EDF	European Development Fund.
EEC	European Economic Community.
EIB	European Investment Bank.
ENI	Ente Nazionale Idrocarburi.
ERP	European Recovery Programme.
EUROPRED	Groupement européen de programmation et d'études générales de développement.
FAC (ACF)	Fonds d'aide et de coopération.
FBI	Federation of British Industries
FCCC	Federation of Commonwealth Chambers of Commerce.
FCCIEA	Federation of Chambers of Commerce and Industry of East Africa.
FIDES/IFESD	Fonds d'investissement pour le développement économique et social.
FLN	Front de libération nationale.
GATT	General Agreement on Tariffs and Trade.
GETAF	Groupement belge pour les études de développement en Afrique.
GIDEC	Groupement international d'études pour le développement du Congo.
IAP	Institut Algérien du pétrole.
IEAEC	Institut d'émission d'Afrique Équatoriale et du Cameroun.
IRHO	Institut de recherches pour les huiles et oléagineux.
MENA	Middle East and North Africa Area.
NCNC	National Council of Nigeria and the Cameroons.
NGO	Non-Governmental Organisation.
NIP	National Indicative Programmes.
NSPMC	Nigerian Security Printing and Minting Company Ltd.
OAS	Organisation de l'armée secrète.
ODA	Official Development Assistance.
OECD	Organisation for Economic Co-operation and Development.

OPEC	Organisation of Petroleum Exporting Countries.
ORSTOM	Office de la recherche scientifique et technique d'outre-mer.
PDCI	Parti démocratique de Côte d'Ivoire.
SAFRAP	Société anonyme française des recherches et d'exploration de pétroles.
SCAF	Compagnie des scieries africaines.
SCC	Social Credit Companies.
SCET	Société centrale pour l'équipement du territoire.
SCOA	Société commerciale de l'Ouest Africain.
SECI	Société d'équipement de la Côte d'Ivoire.
SEDES	Société d'études pour le développement économique et social.
SEMA	Société d'études mathématiques appliquées.
SICOGI	Société ivoirienne de construction et gestion immobilière.
SMI/E	Small and Medium-Sized Industries/Enterprises
SNREPAL	Société nationale de recherche et d'exploitation de pétrole en Algérie.
SOGEFIHA	Société de gestion financière de l'habitat.
SONAFI	Société nationale de financement.
SONATRACH	Société nationale pour la recherche, la production, le transport, la transformation, et la commercialisation des hydrocarbures.
SOPROGI	Société de promotion et de gestion industrielle.
SRA	Société de la raffinerie d'Alger.
SRI	Stanford Research Institution.
SUCCI	Société d'urbanisme et de construction de la Côte d'Ivoire.
TA	Tanganyika Association.
TE	Traction et électricité/Tractionel.
TPN	The Textile Printers of Nigeria Ltd.
UAC	United Africa Company Ltd.
UMHK	Union minière du Haut Katanga.
UN	United Nations.
UNICE	Union of Industrial and Employers' Confederations of Europe.
UNIDO	United Nations Industrial Development Organisation.
WAMU	Western Africa Monetary Union.

Notes on Contributors

Abou B. Bamba teaches History and Africana Studies at Gettysburg College in Pennsylvania, USA. His research is on the diplomatic and transnational relations among the United States, France and Francophone Africa. His first book, *African Miracle, African Mirage: Transnational Politics and the Paradox of Modernization in Ivory Coast* (Ohio University Press, 2016), deals with the interactions among Americans, French and Ivorians over modernisation and socio-political changes in Ivory Coast during the latter's Thirty Glorious Years (1951–1981). This book was a finalist for the 2018 Fage & Oliver Prize of the African Studies Association of the United Kingdom. He is working on two new projects, including one that extends his analysis of US transnationalism to other countries in French-speaking Africa and one that interrogates the presence of French expatriates and residents in postcolonial Ivory Coast.

Poppy Cullen is Lecturer in International History at the University of Loughborough. From 2015 to 2018 she was a lecturer and teaching associate at the University of Cambridge. She was involved in the project 'Afterlives of Empire: Thinking Forward through an Imperial Past' where her research focused on decolonisation and non-governmental organisations in Africa. She is the author of *Kenya and Britain after Independence: Beyond Neo-Colonialism* (Palgrave Macmillan, 2017). She has also published in journals including *Cold War History*, *International History Review* and the *Journal of Imperial and Commonwealth History*.

Andrew Dilley is Senior Lecturer in Imperial and Global History at the University of Aberdeen. He has published extensively on the politics and economics of the British empire, including his first monograph *Finance, Politics and Imperialism: Australia, Canada, and the City of London, c.1899–1914*, published by Palgrave Macmillan in 2010. From 2015 to 2017 he held an AHRC Early Career Fellowship, 'Commerce and the Commonwealth: Business Associations, Political Culture, and Governance, 1886–1975' which supported the research presented in this volume. He is under contract with Oxford University Press to write a monograph, entitled *Commerce and the Commonwealth*.

Véronique Dimier is Associate Professor at the Université Libre de Bruxelles. She held the Chaire Gutenberg in 2015 at SAGE, the Research Centre on Society, Stakeholders and Government in Europe, at the University of Strasbourg. She previously held several other fellowships: the Braudel Fellowship, at the European University Institute in Firenze (2014), Fulbright at the University of New York (2007), Deakin Fellowship (2000) and Marie Curie (2001–2003) at the University of Oxford, St Antony's College. She has published *Le Gouvernement des Colonies, Regards Croisés Franco-Britanniques* (PUB, 2004) and *The Invention of a European Development Bureaucracy: Recycling Empire* (Palgrave, 2014).

Chris Minton completed his PhD 'A partner in progress? Shell-BP's role in Nigeria during the transition to independence, 1946–1967' at the University of Nottingham in 2019. He was a recipient of the John Robinson PhD Studentship in History. His contribution to this book is based on findings from the first two chapters of his PhD thesis.

Marta Musso is a historian working on energy history and digital history. She studies the relation between economic actors, states and international diplomacy, as well as new methods of historical research and heritage preservation in a digital environment. She holds a PhD in Economic History from the University of Cambridge and she was Max Weber Fellow at the European University Institute. She is a teaching fellow at King's College London, and Research Manager for Archives Portal Europe. She is also president of Eogan, the network of oil and gas archives. She has published on the oil politics of the Mediterranean, particularly France and Algeria, energy history and web history.

François Pacquement is presently in charge of History in the French development agency Agence Française de Développement (AFD), where he began working in the late 1970s. He alternated fieldwork with secondments to the Treasury, the European Commission and the Ministry of

Foreign Affairs, and was a member of AFD's board of directors from 2013 to 2019. His scholarly publications include historical analysis of development assistance, monographs about the history of AFD in some specific countries, and critical editions of AFD former general managers' autobiographies.

Sarah Stockwell is a professor of history at King's College London and works on British decolonisation. Her books include *The Business of Decolonization: British Business Strategies in the Gold Coast, 1945–1957* (Oxford University Press, 2000) and *The British End of the British Empire* (Cambridge University Press, 2018), and the edited collections *The British Empire: Themes and Perspectives* (Blackwell, 2007) and (with L.J. Butler) *The Wind of Change: Harold Macmillan and British Decolonization* (Palgrave Macmillan, 2013). As part of a project on Britain in the 1960s and 1970s she is researching the history of British post-colonial development aid, with a particular focus on technical assistance.

Charlotte Strick obtained a Bachelor's degree (2015) in Political Science at the University of Ghent and a Master's degree (2017) in International Relations at the Université Libre de Bruxelles. After her studies, she decided to immerse herself in EU Immigration and Asylum Law and Policy, through her work for Search for Common Ground in Lebanon, the UN Refugee Agency (UNHCR) in Brussels and the European Commission (DG HOME) as a Blue Book Trainee.

Olivier Van den Bossche has a doctorate in contemporary history and is working on the development of agroforestry in public policies. He previously worked for UNESCO and managed projects funded by the French development agency AFD. He completed his PhD on 'A history of EU-ACP private sector development policies (1975–2000)' at the University Paris 3 Sorbonne Nouvelle in 2018. He has published articles in the *Journal of European Integration History* and *Critique Internationale*.

CHAPTER 1

Introduction: New Directions in the History of Business and Development in Post-Colonial Africa

Véronique Dimier and Sarah Stockwell

African states want their countries to be less dependent on their relations with the ex-colonial power. They want to assert their political autonomy, which puts French importers and exporters in a new situation: they have to prepare themselves to face increasing competition. African markets are no more their 'chasse gardée' [private domain]. This evolution is irreversible.

So wrote Michel Debré, the French prime minister, in November 1961. It would be hard to find a better analysis of the situation that French firms faced in Africa following France's withdrawal from its Sub-Saharan African colonies in 1960. Debré was writing to a group of French MPs who were in turn responding to lobbying by the Fédération des industries mécaniques et transfrontalières de métaux, worried about their members' future

V. Dimier (✉)
Université Libre de Bruxelles, Bruxelles, Belgium
e-mail: vdimier@ulb.ac.be

S. Stockwell
King's College London, London, UK
e-mail: sarah.stockwell@kcl.ac.uk

© The Author(s) 2020
V. Dimier, S. Stockwell (eds.), *The Business of Development in Post-Colonial Africa*, Cambridge Imperial and Post-Colonial Studies Series, https://doi.org/10.1007/978-3-030-51106-7_1

1

prospects in France's former African colonies. The French prime minister aimed to reassure them. The French state, he said, could help French enterprises to keep a foothold in Francophone Africa, even though this could no longer be through French administrative control. One way in which it might do so was through the Fonds d'aide et de coopération, at this juncture the main instrument of French aid in Africa, since Debré insisted that conditions be introduced that would ensure that French aid be tied to the purchase of French exports.[1] That Debré wrote this letter at all was a reflection of the very real fears experienced during European decolonisation by French firms, which had hitherto had an effective monopoly on external trade in the French empire. However, it is also illustrative of the new opportunities that—at this key transitional moment from colonialism to the post-colonial era—development aid offered for French, as well as for other European, companies. Development would become one, if not the key, feature of post-colonial relations between the old European colonial powers and their former African colonies as colonialism was effectively reconfigured as aid for the new post-colonial era.

European companies, whether public, private or semi-public, with an established presence in Africa, had been 'socialised' in a particular context: that of the colonial state and its protectionist rules. They operated with certain interests to defend, whether their own commercial ones, those of the colonial powers or, sometimes, those of an African governing elite. European decolonisation consequently presented new uncertainties and risks for them.

Admittedly, new states entered independence with their ability to exercise their new freedom limited by significant structural constraints: the almost complete absence of locally-owned and managed financial institutions; the small scale of an African professional class; and the near-stranglehold exercised by established foreign commercial, mining and oil interests. Crucially, emergent states also remained bound into the financial systems of the former imperial powers. This was most marked in the case of Francophone African states that upon independence retained the Communauté financière d'Afrique currency system as members of the franc zone. In contrast, former British colonies established national currencies issued by new national central banks, but they still entered independence as members of the British-managed sterling area, with currencies linked to, and backed by, sterling.[2] As discussed below, at independence most emergent states also entered into aid agreements with their ex-colonial powers or looked to them for capital aid and technical assistance.

The creation of the European Economic Community (EEC) and the designation in 1957 of the overseas territories of member states as 'associates' (a status retained after decolonisation under the provisions of the Yaoundé [1963] and Lomé [1975] Conventions), allowed other commercial and financial connections between African countries and their ex-colonial rulers to develop under the aegis of the EEC. The arrangements extended to the EEC the colonial preferential trading system between France, Belgium and the Netherlands and their colonies, and, when Britain eventually joined in 1973, also that between Britain and British overseas territories and former colonies. The EEC's new aid instrument, the European Development Fund (EDF), became an additional source of connections between the old European colonial powers and new African states. Together with the fact that new states were anxious to achieve rapid industrialisation, including by the use of the capital and technology of foreign firms, these factors went some way towards mitigating the immediate effects of constitutional decolonisation for European companies.

Yet for all that the ex-imperial powers may have maintained close relationships with their former colonies through financial mechanisms, development aid and trade agreements, they could not offer the same guarantees as before to their companies. The new international order of the 1960s threatened the monopolistic or near-monopolistic positions such companies had previously enjoyed. Expatriate firms were confronted by the willingness of newly-independent African elites to exercise their new sovereignty to exert greater control over their economies (including via the ultimate weapon at their disposal, nationalisation) and to forge new economic and political relations with other foreign countries. At the same time the Cold War created opportunities for African elites to exploit rivalries between West and East and grant privileged access to their markets or resources in exchange for support (whether financial, economic or political).

How, as political actors, did European companies react to these changes? What strategies did they use to maintain their interests when confronted by the potentially hostile economic policies of new African states, or other foreign competition, and the emergence of a new international landscape populated by new supranational political entities like the European Community as well as the United Nations and associated organisations? Some firms chose to manage the risk by diversifying into new geographical areas beyond Africa.[3] This book, however, focuses on those companies that found not just risk but opportunities in decolonisation. By examining the activities of foreign enterprise in various African states, and their strategies to stay in Africa, this book explores how some European companies benefited from features of the new international landscape, particularly those provided by development aid. In doing so, this volume breaks new ground. It is one of the very first to bring the study of foreign companies and development aid to Africa into the same frame of analysis. It brings together research on different European companies (most notably those of former colonial powers) and considers their work or involvement in the development field after European decolonisation. In these ways this book makes an original contribution to post-colonial studies, specifically in relation to development and business.

POST-COLONIAL DEVELOPMENT IN AFRICA

Recent years have seen new interest among historians in the first of these areas: the history of post-colonial development. In line with current historiographical interest in transnationalism, 'experts' and the way they were instrumental in propagating modernisation theories,[4] and in the role of NGOs and charitable foundations in implementing development projects,[5] much of this new historical literature focuses on international agencies (such as the World Bank and those associated with the United Nations) and their role in development.[6] Because of the prominence of the USA in post-colonial aid and the importance of American-domiciled international aid agencies, post-colonial development has also tended to be seen by some as principally an 'American project' to be viewed through a Cold War lens.[7] In recent years there has also been growing interest in the role of Russia and other foreign powers in the provision of aid to newly-independent countries.[8]

The ex-European colonial powers were nonetheless also important, and often the most significant, sources of aid for new states. As Frederick Cooper argues in relation to French West Africa, a 'vertical' axis — an established connection and common language — inclined African politicians to utilise connections to the outgoing colonial powers to access the resources they sought for their own development and state-building projects even as they sought to diversify their external relations.[9] For their part, Britain and France reconfigured established development policies for a new post-colonial era, signed technical assistance agreements with new states, and created new departments and ministries with responsibility for the delivery of overseas aid.

To this end, from 1958 Britain accepted that newly independent Commonwealth African countries should be entitled to British financial aid, for example in the form of Commonwealth Assistance Loans and via access to any unspent funds that they had been allocated under British colonial development legislation. In 1965 the Overseas Development and Service Act brought together funding for colonial development and overseas aid and, from 1963, the Colonial Development Corporation, now restyled as the Commonwealth Development Corporation, was permitted to take on new projects in independent Commonwealth countries. Britain also signed agreements with all its former African colonies to deliver technical assistance to them in the form of the supply of expatriate personnel to fill posts within their public services, educational establishments and other institutions. It reached specific agreements with Ghana, Nigeria and Sierra Leone, the first of Britain's African dependencies (aside from the Sudan, administered as part of an Anglo-Egyptian condominium) to become independent, and in the case of the east, central and southern African states, entered into arrangements under the framework established by the British Overseas Service Aid Scheme established in 1961.[10] These were administered within a new Department of Technical Co-operation. Formed in 1961, this assumed some functions formerly discharged by the Colonial Office. Three years later the new Labour government, which placed more emphasis on overseas development as part of its commitment to internationalism,[11] transformed the Department into a fully-fledged ministry, the Ministry of Overseas Development. This brought under one roof the aid responsibilities of the Department of Technical Cooperation and those that had until this point remained with the Foreign, Commonwealth Relations and Colonial Offices. The new ministry had a chequered history: when the Conservatives were returned to power in 1970, they folded it into the Foreign and Commonwealth Office as the Overseas Development Administration; the administration of British overseas aid went through various institutional reorganisations thereafter until the creation of the Department for International Development in 1997.

All African states that constituted the abortive Communauté française also signed cooperation agreements with France, as voted by the French National Assembly on 9 June 1960. Those agreements largely reflected the strategies and international ambitions of President de Gaulle and encompassed fields as varied as defence, monetary relations, technical assistance and development aid. A whole range of institutional actors were involved in the French relationship with former colonial Africa, most specifically the Secrétariat général pour les affaires africaines et malgaches, created in May 1961 and headed by Jacques Foccart. As the main adviser to the president on African affairs he became the architect of the France-Afrique networks, a system based on personal ties and secret and shadow interventions.[12] A Ministry of Cooperation responsible for aid and cooperation agreements with African states South of Sahara was also created in June 1961. It had at its disposal local agencies on the ground, the 'missions d'aide et de coopération', and a specific instrument for funding development projects, the Fonds d'aide et de coopération (which, as we have seen, Debré thought might also assist French firms in Africa). Other ministries, including Finance, Education and Defence, were also involved, as well as services or agencies, such as the Caisse centrale de coopération économique, which, as Francois Pacquement shows, was tasked with granting African states loans for investment.[13] According to Gérard Bossuat, Marie Christine Kessler and Marie Claude Smouts, one of the specificities of French aid and cooperation was that most French aid was given in the form of outright gifts, and there were also a significant number of French cooperative aid workers (technical experts, aid volunteers, teachers or administrators) on the ground.[14] Other notable features included the opacity of the whole framework,[15] with little public debate about aid until the 1990s, and the practice of tied aid, since much of the material or services for development projects funded through French aid had to be bought in France.[16]

Although the *post-colonial* aid policies of European colonial powers have received less attention from historians than the history of *colonial* development,[17] this is now changing. One element of this emergent literature (and of relevance to the concerns addressed in this book) emphasises the continuities between colonial and post-colonial development.[18] For example, through their prosopograhical studies, Véronique Dimier and Joseph Hodge reveal significant continuities in personnel between the colonial and post-colonial eras. In her pioneering work on the European Community aid bureaucracy, Véronique Dimier shows how former French colonial officials were re-employed in the European Commission's Directorate General for Development and Cooperation, 'recycling' expertise gained during the colonial period. She analyses how the interactions of former French colonial administrators with an African elite in independent Francophone states resembled those of the colonial era.[19] Joseph Hodge points to how former officials previously engaged in the British colonial service, principally in its scientific and technical branches, were recruited to work in post-colonial development via their employment by British and international aid agencies.[20] Sarah Stockwell's book on British domestic institutions during decolonisation reveals other striking continuities between the colonial and post-colonial eras. As part of a discussion of these institutions' role in British technical assistance programmes, she shows how new elites from former colonies were admitted to Colonial Administrative Service training courses at the Universities of Oxford and Cambridge originally devised for white officers; eventually these courses evolved to become part of Britain's contribution to training overseas public administrators before finally, at Cambridge, morphing into a new programme in development studies.[21]

While there are common themes and striking parallels, not least in the timing of new development initiatives, there were also significant differences between the ex-European colonial powers' aid commitments in Africa. In the French case, Africa accounted for an overwhelming proportion of French aid. Even though, as a result of the Jeanneney report on French aid policy produced in 1963 ('la politique de cooperation avec les pays en voie de développement'), President de Gaulle and his government tried for commercial reasons to extend the horizon of French aid and technical cooperation to countries beyond the former French African colonies, these remained the main recipients of French aid. In 1963, Africa (including Algeria, Morocco and Tunisia) received 88.5% of the total French aid budget for developing countries, and in 1971 69% (of which 53.7% went to Sub-Saharan African countries).[22]

In contrast, British aid was dispersed over a wider geographical field. In the financial year 1964–1965 British colonies and Commonwealth states in Africa were provisionally allocated just over 47% of the total of British bilateral financial aid (comprising outright grants and loans) to countries within the empire-Commonwealth, and, when foreign states are included, over 40% of that dispersed to all destinations. Further British aid was directed to Africa in the form of technical assistance and via multilateral programmes, partly as a result of British participation in the Special Commonwealth African Assistance Plan that had been agreed in 1960 by Commonwealth finance ministers.[23] While many new African states were heavily dependent upon British aid, especially in the form of technical assistance,[24] Britain deliberately sought to draw down its aid commitments in post-colonial Africa, as Ichiro Mekawa's recent analysis of post-colonial British aid spending in Africa confirms.[25] From the late 1960s especially, cash-strapped Britain was parsimonious in its provision of capital aid to

Africa, even though it was a significant source of technical assistance to new states, and sometimes found it hard to extricate itself from commitments to them.[26]

The circumstances in which Belgium and Portugal, the other key European regional colonial powers, withdrew from their African colonies were quite different, and neither of these small European states delivered aid to post-colonial Africa on a scale comparable to France or Britain. Belgium's swift withdrawal from the Belgian Congo precipitated a five-year crisis that would become a scene for Cold War rivalries and great power intervention. As shown by Gauthier de Villers, relations between the Congo and Belgium during Mobutu's regime varied from close collaboration, generous aid and support to outright divorce and the imposition of Belgian sanctions.[27] Developmentalism was a significant feature of late Portuguese colonialism in Africa, and Portugal created development instruments and instituted policies broadly similar to those of Britain and France. However, Portugal's African colonies only attained their independence in the mid-1970s when Britain and France had already refashioned their colonial development policies as aid for a post-colonial era. Much of the private investment in Lusophone Africa was also not Portuguese but South African, British and American, a reflection of the ways in which there were in practice empires within empires.[28]

European Business in Colonial and Post-colonial Africa

The other area addressed by this book, the history of foreign business in Africa, has, like the history of European overseas development, attracted more attention from historians of the colonial era than the post-colonial.[29] While focused on the pre-independence period, the resulting body of scholarship includes accounts of European firms during decolonisation that are nevertheless of significance for the themes addressed in this book. In particular, Robert Tignor, Sarah Stockwell and L.J. Butler all explore the ways in which in Anglophone Africa expatriate firms adapted to the new African political context of the 1940s, 1950s and 1960s. Tignor's analysis of the end of empire in Kenya, Egypt and Nigeria leads him to conclude that expatriate businesses not only took a close interest in colonial political change but, where necessary, actively intervened in the decolonisation process.[30] In her account of British businesses in the Gold Coast

(Ghana) in the late colonial period, Stockwell shows just how far British businessmen were willing to go to advance their own interests in the uncertain political climate of the 1940s and 1950s. They developed strategies for decolonisation that entailed investment in public relations and the formation of new business associations. Some firms attempted to shape the Ghanaian political environment, including via backhanders to African politicians.[31] Their attempts to acclimatise to an environment populated by new African political elites prefigured the adjustment foreign firms made to the neo-patrimonial character of newly-independent African states, as discussed later in this introduction. Similarly, L.J. Butler concluded that in Northern Rhodesia (Zambia) the Rhodesian Selection Trust found itself unable to rely straightforwardly on the support of the imperial or colonial state. In these circumstances, its chairman, Sir Ronald Prain, increasingly developed a 'forward-thinking strategy of accommodation to the rise of African nationalism, and to the corresponding eclipse of settler power'.[32]

Histories of French business in colonial Africa reveal similar patterns. While after the Second World War French business circles in Africa continued to oppose any move towards independence, keeping very conservative positions as far as political evolution and social rights for workers were concerned, they nevertheless showed an astonishing capacity for swift adaptation to the context of independence, making sure that, as Catherine Hodeir argues, 'what was good for decolonisation was also good for their interests'.[33] She further argues that they enthusiastically endorsed the first development plans launched by the French government from 1946, recognising them as opportunities to advance their own interests, and accommodated the new African elite, with whom they created alliances in their attempts to bring in more investment. They even played the role of mediator between these elites and the French government, as, for instance, the important French firm Péchiney did when President Sekou Touré of Guinée decided to opt for independence in 1958.[34] Hodeir shows that while French business circles in Africa were originally opposed to the idea of an association between the EEC and African countries, fearing the end of empire and growing competition with German or Italian firms, they increasingly turned to the European project to boost their interests, an approach endorsed by important French figures of the patronat, such as Robert Lemaignen, Edmond Giscard d'Estaing and Luc Durand-Réville. Hence, they succeeded in influencing the negotiation of the Treaty of

Rome on this issue, playing an important role in the Mouvement européen and the Ligue européenne de coopération économique.[35]

While these accounts lay down important markers in terms of the evidence they provide of how businessmen began (with varying degrees of success and in different ways) to forge new connections to African political elites, we have fewer analyses of European firms in the post-colonial era.[36] Of studies that do address the later period, Stephanie Decker's work on West Africa, Andrew Cohen's on Lonrho in Zambia and James Morris on Barclays Bank in Kenya are particularly pertinent to the theme of this book. Decker argues that British firms 'successfully positioned themselves as partners in African development strategies', for instance through advertising that promoted ideas of modernity and economic development, in order to justify 'their presence as first-world businesses in third-world countries'.[37] Andrew Cohen highlights how Lonrho's joint managing director, the controversial Tiny Rowland, similarly sought to ingratiate himself and Lonrho with the Zambian president, Kenneth Kaunda, by aligning with Zambia's development agenda. Rowland developed a web of connections to African ruling elites, and, although Cohen is sceptical about the degree of influence these connections conferred, he nonetheless argues that these African associations helped Rowland himself ride out an attempted boardroom coup against him in 1973.[38] In the case of Barclays, Morris shows how the Bank responded quickly and innovatively to changing political and economic circumstances, reorganising its business model, increasing its local community involvement, and embarking on Africanisation (albeit limited) in response to President Kenyatta's development strategy and emphasis on Kenyanisation.[39]

Thus some historians of European business in Africa offer important insights on the ways in which businessmen both before and after independence instrumentalised the theme of development as a means of maintaining good relations with an African elite.[40] But few explore how firms could exploit the opportunities offered by development aid to advance their own commercial interests in the early years of African independence. Timothy Mitchell on Egypt, Ruben Berrios on USAID procurement[41] and Abou Bamba on the Ivory Coast take the *connection* between development aid and private companies as one of their subjects of investigation, but these accounts are mostly concerned with American actors and aid rather than European.[42] Only a handful of scholars discuss the theme in relation to European actors. One, Elisabetta Bini, shows how the Ente Nazionale Idrocarburi, an Italian-state owned company, not only appealed to oil producers by supporting the discourse of development, but also, by presenting the economic development of the Italian South (Mezzorgiorno) as a model to be exported to decolonising countries, largely promoted and supported Italian development and technological aid. It also made a direct contribution when it established a school (the Graduate School for the Study of Hydrocarbons) to train technicians and elite from developing countries.[43] Like Bini, Emanuele Fantini and Luca Puddu highlight the ways in which foreign firms (here Italian and British) served as 'development brokers', in this case between the Ethiopian government and donor agencies.[44] Beginning from a different perspective, Laurence Badel, in her analysis of French economic diplomacy, shows how at decolonisation France sought to use tied aid and technical assistance to boost domestic economic growth by securing contracts for French firms.[45] Like Bamba, Badel reveals the important role in promoting French businesses played by consultancy organisations specialising in technical assistance created by the French government as para-statal institutions before decolonisation (such as the Bureau central pour les équipements d'Outre-Mer), together with consultants operating in the private sector.[46] Finally, Monika Pohle Fraser analyses how from the 1960s the West German government (and its agencies, most notably the West German development bank) succeeded in securing contracts for German industry through development aid in Egypt, despite their broad endorsement of untying aid. She also demonstrates how German companies used corruption as a way to circumvent the international tenders launched by the local government.[47]

Apart from these scholars, few others have tackled the role of companies and their links with development agencies and local elites in the delivery of development goals.[48] There are studies by development economists that analyse the degree to which aid benefited the economies and firms of donor nations, but these focus on the very late 1970s and after and were written without the use of archival sources.[49]

The Business of Development

In general, then, development and business have tended to generate distinct historiographies that do not always speak to each other. This lack of cross-fertilisation between these two different fields may seem surprising. After all there are obvious interconnections. In the early colonial period European policymakers believed that the development of newly acquired overseas colonies in Africa would principally be undertaken by private enterprise, with the state assuming only a very limited role. They also used colonial development as a vehicle to promote metropolitan industry and commerce. From the 1940s when European colonial powers accepted the need for a greater state role in development, European firms were often beneficiaries. In Nicholas J. White's words, 'Much enlarged public-funding pots for colonial development fell into European business laps'.[50] In the post-colonial period tied aid became a distinctive feature of both French and British bilateral aid.

In the British case even when some (limited) state money was provided to pay for colonial development with the introduction of the 1929 Colonial Development Act, British legislators specifically stipulated that in order to be eligible for funding, projects had to show a benefit to the British economy by generating orders for British manufacturing plants and machinery. This requirement was dropped in subsequent iterations of British development legislation (with the introduction of a more generous and wide-ranging development provision in 1940). However, the expectation that colonial development would benefit metropolitan interests became prominent again after the Second World War, when policymakers hoped to increase colonial export production with a view to sourcing raw materials and expanding colonial foreign exchange earnings for British benefit as much as that of the colonies. The Colonial Development Corporation, created in 1948, was intended to serve precisely this purpose. As well as developing and managing its own projects, it also became a significant partner in numerous manufacturing and commercial enterprises in many former colonies, and from 1969, beyond the Commonwealth. By 1972 it had £165 million invested in 205 projects and ran 54 businesses, over half of which were in Africa.[51]

From the late 1950s several British initiatives aimed specifically at benefiting British business. These included Commonwealth Assistance Loans. Introduced in 1959, these were provided for the purchase of British goods and services. This innovation was followed a few years later by the 'surplus capacity initiative': this linked the provision of additional forms of bilateral aid to the supply of British goods for which there was surplus productive capacity in Britain, and aimed to promote British exports through the provision of aid.[52] By 1974–1975 over 44% of British bilateral assistance was tied to the purchase of British goods and services. A further connection between aid and trade was introduced in 1977 with the Aid and Trade Provision, which aimed to ensure that a small percentage of British bilateral aid would be available to finance development projects which also benefited UK commercial concerns. It was introduced in response to other countries' practice of using 'mixed credit' ('export credits' which coupled an aid element of 35–50% of the export value of a contract with a commercial credit). From 1979 the Conservative government of Margaret Thatcher revised and expanded the Aid and Trade Provision and placed even greater emphasis on the commercialisation of British aid.[53]

Like the Commonwealth Development Corporation (CDC), the Caisse centrale de coopération économique (originally the Caisse centrale de la France Libre, then Caisse centrale de la France d'Outre-Mer), created by Charles de Gaulle in 1941 initially to serve as the treasury and bank of issue for Free France, became after 1946 the key financial institution in charge of investment and development in Francophone colonial Africa. It also became an important actor in encouraging French private investment in post-colonial Africa. The creation of the Fonds d'investissement économique et social (FIDES) by the government of the French Fourth Republic in April 1946 provided the context for its involvement in development plans. The FIDES was intended to facilitate investment and development in the French empire and provided the basis for setting up semi-public local companies, a network of local banks (social-credit companies), and electricity and local housing corporations. The French government anticipated that these companies would enable African 'citizens' to carry out their own agricultural and artisanal projects and create their own private firms. For example, the objective of the social-credit companies, funded by the Caisse, was to contribute to public equipment and to promote the private sector.

After decolonisation, the Caisse continued to provide equity investment and loans (to the African states and private sector) within the framework of new French plans for development aid in Africa. As noted by Victoria Lickert, the aim of its board was then to encourage the operations of French companies which responded to the needs of the local economy.[54] One of the instruments deployed by the Caisse for that purpose was the so called tied-aid loans (les prêts dits d'aide liée), imposing obligations on African states who benefited from its loans to buy their material or services in France. In 1977, the Caisse also set up the Proparco, a subsidiary company whose aim was to encourage projects on which African public authorities and French companies could collaborate, a way to promote French firms with no past experience in Africa. One consequence, Lickert argues, has been a correlation between the main areas of French aid and the main areas of French investment by big French corporations operating in Africa, notably in infrastructure.

The connection between western commercial interests and western development aid remains a consideration today not least as indicated by the ongoing interest of international organisations such as the Development Assistance Committee (DAC) of the Organisation for Economic Co-operation and Development (OECD) in tied aid. A unique international forum, comprising the world's largest aid donors, with the World Bank, the IMF and UNDP as observers, the DAC was created to facilitate the co-ordination and harmonisation of aid policies and practices. Since 1969 tied aid has been the focus of much debate within the DAC, with significant criticism, most notably by the American delegation, of the ways tied aid has led to increased costs, encouraged projects poorly adapted to local needs and circumstances, and created reliance among recipients on the technologies of donor nations.[55] A recommendation adopted in 2001 finally ordered donors to untie their aid for the least developed countries (except in the field of technical assistance and food aid).[56] Most donors agreed, but the way this recommendation should be implemented remains a matter of debate. The loans of the Agence française de développement (the successor of the Caisse centrale de coopération économique) also still largely go to French companies. These continue to win 70 to 80% of the calls for tender.[57] Given the historic and ongoing salience of the issue, using archive-based studies to explore the extent to which development aid was framed to favour European firms is all the more important.

From this point of view, this edited volume will fill a significant gap in the current historiography. Our geographical focus is principally on Africa, one of the main regional focuses of development agencies, and destinations for bilateral and multilateral aid—for all that there were, as we have indicated, disparities between the level of aid spending of different European states. The EDF, the main aid instrument of the EEC/EU, provides the best example of this African focus: it was originally conceived for former colonial territories of France and Belgium in Sub-Saharan Africa, and, although its geographical remit was enlarged to include the Caribbean and the Pacific islands after the UK joined the EEC in 1973, it remained mainly an African affair and continued to be run separately from other EEC development programmes set up for other under-developed countries in the late 1970s.

One particular strength of this book is its comparative approach, incorporating discussion of various European interests, including French,

British, Belgian, German, Italian and American aid and private enterprise. Different chapters highlight national specificities and the rivalries between the business interests of different foreign origin. Historically Africa had been one of the main arenas of rivalry between European powers, and, as various contributions to this volume will show, in the post-colonial era just as in the colonial, this rivalry extended to competition between the companies of different European states. Together the contributors to this volume address themes relating to development and business in relation to north, west, east and central-southern Africa. The discussion also ranges across a variety of different sectors, including oil, finance, construction and retail, and encompasses both established European actors in Africa and newer entrants from the 1950s to the 1980s.

Collectively the chapters in this book highlight one of the main ambiguities of post-colonial states, especially in Africa: while these wanted to assert their autonomy, for example through the Africanisation of their economies and banking systems, and to secure control of their key strategic resources, including oil, they were still heavily reliant on the development agencies, banks and companies of former colonial powers. This is not, of course, a new insight. Scholars and commentators writing from a variety of disciplinary and ideological perspectives have long acknowledged that the transfers of sovereignty did not bring an end to all forms of colonialism, and, more specifically, that European companies and institutions continued to exercise significant power in former European colonies, to an extent that has sometimes been characterised as constituting a form of 'neo-colonialism'.[58] But, as observed earlier, we still lack empirically-based investigations of the post-colonial histories of foreign enterprise in Africa. Analysing the networks linking development agencies, banks, companies and newly-independent African states will be one of the threads of many chapters in this volume. A second, and connected, theme addressed by various contributors concerns the ways in which European development aid offered business opportunities for the companies of former colonial powers, while also engendering competition and confrontation with new actors and powers (notably, from Italy, the USA and Germany). A third theme running through several chapters is the role foreign companies played in propagating, and even devising, a new discourse and paradigm of development in the countries of the former colonial powers during and after constitutional decolonisation.

Francois Pacquement's chapter on the history of the Caisse centrale de cooperation économique bears upon the first of these themes. As former social-credit companies became Africanised, and as national development banks were created in Senegal and the Ivory Coast, sometimes with the help of foreign corporations, the Caisse centrale continued to finance them so that they could distribute credit to local private firms. Pacquement's chapter hence provides ample illustration of the ongoing reliance of new African states, in this case in Francophone Africa, not just on external aid, but on the support of a French colonial institution. As he shows, the financial, political and economic autonomy of emergent post-colonial states was at best relative. Sarah Stockwell's chapter discusses the British equivalent of the Caisse, the CDC. Its activities in post-colonial Anglophone African states provide another example of the way in which a colonial institution was repurposed to become part of British overseas aid.

The chapters by Marta Musso and Christopher Minton deal with one specific sector, oil, but similarly demonstrate the ongoing reliance of new states on external interests, in this case French and British oil companies. For the nationalists who fought for Algerian and Nigerian decolonisation, oil represented the basis from which to build a real independence and to bring prosperity to their country. Musso shows how the Algerians focused their efforts on gaining control over the industry, both on a juridical level by securing sovereignty over their country, and in practice, through the formation of a specialised workforce and managers. However, both the Algerian and Nigerian governments came to rely more and more for their development projects on assistance from the oil companies of the former colonial powers, while, for their part, France and Britain tried to maintain a special relationship with independent Algeria or Nigeria with a view to securing gas and oil supplies.

Turning to Charlotte Strick's discussion of the Congo, we see that it was precisely to avoid this kind of 'dependence' that the new Congolese elite was very sceptical about a development study and company proposed by the Belgian government during the colony's transition to independence. Their scepticism was well founded since, as Strick shows, Belgium considered development as a way to influence the economy of its former colony or, rather, to deprive the new state of its means of control over the economy. With this in mind, the Belgium government had created the Groupement international d'études pour le développement du Congo (GIDEC), a supposedly independent think-tank meant to study the conditions for development in the Congo. The study, which principally involved influential Belgian firms, was to lead to the creation of a development company funded by Belgium and the future Congolese state. As the elite behind Patrice Lumumba (the first democratically elected prime minister in the newly independent Congo) distrusted it, this project never in fact came to fruition.

In many cases, however, despite their rhetoric of political autonomy and independent development, the personal interests of the newly-independent elite—not least their desire to keep themselves in power—led them to collude with foreign companies and governments, including the former European colonial powers. This raises the question of the link between economic and political elites, whether in former colonies or ex-imperial states.[59] As well as Musso and Minton's chapters, several others in this book provide evidence of the willingness of African elites to work with established or new foreign private enterprise, for example, Poppy Cullen's examination of the history of the East African Association, an organisation set up by British businessmen to secure their position in the region after independence; and Abou Bamba's chapter on French agri-business and the import-export industry in the newly-independent Ivory Coast. As they show, foreign companies were eager and quick to adapt to the characteristics of newly-independent African states, and in particular their neo-patrimonialism.[60] Neo-patrimonial states rested on the capacity of local political leaders to 'nurture' clients through the distribution of sinecures and money extracted from external aid and other sources.[61] In these states power and status were garnered by strong leaders and their 'clans', whose patrimonial style of authority and legitimacy rested on a web of very personal relationships, bonds of trust, loyalty, mutual respect and obligation. Opacity of administration (especially financial administration), corruption, bribery and a regime that operated outside the structures of rules were permanent features of neo-patrimonial systems.

Demonstrating the ability of French companies to operate within neo-patrimonial systems is a core concern of Veronique Dimier's chapter in this volume. This focuses on the European Development Fund's contribution to the development and welfare of associated African states within the framework of the Yaoundé and, later, Lomé conventions. The EDF financed specific projects, mostly infrastructural or agricultural. Private companies in both EEC member and associated states were eligible to bid for the contracts available as a result of these projects, and, as Dimier argues, because French companies already had an established network among local African elites and experience in negotiating local practices to obtain contracts (including through resort to bribery), they won a great number of calls for tenders, relative to the firms of other EEC member states, notably Germany.

This leads us to the second theme of this book: development as business. This is at the heart of chapters by Stockwell, Dimier, Musso, Minton and Bamba, who all explore the ways and extent to which development projects, whether financed through national or international agencies, became a good way for the companies of former colonial powers to advance their own commercial interests and to protect their existing privileged positions (and even monopoly) in African states after independence. Stockwell shows how in the 1960s the CDC became a useful resource for some expatriate firms, as well as other foreign manufacturers, as they began to invest in new manufacturing enterprises in newly independent African states. Partnership with CDC and its local development corporations gave access to loan or equity capital as well as to the Corporation's accumulated local experience and to other possible benefits. Unlike the Caisse, the CDC's funds were not tied to the participation of British companies or purchase of British exports. Stockwell asks whether in its selection of projects the Corporation nevertheless favoured British business over companies of other national origin.

As African markets opened to new competitors such as those from the USA, Japan, Italy, Germany, USSR and China, countries which had their own overseas development policies, European firms with established businesses in Africa adopted other new strategies. Dimier particularly shows how, in the case of bids for funding under the EDF, technical assistance was used by French companies to devise development projects (and the technical laws and regulations attached to them) in such a way as to preclude any firms other than French ones from winning the calls for tender. This was a source of permanent complaint among German companies, which wanted to take advantage of the EDF to increase their own presence in, and exports to, Africa. This issue, the so-called discrimination issue, became a bone of contention among the member states, especially France and Germany, which each wanted a fair share of the EDF contracts for 'their' companies. The European Commission of the EEC, which ran the EDF, tried to ease the tensions by making the tendering process more transparent in order to allow for greater competition among the firms of the member states.

In all these cases, we will see that it was not just established foreign firms that readily adjusted to the practices and politics of African states; new business entrants to Africa also adapted to neo-patrimonial systems.

Indeed, Dimier argues that the 'discrimination issue' was eventually resolved not as a result of the European Commission's efforts, but by the adaptation of German firms to local practices. Musso's chapter provides further evidence of this process of acclimatisation. She explains how, during the negotiations between Algeria and France, Italy tried to win the favour of Algerian fighters, by covertly offering economic and diplomatic help in exchange for future oil concessions after independence. Later on, after Algerian independence, Italy and France both hoped, through development projects, to gain the favour of the new Algerian government as the latter also considered the merits of offers made by private multinational oil companies. In this case, as in the case of Nigeria analysed by Minton, development was used by certain companies to secure a privileged position, and by European states to preserve economic domination and prevent other, threatening, interests from securing leverage in the country.

In this game, however, it would be wrong to conclude that local elites were the passive subjects of domination and exploitation by external powers and companies. Dimier argues that African elites used the competition between donors and their companies to sell their development projects and, within the context of the neo-patrimonial state, extort more money from different sides.

This brings us to the third theme dealt with in this book: how for companies, as well as for the elites in power in newly-independent states and former colonial powers, the discourse of development became a useful tool to foster their interests and increase their legitimacy. We can see this in Cullen's examination of the East African Association. She shows that the language and rhetoric of development was prominent in the structure and constitution of the Association, at a time when development was an essential priority for African leaders. For the companies which created and controlled the Association, a central reason for using this language was to make the Association acceptable to East African leaders and secure their own relations with them. In the same way, Musso and Minton show how Italy, France and Britain, though in different ways and under different conditions, offered to implement various development projects in Algeria or Nigeria using the revenue from the oil industry. Like forms of 'corporate social responsibility' today, these projects aimed, at least on paper, to use the massive oil revenues flowing from Europe to producer countries to promote long-term local economic expansion. Through development discourse, both countries and their companies hoped to legitimise their action in Algeria and Nigeria.

In this way corporations could be instrumental in propagating modernising theories as Bamba argues in the case of the Ivory Coast around the moment of independence. He shows how, through their lobbying activities and expertise, and through the circulation and transfer of knowledge, corporations took an active part in devising development plans produced not only by colonial or former colonial powers and by international aid agencies, but also as crafted by newly-independent elites in former colonies. Strick also shows how in the case of the Belgian Congo, Tractionel, a filial of the Société générale de Belgique, one of the most influential Belgian companies in the Congo, actively sought to become and succeeded in becoming part of the GIDEC, the supposedly 'independent' study on the future economic prospects and development of the Congolese state.

It was in order to try to secure this kind of influence that business elites in Britain and the British Commonwealth mobilised at Commonwealth level through the Federation of Commonwealth Chambers of Commerce. According to Andrew Dilley, the end of empire generated a heightened engagement with, as well as shifts in, the rhetoric of development amongst a commercial elite. Not only did the Federation's concern with development intensify after decolonisation, but it also tried to develop a close relationship with the newly founded Commonwealth secretariat and influence the policymaking of the Commonwealth in relation to its development programmes.

While most contributors to this book focus on the early post-colonial era and the period of state developmentalism that lasted until the 1980s, Van den Bossche's contribution to this book picks up some of the issues discussed in other chapters in relation to the 1970s and the more recent past. He shows how from the 1970s a group of European firms involved in Africa ('the group of seven') played an essential role in the negotiation of the Centre de développement industriel (CDI), an EEC institution, whose aim was to favour the private sector in the development field in Africa. Through this example, he analyses the extent to which the interests of European businesses and associations operating in the African market evolved from a narrow nationally-based to a European-wide strategy. Through intense lobbying of the European Commission and within the framework of the neo-liberal ethos of the 1990s, they were also able to influence some of the new measures and paradigms of EEC/EU development policy (most notably the Cotonou agreement, the successor of the Lomé Convention in 2000 and its measures concerning the encouragement of the private sector). However, the definition of this private sector remained a matter of controversy between the African states and the EEC/EU member states, not to mention the European Commission who played the role of intermediary between the two sides and tried to use the CDI to encourage the development of small African firms.

As Van den Bossche's chapter shows, investigating the nexus between overseas development and foreign private enterprise (not least in relation to the aid policies of the European Union) is a task of ongoing importance and relevance. Through their different chapters, the contributors to this volume highlight some of the possible points of intersection between the two. As the first collection to bring together chapters on the history of development and private enterprise in post-colonial Africa, this book will not be the last word on the subject. But it is hoped that it will be richly suggestive of possible further lines of enquiry. Moreover, at the very least, this book shows that development and business, all too often perceived as distinct fields of activity (and which have generated their own discrete historiographies), were intimately connected, with the former of great significance to the ways in which foreign companies succeeded in maintaining established roles in former colonies or in securing new ones despite the political transformations of European decolonisation and the Cold War.

NOTES

1. Archives of the French Foreign Ministry (Nantes), 184 PO/1/296, letter Michel Debré, prime minister, to R. Dusseaux, MP of Seine Maritime, November 1961.
2. See Catherine Schenk, *Britain and the Sterling Area. From Devaluation to Convertibility in the 1950s* (London, 1994).
3. D.K. Fieldhouse, *Merchant Capital and Economic Decolonisation: The United Africa Company 1929–1987* (Oxford, 1994); Nicholas J White: 'Imperial Business Interests, Decolonization, and Post-Colonial Diversification' in Martin Thomas and Andrew S. Thompson (eds.), *The Oxford Handbook of the Ends of Empire* (Oxford, 2018), pp. 639–660.
4. David Ekbladh, *The Great American Mission: Modernization and the Construction of an American World Order* (Princeton and Oxford, 2010); Michael E. Latham, *The Right Kind of Revolution: Modernization, Development and US foreign policy from the Cold War to the Present* (Ithaca, 2011); David Engermann and Corinna Unger, 'Introduction: towards a global history of modernization', *Diplomatic history*, 33, no. 3 (2009),

pp. 375–386; Daniel Speich, 'The Kenyan style of African socialism: development knowledge claims and the explanatory limits of the Cold War', *Diplomatic history*, 33, no. 3 (2009), pp. 449–465; Nick Cullather, *The Hungry World; America's Cold War Battle against Poverty in Asia* (Harvard, 2010); Bradley Simpson R, *Economists with Guns: authoritarian development and US-Indonesian relations, 1960–1968* (Stanford, 2008); Andreas Eckert, Stephen Malinowski and Corinna Unger (eds.), 'Modernizing Missions. Approaches to Developing the Non-Western World after 1945', special issue, *Journal of Modern European History*, 8, no 1 (2010); Robert Tignor, *W. Arthur Lewis and the Birth of Development Economics* (Princeton and Oxford, 2005); Timothy Mitchell, *Rule of Experts, Egypt, Techno-Politics, Modernity* (Berkeley, 2002).

5. Matthew Connelly, *Fatal Misconception. The Struggle to Control World Population* (Harvard, 2010); Gregory Man, *From Empires to NGOs in the West African Sahel* (Cambridge, 2015).

6. Michele Alecevich, *The Political Economy of the World Bank. The Early Years* (Stanford, 2009); Marc Frey, Sonia Kunkel and Corinna Unger (eds.), *International Organizations and Development, 1945–1990* (Basingstoke, 2014); Akira Iriye, *Global Community: The Role of International Organizations in the Making of the Contemporary World* (Berkeley, 2004); Richard Jolly, Louis Emmerij, Dharam Ghai and Frederi Lapeyre, *UN Contributions to Development Thinking and Practice* (Bloomington, 2004); Graig N. Murphy, *The United Nation Development Programme. A Better Way?* (Cambridge, 2006); Nico Schrijver, *Development without Destruction: the UN and Global Resource Management* (Bloomington, 2010); John Shaw, *The UN World Food Program and the Development of Food Aid* (New York, 2001); Patrick Alan Sharma, *Robert McNamara's Other War. The World Bank and International Development* (Philadelphia, 2017); Amy L. Staples, *The Birth of Development: How the World Bank, Food and Agriculture Organization and the World Health Organization Changed the World, 1945–1965* (Athens, Ohio, 2006); Olav Stokke, *The UN and Development. From Aid to Cooperation* (Bloomington, 2009); John Toye and Richard Toye, *The UN and Global Political Economy: Trade, Finance and Development* (Bloomington, 2010).

7. See, for example, David C. Engermann, Nils Gilman, Mark Haefle and Michael E. Latham (eds.), *Staging Growth. Modernization, Development and the Global Cold War* (Amherst, MA, 2003); David Williams, *International Development and Global Politics. History, Theory and Practice* (London, 2012).

8. For example, Constantin Katsakioris, 'Soviet Lessons for Arab Modernization. Soviet educational aid towards Arab countries after 1956' in Andreas Eckert, Stephan Malinowski and Corinna Unger (eds.),

'Modernizing Missions. Approaches to Developing the Non-Western World after 1945', *Journal of Modern European History*, 8, no 1 (2010), pp. 85–105; Corinna Unger, 'Industrialization vs. Agrarian Reform: West German Modernization Policies in India in the 1950s and 1960s', in ibid., pp. 47–63; Deborah Brautigam, *The Dragon's Gift. The Real Story of China in Africa* (Oxford, 2010); Monika Pohle Fraser, '"not the needy but the speedy ones": West German development aid and private investment in the Middle East, 1960–1967', in Helge O. Pharo and Monika Phole Fraser (eds.), *The Aid Rush: Aid regimes in Northern Europe during the Cold War*, Vol 2 (Oslo, 2008), pp. 217–243.

 9. Frederick Cooper, *Citizenship between Empire and Nation: Remaking France and French Africa, 1945–1960* (Princeton and London, 2014), pp. 187–188.

10. Sarah Stockwell, *The British End of the British Empire* (Cambridge, 2018), pp. 78–80.

11. Gerold Krozewski, 'Global Britain and the Post-colonial World: The British Approach to Aid Policies at the 1964 Juncture', *Contemporary British History*, 29, no 2 (2015), pp. 222–240; Charlotte Riley, '"The Winds of Change are Blowing Economically": The Labour Party and British Overseas Development, 1940s–960s' in Chris Jeppesen and Andrew Smith (eds.), *Britain, France and the Decolonization of Africa. Future Imperfect?* (London, 2017), pp. 43–61.

12. Frédéric Turpin, *De Gaulle, Pompidou et l'Afrique: décoloniser et coopérer (1958–1974)* (Paris, 2010); Jean-Pierre Bat, *Le syndrôme Foccart. La politique française en Afrique, de 1959 à nos jours* (Paris, 2012); Xavier Renou, 'A new French policy for Africa', *Journal of Contemporary African Studies*, 20, no 1 (2002), pp. 5–27; Tony Chafer, 'Franco-African Relations: no longer so exceptional?', *African Affairs*, 101(2002), pp. 343–363.

13. François Pacquement, *Histoire de l'agence Française de développement en Côte d'Ivoire* (Paris, 2015).

14. Gérard Bossuat, 'French Development Aid and Co-operation under de Gaulle', *Contemporary European History*, 12, no 4 (2003), pp. 431–456; Marie Christine Kessler, *La politique étrangère de la France: acteurs et processus* (Paris, 1999), ch. 8; Jacques Adda and Marie Claude Smouts, *La France face au Sud. Le miroir brisé* (Paris, 1989).

15. Bossuat, 'True Figures are a Mystery', p. 432.

16. Smouts, *La France*, p. 40.

17. On which see, among many, David Meredith and Michael Havinden, *Colonialism and Development. Britain and its Tropical Colonies 1850–1960* (London, 1993); Stephen Constantine, *The Making of British Colonial Development Policy 1914–1940* (London, 1984); Joseph Hodge, *Triumph of the Expert. Agrarian Doctrines of Development and the Legacies of British*

Colonialism (Athens, Ohio, 2007); Joseph Hodge, Gerald Hodl and Martina Kopf (eds.), *Developing Africa: Concepts and Practices in Twentieth-Century Colonialism* (Manchester University Press, Manchester, 2014); Charlotte Riley, '"Tropical Allsorts": The Transnational Flavor of British Development Policies in Africa', *Journal of World History*, 26, no. 4 (2015), pp. 839–864; Miguel Bandeira Jerónimo, '"A Battle in the Field of Human Relations": The Official Minds of Repressive Development in Portuguese Angola' in Martin Thomas and Gareth Curless (eds.), *Decolonization and Conflict. Colonial Comparisons and Legacies* (London, 2017), pp. 115–136; Monica Van Beusekom, *Negotiating Development: African Farmers and Colonial Exports at the Office du Niger, 1920–1960* (Westport, 2002); Véronique Dimier, 'Politique indigène en France et Grande-Bretagne dans les années 1930: à l'origine de l'idéologie développementaliste', *Politique et société*, 24, no 1 (2005), pp. 73–99; M. Haleh Davis, 'Producing Eurafrica: development, agriculture and race in Algeria, 1958–1965' (Phd, New York University, 2015); special issue, *Contemporary Europan History*, 12, 2, no 4 (2003) edited by Heide–Irene Schmidt and Helga Pharo; special issue, *Outre-Mer*, 102, no. 384–85 (2014) edited by Odile Goerg and Marie-Albane de Suremain; Elena Calandri, 'L'aide au développement. Entre économie, culture et relations internationales', *Relations Internationales*, no 157 (2014), pp.75–95; Catherine Coquery-Vidrovitch, Daniel Hémery and Jean Piel, *Pour une histoire du développement. Etats, sociétés et développement* (Paris, 2007).

18. On which as well as the literature cited below, see also Uma Kothari, 'From colonial administration to development studies: a postcolonial critique of the history of development studies', Uma Kothari (ed.), *A Radical History of Development Studies. Individuals, Institutions, and Ideologies* (Zed Book, London, 2005), pp. 46–66. See also Frederick Cooper, *Decolonization and African Society. The Labor question in French and British Africa* (Cambridge, 1996), and more recently, Miguel Bandeira Jerónimo and Antonio Costa Pinto (eds.), *The Ends of European Colonial Empires: Cases and Comparisons* (Basingstoke, 2015) and Marc Frey and Sönke Kunkel, 'Writing the History of Development: A Review of the Recent Literature', *Contemporary European History*, 20, no 2 (2011), pp. 215–232.

19. Véronique Dimier, 'L'institutionnalisation de la Commission Européenne (DG Développement): du rôle des leaders dans la construction d'une administration multinationale, 1958–1975', *Etudes internationales*, 34, no 3 (2003) pp. 401–428; Véronique Dimier, 'Legitimizing the DG8: a small family business (1958–1975)', European Consortium for Political Research, joint session, Grenoble, 6–10 April 2001; Véronique Dimier, *The Invention of a European Development Aid Bureaucracy. Recycling Empire* (Basingstoke, 2014).

20. At the time of writing this project is ongoing, but see Joseph Hodge, 'British Colonial Expertise, Post-Colonial Careering and the Early History of International Development', in Eckert, Malinowski and Unger (eds.), 'Modernizing Missions. Approaches to Developing the Non-Western World after 1945', special issue of *Journal of Modern European History*, 8, no 1 (2010), pp. 24–44.

21. Stockwell, *British End*.

22. Bossuat, 'French Development Aid and Co-operation under de Gaulle', p. 446.

23. PP. 1960–1961, XXVII, *Technical Assistance from the United Kingdom for Overseas Development* (Cmnd., 1308), paras. 15, 52–56; PP. 1964–1965, Cmnd. 2736. *Ministry of Overseas Development. Overseas Development: The Work of the New Ministry* (HMSO, 1965), table 2.

24. See, for example, Jean Nellie Sindab, 'The impact of expatriates on the Zambian development Process' (PhD, University of Yale, 1984); Poppy Cullen, *Kenya and Britain after independence, beyond neo-colonialism* (Basingstoke, 2017); Stockwell, *British End*.

25. Ichiro Maekawa, 'Neo-Colonialism Reconsidered: A Case study of East Africa in the 1960s and 70s', *Journal of Imperial and Commonwealth History*, 43, no 2 (2015), pp. 317–341.

26. Tony Killick, 'Policy Autonomy and the History of British Aid to Africa', *Development Policy Review*, 23 no 6 (2005), pp. 665–681; Stockwell, *British End*, pp. 75–92.

27. Gauthier de Villers, *De Mobutu à Mobutu. Trente ans de relations Belgique-Zaïre* (Bruxelles, 1995).

28. Miguel Bandeira Jerónimo and Antonio Costa Pinto, 'A Modernizing Empire? Politics, Culture and Economy in Portuguese Late Colonialism' in Miguel Bandeira Jerónimo and Antonio Costa Pinto (eds.), *The Ends of European Colonial Empires: Cases and comparisons* (Basingstoke, 2015), pp. 51–80, esp. 62–63; Crawford Young, 'Imperial Endings and Small States: Disorderly Decolonization for the Netherlands, Belgium, and Portugal' in ibid., pp. 101–125.

29. See, among many, Catherine Coquery-Vidrovitch, 'L'Impact des intérêts coloniaux: SCOA et CFAO dans l'Ouest Africain, 1910–1965', *Journal of African History*, 16 (1975), pp. 595–621; Jacques Marseille, *Empire colonial et capitalisme Français. Histoire d'un divorce* (Paris, 1984); A. G. Hopkins, *An Economic History of West Africa* (Harlow, 1973); idem, 'Imperial Business in Africa. Part I', *Journal of African History*, 17 (1976), pp. 29–48, 'Imperial Business in Africa. Part II', *Journal of African History*, 17 (1976), pp. 267–290; Hubert Bonin, Catherine Hodeir and Jean François Klein (dir.), *L'Esprit économique impérial (1830–1970). Groupes de pression et réseaux du patronat colonial en France et dans l'Empire*

(Publication de la SHOM, 2008). Some studies straddle both eras, for example, D.K. Fieldhouse, *Merchant Capital; Unilever Overseas. The Anatomy of a Multinational 1895–1965* (London, 1978).

30. Robert Tignor, *Capitalism and Nationalism at the End of Empire. State and business in decolonizing Egypt, Nigeria and Kenya, 1945–1963* (Princeton, 1998).

31. Sarah Stockwell, *The Business of Decolonization. British business strategies in the Gold Coast* (Oxford, 2000), chaps. 4–7.

32. L. J. Butler, *Copper Empire: Mining and the Colonial State in Northern Rhodesia, c.1930–1964* (Basingstoke, 2013), esp. p. 459. For a qualification of Butler's argument, see Andrew Cohen, 'Business and Decolonisation in Central Africa Reconsidered', *Journal of Imperial and Commonwealth History*, 36, no 4 (2008) pp. 641–658.

33. Catherine Hodeir, *Stratégie d'empire. Le grand patronat face à la décolonisation, 1945–1963* (Paris, 2003), p. 312.

34. Ibid., p. 255.

35. Ibid., p. 269–301. See also on these organisations: Laura Kottos, *Europe between Imperial Decline and Quest for Integration* (Brussels, 2015).

36. Although the oil industry has attracted more attention than most sectors, for example, Chibuike Uche, 'Oil, British Interests and the Nigerian Civil War', *Journal of African History*, 49 (2008), pp. 111–135.

37. Stephanie Decker, 'Building Up Goodwill: British Business, Development and Economic Nationalism in Ghana and Nigeria, 1945–1977', *Enterprise & Society*, 9, no. 4 (2008), pp. 602–613; idem, 'Corporate Legitimacy and Advertising: British Companies and the Rhetoric of Development in West Africa, 1950–1970', *Business History Review*, 81, no. 1 (2007), pp. 59–86.

38. Andrew Cohen, 'Lonrho and the Limits of Corporate Power in Africa, c. 1961–1973' *South African Historical Journal*, 68, no 1 (2016), pp. 31–49. See also Andrew Cohen, 'Lonrho and Oil Sanctions Against Rhodesia in the 1960s', *Journal of Southern African Studies*, 37, no 4 (2011), pp. 715–730.

39. James Morris, '"Cultivating the African": Barclays DOC and the decolonization of business strategy in Kenya, 1950–1978', *Journal of Imperial and Commonwealth History*, 4, no 4 (2016), pp. 649–671.

40. Hodeir, *Stratégie d'empire*, p. 255.

41. Rubén Berríos, *Contracting for Development. The Role of for-Profit Contractors in US Foreign Development Assistance* (Westport, 2000); Mitchell, *Rule of Experts*.

42. Abou B. Bamba, *African Miracle, African Mirage. Transnational Politics and the Paradox of Modernization in Ivory Coast* (Athens, Ohio, 2016).

43. Elisabetta Bini, 'Fuelling modernization from the Atlantic to the third world', in Alain Beltran, Eric Bussière and G. Garavini (dir.), *L'Europe et la question energétique* (Frankfurt, 2016).
44. Emanuele Fantini and Luca Puddu, 'Ethiopia and International Aid: Development between High Modernism and Exceptional Measures', in Tobias Hagmann and Filip Reyntjens (eds.), *Aid and Authoritariarism in Africa. Development without Democracy* (London, 2016), pp. 91–108.
45. Laurence Badel, *Diplomatie et grands contrats. L'Etat français et les marchés extérieurs au XXème siècle* (Paris, 2010), p. 196.
46. Ibid., p. 226; Abou Bamba, *African Miracle*.
47. Fraser, '"not the needy but the speedy ones…"', pp. 229–230.
48. With a couple of exceptions: in his account of the implementation of the European Development Fund in Senegal, Martin Rempe mentions the involvement of societal actors (including firms and NGOs), and the way they interacted with the local elite. Martin Rempe, *Entwicklng im konflikt. Die EWG und des Senegal, 1957–1975* (Böhlau, Köln, 2012). On the role of French companies in the Turkwel project in Kenya and the collusion between economic and political elite, see also: Elisabeth Kleemeier, 'La France et l'argent noir du Kenya', *Politique africaine*, 40 (1990), pp. 130–138.
49. For example, Ranald S. May, Dieter Schumacher and Mohammed H. Malek, *Overseas Aid. The Impact on Britain and Germany* (Hemel Hempstead, 1989).
50. White, 'Imperial Business Interests', p. 641.
51. Michael McWilliam, *The Development Business. A History of the Commonwealth Development Corporation* (Basingstoke, 2001); Chistopher Brain and Michael Cable, *Pioneering Development, 1948–2008* (2nd edn., London, 2018), p. 102.
52. Barry Ireton, *Britain's International Development Policies. A History of DfID and Overseas Aid* (Basingstoke, 2013), pp. 23–25, 187–195.
53. Gordon Cumming, *Aid to Africa. French and British Policies from the Cold War to the New Millenium* (Aldershot, 2001), pp. 24, 74, table 4.6, p. 90; John Toye, 'The Aid and Trade Provision of the British Overseas Aid Programme' in Anuradha Bose and Peter Burnell eds., *Britain's Overseas Aid Since 1979. Between Idealism and Self-Interest* (Manchester, 1991), pp. 97–124.
54. Victoria Lickert, 'Les milieux d'affaires français, l'AFD et l'Afrique dans les années 1990' in *75 ans au service du développement. L'AFD des origines à nos jours* (Publication de l'AFD, Paris, 2017), pp. 175–179. See also: Pacquement, *Histoire*.

55. OCDE, Le deliement de l'aide aux pays les moins avancés, l'Observateur de l'OCDE, 2001; http://www.oecd.org/fr/cad/aide-deliee/35919775.pdf.
56. Later on, this recommendation was extended to the Heavily Indebted Poor countries. The revised text was approved by DAC on 21 July 2014 following a written procedure: revised DAC recommendation on untying ODA to the least developed countries and Heavily Indebted Poor countries: DCD/DAC (2014) 37/FINAL.
57. Lickert, *Les milieux d'affaires français,* p. 179.
58. See Kwame Nkrumah, *Neo-Colonialism. The Last Stage of Imperialism* (1965); Gary Wasserman, *The Politics of Decolonization: Kenya, Europe and the Land Issue, 1960–1965* (Cambridge, 1976).
59. On this see, for example, Antoinette Handley, *Business and State in Africa. Economic policy-making in the neo-liberal era* (Cambridge, 2008), ch. 4. See also Béatrice Hibou, *The Force of Obedience. The political economy of repression in Tunisia* (Cambridge, 2011).
60. Jean François Médard, 'The Underdeveloped State in Tropical Africa: Political Clientelisme or Neo-Patrimonialisme?'in C. Clapham (ed.), *Private Patronage and Public Power: Political clientelism in the Modern State* (London, 1982).
61. Jean François Bayart, *L'Etat en Afrique. La politique du ventre* (Fayard, Paris, 1989). On the way this neo-patrimonial system changed over time, see Thomas Bierschenk and Jean-Pierre Olivier de Sardan (eds.) *States at Work. Dynamics of African Bureaucracies* (Leiden, 2014).

REFERENCES

Adda, Jacques, and Marie Claude Smouts, *La France face au Sud. Le miroir brisé* (Karthala, Paris, 1989).
Alecevich, Michele, *The Political Economy of the World Bank. The Early Years* (Stanford University Press, Stanford, 2009).
Badel, Laurence, *Diplomatie et grands contrats. L'etat français et les marchés extérieurs au XXème siècle* (Publication de la Sorbonne, Paris, 2010).
Bandeira Jerónimo, Miguel, and Antonio Costa Pinto (eds.), *The Ends of European Colonial Empires: Cases and Comparisons* (Palgrave Macmillan, Basingstoke, 2015).
Bandeira Jerónimo, Miguel, and Antonio Costa Pinto, 'A Modernizing Empire? Politics, Culture and Economy in Portuguese Late Colonialism', in Miguel Bandeira Jerónimo and Antonio Costa Pinto (eds.), *The Ends of European Colonial Empires: Cases and Comparisons* (Palgrave Macmillan, Basingstoke, 2015), pp. 51–80.

Bandeira Jerónimo, Miguel, 'A Battle in the Field of Human Relations': The Official Minds of Repressive Development in Portuguese Angola', in Martin Thomas and Gareth Curless (eds.), *Decolonization and Conflict. Colonial Comparisons and Legacies* (Bloomsbury Academic, London, 2017), pp. 115–136.

Bamba, Abou B., *African Miracle, African Mirage. Transnational Politics and the Paradox of Modernization in Ivory Coast* (Ohio University Press, Athens, OH, 2016).

Bat, Jean-Pierre, *Le syndrôme Foccart. La politique française en Afrique, de 1959 à nos jours* (Gallimard, Paris, 2012).

Bayart, Jean François, *L'Etat en Afrique. La politique du ventre* (Fayart, Paris, 1989).

Berríios, Rubén, *Contracting for Development. The Role of For-Profit Contractors in US Foreign Development Assistance* (Praeger, Westport, 2000).

Bini, Elisabetta, 'Fuelling Modernization from the Atlantic to the Third World', in Alan Beltran, Eric Bussièr and G. Garavini (dir.), *L'Europe et la question energétique* (P. Lang, Brussels, 2016).

Bierschenk, Thomas, and Jean-Pierre Olivier de Sardan (eds.), *States at Work. Dynamics of African Bureaucracies* (Brill, Leiden, 2014).

Bonin, Hubert, Catherine Hodeir, and Jean François Klein, *L'Esprit economique impérial (1830–1970). Groupes de pression et réseaux du patronat colonial en France et dans l'empire* (Publication de la SHOM, 2008).

Bossuat, Gérard, 'French Development Aid and Co-operation Under de Gaulle', *Contemporary European History*, 12, no. 4 (2003), pp. 431–456.

Brain, Christopher, and Michael Cable, *Pioneering Development, 1948–2008*, 2nd Edition (CDC Group plc, London, 2018).

Butler, L.J., *Copper Empire: Mining and the Colonial State in Northern Rhodesia, c.1930–1964* (Palgrave Macmillan, Basingstoke, 2013).

Brautigam, Deborah, *The Dragon's Gift. The Real Story of China in Africa* (Oxford University Press, Oxford, 2010).

Calandri, Elena, 'L'Aide au développement. Entre économie, culture et relations internationales', *Relations Internationales*, I, no. 157 (2014), pp. 75–95.

Chafer, Tony, 'Franco-African Relations: No Longer So Exceptional?', *African Affairs*, 101 (2002), pp. 343–363.

Cohen, Andrew, 'Business and Decolonisation in Central Africa Reconsidered', *Journal of Imperial and Commonwealth History*, 36, no. 4 (2008), pp. 641–658.

Cohen, Andrew, 'Lonrho and Oil Sanctions Against Rhodesia in the 1960s', *Journal of Southern African Studies*, 37, no. 4 (2011), pp. 715–730.

Cohen, Andrew, 'Lonrho and the Limits of Corporate Power in Africa, c. 1961–1973', *South African Historical Journal*, 68, no. 1 (2016), pp. 31–49.

Coquery-Vidrovitch, Catherine, 'L'Impact des intérêts coloniaux: SCOA and CFAO dans l'Ouest Africain, 1910–1965', *Journal of African History*, 16 (1975), pp. 595–621.

Coquery-Vidrovitch, Daniel Hémery, and Jean Piel, *Pour une histoire du développement. Etats, sociétés et développement* (L'Harmattan, Paris, 2007).

Connelly, Matthew, *Fatal Misconception. The Struggle to Control World Population* (Harvard University Press, Cambridge, MA, 2010).

Constantine, Stephen, *The Making of British Colonial Development Policy 1914–1940* (Routledge, London, 1984).

Cooper, Frederick, *Decolonization and African Society. The Labor Question in French and British Africa* (Cambridge University Press, Cambridge, 1996)

Cooper, Frederick, *Citizenship between Empire and Nation: Remaking France and French Africa, 1945–1960* (Princeton University Press, Princeton and London, 2014).

Cullather, Nick, *The Hungry World: America's Cold War Battle against Poverty in Asia* (Harvard University Press, Cambridge, MA, 2010).

Cullen, Poppy, *Kenya and Britain after Independence. Beyond Neo-Colonialism* (Palgrave Macmillan, Basingstoke, 2017).

Cumming, Gordon, *Aid to Africa. French and British Policies from the Cold War to the New Millenium* (Ashgate, Aldershot, 2001).

Davis, Haleh M., 'Producing Eurafrica: Development, Agriculture and Race in Algeria, 1958–1965' (PhD, NYU, 2015).

Decker, Stephanie, 'Building Up Goodwill: British Business, Development and Economic Nationalism in Ghana and Nigeria, 1945–1977', *Enterprise & Society*, 9, no. 4 (2008), pp. 602–613.

Decker, Stephanie, 'Corporate Legitimacy and Advertising: British Companies and the Rhetoric of Development in West Africa, 1950–1970', *Business History Review*, 81, no. 1 (2007), pp. 59–86.

Decker, Stephanie, 'Decolonising Barclays DCO? Corporate Africanisation in Nigeria, 1945–1969', *The Journal of Imperial and Commonwealth History*, 33, no. 3 (2005), pp. 419–440.

De Villers, Gauthier, *De Mobutu à Mobutu. Trente ans de relations Belgique-Zaïre* (De Boeck, Bruxelles, 1995).

Dimier, Véronique, 'Politique indigène en France et Grande-Bretagne dans les années 1930: à l'origine de l'idéologie développementaliste', *Politique et Société*, 24, no. 1 (2005), pp. 73–99.

Dimier, Véronique, 'L'Institutionnalisation de la Commission Européenne (DG Développement): du rôle des leaders dans la construction d'une administration multinationale, 1958–1975', *Etudes internationales*, 34, no. 3 (2003), pp. 401–428.

Dimier, Véronique, 'Legitimizing the DG8: a small family business (1958–1975)', European Consortium for Political Research, joint session, Grenoble, 6–10 April 2001.

Dimier, Véronique, *The Invention of a European Development Aid Bureaucracy. Recycling Empire* (Palgrave Macmillan, Basingstoke, 2014).

Eckert, Andreas, Stephen Malinowski, and Corinna Unger (eds.), 'Modernizing Missions. Approaches to Developing the Non-Western World after 1945', special issue, *Journal of Modern European History*, 8, no. 1 (2010).

Ekbladh, David, *The Great American Mission: Modernization and the Construction of an American World Order* (Princeton University Press, Princeton and Oxford, 2010).

Engermann, David C., Nils Gilman, Mark Haefle, and Michael E. Latham (eds.), *Staging Growth. Modernization, Development and the Global Cold War* (University of Massachusetts Press, Amherst, MA, 2003).

Engermann, David C., and Corinna Unger, 'Introduction: Towards a Global History of Modernization', *Diplomatic History*, 33, no. 3 (2009), pp. 375–386.

Fantini, Emanuele, and Luca Puddu, 'Ethiopia and International Aid: Development between High Modernism and Exceptional Measures', in Tobias Hagmann and Filip Reyntjens (eds.), *Aid and Authoritarianism in Africa. Development without Democracy* (Zed Books, London, 2016), pp. 91–108.

Fieldhouse, David K., *Black Africa 1945–80: Economic Decolonization and Arrested Development* (Allen & Unwin, London, 1986).

Fieldhouse, David K., *Merchant Capital and Economic Decolonization: The United Africa Company 1929–1989* (Oxford University Press, Oxford, 1994).

Fieldhouse, David K., *Unilever Overseas. The Anatomy of a Multinational 1895–1965* (Crom Helm, London, 1978).

Fraser, Monika Pohle, 'Not the Needy but the Speedy Ones': West German Development Aid and Private Investment in the Middle East, 1960–1967', in Helge Pharo and Monika Phole Fraser (eds.), *The Aid Rush: Aid Regimes in Northern Europe during the Cold War*, Volume 2 (Oslo Academic Press, Oslo, 2008), pp. 217–243.

Frey, Marc, and Sönke Kunkel, 'Writing the History of Development: A Review of the Recent Literature', *Contemporary European History*, 20, no. 2 (2011), pp. 215–232.

Frey, Marc, Sonia Kunkel, and Corinna Unger (eds.), *International Organizations and Development, 1945–1990* (Palgrave Macmillan, Basingstoke, 2014).

Handley, Antoinette, *Business and State in Africa. Economic Policy-Making in the Neo-Liberal Era* (Cambridge University Press, Cambridge, 2008).

Hibou, Béatrice, *The Force of Obedience. The Political Economy of Repression in Tunisia* (Polity Press, Cambridge, 2011).

Hodeir, Catherine, *Stratégie d'Empire. Le Grand patronat face à la décolonisation, 1945–1963* (Belin, Paris, 2003).

Hodge, Joseph, *Triumph of the Expert. Agrarian Doctrines of Development and the Legacies of British Colonialism* (Ohio University Press, Athens, OH, 2007).

Hodge, Joseph, Gerald Hodl, and Martina Kopf (eds.), *Developing Africa: Concepts and Practices in Twentieth-Century Colonialism* (Manchester University Press, Manchester, 2014).

Hodge, Joseph, 'British Colonial Expertise, Post-Colonial Careering and the Early History of International Development', in Andreas Eckert, Stephen Malinowski, and Corinna Unger (eds.), 'Modernizing Missions. Approaches to Developing the Non-Western World after 1945', special issue, *Journal of Modern European History*, 8, no. 1 (2010).

Hopkins, Anthony G., *An Economic History of West Africa* (Longman, Harlow, 1973).

Hopkins, Anthony G., 'Imperial Business in Africa. Part I', *Journal of African History*, 17 (1976a), pp. 29–48.

Hopkins, Anthony G., 'Imperial Business in Africa. Part II', *Journal of African History*, 17 (1976b), pp. 267–290.

Ireton, Barry, *Britain's International Development Policies. A History of DFID and Overseas Aid* (Palgrave Macmillan, Basingstoke, 2013).

Iriye, Akira, *Global Community: The Role of International Organizations in the Making of the Contemporary World* (Columbia University Press, New York, 2004).

Jolly, Richard, Louis Emmerij, Dharam Ghai, and Frederic Lapeyre, *UN Contributions to Development Thinking and Practice* (Indiana University Press, Bloomington, 2004).

Katsakioris, Constantin, 'Soviet Lessons for Arab Modernization. Soviet Educational aid Towards Arab Countries after 1956', in Andreas Eckert, Stephan Malinowski, and Corinna Unger (eds.), 'Modernizing Missions. Approaches to Developing the Non-Western World after 1945', *Journal of Modern European History*, 8, no. 1 (2010), pp. 85–105.

Kessler, Marie Christine, *La Politique étrangère de la France: acteurs et processus* (Presses FNSP, Paris, 1999).

Killick, Tony, 'Policy Autonomy and the History of British Aid to Africa', *Development Policy Review*, 23, no. 6 (2005), pp. 665–681.

Kleemeier, Elisabeth, 'La France et l'argent noir du Kenya', *Politique Africaine*, 40 (1990), pp. 130–138.

Kothari, Uma, 'From Colonial Administration to Development Studies: A Postcolonial Critique of the History of Development Studies', in Uma Kothari (ed.), *A Radical History of Development Studies. Individuals, Institutions, and Ideologies* (Zed Book, London, 2005), pp. 46–66.

Kottos, Laura, *Europe between Imperial Decline and Quest for Integration* (P. Lang, Brussels, 2015).

Krozewski, Gerold, 'Global Britain and the Post-colonial World: The British Approach to Aid Policies at the 1964 Juncture', *Contemporary British History*, 29, no. 2 (2015), pp. 222–240.

Latham, Michael E., *The Right Kind of Revolution: Modernization, Development and US Foreign Policy from the Cold War to the Present* (Cornell University Press, Ithaca, 2011).

Lickert, Victoria, 'Les milieux d'affaires français, l'AFD et l'Afrique dans les années 1990', in *75 ans au service du développement. L'AFD des origines à nos jours* (Publication de l'AFD, Paris, 2017).

Maekawa, Ichiro, 'Neo-colonialism Reconsidered: A Case Study of East Africa in the 1960s and 70s', *Journal of Imperial and Commonwealth History*, 43 no. 2 (2015), pp. 317–341.

Man, Gregory, *From Empires to NGOs in the West African Sahel* (Cambridge University Press, Cambridge, 2015).

Marseille, Jacques, *Empire colonial et capitalisme Français. Histoire d'un divorce* (Albin Michel, Paris, 1984).

May, Ranald S. Dieter Schumacher, and Mohammed H. Malek, *Overseas Aid. The Impact on Britain and Germany* (Harvester Wheatsheaf, Hemel Hempstead, 1989).

McWilliam, Michael, *The Development Business. A History of the Commonwealth Development Corporation* (Palgrave Macmillan, Basingstoke, 2001).

Médard, Jean François, 'The Underdeveloped State in Tropical Africa: Political Clientelism or Neo-patrimonialism?', in C. Clapham (ed.), *Private Patronage and Public Power: Political clientelism in the Modern State* (Frances Pinter Ltd., 1982).

Meredith, David, and Michael Havinden, *Colonialism and Development. Britain and its Tropical Colonies 1850–1960* (Routledge, London, 1993).

Mitchell, Timothy, *Rule of Experts, Egypt, Techno-Politics, Modernity* (University of California Press, Berkeley, 2002).

Morris, James, '"Cultivating the African": Barclays' DOC and the Decolonization of Business Strategy in Kenya, 1950–1978', *Journal of Commonwealth history*, 4, no. 4 (2016), pp. 649–671.

Murphy, Graig N., *The United Nations Development Programme. A Better Way?* (Cambridge University Press, Cambridge, 2006).

Nkrumah, Kwame, *Neo-Colonialism. The Last Stage of Imperialism* (first pub. 1965; this edn. Panaf Books, London, 1974).

Pacquement, François, *Histoire de l'agence Française de développement en Côte d'Ivoire* (Karthala, Paris, 2015).

Rempe, Martin, *Entwicklung im Konflikt. Die EWG und des Senegal, 1957–1975* (Böhlau, Köln, 2012).

Renou, Xavier, 'A New French Policy for Africa', *Journal of Contemporary African Studies*, 20, no. 1 (2002), pp. 5–27.

Riley, Charlotte, "The Winds of Change are Blowing Economically': The Labour Party and British Overseas Development, 1940s–960s', in Chris Jeppesen and Andrew Smith (eds.), *Britain, France and the Decolonization of Africa. Future Imperfect?* (UCL Press, London, 2017), pp. 43–61.

Riley, Charlotte, '"Tropical Allsorts": The Transnational Flavor of British Development Policies in Africa', *Journal of World History* (2015), 26, no. 4, pp. 839–864.

Schenk, Catherine, *Britain and the Sterling Area. From Devaluation to Convertibility in the 1950s* (Routledge, London, 1994).

Schrijver, Nico, *Development without Destruction: The UN and Global Resource Management* (Indiana University Press, Bloomington, 2010).

Shaw, John, *The UN World Food Programme and the Development of Food Aid* (Palgrave Macmillan, New York, 2001).

Sharma, Patrick Alan, *Robert McNamara's other War. The World Bank and International Development* (University of Pennsylvania Press, Philadelphia, 2017).

Simpson, Bradley R., *Economists with Guns: Authoritarian Development and US-Indonesian Relations, 1960–1968* (Stanford University Press, Stanford, 2008).

Sindab, Jean Nellie, 'The Impact of Expatriates on the Zambian Development Process' (PhD, University of Yale, 1984).

Speich, Daniel, 'The Kenyan Style of African Socialism: Development Knowledge Claims and the Explanatory Limits of the Cold War', *Diplomatic History,* 33, no. 3 (2009), pp. 449–465.

Staples, Amy L., *The Birth of Development: How the World Bank, Food and Agriculture Organization and the World Health Organization Changed the World, 1945–1965* (The Kent State University Press, Athens, OH, 2006).

Stockwell, Sarah, *The Business of Decolonization. British Business Strategies in the Gold Coast* (Oxford University Press, Oxford, 2000).

Stockwell, Sarah, *The British End of the British Empire* (Cambridge University Press, Cambridge, 2018).

Stokke, Olav, *The UN and Development. From Aid to Cooperation* (Indiana University Press, Bloomington, 2009).

Tignor, Robert, *Capitalism and Nationalism at the End of Empire. State and Business in Decolonizing Egypt, Nigeria and Kenya, 1945–1963* (Princeton University Press, Princeton and Oxford, 1998).

Tignor, Robert, *W. Arthur Lewis and the Birth of Development Economics* (Princeton University Press, Princeton and Oxford, 2005).

Toye, John, 'The Aid and Trade Provision of the British Overseas Aid Programme', in Anuradha Bose and Peter Burnell (eds.), *Britain's Overseas Aid Since 1979. Between Idealism and Self-Interest* (Manchester University Press, Manchester, 1991), pp. 97–124.

Toye, John, and Richard Toye, *The UN and Global Political Economy: Trade, Finance and Development* (Indiana University Press, Bloomington, 2010).

Turpin, Frédéric, *De Gaulle, Pompidou et l'Afrique: décoloniser et coopérer (1958–1974)* (Indes Savantes, Paris, 2010).

Uche, Chibuike, 'Oil, British Interests and the Nigerian Civil War', *Journal of African History*, 49 (2008), pp. 111–135.

Unger, Corinna, 'Industrialization vs. Agrarian Reform: West German Modernization Policies in India in the 1950s and 1960s', in Andreas Eckert, Stephan Malinowski, and Corinna Unger (eds.), 'Modernizing Missions. Approaches to Developing the Non-Western World after 1945', *Journal of Modern European History*, 8, no. 1 (2010), pp. 47–63.

Van Beusekom, Monica, *Negotiating Development: African Farmers and Colonial Exports at the Office du Niger, 1920–1960* (Heinemann, Westport, 2002).

Wasserman, Gary, *The Politics of Decolonization: Kenya, Europe and the Land Issue, 1960–1965* (Cambridge University Press, Cambridge, 1976).

White, Nicholas J., 'Imperial Business Interests, Decolonization, and Post-Colonial Diversification', in Martin Thomas and Andrew S. Thompson (eds.), *The Oxford Handbook of the Ends of Empire* (Oxford University Press, Oxford, 2018), pp. 639–660.

Williams, David, *International Development and Global Politics. History, Theory and Practice* (Routledge, London, 2012).

Young, Crawford, 'Imperial Endings and Small States: Disorderly Decolonization for the Netherlands, Belgium, and Portugal', in Miguel Bandeira Jerónimo and Antonio Costa Pinto (eds.), *The Ends of European Colonial Empires: Cases and Comparisons* (Palgrave Macmillan, Basingstoke, 2015), pp. 101–125.

CHAPTER 2

Business, the Commonwealth and the Rhetoric of Development: The Federation of Commonwealth Chambers of Commerce and Africa, 1945–1974

Andrew Dilley

In the decades after 1945 development rose dramatically up the global political agenda.[1] European empires pursued colonial growth, exports and welfare both to legitimate their existence and to facilitate metropolitan post-war reconstruction, not least via the acquisition of dollar-earning exports.[2] Decolonisation then transferred power to anti-colonial nationalists whose aspirations were usually also heavily developmental, pursuing sovereignty to transform economies and societies.[3] In the context of the Cold War, the Western Bloc sought to prevent communist infiltration of the 'third world', and by raising living standards there sought to buttress and validate capitalism.[4] These forces produced fluid languages and practices of development, themselves grounded in ideas about the relationship between the global north and south. This *praxis* of development played

A. Dilley (✉)
University of Aberdeen, Aberdeenshire, UK
e-mail: a.dilley@abdn.ac.uk

© The Author(s) 2020
V. Dimier, S. Stockwell (eds.), *The Business of Development in Post-Colonial Africa*, Cambridge Imperial and Post-Colonial Studies Series, https://doi.org/10.1007/978-3-030-51106-7_2

37

out not only in the actions of states and politicians, but also in those of multinational organisations like the United Nations and the Commonwealth of Nations, and in the activities of NGOs including businesses and business associations.[5]

Africa played a central role in the shifting development agenda. It was a crucial sphere of European colonialism and a significant potential arena in the Cold War. The second African-centred wave of decolonisation reconfigured relations between the north and south not only through the creation of numerous new states but also more generally by transforming global institutions, tipping the membership of supranational bodies like the UN or the Commonwealth of Nations firmly in the direction of the global south.[6] Decolonisation altered not only the institutions connecting north and south, but the ideas underpinning north-south relations. Frederick Cooper has pointed out that whereas the late colonial period 'provided people in the colonies with a basis for making claims upon imperial powers', independence, precisely by ceding state sovereignty, turned 'entitlement into supplication' within the framework of foreign relations between sovereign states. However, he also observed that this transition from imperial 'entitlement' to post-imperial 'supplication' was not instantaneous. Rather, 'alternative "we's" to both imperial incorporation or national separation appeared on the horizon for a time' (i.e. alternative notions of community on which to make and validate south-north claims), even if they proved—in Cooper's judgement—to be chimerical.[7] Thus, African decolonisation played a crucial role in shaping the possibilities and limitations of the post-imperial global framework within which development would be pursued. Business and the development agenda would interact within that framework. Close attention is required to the possibilities, and limitations, of those 'alternative we's'.

The Commonwealth of Nations was one 'alternative we'. The role the post-imperial Commonwealth came to play in development, and the *non-governmental* elements it could mobilise, was shaped by decolonisation.[8] This chapter explores how business associations, whose Commonwealth-level mobilisation originated in an older white-dominions focused incarnation of the Commonwealth, sought (and failed) to engage with this African moment. It focuses on the Federation of Commonwealth Chambers of Commerce (FCCC), as it became in the early 1960s, which in 1945 was the largest and leading pan-Empire Commonwealth business association.[9] It shows how political changes placed a reconfigured rhetoric of development focused on Africa at the heart of the organisation's activities. By the mid-1960s, to be a legitimate Commonwealth organisation of necessity required an engagement with both development and Africa. Yet the pre-existing Anglo-dominion networks could not easily be refocused on Africa. Political imperative lacked underlying economic rationale. In the end, this contradiction undermined the Federation in 1974. Thus, while the Commonwealth would persist as a quasi-governmental entity with (as is often noted) a significant penumbra of associated NGOs, business consciously mobilising at Commonwealth level would not be part of that penumbra.[10]

The failure of the Federation's engagement with development in Africa thus reveals a crucial limit to the Commonwealth's development drive. Moreover, it shows an important limitation in the engagement of global business with post-colonial African development. In the 'old' Commonwealth the dense social networks reflected in organisations like the FCCC played an important role in generating new economic opportunities, facilitating inflows of capital and labour and exchanges of goods and services.[11] The failure of a Commonwealth business 'we' meant that post-independence Africa would not have access to the same kinds of networks. This configured the global business presence and economic opportunities available to the continent following decolonisation.

I

The Commonwealth of Nations emerged from the inter-war British Commonwealth of Nations. The term British Commonwealth of Nations, although it had some antecedents, was first officially deployed in the 1921 Anglo-Irish Treaty. Membership comprised Britain, the self-governing dominions (including Eire) and India, all of which had full status at the imperial conferences which had emerged from the end of the nineteenth century. India had been included by Resolution IX of the 1917 Imperial War Conference. But the interwar Commonwealth fundamentally centred on Britain and the self-governing dominions, including South Africa, and focused on economic, constitutional and strategic relations between these entities.[12]

The interwar Commonwealth possessed a deep civil society—clusters of organisations that fostered and embodied less formal networks and gave depth and some degree of organic substance to the association. These overlapped with or were indistinguishable from broader pan-imperial networks, many of them concentrated in the British Commonwealth of

Nations. Empire remained the term of choice.[13] This was true of the Federation of Chambers of Commerce of the British Empire (as the FCCC was then called), the pan-empire-Commonwealth business association which achieved the most significant engagement from businesses beyond Britain.[14]

The Federation drew support from chambers of commerce across the empire, but principally from the UK, Canada, the antipodes and (to a lesser extent) South Africa. It was organised by the London chamber of commerce. It is difficult and misleading to over-generalise about the kinds of businesses represented. Chambers of commerce in the Anglophone world function on a voluntary basis and their composition varies. They are unified by the goal of projecting a 'local voice' and generally represent the leading economic interests in particular areas, although they tend to focus on trade, commerce and services since manufacturers and retailers (e.g. in the UK, Canada, and Australia) tend to form their own associations.[15] Chambers' pre-1939 mobilisation at empire-commonwealth level brought together chambers to formulate shared views on matters of imperial governance, especially the totemic policy of imperial preference. This took place particularly through quasi-parliamentary Congresses involving hundreds of delegates from chambers to formulate resolutions taken forward by the Federation. Debates and participation at these Congresses and hence in the Federation were overwhelmingly concentrated on the UK and the old dominions, that is, on the core of the British Commonwealth of Nations.[16]

The proceedings of the Federation's 1939 congress reveal the degree and nature of representation of Africa and of colonial development. Of 159 chambers which were members of the Federation, 27 were from Africa of which 15 were from South Africa and a further three from Southern Rhodesia. Fifteen sent delegates to the congress, nine from South Africa, two from the Rhodesias and none from West Africa. All except Leon C. Ishmael of Uganda seem to be European expatriates. Of the 27 resolutions adopted, only a scattering centred on the colonial empire: one urging the UK government to consider the interests of the colonies in trade agreements, two calling for the continuation of empire preference in citrus fruit and petroleum, and one criticising the Crown Agents' (official purchasers) monopoly in procuring colonial stores. At one point Sir Arthur J. Aiton of Derby argued that 'a very slight increase in the standard of living of the black races of Africa would produce a very fine market, and the same was true of the West Indies'.[17] But such references were only incidental. Colonial development, like African representation, was marginal within the Federation until 1939.

II

During the 1940s, development simultaneously rose up the agenda globally, at Commonwealth level, and within the Federation. It did so in two phases pivoting respectively around the Second World War and the period of the 'second colonial occupation', and political decolonisation at the turn of the 1960s.[18] The immediate post-war prominence of development became quickly apparent when in October 1945 the Federation held a conference in London to discuss the post-war world. The conference included delegations from the UK, the Dominions, India and Southern Rhodesia, plus further delegates from 'associations or provincial chambers in the larger colonies' including the president of the Lagos chamber of commerce and further representatives from the associated chambers of Northern Rhodesia and East Africa. Including South Africa, the seemingly exclusively expatriate 'representatives' of Africa accounted for a quarter of the total of 44 delegates combined with larger numbers for the West Indies and India. Thus Africa immediately assumed greater prominence than before the war.[19]

Colonial development also assumed a new importance. The topic was the subject of a discrete section of the 1945 conference's approved report, which synthesised the now unrecorded discussions. Discussion of the 1940 and 1945 Colonial Development Acts (CDAs) revealed business representatives echoing the mix of welfare-ism and economic imperatives which underlay the so-called second colonial occupation. Equally, a racially-inflected paternalism revealed itself in an account of the evolution of colonial economic governance.[20] Thus, the congress rejected the laissez-faire approach to colonial economies because the 'indigene was quite incapable of protecting his own interests in a deal with the white man'. Modernisation therefore had to be managed by the state and at a slow pace since 'The shattering of old beliefs, the changes in traditional ways of life which necessarily follow from contact with white civilisation, must not be allowed to make too great a demand on the indigene's powers of adaption, otherwise his society will not develop it will disrupt'. Building on this it was therefore 'now a far step from recognising the obligation to protect the population from exploitation to the acceptance of responsibility to assist them in the development of themselves and their country'. The conference supported the 1945 CDA as a means to enable colonies to 'stand on their own two feet' as a prelude to 'maturity and nationhood...alongside the other sovereign nations within the framework of empire'. Money should be spent (generally, they argued, by better informed local governments) on 'social services' (medicine, education) and on promoting 'balanced agriculture' to avoid dependence on one cash crop.[21]

The conference revealed early anxiety about political change. It asserted that mandated territories and protectorates should not be transferred from 'one sovereign power to another'. 'In primitive communities', it continued, 'the economic factor was frequently of far greater interest to the welfare of the people than the political'. Hence such transfers might block existing channels of trade and do 'severe damage' to an economy 'incapable of sustaining so severe a shock'. The Federation endorsed a call for the unification of Britain's central African territories encompassing not only the Rhodesias and Nyasaland (what became the Central African Federation) but also Northern Bechuanaland, Tanganyika, Kenya and Uganda. These territories' 'low population density' created a 'severe handicap to any attempt to develop primary production'. Amalgamation would create a 'worthwhile internal market'.[22] Thus, chambers of commerce leaders articulated a model of development derived from government, seasoned with racially-inflected paternalism, influenced by Southern Rhodesian and (perhaps) South African expatriate colonialism.

The growth in attention to Africa continued into the late 1940s. In 1948 the Federation held its first full congress since the war in Johannesburg. The congress coincided with the election of F. D. Malan's National Party, which reaffirmed the Smuts government's invitation. The Mayor of Johannesburg's opening address asserted that the event showed a 'growing recognition of Africa in international affairs and in international commerce'. He thought it also an opportunity to 'disprove' the 'maliciously misleading information' which circulated on the Union's 'treatment of minority and native races'. Delegates, he continued, would see the 'real and true position of our relationship with other peoples in our multilateral civilisation'.[23]

The congress strongly articulated a late-colonial vision of development centred on Africa. As the Federation's then president, Lord Balfour of Inchrye, explained: 'there is one direction of real hope for productive expansion, such as will enable standards of living in the Commonwealth to be sustained and then raised. It lies in a bold Commonwealth and Colonial Empire development policy pursued enthusiastically by all partners in agreement, each with the other'. The 1948 congress's report again devoted a section to 'colonial development'. This highlighted the real potential for 'new dollar industries in African chrome, copper, and manganese'. It reiterated that businessmen from 'all parts of the empire' supported the proposed federation of the Rhodesias and Nyasaland, and endorsed the need to overturn the Congo Basin Treaties to ensure the proposed entity had full tariff sovereignty. The problems of the Tanganyika Ground Nut Scheme showed the need for 'exhaustive planning', 'cooperation between members of the Commonwealth', the management of labour, the use of technical experts to 'train native labour', and capital. The report continued that to secure the necessary investment, capital needed the 'maximum protection possible' when 'political change is bought about' since 'confidence' could easily be 'rudely shaken'. It also criticised some exploitative practices, particularly bulk purchasing at 'below world price'. The congress also endorsed a call for dollars to be 'equitably shared' with the colonial empire.[24] Thus, a more fully-fledged vision of development based on capital investment and technical expertise overseen by Europeans permeated the 1948 report—with Balfour's term 'partnership' imbued with an essentially hierarchical meaning.[25] African development required Africans' continued subordination.

Such an approach emphasising the need for capital investment, the potential of economic integration in Central Africa and the role of Europeans persisted through to the late 1950s.[26] So too did concerns about the supposedly destabilising effects of political change. Thus the report of the 1957 congress, held two months after Ghanaian independence, called for a bipartisan policy between the Conservatives and Labour on self-government as the 'current practice of conceding independence when colonies were capable of managing their own affairs' left 'too wide an area of *potential* [my italics] disagreement'. The concern was not that the two parties differed so much as that there was not enough clarity on when these conditions would be deemed to be met in particular colonies. Hence the report explained that there was

> no sense of security but instead a considerable measure of uncertainty which militates against capital investment in the colonies, discourages the immigra-

tion of those who could help guide the territories in their way of life, and acts as a deterrent to the development of that prosperous trade which is fundamental to the well-being of both the colonial peoples as well as of the Commonwealth as a whole.

The congress therefore asked the parties to agree on a 'definite programme of development' which would be pursued regardless of who held power. This would exert a 'profound and stabilising influence' and hence create the conditions for 'optimum development'.[27] Political decolonisation, and its unpredictable nature and timing, thus continued to be imagined as a destabilising threat to development through capital investment and the application of European expertise: as a potential threat to partnership.

Southern Rhodesian participation in the Federation helped sustain these suspicions of colonial nationalism. In September 1952, Roy Welensky, soon to be prime minister of the new Central African Federation, addressed an audience at the London chamber composed of the representatives of over 60 firms, along with the *Financial Times*, Manchester *Guardian*, and *East African Standard*. Welensky distilled the hierarchical settler conception of partnership. He asserted that 'only a handful of Africans would be capable of playing any real part in the government of central Africa for some considerable time' and perhaps 'only a dozen could be compared with adult Europeans today'. African nationalism should be 'recognised and used for the good of central Africa' while those opposing federation represented a 'small element' determined to further their 'own ends'. He warned (not un-prophetically) that the failure of the Central African Federation would 'spawn European nationalism and there would be a clash'. In discussion he added that opposition was generally due to a 'lack of understanding rather than nationalism' since less than 10% of African adults could write, and that after 30 to 40 years of 'the African [being] told what was good for him, now he was being asked what he would like to do—he could not therefore make up his own mind...nor did he want to do so'. None of this proved controversial with the audience, and the chairman of the meeting merely commented that the case for a central African federation was 'unanswerable'.[28]

Welensky's address exemplifies the way in which the networks underlying the FCCC remained white and expatriate dominated, notwithstanding the first wave of decolonisation in Asia. The 1945 London conference had been denounced by the Federation of Indian Chambers of Commerce and Industry (drawing together South Asian-dominated chambers of commerce) for making claims about India in the absence of genuine Indian representatives other than the expatriate-dominated Association of Indian Chambers of Commerce and Industry.[29] In the early 1950s the FCCC executive considered, somewhat inconclusively, the degree to which they should admit the Indian and Pakistani federations of chambers (after partition, both Pakistan and India retained more expatriate-dominated 'associations' of chambers and rival south Asian 'federations'). The Pakistani federation in particular was thought to be 'somewhat anti-British' due to a 'violent outburst against imperial preference' and its view that the Pakistan association was 'anti-Pakistan'.[30] Eventually a compromise was brokered in 1956 to allow Indian chambers to join only with the approval of the Indian federation on the informal understanding that Indian chambers would not 'swamp' the FCCC through 'unfettered admissions'.[31]

The Federation took an equally ambivalent approach to overtures from non-settler Africa. In 1952 an application from the African Chamber of Commerce in the Gold Coast was 'deferred' pending 'replies to a number of very searching questions regarding its status and activities'.[32] A year later a further dilemma arose when the Federation of Chambers of Commerce and Industry of East Africa sought admission. The FCCIEA was 'Asiatic' and the (expatriate-dominated) 'multi-racial' association of chambers in the region was to be 'sounded out' for advice.[33] Negotiation between the two East African bodies broke down. In 1958 the new chair of the FCCC, Lord Lloyd (son of Selwyn Lloyd, until 1957 the undersecretary for the colonies and Federation president from 1958–1962), concluded that it was 'not wise' to allow the FCCIEA's accession since membership 'should be confined to chambers or associations which represented the whole and not merely racial sections of the mercantile community'.[34]

The Federation adopted a distinctive and ultimately less reticent approach to West Africa. The London-based High Commissioner of newly-independent Ghana expressed 'disappointment' that the Ghana chamber of commerce, which was 'entirely African in character', was not a member. Soon after the Liverpool chamber (which had strong connections in the region) passed on information from the Accra chamber that the Ghana and Accra chambers were soon likely to merge. This would form a combination of chambers representing 'larger companies' (Accra) and smaller traders (Ghana), and reflected that Accra thought the Ghana chamber 'worthy of membership'. Nevertheless, the still cautious

Federation decided to consult Accra directly.[35] When the application came, Ghana's admission was adopted after a 'spirited discussion'.[36]

Nigeria, Ghana's West African rival, developed stronger links between the Federation and non-expatriate African business. In particular, the Nigerian politician and businessman Chief S. L. Edu became the lynchpin of a significant connection. Edu rose in the shipping industry and by the late 1950s was transporting oil for British Petroleum. He became a major figure (by the mid-1960s, the president) of the originally expatriate-dominated Lagos chamber of commerce.[37] He first established contact with the Federation in 1953 through a meeting with its secretary at the London chamber of commerce during a visit to London. He was already a member of the Lagos House of Deputies as well as the Lagos chamber of commerce,[38] and attended the 1957 congress. He was to become the most prominent African figure in the Federation over the next ten years. Edu's growing stature coincided with a broader reform designed to make the Federation 'truly representative'.[39] This project required intensification of African connections and re-conceptualised the rhetoric of development, especially shifting the language of partnership into one of equal collaboration between Africans and Europeans. To understand this moment, it is necessary to retrace our steps through the evolution of the post-1945 Commonwealth.

III

In 1945 a white dominion-centred conception of the (still) British Commonwealth of Nations remained dominant. Yet first Asian and then African decolonisation radically altered the association which grew from 8 members in 1939 to 11 in 1960. In that year the admission of Cyprus (and hence all small former colonies) paved the way for a further dramatic expansion to 32 by 1960.[40] The changing scale and composition disturbed the concept of the Commonwealth, ushering in, from the late 1940s, a period of flux through the 1950s, reflected for example in the subtle dropping of 'British' from the official lexicon and (with varied and often heavily lagged timing) from civil society nomenclature.[41] The (re)-admission of India as a republic under the 1949 Declaration of London cemented this re-imagination of the Commonwealth as 'multi-racial'. Asian decolonisation produced a still-small but widened circle—the 'Nehru Commonwealth'—that could still be imagined as a close-knit, distinct and (at least potentially) coordinated entity.[42] This operated in combination with the continuation of other key integrating economic elements, the frozen but not yet abolished imperial preferences, and the Commonwealth-dominated sterling area.[43]

The second wave of decolonisation centred on Africa resulted in a larger Commonwealth with a much-expanded membership. The sheer proliferation of voices and the increasingly contrasting nature of the member states in and of themselves altered the nature of the entity.[44] The establishment of the Commonwealth Secretariat, particularly as a result of pressure exerted by Nkrumah, formalised the decoupling of the association from the UK state. It symbolised the need for the official and unofficial Commonwealth to eschew connections with 'neo-colonialism'. The departure first of South Africa from the Commonwealth in 1961 and then Rhodesia in 1965 further ensured a (increasingly vehement) rejection of settler-centric conceptions of development and politics. Increasingly, settlers in Africa became part of the problem and not part of the solution.[45]

The economics of the Commonwealth shifted with the changed political composition. The winding down of the sterling area as a managed currency bloc from the late 1950s significantly loosened economic coordination, not least in Africa where the Commonwealth and the sterling area virtually coincided.[46] The erosion of the value and relevance of imperial preference in the context of shifting patterns of world trade, and in particular as a result of Britain's applications to the EEC from the early 1960s, removed a further symbolic and practical expression of economic cooperation.[47] These economic changes, in combination with political decolonisation and its developmental aspirations, of necessity placed development ever more at the centre of the official Commonwealth agenda.[48] At the same time, political independence necessarily altered the rhetoric of development. Very different conceptions of partnership came to the fore emphasising the equality, inclusion and empowerment of Africans (especially through education).[49]

These changes necessarily had a powerful impact within business circles. In the late 1950s and early 1960s the FCCC sought to catch up with the political changes in the Commonwealth. As a Commonwealth-level organisation, it could only retain legitimacy by responding to this shifting Commonwealth-level political and economic agenda. This required a significant and altered engagement with the development agenda and with Africa. From the late 1950s, building on the initial overtures in West Africa, the Federation pursued a programme of internal reform to respond to the rapidly changing Commonwealth. The programme was led by

Lloyd, who explained the need to change at the 1959 annual meeting. In a 'bewildering' age, he said, the association faced a 'dangerous time' with a 'real risk' that a newly independent nation would '[shift] out of the Commonwealth'. Lloyd implied that this might also mean embracing communism since, in contrast to the old dominions which shared 'ideals' of 'democracy, freedom and justice' (classic Cold War lexicon), in the newly independent post-colonial world there were 'rather disturbing signs that those ideals are very rapidly forgotten as soon as direct British guidance is removed'. In this context, Britain must play a 'leading part in the development' of underdeveloped members as the 'surest means to cement the Commonwealth'. The Federation, he asserted, could facilitate this goal.[50]

Lloyd proposed reforms designed to 'adapt…to the changed pattern' of the Commonwealth and hence enable the Federation 'to play its proper role in coining commercial and industrial opinion' by making it 'truly representative'. The organisation could no longer 'continue to restrict its membership to British chambers of commerce'.[51] Borrowing from the model of the International Chamber of Commerce, new national or regional committees would be formed where national associations did not exist to handle membership and thus to prevent the London headquarters of the Federation from being placed in an awkward position by continuing to have to act as adjudicate on admissions, as had been the case with the FCCIEA. These regional committees were also intended to promote deeper bilateral connections.[52] The Federation's budget would increase tenfold, largely through increased UK and 'old' Commonwealth contributions—introducing a disjuncture between the membership and financing that was to prove problematic. The changes required a re-imagination of 'partnership'. As Lloyd explained:

> If we are to play a part in the development of the new Commonwealth, and if we are to capture the imagination and goodwill of these people…we have got to treat them on terms of equality. We can no longer tell them what to do. We can only persuade them that our ideas are the right ideas and by giving them all the help we can, and by showing our goodwill build up the necessary confidence and trust.[53]

Reform was thus not only administrative but also involved a re-imagination of the Federation for a 'multi-racial' Commonwealth, a re-imagination that inevitably placed development centre stage. Lloyd's programme of reform was ratified at the 1960 congress in Canberra, with some disquiet leading to a short-lived compromise over the proposal to drop the word 'British' from the Federation's title.[54]

Queen Elizabeth II inaugurated the reformed organisation at the opening of the 1962 congress, praising the 'vitality which your Federation has shown in adapting itself'.[55] The change was symbolised in a photograph of Lloyd introducing Edu to the Queen reproduced in the *Chamber of Commerce Journal*.[56] In a further symbolic act in 1962, the venue of the next (now biennial) congress to be held in 1964 was shifted from Rhodesia to Port of Spain in Trinidad. As Lloyd explained, 'congress had hitherto been held in the largest commercial centres of the Commonwealth'. Hence 'the time had come to spread the net rather wider'. Although Rhodesia had already asked to host the congress, they had to consider 'what is best planning and what is best for the Commonwealth'.[57]

The reconstituted FCCC acquired a wider membership across the new Commonwealth. In Africa in particular it built connections in Nigeria and Kenya where the post-independence governments adopted a private sector, export-orientated approach to development in combination with indigenisation policies.[58] Ghana conversely (where Nkrumah favoured a more statist and closed approach) ceased membership with the formation of a new state-run Ghanaian National Chamber.[59] In 1961 South Africa's departure from the Commonwealth obliged South African chambers to leave the FCCC, whose membership cleaved to formal Commonwealth membership, notwithstanding the continued close connections with British business and through the sterling area.[60] South African withdrawal, with the marginalisation of Rhodesia, reduced African settler representation.

By 1965 the Federation showed signs of success in its quest for African engagement. By 1965, the FCCC's African membership beyond South Africa had increased from 15 in 1957 to 49 in 1965, or from 9% to 16% of the total membership. Of those chambers, 11 came from Nigeria, matching Rhodesia's total. No other region of the Commonwealth saw such an increase, although in the Caribbean membership also advanced from 11 to 22. Eight African chambers sent delegates to the 1964 congress, the highest total (excluding South Africa) in the Federation's history. Sixteen per cent of sub-Saharan African member chambers participated, compared to only 10% of UK member chambers (which made Port of Spain the lowest UK turnout in the Federation's history) and only 4.5% of Australasian members.[61]

Just as patterns of membership and participation shifted, so too did the rhetoric of development. The congresses of the 1960s devoted more attention to—and crucially reconceived the 'we' at the heart of—development. The changes reached fruition at the 1964 congress in Port of Spain, which coincided with the establishment of the United Nations Conference on Trade and Development.[62] In that context, the symbolism of the holding of the first congress in a developing part of the Commonwealth was picked up by the island's governor Sir Solomon Hochoy, who opened the congress by bemoaning the growing gap between rich and poor countries and the way in which trade increasingly bypassed the latter. The Federation's president, Canadian Major-General Alfred Walford, echoed this and asserted that 'We here all accept and we fully understand the complete independence of [Commonwealth] members, although other countries seem to find it hard to believe in some cases that elements of neo-colonialism does not persist'.[63]

Elements of continuity and change in discourses on development were well on display in 1964. The section of the report on development opened by stressing the 'great urgency' in narrowing gaps in living standards. It considered a major problem to be the need to promote domestic capital formation to a 'self-supporting point' supplemented by official aid and outside investment, thus for the first time placing prime emphasis on domestic resources. The congress still called for an increase in outside private investment, restating the 'fear of social, political, and economic instability', and hence asserting the necessity to demonstrate 'profitable investment opportunities and reasonable social, monetary and political stability'. It urged chambers to pressure their governments to do this by adopting 'fiscal and monetary policies' to 'ensure stability', and to encourage 'technical, managerial, and professional know-how', while using 'expatriates where it can be shown that local expertise has not yet developed'; to impose 'no discrimination between local and foreign capital'; encourage savings institutions that invest in profitable activities; encourage 'joint ventures' using 'indigenous and external resources'; control 'population expansion'; 'avoid excessive protection'; pursue the 'objective of liberalisation and integration with the rest of the Commonwealth' and encourage 'indigenous production' to achieve 'greater self-sufficiently and increased export trade'.[64] Thus a vision of the centrality of private enterprise and investment within a stable political framework remained at the heart of FCCC discourses of development.

This vision now also emphasised local as well as expatriate and multinational business. This in turn led to a desire to help build stronger chambers in the new Commonwealth. As a result, the FCCC engaged (on perhaps a low scale) with a more general trend at the end of empire (now thoroughly reconstructed by Sarah Stockwell) of British institutions facilitating the transfer of expertise to the developing Commonwealth to substitute domestic for expatriate labour.[65] The 1962 congress called for chambers of commerce in 'developed countries' to offer 'prolonged training periods' for chambers officials from the new Commonwealth. The 1964 report called for exchanges of personnel between members of the developing and developed Commonwealth.[66] The extent of what would inevitably be ad hoc exchanges remains difficult to chart, but in 1968 the London chamber of commerce hosted four long exchanges.[67]

The reconstituted Federation sought to be a crucible for intra-Commonwealth business networking. As Walford explained in opening the 1964 congress, 'the expansion of Commonwealth trade is too often thought of merely as trade between other Commonwealth countries and the UK, whereas the mutual development of trade between any and all Commonwealth countries is the objective which must always be before us'.[68] The hope had been to promote increased bilateral exchanges. Some took place. In 1964 a UK delegation visited Lagos for discussions with Nigeria, discussions which continued in London in 1965 with a further bilateral meeting and a luncheon in honour of visiting Prime Minister Abubakar Tafawa Balewa.[69] However, the FCCC's annual reports also reveal relatively few bilateral connections being formed with tropical Africa. Beyond the mid-1960s engagement with Nigeria, there was only one further visit by the FCCC's UK Committee to Africa, to Ghana in 1967, occasioned by Nkruhmah's fall from power. No other 'old' Commonwealth chamber visited the continent, and beyond Canadian—Caribbean connections, few other north-south connections emerged, and none specifically due to the Federation. South-south connections were virtually absent.[70]

With the FCCC only a weak crucible for bilateral exchanges, the congresses remained the key venue within which new connections might be formed. The location of the congress and the goals of the FCCC leadership were therefore closely entwined. It was revealing that the 1964 congress agreed, after deliberations by what the report described as 'a council of elders', that the next congress would definitely take place in Africa, but in Nigeria rather than Southern Rhodesia as had previously been proposed. One Nigerian delegate explained the benefits to Nigeria in an interesting (and perhaps unconscious) echo of the language of the 'young country' once applied to the old dominions:[71] '[Africa] is a new and important continent and I believe you will learn a great deal', and that 'We…would like you to give us the opportunity to show you the vastness of our country and the difficulties which we are having at the moment and the way we rise to the challenge of the issues involved'. The Rhodesians acquiesced in the shift of the congress venue to Lagos since 'we have been resolute that the next congress should be in Africa'.[72] The attempt to hold a congress in Lagos, however, was to reveal how the changing Commonwealth, and the development agenda the decision reflected, was detaching the Federation from its base in the UK and the old dominions.

IV

The FCCC's shift in focus to Africa and development ran counter to broader economic developments during the 1960s. First intra-Commonwealth trade declined as a proportion of total Commonwealth trade from 39% and 36% of imports and exports in 1960 to 14% in 1970. The UK and old dominions saw their trade with the US and continental Europe outpace trade with each other and the new Commonwealth, part of a re-orientation of post-war global trade towards intensifying north-north exchanges.[73] The proportion of UK imports and exports with the developing Commonwealth in Africa was low and relatively static: 4.5% and 5.2% in 1961, and 3.6% and 4% in 1970. Such countries were marginal for both antipodean and Canadian trade.[74] While volumes of Commonwealth trade declined, the liberalisation of the sterling area, the freezing of imperial preference under GATT, and the UK's courtship of the EEC all challenged the concept of the Commonwealth as an entity within which economic governance would be practised. Thus, the need to lobby at Commonwealth level declined for UK and old dominions chambers, and with it the rationale for the Federation.[75] Meanwhile the development agenda focused on both a political economy and spheres of economic activity in Africa which were marginal to UK and old dominion chambers. The politics of development ungirded the FCCC from any underlying economic or political rationale.

The proposed Lagos congress revealed the difficulties in this context of sustaining a pan-Commonwealth business association refocused on Africa and the development agenda. That only 15% of member chambers sent delegates to Port of Spain already highlighted the risk that shifting to the developing Commonwealth would weaken interest in the Federation. Even so, its leadership failed to recognise the potential weakness. Preparations for the Lagos congress continued apace through 1965, with key figures visiting to inspect what were seen as largely satisfactory arrangements.[76] However, by June 1966 it became clear that the congress was not attracting interest. Only the UK, the Caribbean and New Zealand had contributed any resolutions to the agenda, and the latter two were unable to send delegates, and neither were Australia, Hong Kong, Singapore or any other African country. Only Canada, India and the UK had committed to sending representatives. As the FCCC executive considered how to proceed, Edu complained that since 'all countries had agreed to hold these congresses in different Commonwealth countries, that all countries would have made an effort to be represented'.[77] A month later, in Edu's absence, the leadership concluded that while undesirable, cancellation 'would be wise if possible to avoid risking a failure'.[78]

The forces undermining the attempt to connect the old pan-commonwealth chambers movement to development and Africa were laid bare in internal discussions on the reasons for the failure in Lagos. The military coup in January of that year and the subsequent political instability (which ultimately culminated in the Nigerian Civil War from 1967) may have played a role in deterring delegates. That Edu had to be reassured that the lack of uptake was not 'in any way due to the present military regime or recent events in Nigeria' should perhaps not be taken at face value. Nonetheless, the FCCC's council believed that the underlying cause was the 'present attitude towards Commonwealth trade', that trade within the Commonwealth was not increasing, and that increasingly the Commonwealth was not conceived of as a 'trading entity'. On a practical level, attendance was low because delegates could only afford to attend congresses by justifying them as a 'business expense'. Hence 'in the case of Commonwealth countries which had little trade with Nigeria it was extremely difficult to fund delegates who were able to go'.[79] The Associated Chambers of Commence of New Zealand struggled in vain to find members likely to be present.[80] The relatively low proportions of trade between most Commonwealth countries and Nigeria, along with expectations especially in the context of political instability that trade was unlikely to expand, made it hard to attract delegates there, even from other African states. In response to the Lagos failure and disillusionment in the old Commonwealth, the FCCC was plunged into a holding pattern, with a much reduced budget, and its activities purely focused on congresses.[81] The limits of the project of connecting 'old Commonwealth' trade networks to a 'new Commonwealth' development agenda—of engaging private enterprise the Commonwealth as an alternative 'we'—were becoming clear.

Yet the project did not end in 1966. The FCCC found a new ally in the Commonwealth secretariat. Initial contact had been established soon after the Secretariat was founded in 1965.[82] The new secretary-general Arnold Smith addressed the 1968 congress and hosted a reception at Marlborough House, as well as attending what was to prove the last congress.[83] By 1972 the Secretariat was keen to preserve Commonwealth-wide meetings of businessmen. The Federation's director believed that 'the link with the Commonwealth Secretariat was the most useful thing that had happened to the FCCC since the war'. Smith was particularly keen for more to be done to finance and facilitate training in developing countries.[84] The development trajectory was further reinforced when in 1970 Malcolm Macdonald became the Federation's last president, which ended a long pan-Commonwealth career that included serving as governor and then second British High Commissioner in Kenya from 1963 to 1964, and from 1967 to 1969 serving as a roving ambassador in Africa for Wilson's Labour government.[85]

Development became the primary focus of the final congresses. The 1968 congress adopted 'the Commonwealth in the context of possible world economy groupings' as its theme. Arnold Smith used his address to outline the need for an open commonwealth which would bridge the developed and developing worlds.[86] In 1970 a congress in Hong Kong took as its theme a 'Focus on Constructive Commonwealth Cooperation'. Even more than in 1968 the report focused again on the need to foster development through private sector cooperation. The 1972 congress took as its theme 'Commonwealth Development through Business Enterprise', and emphasised the need to improve business education, secure increased investment and promote exports.[87]

Some old dominion members viewed this development agenda with scepticism. In 1970 the general manager of the Melbourne chamber of commerce thought the Federation 'lacked cohesion', and a year later that chamber's president complained that 'the benefits which accrued through the FCCC were mainly derived by the developing countries of the Commonwealth'. Australian chambers were not opposed to forging connections and fostering development. This period saw a serious

2 BUSINESS, THE COMMONWEALTH AND THE RHETORIC...   55

engagement with Asian countries through the Confederation of Asian Chambers of Commerce and Industry, and also with the Pacific Basin Economic Council (a pan-Pacific business association).[88] However, an Afro-centric Commonwealth was of less interest than the newly emerging possibilities in the Asia-Pacific region. There, and elsewhere, regional as opposed to all-Commonwealth business associations provided the more obvious framework within which to pursue such activities.

The UK's courtship of the EEC remained an area where the Commonwealth level retained economic relevance. The issue had implications for all member countries, and EEC membership placed in jeopardy many of the remaining pan-Commonwealth economic frameworks such as preferential trade and the Commonwealth Sugar Agreement. Europe had drawn the attention of congresses since the late 1950s. In 1962, amidst the first application, the Federation's congress had supported the UK's application (reflecting its strong UK membership) but reiterated the need for the UK to take account of the interests of other Commonwealth members.[89]

When the UK resumed pursuit of membership in the late 1960s, the EEC issue and the development agenda coalesced. In response, the FCCC—like Arnold Smith's Secretariat—gave particular attention to the developing Commonwealth.[90] Hence, the 1968 congress asserted that 'Britain had a duty to those Commonwealth countries whose trading patterns had developed on the basis of Commonwealth preference and whose total trade or individual products were particularly vulnerable'. That of course could include New Zealand but the report went on to call specifically on the UK to work from within to persuade the EEC to make 'generous concessions to exports of manufactured goods from the developing countries'.[91] At the last congress in 1972, Smith addressed the Congress and on the EEC urged for the interests of developing nations to be taken into account. Responding, Michael Noble, UK minister for trade, reassured the delegates that 'strong emphasis was laid on the vital importance of recognising the special needs of the developing and developed countries in respect of sensitive commodities', pointing to arrangements being made for sugar producers. Similarly, George Bertoin, EEC Ambassador in the UK, took the opportunity to outline the advantages for developing countries of association with the EEC through the second Yaoundé convention, emphasising the degree to which protection was still possible to promote industrialisation.[92]

The strong emphasis on the EEC in 1972 shows how, temporarily, the issue gave the Federation some impetus. Although it did not then have the resources to lobby actively for its members, it did circulate a fortnightly newsletter to members entitled 'Commonwealth and European Focus' offering the latest intelligence.[93] Yet, that impetus was temporary. In 1972 Noble pointed out that worries about EEC protection might be addressed through a new round of GATT talks and through the renegotiation of the Yaoundé conventions (which eventually led to the Lomé Convention of 1975).[94] Noble inadvertently highlighted how in future developed Commonwealth countries would relate to the UK and EEC through different frameworks. The moment of unity around Britain's EEC entry could not be expected to last.

The Federation did not last long after the UK joined the EEC: it ceased activity in 1974. As recounted elsewhere, the shifting patterns of trade, the erosion of Commonwealth economic governance and the EEC application all played a role in the Federation's demise. There was nonetheless a strong African dimension in precipitating the final crisis, in effect a repeat of Lagos 1966.[95] This reflected the continued pull of the development agenda. Doubtless as a result of Macdonald's East African connections (perhaps not least his friendship with Jomo Kenyatta), the Federation committed itself to holding a congress in 1974 in Nairobi. Kenya, like Nigeria, had adopted a broadly open private enterprise-orientated approach to development. Support was secured from the Kenyan government. Kenyatta would open the event and Arnold Smith too agreed to speak.[96] By July 1973 it emerged that Australia and New Zealand would only send 'small delegations' and that it was necessary to do 'everything possible to encourage representation'.[97] By spring 1974 prospects for both the FCCC and the Nairobi congress became grim. By March 1974 only 50 delegates had agreed to attend, half the number needed to break even.[98] Even some of these subsequently withdrew and by 4 July there were only 18 firm delegates, with 25 more possibles. As the FCCC treasurer explained, 'one reason for the lack of support for the congress was the location. A delegate would want to take in the congress whilst on a business trip. [In] some important countries chambers of commerce members saw insufficient opportunity of combining the two in Kenya'. An event that relied on pre-existing networks for its success could not be used to transform the position of a country like Kenya which those networks largely bypassed. The congress was cancelled.[99]

As with Lagos in 1966, the Nairobi congress was organised against the backdrop of a deeper financial crisis in the Federation. This had been made acute by a decision by the London chamber of commerce to withdraw its long-standing subsidy in cash and services. This led to dramatic increases in the proposed contributions from the UK and old dominions. These were opposed by Australia and New Zealand, and were met with luke-warm enthusiasm at best by Canada.[100] When the future was discussed in May 1974, the new director reported that there was 'enthusiasm for the continuation of the FCCC but not in the old Commonwealth'. One member of the governing council reflected that 'there were many organ-isations trying to help developing countries: was the Federation a viable one?' Another commented that 'Britain's membership of the EEC had probably not received a favourable reception from a number of mem-bers'.[101] While supportive, the Commonwealth Secretariat could only help out financially if the organisation applied to the Commonwealth Foundation to undertake a specific project. No application was forthcom-ing. The FCCC ceased activity in summer 1974,[102] and thus ended the most prominent attempt to harness the business networks of the old Commonwealth to promote development in the new Commonwealth.

V

This chapter has charted how a possibility of connecting business and development in Africa through the Commonwealth first erupted and then eroded from 1945 to 1975. It has done so by examining both the net-works and languages of development that ran through the leading pan-Commonwealth business association, the Federation of Commonwealth Chambers of Commerce. First, after 1945 the exigencies of the post-war world and the late colonial development drive pulled the previously heav-ily Anglo dominion-focused Federation's attention towards development and Africa, with a hierarchical understanding of the development process heavily inflected by ideas emerging from settlers in southern Africa. The package imagined down to the mid-1950s combined heavy investment, the use of private enterprise, and leadership and the provision of technical expertise by Europeans. At the same time, although it was never entirely racially exclusive, the FCCC did little to encourage, and much to impede, the entry of significant numbers of non-Europeans into its networks.

Much of this changed in a second phase ushered in from the mid- to late 1950s. Political decolonisation placed the so-called new

Commonwealth at the heart of the conception of and activities surrounding the Commonwealth as a whole. This and the decline of other aspects of Commonwealth economic cooperation made development an ever more central issue. These changes drove a Federation whose members were still, in the late 1950s, convinced of the likely significance of the Commonwealth to engage more explicitly with a development agenda in which partnership was (at least superficially) reconceived as being between equals. Political decolonisation indeed generated a potential alternative 'we', as described by Cooper. The FCCC actively courted connections with Africans in chambers of commerce and countries broadly sympathetic to a conception of development still attached to an open economic vison centred on trade, investment and now-collaborative application of technical expertise. However, the attempt to weld a strong African connection and development dimension into the heart of an association sitting atop old Commonwealth business connections proved unsustainable. It proved difficult to attract old dominion members to the new development-centred agenda, especially as other older forms of economic cooperation eroded. The proposed 1966 and 1974 congresses served as the lenses through which this new reality came to be glimpsed.

Ungirded from a strong grounding in economics and governance, the alternative 'we' of the Commonwealth proved chimerical at least for businesses. Development economics as far as they were pursued at Commonwealth level would be left almost exclusively to state aid and NGOs. The Commonwealth would not therefore become a significant intermediary through which business would connect Africa to the global economy. The fluid networking between Britain and the old dominions from the late nineteenth century had played a crucial role in their ability to attract investment, forge trading connections, and bargain for forms of preferential treatment by the UK which helped foster economic success.[103] The failure of the Federation of Commonwealth Chambers of Commerce as it attempted to refocus on the development agenda reinforced and epitomised the tendency for a more confined set of multilateral companies to connect Africa to the world economy. This in turn promoted the enclave economies that so characterised, and perhaps held back, much postcolonial African development.[104] The failure of this alternative 'we' to marshal the private sector was of more than incidental consequence.

Notes

1. For overviews, see the introduction to this volume and Marc Frey and Sönke Kunkel, 'Writing the History of Development: A Review of the Recent Literature', *Contemporary European History*, 20, no. 2 (2011).
2. Michael Havinden and David Meredith, *Colonialism and Development: Britain and Its Tropical Colonies, 1850–1960* (London; New York, 1993); Jessica Pearson-Patel, 'Promoting Health, Protecting Empire: Inter-Colonial Medical Cooperation in Postwar Africa', *Monde(s)*, 7, no. 1 (2015).
3. Anthony Hopkins, 'Development and the Utopian Idea' in Robin Winks (ed.), *Oxford History of the British Empire*: Vol. 5: *Historiography* (Oxford, 1999), 642–643. See, for example, Kwame Nkrumah, *Africa Must Unite* (New York, 1963).
4. Mark Bradley, 'Decolonization, the Global South, and the Cold War, 1919–1962' in Melvyn Leffler and Odd Arne Westad eds. *The Cambridge History of the Cold War:* Volume 1: *Origins, 1945–1962* (Cambridge, 2010); Matthew Connelly, 'Taking Off the Cold War Lens: Visions of North-South Conflict During the Algerian War for Independence', *American Historical Review*, 105, no. 3 (2000), p. 74; Ademola Adeleke, 'Playing Fairy Godfather to the Commonwealth: The United States and the Colombo Plan', *Commonwealth & Comparative Politics*, 42, no. 3 (2004); William Roger Louis and Ronald Robinson, 'The Imperialism of Decolonization', *Journal of Imperial and Commonwealth History*, 22 (1994).
5. Amy Staples, *The Birth of Development: How the World Bank, Food and Agriculture Organization and the World Health Organization Changed the Worlds* (Ohio, 2006); Olav Stokke, *The UN and Development: From Aid to Cooperation* (Bloomington, Ind., 2009).
6. Krishnan Srinivasan, 'Nobody's Commonwealth? The Commonwealth in Britain's Post-Imperial Adjustment', *Commonwealth and Comparative Politics*, 64 (2006). On the UN, see Mark Mazower, *No Enchanted Palace: The End of Empire and the Ideological Origins of the United Nations* (Princeton, 2009), pp. 197–199; M. Adeleye Ojo, 'Africa and the United Nations' System: Decolonization and Development', *Présence Africaine*, no. 119 (1981).
7. Frederick Cooper, 'Writing the History of Development', *Journal of Modern European History*, 8, no. 1 (2010), pp. 14–16.
8. Srinivasan, 'Nobody's Commonwealth?'; Yusuf Bangura, *Britain and Commonwealth Africa: The Politics of Economic Relations 1951–1975* (Manchester, 1983).

9. The Federation had four different titles in the period. For simplicity, it will be termed 'the Federation' or FCCC throughout.

10. W. David McIntyre, *The Significance of the Commonwealth, 1965–1990* (Basingstoke, 1991), pp. 174–243.

11. Gary Magee and Andrew Thompson, *Empire and Globalisation: Networks of People, Goods and Capital in the British World, c.1850–1914* (Cambridge, 2010); David Thackeray, *Forging a British World of Trade: Culture, Ethnicity, and Market in the Empire-Commonwealth, 1880–1975* (Oxford, 2019).

12. W. David McIntyre, *The Commonwealth of Nations: Origins and Impact, 1869–1971* (Minneapolis, 1977); Robert Holland, *Britain and the Commonwealth Alliance, 1918–1939* (London, 1981); Ian Drummond, *Imperial Economic Policy, 1917–1939* (London, 1974).

13. Claude Scott, 'Caring About the British Empire: British Imperial Activist Groups, 1900–1967' (Ph.D. Thesis, King's College London, 2014). See also the literature on the 'British world', cited and critiqued in Rachel Bright and Andrew Dilley, 'After the British World', *Historical Journal*, 60, no. 2 (2017).

14. See Andrew Dilley, *Commerce and the Commonwealth* (Oxford, forthcoming).

15. Robert Bennett, *The Local Voice: The History of Chambers of Commerce in Britain, Ireland, and Revolutionary America, 1760–2011* (Oxford, 2011).

16. Andrew Dilley, 'The Politics of Commerce: The Congress of Chambers of Commerce of the Empire, 1886–1914', *SAGE Open*, 3, no. 4 (2013); Andrew Dilley, 'Trade after the Deluge: British Commerce, Armageddon, and the Political Economy of Globalization, 1914–1918' in Andrew Smith and Kevin Tennant eds. *The Impact of the First World War on International Business* (London, 2016).

17. London Metropolitan Archive, Federation of Commonwealth Chambers of Commerce Papers [FCCC Papers hereafter], CLC/B/082/MS18287/9 *Congress Report*, 1939, pp. 4–14, 29.

18. John Lonsdale and Donald Anthony Low, 'Towards the New Order 1945–1963' in Donald Anthony Low and Alison Smith eds. *History of East Africa* (Oxford, 1976).

19. FCCC Papers, CLC/B/082/MS18287/10, *Conference Report*, 1945, pp. 1–2

20. On the ideas underpinning the second colonial occupation, see Frederick Cooper, *Africa since 1940: The Past of the Present* (Cambridge, 2002), p. 31.

21. *Conference Report*, 1945, pp. 10–11

22. Ibid., pp. 10–11.

23. FCCC Papers, CLC/B/082/MS18287/11, *Congress Report,* 1948, p. 18.
24. Ibid., pp. 28, 53–56.
25. On the role of 'expertise' in development, see Joseph Hodge, Gerald Hodl, and Martina Kopf (eds.), *Developing Africa: Concepts and Practices in Twentieth-Century Colonialism* (Manchester, 2014).
26. FCCC Papers CLC/B/082/MS18287/12–14, *Congress Reports,* 1951, 1954, 1957.
27. Ibid., 1957, pp. 41–42.
28. FCCC Papers CLC/B/082/MS18283/4, Minutes of Address, 22 September 1952, *Minute Book 4,* pp. 39–40.
29. Andrew Dilley, 'Un-Imagining Markets: Chambers of Commerce, Globalisation and the Political Economy of the Commonwealth, 1945–1974' in David Thackaray, Andrew Thompson, and Richard Toye eds. *Imagining Britain's Economic Future, C.1800–1975: Trade, Consumerism, and Global Markets* (Basingstoke, 2018), 261; Maria Misra, *Business, Race, and Politics in British India, c.1850–1960* (Oxford, 1999).
30. FCCC Papers CLC/B/082/MS18283/4, *Minute Book,* B. R. Graham to A. V. Leigh, 20 April 1951; Executive Committee, 4 May 1951, p. 3.
31. Ibid., Executive Committee, 31 October 1956, pp. 145–146.
32. Ibid., Council, 14 March 1952, pp. 25–27.
33. FCCC Papers CLC/B/082/MS18283/5, *Minute Book,* Council Meeting, 25 July 1957, p. 21.
34. Ibid. Executive Committee, 1 May 1958, pp. 37–38.
35. Ibid. Council, 25 July 1957, p. 21.
36. Ibid. Council Meeting, 15 June 1960, p. 83
37. Siyan Oyeweso, *Journey from Epe: Biography of S.L. Edu* (Ilupeju, Lagos, 1996).
38. FCCC Papers, CLC/B/082/MS18283/4, Minute Book 4, 'Work of the Federation since November 1952', 22 May 1952, p. 4.
39. *Minute Book* 4, Council Meeting, 3 June 1959, pp. 71–72.
40. W. David McIntyre, 'The Admission of Small States to the Commonwealth', *Journal of Imperial and Commonwealth History,* 24, no. 2 (1996).
41. Christopher Prior, "This Community Which Nobody Can Define': Meanings of Commonwealth in the Late 1940s and 1950s', ibid. (2019); Patrick Gordon Walker, *The Commonwealth,* (London, 1962).
42. Robin Moore, *Making the New Commonwealth* (Oxford, 1987).
43. Francine McKenzie, *Redefining the Bonds of Commonwealth, 1939–1948: The Politics of Preference* (Basingstoke, 2002); Catherine R. Schenk,

Britain and the Sterling Area: From Devaluation to Convertibility in the 1950s (London, 1994).

44. Srinivasan, 'Nobody's Commonwealth?'.

45. Philip Alexander, 'A Tale of Two Smiths: The Transformation of Commonwealth Policy, 1964–1970', *Contemporary British History*, 20, no. 3 (2006).

46. Bangura, *Britain and Commonwealth Africa*, pp. 72–88.

47. Richard Toye, 'Words of Change: The Rhetoric of Commonwealth, Common Market and Cold War, 1961–1963' in Larry Butler and Sarah Stockwell (eds.), *Winds of Change: Harold Macmillan and British Decolonisation* (Basingstoke, 2013).

48. Bangura, *Britain and Commonwealth Africa*.

49. Stephanie Decker, 'Corporate Legitimacy and Advertising: British Companies and the Rhetoric of Development in West Africa, 1950–1970', *Business History Review*, 81, no. 1 (2011).

50. *Minute Book* 5, Annual Meeting, 27 November 1958, p. 51.

51. Ibid. Council Meeting, 3 June 1959, 'Reconstructing the Federation', June 1959, pp. 71–72.

52. *Minute Book 5*, Council Meeting, 29 November 1962, Executive Committee, 19 Feb. 1963, pp. 52–53, 72; FCCC Papers CLC/B/082/MS18296.

53. *Minute Book 5*, Annual General Meeting, November 1959, p. 106.

54. FCCC Papers CLC/B/082/MS18296, 'Proposals for Reorganisation', 1960.

55. FCCC Papers CLC/B/082/MS18287/16, *Congress Report*, 1962, p. 14.

56. *Chamber of Commerce Journal*, June 1962, p. 3.

57. *Congress Report*, 1962, p. 34.

58. Bangura, *Britain and Commonwealth Africa*, pp. 194–197.

59. FCCC Papers CLC/B/082/MS18283/6, *Minute Book 6*, Executive Committee, 15 February 1962, pp. 43–44.

60. Ibid. Council Meeting, 31 May 1961, pp. 14–15.

61. Calculated from *Congress Report*, 1957, pp. 7–10; FCCC Papers, CLC/B/082/MS18285, FCCC, *Directory*, 1965.

62. Sara Lorenzini, *Global Development: A Cold War History* (Princeton, 2019), pp. 101–103.

63. in FCCC Papers CLC/B/082/MS18287/17, *Congress Report*, 1964, p. 11

64. Ibid., pp. 20–21.

65. *Congress Report*, 1962, p. 22; Sarah Stockwell, *The British End of the British Empire* (Cambridge, 2018).

66. *Congress Report*, 1962, p. 26.

67. FCCC UK Committee, FCCC Papers, CLC/B/082/MS18287/17, Annual *Report*, 1967, p. 5.
68. Congress Report, 1964, p. 12.
69. FCCC Papers, CLC/B/082/MS18287/17, FCCC UK Committee, *Annual Report*, 1964, 8–9; *Annual Report*, 1965, pp. 3–7.
70. FCCC Papers, CLC/B/082/MS18282/004, FCCC Annual Reports, 1961–1969.
71. Peter Cain, 'Afterword: The Economics of the 'British World'', *Journal of Imperial and Commonwealth History*, 41, no. 1 (2013).
72. *Congress Report*, 1964, p. 27.
73. David Fieldhouse, 'The Metropolitan Economics of Empire' in Judith Brown and William Roger Louis eds. *Oxford History of the British Empire*. Vol. 4. *The Twentieth Century* (Oxford, 1999), pp. 103–111.
74. Ghana, Nigeria, Malawi, Zambia, Rhodesia and Kenya only, *Commonwealth Trade, 1965*, (London, 1966), pp. 23. 25, 27, 29, 31, 33, 37–28; Gambia, Ghana, Kenya, Malawi, Nigeria, Tanzania, Uganda, Zambia, *Commonwealth Trade, 1970* (London, 1971), pp. 37, 39, 44, 46, 85–86, 110, 112.
75. Dilley, 'Un-Imagining Markets'.
76. *Minute Book 6*, Executive Committee, 22 June 1966, pp. 176–177.
77. Ibid. Council Meeting, 6 June 1966, p. 184.
78. FCCC Paper CLC/B/082/MS19296, 'The Future of the Federation', 4 July 1966, p. 4.
79. Ibid., p. 4; *Minute Book 6*, p. 184.
80. Turnbull Library, Wellington, Wellington Regional Chamber of Commerce Papers, 94-170-09, Associated New Zealand Chambers Executive Committee, *Minute Book*, 11 March 1966, p. 11.
81. 'Future of the Federation', pp. 2–3.
82. Commonwealth Secretariat Archive, London, Arnold Smith Papers [Smith Papers hereafter], 1997/10 (Federation of Commonwealth Chambers of Commerce), F. H. Tate to Arnold Smith, 6 July 1965, 6 July 1965–1916 July 1972.
83. Ibid. Noel Salter to William Luxton, 29 February 1972; FCCC Papers CLC/B/082/MS18287/18, *Congress Report*, 1968, pp. 6–7.
84. Smith Papers, 1997/10, Noel Slater, 'Record of Meeting between the Commonwealth Secretary-General and the Director of the Federation of Commonwealth Chambers of Commerce', 5 May 1972.
85. Clyde Sanger, *Malcolm Macdonald: Bringing an End to Empire* (Liverpool, 1995).
86. *Congress Report*, 1968, pp. 4–7 in FCCC Papers CLC/B/082/MS18287/18.

87. *Congress Reports*, 1968, 1970, 1972 in FCCC Papers CLC/B/082/MS18287/18–20.
88. Dilley, 'Un-Imagining Markets', p. 268.
89. *Congress Report*, 1962, pp. 20–21.
90. Arnold Smith, *Stitches in Time: The Commonwealth in World Politics* (London, 1981), pp. 175–203.
91. *Congress Report*, 1968, 8. See also *Congress Report*, 1970, pp. 17, 26–28.
92. *Congress Report*, 1972, pp. 5, 34–36, 41–42.
93. For example, FCCC Papers, CLC/B/082/MS18286, *Commonwealth and European Focus*, 1 August 1972.
94. *Congress Report, 1972*, p. 37.
95. Dilley, 'Un-Imagining Markets', pp. 263–271.
96. Ibid. Executive Committee, 15 January1974, p. 52.
97. FCCC Papers CLC/B/082/MS18283/7, Minute Book 7, Council Meeting, 4 July 1973, p. 45 in.
98. Ibid. Executive Committee, 14 March 1974, pp. 55–66.
99. Ibid., Council Meeting, 4 July 1974, p. 71, 'Note by Sir Garnett Gordon on a telephone conversation with Mr Arnold Smith', 18 July 1974, p. 77.
100. Ibid., Executive Committee, 14 March 1974, pp. 55–56.
101. Ibid. Executive Committee, 23 May 1974, pp. 58–59; Council Minutes, 4 July 1974, p. 73.
102. Ibid., 'Minute of Meeting with H. Wire and B. D. Jayal', 30 July 1974, p. 77.
103. Magee and Thompson, *Empire and Globalisation*.
104. See, for example, David Fieldhouse, *The West and the Third World: Trade, Colonialism, Dependence, and Development* (Oxford, 1999), p. 254.

References

Adeleke, Ademola, 'Playing Fairy Godfather to the Commonwealth: The United States and the Colombo Plan', *Commonwealth & Comparative Politics*, 42 (2004), pp. 393–411.

Alexander, Philip, 'A Tale of Two Smiths: The Transformation of Commonwealth Policy, 1964–1970', *Contemporary British History*, 20 (2006), pp. 303–321.

Bangura, Yusuf, *Britain and Commonwealth Africa: The Politics of Economic Relations 1951–1975* (Manchester University Press, Manchester, 1983).

Bennett, Robert J., *The Local Voice: The History of Chambers of Commerce in Britain, Ireland, and Revolutionary America, 1760–2011* (Oxford University Press, Oxford, 2011).

Bradley, Mark Philip. 'Decolonization, the Global South, and the Cold War, 1919–1962', in Melvyn P. Leffler and Odd Arne Westad (eds.), *The Cambridge*

History of the Cold War: Volume 1: *Origins, 1945–1962* (Cambridge University Press, Cambridge, 2010).

Bright, Rachel K. and Andrew R. Dilley, 'After the British World', *Historical Journal,* 60 (2017), pp. 547–568.

Cain, Peter, 'Afterword: The Economics of the 'British World'', *Journal of Imperial and Commonwealth History,* 41 (2013), pp. 98–103.

Committee, Commonwealth Economic, *Commonwealth Trade, 1965* (H.M.S.O., London, 1966).

Committee, Commonwealth Economic, *Commonwealth Trade, 1970* (H.M.S.O., London, 1971).

Connelly, Matthew, 'Taking Off the Cold War Lens: Visions of North-South Conflict During the Algerian War for Independence', *American Historical Review,* 105 (2000), pp. 739–769.

Cooper, Frederick, *Africa since 1940: The Past of the Present* (Cambridge University Press, Cambridge, 2002).

Cooper, Frederick, 'Writing the History of Development', *Journal of Modern European History,* 8 (2010), pp. 5–23.

Decker, Stephanie, 'Corporate Legitimacy and Advertising: British Companies and the Rhetoric of Development in West Africa, 1950–1970', *Business History Review,* 81 (2011), pp. 59–86.

Dilley, Andrew, 'The Politics of Commerce: The Congress of Chambers of Commerce of the Empire, 1886–1914', *SAGE Open,* 3 (2013), pp. 1–12.

Dilley, Andrew, 'Trade after the Deluge: British Commerce, Armageddon, and the Political Economy of Globalization, 1914–1918', in Andrew Smith and Kevin Tennant (eds.), *The Impact of the First World War on International Business* (Routledge London, 2016), pp. 25–46.

Dilley, Andrew, 'Un-Imagining Markets: Chambers of Commerce, Globalisation and the Political Economy of the Commonwealth, 1945–1974', in Thackaray, David, Andrew Thompson and Richard Toye (eds.), *Imagining Britain's Economic Future, c.1800–1975: Trade, Consumerism, and Global Markets* (Palgrave Macmillan, Basingstoke, 2018), pp. 253–277.

Drummond, Ian Macdonald, *Imperial Economic Policy, 1917–1939* (Allen and Unwin, London, 1974).

Fieldhouse, David K. 'The Metropolitan Economics of Empire', in Judith M. Brown and William Roger Louis (eds.), *Oxford History of the British Empire:* Vol. 4: *The Twentieth Century* (Oxford University Press, Oxford, 1999).

Fieldhouse, David K., *The West and the Third World: Trade, Colonialism, Dependence, and Development* (Blackwell, Oxford, 1999).

Frey, Marc, and Sönke Kunkel, 'Writing the History of Development: A Review of the Recent Literature', *Contemporary European History,* 20 (2011), pp. 215–232.

Havinden, Michael Ashley, and David Meredith, *Colonialism and Development: Britain and Its Tropical Colonies, 1850–1960* (Routledge, 1996, London; New York, 1993).

Hodge, Joseph M., Gerald Hodl, and Martina Kopf (eds.), *Developing Africa: Concepts and Practices in Twentieth-Century Colonialism* (Manchester University Press, Manchester, 2014).

Holland, Robert F., *Britain and the Commonwealth Alliance, 1918–1939* (Macmillan, London, 1981).

Hopkins, Anthony G., 'Development and the Utopian Idea', in Robin W. Winks (ed.), *Oxford History of the British Empire*. Vol. 5, *Historiography* (Oxford University Press, Oxford, 1999).

Lonsdale, John and Donald Anthony Low. 'Towards the New Order 1945–1963', in Donald Anthony Low and Alison Smith Smith (eds.), *History of East Africa* (Clarendon Press, Oxford, 1976), pp. 1–64.

Lorenzini, Sara, *Global Development: A Cold War History* (Princeton University Press, Princeton, 2019).

Louis, William Roger, and Ronald Robinson, 'The Imperialism of Decolonization', *Journal of Imperial and Commonwealth History*, 22 (1994), pp. 462–512.

Magee, Gary, and Andrew Thompson, *Empire and Globalisation: Networks of People, Goods and Capital in the British World, C.1850–1914* (Cambridge University Press, Cambridge, 2010).

Mazower, Mark, *No Enchanted Palace: The End of Empire and the Ideological Origins of the United Nations* (Princeton University Press, Princeton, NJ, Oxford, 2009).

McIntyre, W. David, 'The Admission of Small States to the Commonwealth', *Journal of Imperial and Commonwealth History*, 24 (1996), pp. 244–277.

McIntyre, W. David, *The Commonwealth of Nations: Origins and Impact, 1869–1971* (University of Minnesota Press, Minneapolis, 1977).

McIntyre, W. David. *The Significance of the Commonwealth, 1965–1990* (Macmillan Academic and Professional, Basingstoke, 1991).

McKenzie, Francine, *Redefining the Bonds of Commonwealth, 1939–1948: The Politics of Preference* (Palgrave Macmillan, Basingstoke, 2002).

Misra, Maria, *Business, Race, and Politics in British India, C.1850–1960* (Clarendon, Oxford, 1999).

Moore, Robin James, *Making the New Commonwealth* (Clarendon, Oxford, 1987).

Nkrumah, Kwame, *Africa Must Unite* (Frederick A Praeger, New York, 1963).

Ojo, M. 'Adeleye, 'Africa and the United Nations' System: Decolonization and Development', *Présence Africaine* (1981), pp. 72–89.

Oyeweso, Siyan, *Journey from Epe: Biography of S.L. Edu* (West African Book Publishers, Ilupeju, Lagos, 1996).

Pearson-Patel, Jessica, 'Promoting Health, Protecting Empire: Inter-Colonial Medical Cooperation in Postwar Africa', *Monde(s)*, 7 (2015), pp. 213–230.

Prior, Christopher, "'This Community Which Nobody Can Define': Meanings of Commonwealth in the Late 1940s and 1950s', *Journal of Imperial and Commonwealth History* (2019), pp. 1–23.

Sanger, Clyde, *Malcolm Macdonald: Bringing an End to Empire* (Liverpool University Press, Liverpool, 1995).

Schenk, Catherine R., *Britain and the Sterling Area: From Devaluation to Convertibility in the 1950s* (Routledge, London, 1994).

Scott, Claude Fredrick. 'Caring About the British Empire: British Imperial Activist Groups, 1900–1967', in, 2014).

Smith, Arnold, *Stitches in Time: The Commonwealth in World Politics* (Andre Deutsch, London, 1981).

Srinivasan, Krishnan, 'Nobody's Commonwealth? The Commonwealth in Britain's Post-Imperial Adjustment', *Commonwealth and Comparative Politics*, 64 (2006), pp. 257–269.

Staples, Amy L., *The Birth of Development: How the World Bank, Food and Agriculture Organization and the World Health Organization Changed the Worlds* (Kent State University Press, Ohio, 2006).

Stockwell, Sarah, *The British End of the British Empire* (Cambridge University Press, Cambridge, 2018).

Stokke, Olav, *The UN and Development: From Aid to Cooperation* (Indiana University Press, Bloomington, IN, 2009).

Thackeray, David, *Forging a British World of Trade: Culture, Ethnicity, and Market in the Empire-Commonwealth, 1880–1975* (Oxford University Press, Oxford, 2019).

Toye, Richard. 'Words of Change: The Rhetoric of Commonwealth, Common Market and Cold War, 1961–1963', in Larry J. Butler and Sarah Stocckwell (eds.), *Winds of Change: Harold Macmillan and British Decolonisation* (Palgrave Macmillan, Basingstoke, 2013), pp. 140–158.

Walker, Patrick Gordon, *The Commonwealth* (Secker and Warburg, London, 1962).

CHAPTER 3

Adapting to Independence: The East Africa Association, Post-Colonial Business Networks and Economic Development

Poppy Cullen

The relationship between British business and decolonisation has been much examined, with the most convincing arguments showing that business did not lead decolonisation, and that relationships between officials in the Colonial Office and British businessmen were not always close.[1] Nonetheless, businesses had to find ways to respond to the changes brought about by decolonisation. This chapter looks at one way that business leaders sought to do so: the formation of the East Africa Association in 1964, covering Britain's former colonies of Tanganyika (joining with Zanzibar to become Tanzania in 1964), Uganda and Kenya. The independence of these countries in the early 1960s had repercussions for business relations. Before independence, businessmen had been able to rely upon British colonial policies to ensure a secure and profitable environment for themselves; in the post-colonial era, businessmen feared, the British

P. Cullen (✉)
Loughborough University, Loughborough, UK
e-mail: C.P.Cullen@lboro.ac.uk

© The Author(s) 2020
V. Dimier, S. Stockwell (eds.), *The Business of Development in Post-Colonial Africa*, Cambridge Imperial and Post-Colonial Studies Series, https://doi.org/10.1007/978-3-030-51106-7_3

69

government would no longer be able to promote their interests to such a degree, and government interests might differ from their own. Companies would also be operating in newly independent nation-states which were increasingly keen to assert their independence on the world stage, and critical of what they perceived as economic neo-colonialism and dependency.[2] In dealing with these challenges, British businesses showed that they could adapt to the circumstances of independence. In spite of David Fieldhouse's assertion that 'British business firms never thought very clearly about the prospects of decolonization', British businesses did make plans.[3] By the time independence came to Britain's East African colonies in the early 1960s, businesses had experienced these changes in former British colonies in other parts of the world. The work of Nicholas White on Malaya, Sarah Stockwell on the Gold Coast/Ghana, and Stephanie Decker on Nigeria and Ghana clearly shows the adaptability of businesses in responding to independence.[4]

The formation of the East Africa Association (EAA) in 1964 constitutes a further striking example of how expatriate businesses were quick to adapt to a fast-changing political context. The EAA was created after the three territories it operated in had achieved independence, but discussions began much earlier. This chapter will explore the ideas which lay behind the foundation of the Association, as business leaders sought to create an organisation which would promote and protect their interests. There has been little scholarly consideration of business associations in the decolonisation era. The obvious exception is Stockwell's work on the West Africa Committee, although she does not discuss the Committee's activities after Ghanaian independence.[5] But the East Africa Association discussed here, as well as the India, Pakistan and Burma Association, seems to have received limited attention.[6] This chapter argues that business associations are worthy of study as sites where business leaders together discussed their concerns and considered how to respond to decolonisation. They can thus reveal the anxieties and priorities of business leaders as they sought to adapt to independence and foster relations with new governments.

As the introduction to this volume shows, it has not been common for scholars to examine expatriate businesses and development in the post-colonial era in the same frame. However, for businesses which had to adapt to a post-colonial environment, development narratives could provide a key strategy through which to do so. In order to gain good relations with African governments, foreign businesses had to convince them that they were committed to long-term development and not just profit-seeking. Expatriate companies would also potentially need to maintain a low profile that would not attract criticism. Additionally, they would have to show that they were non-racist, despite the fact that they were externally owned. This would mean Africanising staff—a central development concern of African governments, and with the additional complicating factor of European and Asian minorities in East Africa. Highlighting development was, for the EAA and its members, an attempt to appeal to East African governments in order to gain good relations. These relations would in turn—or so it was hoped—give them some influence on East African policies towards business, and thereby prevent hostile policies or nationalisations which were the most significant threats to them.[7]

The EAA's direct engagement with the concept of development was clear, with development the stated primary aim of the Association. The EAA had, though, a particular interpretation of development, based on earlier colonial models. Understanding the continuities between colonial and post-colonial development helps to explain the EAA's ideas.[8] Since the 1940s, colonial development had been the centrepiece of British colonial policy. The way that colonial development was framed by colonial officials, and the context of the 'second colonial occupation',[9] meant that it was intended to be beneficial to both colonial economies and the British. This understanding of development as having a dual purpose was echoed by the EAA: the development they offered would benefit both East African economies and themselves, with seemingly little thought given to potential contradictions. Their interpretation of economic development assumed that it would directly follow foreign investment. This justified their involvement to the most important audiences they needed to cultivate: independent East African governments. Decker has rightly argued that 'Imperial businesses derived new legitimacy from ...development efforts'.[10] Many members of the EAA were keen to capitalise on the potential benefits to be gained through their engagement with development.

This chapter argues that in the creation of the EAA the three themes of this book—business, decolonisation and development—are brought together. The language of development was central to framing the EAA as businesses thought about their future in the era of decolonisation. The chapter first considers the earlier Tanganyika Association, and then the discussions around forming an East African group. It moves on to consider membership issues, including Africanisation policies, and finally explores the EAA's explicit concern with development in its attempt to cultivate relationships with new governments.

The EAA has no archives. The chapter is therefore based on material from the British National Archives and the archives of various companies which were involved in the formation of the Association. The EAA continues to exist, suggesting that businesses perceive it to have been and remain useful. While it has undergone certain name changes over the years since its establishment (becoming the East Africa and Mauritius Association and then the Eastern Africa Association), the EAA has persisted, and in its current form is much larger than the organisation discussed here, with over 350 members and covering an expanded range of countries.[11] In the current Eastern Africa Association, development remains the organisation's stated aim, and the language used has hardly changed from that used by the Association at the time of its inception.[12]

THE TANGANYIKA ASSOCIATION AND DECOLONISATION IN EAST AFRICA

The EAA was officially created in 1964, but the idea of having a business association within the region has a longer history. Indeed, there was a direct precursor to the EAA in the Tanganyika Association (TA) suggested in 1957 and set up in 1958.[13] The Governor of Tanganyika, Sir Edward Twining, made the initial suggestion for such an organisation at a meeting with representatives from prominent companies operating in the colony.[14] Twining argued that, due to political changes in Tanganyika, representation of overseas business interests would decrease and so 'suggested that they should employ a high-powered representative' to 'generally be a liaison between the Government and business interests'.[15] The original motives for such an organisation were thus highly political. The TA aimed to encourage foreign investment in a changing political climate: 'we hope to exert whatever beneficial influence we can in creating confidence in the future of the country among investors'.[16] The main function of the TA was carried out by its representative living in Tanganyika who would 'maintain a two-way traffic of advice and information'.[17] The representative would act as a middle-man, sending reports to TA members and representing the interests of the TA to the Tanganyikan government.[18]

Already at this stage, development was important to framing the TA: 'the object was the encouragement of economic development and further investment in the Territory'.[19] The businessmen aimed to promote overseas investment, with the expectation that this would stimulate economic development. For those setting up the TA, the existence of such an Association with its resident representative was in itself believed to be a contribution to development. Earl de la Warr, from the Standard Bank Ltd., argued that if 'an individual of the quality contemplated' was appointed, the TA 'will indeed be making a very real contribution towards the development of the economic resources of the country and will also be providing some measure of encouragement for the introduction of new capital'.[20] Encouraging foreign investment, and providing businessmen in London with information about Tanganyika, was the way that the TA's contribution to development was understood by its founders.

Nonetheless, for companies, their own interests were their prime concern. Minutes from one of the earliest meetings in June 1957 noted that 'The main objective was to expand production and to safeguard interests in property irrespective of what political developments might take place'.[21] This was about their interests, not just about development. It was in many ways this attitude which led to the critiques of multinational corporations in Africa in the 1960s and 1970s.[22] This contradiction was, to an extent, recognised by the TA in 1960: 'It is admitted that there is an element of self-interest implicit in membership, but it would be false to suggest that members are unmindful or careless of the wider interests of the country and the economic, social and political advancement of its inhabitants'.[23] While their own concerns were paramount, it is perhaps also over-simplistic to ignore this statement: businessmen could care about wider issues. This has been explored elsewhere, for example in L. J. Butler's work on Ronald Prain, Chairman of the Rhodesian Selection Trust, where, as Butler argues, 'Prain was not merely paying lip service to fashionable developmental priorities'.[24] Attitudes and commitments to development differed among the TA's members. For the Association as a whole, however, and later the EAA, development was primarily associated with encouraging overseas investment.

The discussions dating from this period make clear how quickly things were changing. The initial meeting in 1957 to set up the TA expected 'Self-Government in the next twenty or thirty years: some thought it would come sooner than that'.[25] The speed of change in the colony was by no means expected by businessmen, or indeed by the British government at that time. At a government meeting at Chequers in 1959, independence was suggested for Tanganyika in around 1970 and Uganda and Kenya in perhaps 1975.[26] This thinking was very quickly outdated and Tanganyika became independent in 1961, Uganda in 1962 and Kenya in

1963. There were also hopes for political and economic unity between the three territories. In 1948, the East Africa High Commission had been formed, creating common laws regulating duties and taxes and setting up a common market. In 1961, with the independence of Tanganyika, this was turned into the East African Common Services Organisation.[27] Political federation was also a possibility. The idea had a long history of British government support, as colonial officials believed that larger territorial units would be more viable and prosperous at independence.[28] In June 1963, East African leaders 'announced their determination to establish an East African Federation' by the end of the year.[29] It was not long, however, before this commitment had dissolved, and it became clear that federation was not likely in the near future, although the common market remained in place.[30]

The changing political situation meant changing economic projections and assessments. In 1960, there was a flight of capital from the region, especially Kenya, after the announcement by Colonial Secretary Iain Macleod that Kenya would achieve majority rule. The Standard Bank estimated transfers of capital from its East African branches from 1961 to 1963 at £9,243,729 in inward remittances and £26,709,121 outward.[31] There was a lack of confidence among Kenya's white European population, as well as among investors. In 1961, the Mowlem Construction Company complained of 'practically no commercial work coming out to tender at present owing to the political uncertainties', though they remained reasonably optimistic about the future.[32] The United Africa Company Ltd. suggested in October 1961 that 'Kenya was the territory which would remain the key to our business if it was worth while going on at all'.[33] They were not confident about their future in East Africa. In April 1962, Kenya was downgraded from a 'B' to 'C' risk area, a clear signal that investors lacked confidence in the country's economic future.[34] This confidence was restored fairly quickly, however. By July 1962, the United Africa Company was more hopeful,[35] and in September 1964, 'by and large the East African business had never been as healthy as it was at the moment'.[36] Projections for the region changed as investors grew more confident and recognised that independence would not be too damaging.

For expatriate businesses, the common market and possible federation would be particularly useful. In 1961, the United Africa Company considered that 'On the question of Federation…the alternative was too hard to contemplate'.[37] When this became unlikely, the Chairman of Barclays Bank Dominion Colonial and Overseas (DCO) Ltd. noted that: 'Our main hope is that at least the common services will be maintained'.[38] East Africa was a valuable market when taken as a whole; the individual countries were much less so. As the United Africa Company discussed in 1964 when considering setting up a bike factory, 'the profitability aspect would depend on the extent to which we were allowed to view the three territories as one'.[39] Both the British government and British businesses favoured regionalism which they hoped would foster greater economic and political stability and a wider economic market. This would make an organisation covering just one country much less useful, and when the time came for reassessment, the idea of continuing the TA just in Tanganyika was not seriously considered.

A Possible East Africa Committee

In 1962, meetings of the TA discussed the possibility of extending the Association to cover East Africa. The companies which took the lead were James Finlay & Co. Ltd., Shell International Petroleum Co., Barclays DCO, the United Africa Company and the Inchcape Group.[40] A draft was prepared in August 1962 for a potential East Africa Committee which argued that 'the time has come for a spontaneous coming-together of business concerns having interests in the East African territories to maintain and if possible increase their existing interests, to provide a forum for the discussion and correlation of their problems and generally to promote the economic development of the territories'.[41] This combination of interests was very similar to that which had characterised the TA, and development remained a part of this, further discussed below. The intention was to follow the model of the TA, with the ideal being to appoint three representatives, one for each country.

In making their plans for a possible East Africa Committee, the TA members had several questions to discuss. One was whether an expanded organisation would or should have any political role. The TA had been set up with an explicit political focus. But when the Governor of Tanganyika wanted to appoint the TA's representative to the Legislative Council, members in London resisted, concerned that 'it was very important not to give [Julius] Nyerere and his [Tanganyika African National Union] party the least chance of saying that the representative of overseas capitalists had been put in a position to interfere with local affairs'.[42] The representative remained formally out of politics. There also existed the more political Joint East and Central African Board, which represented European settler and business views, and was involved in the founding of the TA. There was some consideration of merging the TA into the Board. Many businessmen, however, wanted an apolitical organisation. Brian Macdona from Barclays DCO, for example, preferred a separate business association, which he 'strongly urged'.[43] With the independence of the territories, an explicitly political role would not have been welcomed by the new governments and would have made relations more difficult. There was agreement that any organisation set up would not have a political role, but would solely represent business interests.

The central consideration, however, was about the cost of such an expanded group. The TA had cost around £7,500 annually.[44] The proposed East Africa Committee would cost £28–30,000 per year.[45] This would mean recruiting more members and soliciting higher contributions from existing ones. This was the stumbling block for many, and in the discussions, 'financial considerations predominated'.[46] By November 1962, it was clear that although an East Africa Committee 'was regarded as the ideal development by many members, the necessary money to finance it would not be forthcoming at present'.[47] The idea was shelved, and members decided that the TA should be closed at the end of April 1963 when the representative's contract ended.[48] The TA was wound up, with the 'final accounts' sent to members in December 1963.[49] At this point, therefore, the idea of an organisation which would work across the three territories was favoured by business leaders, but not enough to make them willing to pay for it. Although the TA representative was admired and had good relationships with Nyerere and others,[50] his role was not so necessary as to make business leaders believe that they could not do without it.

Nevertheless, the idea did not lie fallow for long. In January 1964, Julian Crossley, Chairman of Barclays DCO, had lunch with Fred Pedler of the United Africa Company 'to discuss the question of the formation of an East African Committee'.[51] Personal networks of businessmen in London facilitated business coordination. Crossley recorded in his diary that 'it seems obvious, I think, with all three East African territories now independent we ought to change things as British commercial interests really need a direct access to the new Governments. The point of contact must be there rather than in Whitehall'.[52] He favoured the creation of a new organisation, as did Pedler, who argued 'that its basic purpose should be to secure direct representation of private investment thinking with the African governments'.[53] Both of them believed that they needed a new way of accessing East African governments beyond their connections in the British government.

Discussions and action quickly followed. An initial committee was set up in London, and on 16 April, the decision was taken to form the EAA.[54] Sixty-five firms had been invited and forty-four were represented at this meeting.[55] In June, the constitution was established. This made provision for an executive committee of 11–16 members, which planned 'as far as possible to represent inter alia Plantations, Industrial, Trading, Shipping, Petroleum, Banking, Insurance and Professional interests'.[56] As this shows, the organisers hoped to be representative of the multiple types of business interests within East Africa. Annual subscriptions were to be paid at a minimum of £50, though the larger companies and banks paid £500.[57] At this initial stage, there was not enough money to appoint overseas representatives. In November 1964, the EAA appointed its first Director, Sir Kenneth Maddocks, formerly of the colonial service, who had worked in Nigeria, and then as Governor of Fiji. The EAA had initially hoped that Maddocks would be stationed in Nairobi, but he 'obtained their agreement to being based in London, where I should be in close touch with government departments, on the understanding that I would fly out as often as necessary'.[58] It was not until 1967 that the EAA set up an office in Nairobi with a full-time representative.[59]

Membership and Benefits of the EAA

The EAA was set up by businessmen who believed it to be in their interests to create such an organisation. The idea of collective action must have appealed to businessmen, who believed that they could gain certain benefits from business associations which they could not achieve as successfully alone.[60] As Stockwell has argued about West Africa, the 'business community…debated common concerns, orchestrated business negotiations with Whitehall, and sought to present a united front to government in London and in Accra'.[61] The EAA followed the same pattern. Some of its members may have been competitors, but they also faced similar challenges, and sometimes benefited from working collectively.[62] There were nine founder members of the EAA: Arbuthnot Latham & Co., Ltd. Barclays DCO, Shell, the British & Commonwealth Shipping Co., Ltd., James Finlay & Co., Smith Mackenzie & Co., Ltd., the Standard Bank, the United Africa Company and Wigglesworth & Co., Ltd.[63] Eight of them had been in the TA (one, Inchcape, as a parent company of Gray,

Dawes and Co. Ltd. and then of Smith Mackenzie and Co.).[64] By September, there were forty-five members,[65] and by December, fifty-nine.[66]

The EAA was by no means the only business association set up in Britain's empire or former colonies. Apart from the TA, the closest model followed by the EAA was that of the West Africa Committee. This was a much larger organisation than the EAA ever intended to be, and, costing approximately £50,000 per annum, much more expensive.[67] The intention for the EAA was 'definitely on a much more modest scale'.[68] Another important precursor to the EAA was the India, Pakistan and Burma Association, and 'the Committee proposes to follow closely the models' of both.[69] The links between these organisations in terms of personnel and companies were clear. The initial chairman of the EAA, Sir John Burns, had 'close associations' with the India, Pakistan and Burma Association from time spent in Bombay.[70] Maddocks had known the West African Committee in Nigeria.[71] Many of the companies who joined the EAA were also represented on the West Africa Committee and some were members of the India, Pakistan and Burma Association.[72] They thus already had experience of this kind of organisation and the potential benefits it could offer. Setting up a business association was an established method of seeking to encourage investment and promote interests.

The EAA offered its members a forum for sharing and reporting information. The director sent reports, and members who travelled to East Africa sometimes shared their views with the group.[73] The eventual resident representatives sent reports which were confidentially circulated among members, giving their impressions as well as detailed information about policies.[74] These reports were 'not to be sent to East Africa' and were intentionally not labelled so that the EAA could not be identified as their source 'if a copy were to go astray'.[75] This was to encourage frank reporting, while ensuring that relations could not be damaged by any criticism. The EAA's meetings in London also offered a forum for sharing information about the region, and this could be useful for members as they learned about the thinking and practices of others.[76] Tanzania's Foreign Investments Protection Bill, for example, was discussed by the EAA, 'which has managed to gather a broad picture from the information supplied by members'.[77] The Association facilitated discussion and knowledge exchange. It could offer its members new information and alternative perspectives.

Businessmen, however, had differing assessments of the usefulness and necessity of the EAA's functions. For smaller companies which did not have their own representatives in East Africa, the benefits were most obvious, and some indeed suggested about the TA that 'perhaps its benefit had been greatest to the smaller subscribers'.[78] For some of the larger companies, the EAA's roles of providing information and representing interests within East Africa were not so essential because they had their own representatives in the region. In initial discussions, Shell's representative 'implied that in a large organisation such as theirs, the top personnel were quite capable of maintaining friendly relations with Ministers', and they therefore did not need a middle-man.[79] Similarly, J. F. Pearcy was also somewhat sceptical, as his company Consolidated Petroleum Co. Ltd. was 'better able than some to keep an adequate cadre of high calibre staff in East Africa and he thought frankness required him to assert that much of the help which an association could give to smaller companies would not apply'.[80] The larger companies had enough money and personnel to conduct their own reporting and relationships. Still, there was potential value in having a joint representative who would not be linked to any individual company, and 'the importance of a separate and disinterested representative, not suspected of having a strong individual or sectional interest was admitted'.[81] The benefits of joint representation were particularly obvious for the smaller companies, but even for larger ones there could be advantages in having someone disassociated from their company make representations on difficult issues.

A further incentive for some was to be part of any organisation which was set up and might prove useful. The Standard Bank, when considering this in April 1964, commented about the TA's resident representative that 'his monthly reports did not give the Bank more information than was available from its own seniors in East Africa and that, save on rare occasions, he was not able to exercise over-great influence on Ministers, though he was on very good terms with them'.[82] Despite this limited benefit, and that the Bank had its own East Africa board and representatives, it remained 'important that the Bank should be represented on the temporary committee and that it should be a founder member'.[83] Even if there were few quantifiable benefits to be gained, the Bank still believed that it was necessary to be a part of and shape any planned organisation, and to be thereby recognised as one of the major businesses operating in the region. Pearcy raised a similar point: despite seeing limited value for his company, 'he was confident they [Consolidated Petroleum] would sympathetically consider giving support'.[84] This may have encouraged others to join too. This logic did not work for all, however, and two major firms operating in the region,

Mitchell Cotts & Company Ltd. and the Uganda Company Ltd., initially did not join. The Commonwealth Relations Office (CRO) suggested that 'these companies wanted to assess the Association's value over a period of time before deciding to join'.[85] It was not self-evident to all that the EAA would be useful. The TA had not proved essential, and the discussion over whether it was worth establishing an East African equivalent, with the initial decision not to, suggests that there was little certainty about how useful such an organisation would prove to be. More than a year after its founding, the Standard Bank was still 'sceptical about whether the Association will be any more successful than the old Tanganyika Association'.[86] As this indicates, being part of the group was more important to the Bank than specific benefits.

The key question regarding membership was whether it should be open only to British business interests or to international businesses as well. In particular, this would shape the kind of relationship the EAA would have with the British government. In an early discussion, the TA's Deputy Chairman argued that 'British High Commissioners would only be able to concern themselves with British interests so that in the long term he thought any association should be exclusively British in membership'.[87] Once the EAA was created, but with this discussion still ongoing, the British High Commission in Kenya made the same arguments, suggesting that their attitude towards an association with international membership 'would have to be very much more informal than with a specifically British business association', although 'we would not wish to dictate to the Association what its membership should be'.[88] However, businessmen were keenly aware that the priorities of government were likely to differ from their own. The British government could not necessarily be relied upon to protect business interests in the ways that businesses might have hoped. As the Standard Bank considered, the government 'would be more concerned with pushing British exports than with protecting local British interests. They would have to pursue towards local Governments the policy laid down by Whitehall, which might not be in the interests of British businessmen in East Africa'.[89] Business leaders realised that they would have to act to protect their own interests and could no longer rely on the government to do this for them. For the businesses involved, therefore, sectoral interests predominated, and the decision was taken to include non-British expatriate firms, with the Algemene Bank Nederland joining as the first non-British firm by December 1964.[90] By December 1965, there were members from Britain, America, Canada and six other European countries.[91]

The decision to include non-British members clearly speaks to the divergence between business and government interests. For the EAA, relations with the British government were important, but not their primary concern. The EAA took a conscious decision to have looser relations with the British government in order to have a wider membership. The British government was informed about the EAA, but the CRO's response to the Association was reactive. Indeed, in April 1964, the High Commission in Uganda noted that 'firms in London are moving rather faster' than they had anticipated.[92] The CRO, when informed, was 'very glad to know of the formation of this Association. We welcome your assurance that the Association will be anxious to co-operate and assist, and we for our part entirely reciprocate these sentiments'.[93] This was something which could be useful to British government officials if it helped to secure British interests. The government considered that 'If an association is set up on the right lines we should welcome it, and I think that on the whole we can rely on the good sense of the City to ensure that if it is set up it will be on the right lines'.[94] While this does suggest something of Cain and Hopkins' 'gentlemanly capitalism' model, highlighting the similarities between officials in government and the City, this is too simplistic a picture.[95] Businesses perceived their interests to differ from those of government and the decision to include non-British members was clear evidence of this.

In the EAA's consideration of membership, another crucial issue was raised: whether to include locally-based Asian firms. Like the decision to include non-British businesses, this debate had wider implications, touching on issues of race, Africanisation and the place of Asians in East Africa.[96] In discussions with the British government in September 1964, the EAA 'had not yet decided whether to invite Indian [local Asian] firms or not. We warned them of the dangers of racial exclusiveness and they assured us that they were fully aware of these'.[97] Race was an important issue in the context of newly independent East Africa, and the British government did not want 'to appear as champions of an expatriate, i.e. European, organisation'.[98] By January 1965, the EAA had decided that Japanese or Indian firms might be 'allowed' to join, but this decision was 'obviously drawing a distinction between firms of that sort established in India and local Asian firms whose capital is predominantly local'.[99] Local Asian businesses were thus not included.

Africanisation agendas considerably affected the thinking of business leaders in this decision. Africanisation was a policy of removing expatriates and replacing them with Africans in areas including politics, civil service and business. For newly independent East African governments, Africanisation was an important part of their development agenda as they sought to gain greater African control over the levers of power and to increase African employment more widely. For business interests, Africanisation was one of the major challenges they faced with decolonisation. Many expatriate firms employed expatriate staff, and increasing the number of Africans they employed became a priority from the 1950s.[100] The East African governments explicitly encouraged foreign enterprises to Africanise their staff. For example, Uganda's 1964 Industrial Charter stated that the government 'will expect an Approved Enterprise to train and employ as high a proportion of Uganda[ns] as is reasonably possible, at all levels, and specifically to draw all its unskilled workers from Uganda'.[101] The companies which formed the EAA had to respond to such calls, and indeed try to get ahead of them; this would be read as an indication of their commitment to development. The United Africa Company in 1964 reported on its progress: 'Some promising Africans were now emerging, of potential managerial quality. There were 35 in Kenya, 6 in Tanganyika and 7 in Uganda, a total of 48 against a target of 120 by January 1966'.[102] Despite some hesitancy about these Africans, they were well aware of the need to change the composition of their workforce. Within this Africanisation agenda, the Asian population was a particular concern. Although policies might be framed as, for example, Kenyanisation, they often meant employing Africans rather than Asians, regardless of citizenship. This was potentially problematic for expatriate companies because many employed Asian staff who had received better education during the colonial period. Barclays DCO noted in April 1965 that 'We are still extremely dependent on the service and the loyalty of our Asian staff'.[103] Meanwhile, the United Africa Company 'had a distinct uneasiness in regard to the vulnerability of certain branches of the business where there was a preponderance of Asians employed'.[104] This would not necessarily correspond to the popular East African view of Africanisation and could therefore lead to criticism.

Africanisation policies also affected East African attitudes towards Asian-owned businesses. Many Asians in East Africa were small traders, such as shopkeepers, and their businesses were often those that East African governments wanted to be quickly taken over by Africans. For

example, one Tanzanian MP in July 1964 'single[d] out Asian firms …
The implementation of this policy will, I am afraid, result in displacing the
number of existing traders, particularly Asian traders'.[105] The larger companies run by expatriates and requiring more highly skilled workers would
be harder to immediately Africanise without further training, but the low-
or semi-skilled Asian businesses were easier targets. This meant that
including local Asian businesses within the EAA could make relations with
East Africa's governments difficult: if the Association sought to represent
the interests of Asian members, it could come into conflict with the governments. Due to this, the EAA decided that it was 'not interested in
members from countries which might at some time be "persona non
grata" with the … authorities'.[106] The constitution of the EAA thus stated
that membership was open to those 'normally resident outside the countries', or 'whose share and/or loan, capital is derived mainly from outside
the countries'.[107] This excluded local Asian businesses, even if not explicitly targeting them. This decision was shaped by the desire for good relations with East African governments and a wider East African public.
Africanisation was a crucial part of the development agenda of newly independent East African governments. In responding to this, EAA members
sought to Africanise their own staffs and to set rules of membership for the
Association which would fit this agenda.

DEVELOPMENT AND PERSONAL NETWORKS

As discussed above, the TA explicitly engaged with the concept of development, believing that the Association would encourage economic investment and therefore development. These ideas continued into the formation
of the EAA. Early discussions suggested that an association was 'likely to
meet no obstruction from African politicians, who will realise that an association of this kind should not only help overseas investors to make their
maximum contribution to the further development of the region, but is
likely to formulate ideas helpful to a newly-formed independent
Government'.[108] The drafters expected that, because of the East African
governments' focus on development, such an organisation would be welcomed by them—and also, paternalistically, that they would require external assistance. It is certainly true that development was a priority of the
new East African governments. Michael Jennings has argued that
Tanganyika 'was to be a developmental state, with every ounce of its
energy and attention, its intellectual and material resources, dedicated to

raising standards of living'.[109] As he suggests, however, this was not identical to colonial development, but had a wider purpose aimed at improving social welfare as well as developing economically. Within economic development, industrialisation was prioritised,[110] and to achieve this, East African governments were seeking to attract foreign investment. Uganda's Industrial Charter, for instance, stated that 'in its determination to accelerate the pace of Uganda's economic progress, [the government] seeks local and overseas investment in the industrial development of Uganda'.[111] All three governments offered formal protection for foreign investments in 1964.[112] Although policies would change, especially in Tanzania, it seemed when the EAA was set up that foreign investment was welcomed and protected, and therefore that the region would continue to be profitable for external businesses.

The EAA explicitly engaged with development in its attempt to show commitment to the newly independent countries and foster good relations with East African leaders. The constitution written in June 1964 stated that the Association's objective was:

> To provide an organisation to facilitate participation in the economic development of the East African countries of Kenya, United Republic of Tanganyika and Zanzibar, and Uganda by persons (including firms and companies) from other countries to the mutual economic advantage of such East African countries and of the members of such organisation.[113]

In addition, those 'eligible for membership' were those 'whose business or professional activities represent an actual or potential contribution to the economic development of those countries'.[114] This focus on development echoed the constitutions of the West Africa Committee and TA.[115] The type of development promoted here was specifically 'economic development' rather than a wider social programme. It was also development 'to the mutual economic advantage' of external businesses and East Africa. This closely resembled colonial ideas: development was to benefit distinct groups with very different aims and needs. Businesses sought to boost their profits and protect their investments; East African governments to improve the social welfare of their populations and increase the wealth of their countries. These aims could not necessarily be easily unified, as had been found by colonial governments who had faced the increasing costs of development and found that their initial ideas were co-opted by Africans to argue against colonial rule rather than serving as its justification.[116]

The focus on development was intended to assist the EAA in achieving its central aim of fostering good relationships with East African governments. Connections with East African elites were both a business necessity, as they would be customers, and a political necessity, as these elites controlled the environment in which the companies would operate. As Andrew Cohen has argued about Lonrho, one of the EAA's members, 'Far from being able to dictate terms to African governments, Lonrho was reliant on their good will'.[117] Personal relations were particularly important because of these states' neo-patrimonialism. Although formal structures were in place, clientelism was often more significant, and, as Christopher Clapham has argued, those with official positions 'exercise those powers, so far as they can, as a form not of public service but of private property'.[118] Having good relations with influential East Africans who controlled business activities was crucial, and the EAA was a means by which such connections could be fostered, creating networks between expatriate businessmen and East Africans.

These overseas businessmen also hoped that the EAA would lobby East African governments and influence their policies to the benefit of EAA members. The EAA's representatives, like the TA's earlier, were intended to foster such relations and exert influence. As H. D. Roberts from the Standard Bank commented during an early discussion, 'The key to the proposal lay in having first-class men in the three territories who could, by their ability and their manner, win the confidence of local ministers and officials and use it unobtrusively to influence official action and policy'.[119] Personal networks were one of the ways that foreign companies could have influence. Maddocks, the EAA's first director, later argued that this had been successful, though he may have been overstating his own influence. 'By pointing out to African Ministers and their Permanent Secretaries the difficulties being experienced or likely to be experienced by overseas investors as a result of existing or proposed legislation...the governments could be persuaded to think again and sometimes to make useful concessions'.[120] The EAA made representations to the East African governments over concerns such as the Tanzanian nationalisation of banks and Kenyan Trade Licensing Bill, both in 1967.[121] While these approaches were not very successful, lobbying and promoting business interests directly to East African governments was one of the main benefits that the EAA could offer.

The first official visit representing the EAA was made by its director in January-February 1965 and offered a key occasion to establish personal relations. Maddocks visited all three countries and received positive reactions from ministers in Kenya and Uganda.[122] These ministers particularly liked the idea of having an organisation with which they could meet in London where they could further foster their personal networks. Maddocks' reception in Tanzania was 'less happy than in either Kenya or Uganda', and the Association did not host a cocktail party—an important signal as these were significant business and diplomatic occasions.[123] The High Commission in Tanzania reported that 'the East Africa Association is right to proceed very cautiously'.[124] However, in Maddocks' report of his visit, he believed that it had gone reasonably well and that although ministers had initially been 'very cautious…[they] appeared eventually convinced that the Association was likely to be helpful'.[125] British relations with Uganda and Kenya were warmer at this point than those with Tanzania, which explains why reactions differed.[126]

In order to try to establish positive relations, the EAA highlighted its commitment to development. The Ugandan, Tanzanian and Kenyan High Commissioners in London were informed that the EAA had been created in June 1964, and the Chairman, Burns, was 'anxious that you should hear from us about the matter and not from any other source'.[127] Burns wanted to create the right impression of seeking to work with the East African governments, not purely acting in the interests of external capital. His letter continued to 'assure' the High Commissioners 'that the Association will be ready to offer any co-operation and assistance which it can at any time' and quoted the constitution's statement on development.[128] Development was thus instrumentalised as a way to promote the EAA to the East African governments. In response to Tanzania's hostility towards British business and the EAA, the British High Commissioner recommended that the EAA 'emphasise' its focus on development.[129] As he suggested, if the EAA and businesses could show that they would assist development, they were much more likely to find acceptance and approval from the East African governments for whom this was a priority, and whom the association needed to persuade of its value.

However, for businesses in the EAA, their interest in development was always bound up with their own interests. In 1965, the EAA presented a memorandum to the East African Commission on the future of the common market. This made several arguments as to why the common market was good for development, and concluded that these 'are put forward in the sincere belief that they are of great importance to the economic development of East Africa. Our members have the greatest possible interest in the future prosperity of these three countries since their own prosperity is bound up with it'.[130] As this suggests, economic development was in their own interest, and their self-interest was used to justify their concern with development. Africanisation policies, and the training schemes which accompanied them, could also boost companies' reputations within the region. Training schemes served a dual purpose, the United Africa Company recognised in June 1964, of 'having a very good public relations value, apart from producing trained Africans for the future'.[131] The publicity value of associating companies with development was part of why Africanisation programmes, training, and commitments to development were so prominent at this time.

Although the EAA pledged a commitment to development, there were no obvious criteria or ways that this would be measured. At an initial meeting, members agreed that 'it should be mentioned that the steering committee were in favour of the Association arranging training schemes for Africans' in Britain.[132] It is not, however, clear that the EAA had any training schemes of its own. The criterion for membership—'an actual or potential contribution' to development—could also be very widely interpreted. It is likely that this was open to any and all foreign business. The EAA seems to have continued to hold the view that development would follow overseas investment, and thus that their presence and activity automatically contributed to it. It does not seem that the organisation had a substantive development agenda of its own, although individual companies did have specific programmes. The EAA's main role was one of fostering connections with East African governments and thereby protecting the interests of its members, whose investments, it was expected, would naturally lead to economic development.

CONCLUSION

The discussions surrounding the establishment of the EAA reveal the ways in which expatriate businesses sought to adapt to political change in East Africa using ideas of development. The kind of development the Association promoted followed colonial ideas: that development would serve two distinct communities—East Africans and expatriate businessmen—and that economic development would automatically follow from external investment. These were not unproblematic assertions, as is now well acknowledged, but in the discussions to set up the EAA there was little consideration of any potential contradictions. Rather, the focus on development was intended to help foster relations with East African governments. These relations were the priority for the businessmen involved in setting up the EAA, as East Africa's neo-patrimonialism increased the importance of personal relationships, and independence meant that the British government would no longer be as useful to businesses as it had previously been.

The commitment of the EAA to development was clearly stated in its constitution, conditions of membership and in communications with the East African governments. This was also aided by commitments to Africanisation. Their concern with development shows them to be aware of the priorities of East African governments and unwilling to take steps which might prejudice relations. Focusing on development was one way for businesses to foster relations with East African elites who might otherwise be suspicious of their continued presence after independence. Many of these companies also operated in other former colonies, and so had gone through this process of transition elsewhere. This was not, therefore, an entirely new experience for them. Nonetheless, there were still uncertainties, as the political situation and choices of the new governments had the potential to change. The East African mutinies in January 1964 were evidence of instability which could prove detrimental to investment. More significantly, Tanzania nationalised banks in 1967. Businesses did therefore have some reason to be nervous about their futures. The EAA was part of their response, and the Association instrumentalised development in its attempt to maintain support from East African governments now that British businesses and government no longer controlled the environment in East Africa.

NOTES

1. See, for examples, D. K. Fieldhouse, *Black Africa 1945–1980: Economic Decolonization and Arrested Development* (London: Allen & Unwin, 1986); Nicholas J. White, 'The business and the politics of decolonization: The British experience in the twentieth century', *Economic History Review* 53, no. 3 (2000), pp. 544–564; Sarah Stockwell, 'Trade, empire, and the fiscal context of imperial business during decolonization', *Economic History Review* LVII, no. 1 (2004), pp. 142–160.
2. See Kwame Nkrumah, *Neo-Colonialism: The Last Stage of Imperialism* (London: Nelson, 1965).
3. Fieldhouse, *Black Africa 1945–1980*, p. 9.

4. See Nicholas J. White, 'The survival, revival and decline of British economic influence in Malaysia, 1957–1970', *Twentieth Century British History* 14, no. 3 (2003), pp. 222–242; Sarah Stockwell, *The Business of Decolonization: British Business Strategies in the Gold Coast* (Oxford: Clarendon Press, 2000); Stephanie Decker, 'Building up goodwill: British business, development and economic nationalism in Ghana and Nigeria, 1945–1977', *Enterprise and Society* 9, no. 4 (2008), pp. 602–613.
5. Stockwell, *Business of Decolonization*, pp. 111–134.
6. For brief exceptions, see Colin Leys, *Underdevelopment in Kenya: The Political Economy of Neo-Colonialism 1964–1971* (London: Heinemann, 1975), p. 140; Maria Misra, *Business, Race, and Politics in British India, c. 1850–1960* (Oxford: Oxford University Press, 1999), pp. 178–179.
7. See Chibuike U. Uche, 'British government, British businesses, and the indigenization exercise in post-independence Nigeria', *Business History Review* 86 (2012), p. 750.
8. See Frederick Cooper, *Africa since 1940: The Past of the Present* (Cambridge: Cambridge University Press, 2002), pp. 91–132.
9. D. Low and J. Lonsdale, 'Introduction', in D. Low and A. Smith, eds. *The Oxford History of East Africa* (Oxford: Oxford University Press, 1976), pp. 1–64.
10. Stephanie Decker, 'Corporate legitimacy and advertising: British companies and the rhetoric of development in West Africa, 1950–1970', *Business History Review* 81, no. 1 (2007), p. 62.
11. http://www.eaa-lon.co.uk/ accessed 14 December 2018.
12. The current website states that: 'We aim to facilitate successful participation in the economic development of Eastern Africa by member companies'; this is remarkably similar to the 1964 constitution discussed below. http://www.eaa-lon.co.uk/index.php/home/aims-a-purposes accessed 14 December 2018.
13. Record of a meeting to consider the representation of overseas interests in Tanganyika, 19 June 1957, London Metropolitan Archives (hereafter, LMA) CLC/B/207/STO3/07/01/008.
14. Extract of letter from Governor to OAG, 20 June 1957, The National Archives, Kew (hereafter, TNA) FCO 141/17931/1.
15. Ibid.
16. Tanganyika Association, Statement by the Chairman, 25 October 1958, LMA CLC/B/207/STO3/07/01/007.
17. Ponsonby, Tanganyika Association, January 1958, LMA CLC/B/207/STO3/07/01/14.
18. Tanganyika Association, Statement by the Chairman, 25 October 1958, LMA CLC/B/207/STO3/07/01/007.

19. Minutes of the Tanganyika Committee, 4 July 1957, LMA CLC/B/207/ STO3/07/01/008.
20. De la Warr to Tyrrell, 22 July 1957, LMA CLC/B/207/ STO3/07/01/008.
21. Minutes of the (Tanganyika) Sub-Committee, 19 June 1957, TNA FCO 141/17931/3.
22. See, for examples, Leys, *Underdevelopment in Kenya*; Alice Hoffenberg Amsden, *International Firms and Labour in Kenya: 1945–1979* (London: Cass, 1971).
23. Tanganyika Association, Second annual report of the Executive Committee covering the year ended 30 April 1960, LMA CLC/B/207/ STO3/07/01/009.
24. L. J. Butler, 'Business and British decolonisation: Sir Ronald Prain, the mining industry and the Central African Federation', *Journal of Imperial and Commonwealth History* 35, no. 3 (2007), p. 466.
25. Record of a meeting to consider the representation of overseas interests in Tanganyika, 19 June 1957, LMA CLC/B/207/STO3/07/01/008.
26. David Percox, *Britain, Kenya and the Cold War: Imperial Defence, Colonial Security and Decolonisation* (London: I.B. Tauris, 2004), p. 187.
27. A. M. Akiwumi, 'The development of the legislative process in East African integration', *Africa Spectrum* 7, no. 3 (1972), pp. 30–47.
28. See N. J. Westcott, 'Closer Union and the future of East Africa, 1939–1948: A case study in the 'official mind of imperialism'', *Journal of Imperial and Commonwealth History* 10, no. 1 (1981), pp. 67–88; Michael Collins, 'Decolonisation and the "Federal Moment"', *Diplomacy & Statecraft* 24, no. 1 (2013), pp. 21–40.
29. Brief for Secretary of State's meeting with Mr Obote on 8 June 1963: East African Federation, TNA CO 822/3194/7.
30. See Joseph S. Nye, 'East Africa: From Common Market to federation', *Africa Report* 8, no. 8 (1963) pp. 3–6.
31. Capital remittances overseas, estimated transfers of capital from East Africa by branches of the Standard Bank Ltd. 1960/1963 and inward capital remittances received by East African Branches of the Standard Bank Ltd. 1961/1963, LMA CLC/B/207/STO3/02/37/004.
32. Jonas and Anderson to the Directors, Board Memorandum no. 1138, 27 September 1961, United Africa Company collection, Unilever Archives, Port Sunlight (hereafter, UAC) 1/2/5/6/2.
33. Minutes of Chairman's Committee, 2 October 1961, UAC 1/1/2/1/3/27.
34. Percival to Partridge, 4 April 1962, TNA T 312/2229/1.
35. Minutes of Chairman's Committee, 9 July 1962, UAC 1/1/2/1/3/27.

36. Minutes of Chairman's Committee, 29 September 1964, UAC 1/1/2/1/3/27.
37. Minutes of Chairman's Committee, 2 October 1961, UAC 1/1/2/1/3/27.
38. Crossley, Chairman diaries, Notes for week ending 30 November 1963, Barclays Group Archives, Manchester (hereafter, BGA) 38/209.
39. Minutes of Chairman's Committee, 7 September 1964, UAC 1/1/2/1/3/27.
40. Minute, East African Association, 30 September 1964, TNA DO 214/75/25.
41. Draft, Proposed East Africa Committee, 24 August 1962, LMA CLC/B/207/STO3/07/01/015.
42. Ponsonby to Turnbull, 15 October 1958, TNA FCO 141/17931/37.
43. Standard Bank, Note for the general manager, 'Tanganyika Association, meeting of Executive Committee', 17 July 1962, LMA CLC/B/207/STO3/07/01/015.
44. Notes on meeting of the Tanganyika Committee, 8 January 1958, LMA CLC/B/207/STO3/07/01/008.
45. Draft, Proposed East Africa Committee, 24 August 1962, LMA CLC/B/207/STO3/07/01/015.
46. Standard Bank, Note for the Chairman, Proposed East Africa Committee, 19 September 1962, LMA CLC/B/207/STO3/07/01/015.
47. Minutes of the Executive Committee of the Tanganyika Association, 20 November 1962, LMA CLC/B/207/STO3/07/01/015.
48. Minutes of the council of the Tanganyika Association, 9 January 1963, LMA CLC/B/207/STO3/07/01/009.
49. Stanley-Smith to all former members of the Tanganyika Association, 18 December 1963, LMA CLC/B/207/STO3/07/01/010.
50. Williams, Board Memorandum, Tanganyika Association, 23 December 1959, LMA CLC/B/207/STO3/07/01/013.
51. Crossley, Chairman diaries, Notes for week ending 18 January 1964, BGA 38/209.
52. Ibid.
53. Pedler to Crossley, 28 January 1964, BGA 80/3583/3.
54. Burns to de Freitas, 21 April 1964, TNA DO 214/75/6.
55. Lamarque to Preston, 8 May 1964, TNA DO 214/75/11.
56. EAA, Constitution and Rules, June 1964, TNA DO 214/75/22.
57. Ibid.; Memorandum for the Standard Bank Standing Committee, 'East Africa Association', 14 September 1965, LMA CLC/B/207/STO3/07/01/011.

58. Kenneth Maddocks, *Of No Fixed Abode: An account of Colonial Service in Nigeria and Fiji and of subsequent work in London and East Africa* (Aldeburgh, [the author], 1988), p. 155.

59. Ibid., p. 159.

60. There have been many attempts to theorise about why such associations were appealing. See, for examples, Mancur Olson, *The Logic of Collective Action: Public Goods and the Theory of Groups* (Cambridge, MA: Harvard University Press, 1965); Jeffrey Pfeffer and Ferald R. Salancik, *External Control of Organizations: A Resource Dependence Perspective* (Stanford: Stanford University Press, 2003); Virginia Gray and David Lowery, 'Environmental limits on the diversity of state interest organization systems: A population ecology interpretation', *Political Research Quarterly* 49, no. 1 (1996), pp. 103–118.

61. S. E. Stockwell, 'Political strategies of British business during decolonization: The case of the Gold Coast/Ghana, 1945–57', *Journal of Imperial and Commonwealth History* 23, no. 2 (1995), p. 279.

62. An example of this was the coordination of the banks over the flight of capital in 1960; see Standard Bank general manager in East Africa to general manager in London, 9 March 1960, LMA CLC/B/207/STO3/02/37/004.

63. EAA, Constitution and Rules, June 1964, TNA DO 214/75/22.

64. Memorandum for Roberts, 'List of companies having East African connections and capable of paying at least £500 per annum', LMA CLC/B/207/STO3/07/01/015. On Inchcape, see Stephanie Jones, *Two Centuries of Overseas Trading: The Origins and Growth of the Inchcape Group* (Basingstoke: Macmillan, 1986).

65. EAA, list of members, 3 September 1964, TNA DO 214/75/22.

66. EAA, list of members, 31 December 1964, TNA DO 214/75/35.

67. Standard Bank, Note for the general manager, 'Tanganyika Association, meeting of Executive Committee', 17 July 1962, LMA CLC/B/207/STO3/07/01/015.

68. Collings to Kennaway, 27 February 1964, TNA DO 214/75/2.

69. Lamarque to Preston, 8 May 1964, TNA DO 214/75/11.

70. Ibid.

71. Maddocks, *Of No Fixed Abode*, p. 155.

72. See Stockwell, 'Political strategies of British business', p. 285.

73. See, for example, EAA, Notes on a visit to Tanzania in July 1965, UAC 1/3/5/6/2.

74. See, for example, the East Africa and Mauritius Association, reports on East Africa, April 1972, TNA FCO 31/1077/1.

75. EAA to all members, 11 May 1973, TNA FCO 31/1437/7.

76. For example, see Coleman to Pedler, 19 November 1964, UAC 1/3/5/6/2.

77. Coleman to Ball, 'Tanzania—Foreign Investments Protection Bill', 30 December 1964, UAC 1/9/4/8/1.
78. Minutes of the council of the Tanganyika Association, 9 January 1963, LMA CLC/B/207/STO3/07/01/009.
79. Standard Bank, Note for the Chairman, Proposed East Africa Committee, 19 September 1962, LMA CLC/B/207/STO3/07/01/015.
80. Minutes of the Executive Committee of the Tanganyika Association, 18 September 1962, LMA CLC/B/207/STO3/07/01/015.
81. Ibid.
82. Standard Bank, Note for Martin, 10 April 1964, LMA CLC/B/207/STO3/07/01/015.
83. Ibid.
84. Minutes of the Executive Committee of the Tanganyika Association, 18 September 1962, LMA CLC/B/207/STO3/07/01/015.
85. Lamarque to Stanley, 17 September 1964, TNA DO 214/75/23.
86. Standard Bank, Rob to Smith, 23 September 1965, LMA CLC/B/207/STO3/07/01/011.
87. Minutes of the Executive Committee of the Tanganyika Association, 18 September 1962, LMA CLC/B/207/STO3/07/01/015.
88. Stanely to Lamarque, 4 September 1964, TNA DO 214/75/17.
89. Standard Bank, Note for the Chairman, Proposed East Africa Committee, 19 September 1962, LMA CLC/B/207/STO3/07/01/015.
90. EAA, list of members, 31 December 1964, TNA DO 214/75/35.
91. Burns, 'Memorandum presented to the East African Commission on the future of the Common Market and Common Services', 23 December 1965, LMA CLC/B/207/STO3/07/01/011.
92. Preston to Kennaway, 23 April 1964, TNA DO 214/75/6.
93. Walsh Atkins to Burns, 8 July 1964, TNA DO 214/75/16.
94. Minute, Lamarque to Walsh Atkins, 10 April 1964, TNA DO 214/75.
95. P. J. Cain and A. G. Hopkins, *British Imperialism, 1688–2000*, Second Edition (Harlow: Longman, 2002). For a recent critique, see Andrew Dilley, 'The Elisions and Elusions of Gentlemanly Capitalism', *History of Global Arms Transfer* 5 (2018), pp. 37–48.
96. On these issues more widely see Gijsbert Oonk, *Settled Strangers: Asian Business Elites in East Africa (1800–2000)* (Los Angeles: SAGE, 2013).
97. Lamarque to Stanley, 17 September 1964, TNA DO 214/75/23.
98. Stanely to Lamarque, 4 September 1964, TNA DO 214/75/17.
99. Preston to Griffith, 13 January 1965, TNA DO 214/75/36.
100. See James Morris, "Cultivating the African': Barclays DCO and the decolonisation of business strategy in Kenya, 1950–1978', *Journal of Imperial and Commonwealth History* 44, no. 4 (2016), pp. 649–671; Stephanie Decker, 'Decolonising Barclays Bank DCO? Corporate

Africanisation in Nigeria, 1945–1969', *Journal of Imperial and Commonwealth History*, 33, no. 3 (2005), pp. 419–440.

101. Government of Uganda, Industrial Charter, July 1964, UAC 1/9/4/8/1.
102. Minutes of Chairman's Committee, 20 July 1964, UAC 1/1/2/1/3/27.
103. Wilkinson, Visit to East Africa, 20 March–8 April 1965, BGA 29/605.
104. Minutes of Chairman's Committee, 25 May 1964, UAC 1/1/2/1/3/27.
105. Speech by Kasambala, Minister for Commerce and Co-operatives, to the Dar es Salaam Chamber of Commerce, 30 July 1964, UAC 1/3/5/6/2.
106. Preston to Kennaway, 12 December 1964, TNA DO 214/75/31. This occurred when Idi Amin expelled Uganda's Asian population in 1972.
107. EAA, Constitution and Rules, June 1964, TNA DO 214/75/22.
108. Draft, Proposed East Africa Committee, 24 August 1962, LMA CLC/B/207/STO3/07/01/015.
109. Michael Jennings, '"A Very Real War": Popular participation in development in Tanzania during the 1950s & 1960s', *International Journal of African Historical Studies* 40, no. 1 (2007), p. 71.
110. Miatta Fahnbulleh, 'In search of economic development in Kenya: Colonial legacies & post-independence realities', *Review of African Political Economy* 33, no. 107 (2006), p. 33.
111. Government of Uganda, Industrial Charter, July 1964, UAC 1/9/4/8/1.
112. Watt to Coleman, 29 July 1964, UAC 1/9/4/8/1.
113. EAA, Constitution and Rules, June 1964, TNA DO 214/75/22.
114. Ibid.
115. Tanganyika Association, Constitution, January 1958, LMA CLC/B/207/STO3/07/01/14.
116. See Cooper, *Africa since 1940*.
117. Andrew Cohen, 'Lonrho and the limits of corporate power in Africa, c. 1961–1973', *South African Historical Journal* 68, no. 1 (2016), p. 39.
118. Christopher Clapham, *Third World Politics: An Introduction* (London: Croom Helm, 1985), p. 48.
119. Minutes of the Executive Committee of the Tanganyika Association, 18 September 1962, LMA CLC/B/207/STO3/07/01/015.
120. Maddocks, *Of No Fixed Abode*, p. 158. See also Pedler to Smith, 10 February 1967, UAC 1/3/5/6/2.
121. Chairman of the East Africa and Mauritius Association to Kawawa, 10 February 1967, UAC 1/3/5/6/2; East Africa and Mauritius Association, 'Memorandum presented to the Minister for Commerce and Industry: The Trade Licensing Bill 1967', 15 November 1967, UAC 1/5/1/2/8.
122. Report on the Director's visit to East Africa, 4 January to 9 February 1965, TNA DO 214/75/38.
123. Miles to Aspin, 13 February 1965, TNA DO 214/75/37.
124. Ibid.

125. Report on the Director's visit to East Africa, 4 January to 9 February 1965, TNA DO 214/75/38.
126. See Cranford Pratt, 'Foreign-policy issues and the emergence of socialism in Tanzania 1961–1968', *International Journal* 30, no. 3 (1975), pp. 445–470.
127. Burns to Karanja, 29 June 1964, TNA DO 214/75/22.
128. Ibid.
129. Miles to Kennaway, 7 December 1964, TNA DO 214/75/30.
130. Memorandum presented to the East African Commission on the future of the Common Market and Common Services, 23 December 1965, LMA CLC/B/207/STO3/07/01/011.
131. Coleman to Lindsay, 1 June 1964, UAC 1/3/5/6/2.
132. EAA, minutes of the provisional steering committee, 29 April 1964, TNA DO 214/75/12.

References

Akiwumi, A.M., 'The Development of the Legislative Process in East African Integration', *Africa Spectrum,* 7, no. 3 (1972), pp. 30–47.

Amsden, Alice Hoffenberg, *International Firms and Labour in Kenya: 1945–1979* (Cass, London, 1971).

Butler, L.J., 'Business and British Decolonisation: Sir Ronald Prain, the Mining Industry and the Central African Federation', *Journal of Imperial and Commonwealth History,* 35, no. 3 (2007), pp. 459–484.

Cain, P.J., and A.G. Hopkins, *British Imperialism, 1688–2000,* Second Edition (Longman, Harlow, 2002).

Clapham, Christopher, *Third World Politics: An Introduction* (Croom Helm, London, 1985).

Cohen, Andrew, 'Lonrho and the limits of corporate power in Africa, c. 1961–1973', *South African Historical Journal,* 68, no. 1 (2016), pp. 31–49.

Collins, Michael, 'Decolonisation and the "Federal Moment"', *Diplomacy & Statecraft,* 24, no. 1 (2013), pp. 21–40.

Cooper, Frederick, *Africa since 1940: The Past of the Present* (Cambridge University Press, Cambridge, 2002).

Decker, Stephanie, 'Decolonising Barclays Bank DCO? Corporate Africanisation in Nigeria, 1945–1969', *Journal of Imperial and Commonwealth History,* 33, no. 3 (2005), pp. 419–440.

Decker, Stephanie, 'Corporate Legitimacy and Advertising: British Companies and the Rhetoric of Development in West Africa, 1950–1970', *Business History Review,* 81, no. 1 (2007), pp. 59–86.

Decker, Stephanie, 'Building Up Goodwill: British Business, Development and Economic Nationalism in Ghana and Nigeria, 1945–1977', *Enterprise and Society,* 9, no. 4 (2008), pp. 602–613.

Dilley, Andrew, 'The Elisions and Elusions of Gentlemanly Capitalism', *History of Global Arms Transfer* 5 (2018), pp. 37–48.

Fahnbulleh, Miatta, 'In Search of Economic Development in Kenya: Colonial Legacies & Post-independence Realities', *Review of African Political Economy,* 33, no. 107 (2006), pp. 33–47.

Fieldhouse, D.K., *Black Africa 1945–1980: Economic Decolonization and Arrested Development* (Allen & Unwin, London, 1986).

Gray, Virginia, and David Lowery, 'Environmental Limits on the Diversity of State Interest Organization Systems: A Population Ecology Interpretation', *Political Research Quarterly,* 49, no. 1 (1996), pp. 103–118.

Jennings, Michael, '"A Very Real War": Popular Participation in Development in Tanzania During the 1950s & 1960s', *International Journal of African Historical Studies,* 40, no. 1 (2007), pp. 71–95.

Jones, Stephanie, *Two Centuries of Overseas Trading: The Origins and Growth of the Inchcape Group* (Macmillan, Basingstoke, 1986).

Leys, Colin, *Underdevelopment in Kenya: The Political Economy of Neo-Colonialism 1964–1971* (Heinemann, London, 1975).

Low, D., and J. Lonsdale, 'Introduction', in D. Low and A. Smith, eds. *The Oxford History of East Africa* (Oxford University Press, Oxford, 1976), pp. 1–64.

Maddocks, Kenneth, *Of No Fixed Abode: An Account of Colonial Service in Nigeria and Fiji and of Subsequent Work in London and East Africa* (Aldeburgh, [the author], 1988).

Misra, Maria, *Business, Race, and Politics in British India, c. 1850–1960* (Oxford University Press, Oxford, 1999).

Morris, James, '"Cultivating the African": Barclays DCO and the Decolonisation of Business Strategy in Kenya, 1950–1978', *Journal of Imperial and Commonwealth History,* 44, no. 4 (2016), pp. 649–671.

Nkrumah, Kwame, *Neo-Colonialism: The Last Stage of Imperialism* (Nelson, London, 1965).

Nye, Joseph S., 'East Africa: From Common Market to Federation', *Africa Report,* 8, no. 8 (1963), pp. 3–6.

Olson, Mancur, *The Logic of Collective Action: Public Goods and the Theory of Groups* (Harvard University Press, Cambridge, MA, 1965).

Oonk, Gijsbert, *Settled Strangers: Asian Business Elites in East Africa (1800–2000)* (SAGE, Los Angeles, 2013).

Percox, David, *Britain, Kenya and the Cold War: Imperial Defence, Colonial Security and Decolonisation* (I.B. Tauris, London, 2004).

Pfeffer, Jeffrey, and Ferald R. Salancik, *External Control of Organizations: A Resource Dependence Perspective* (Stanford University Press, Stanford, 2003).

Pratt, Cranford, 'Foreign-Policy Issues and the Emergence of Socialism in Tanzania 1961–1968', *International Journal,* 30, no. 3 (1975), pp. 445–470.

Stockwell, Sarah, 'Political Strategies of British Business During Decolonization: The Case of the Gold Coast/Ghana, 1945–1957', *Journal of Imperial and Commonwealth History* 23, no. 2 (1995), pp. 277–300.

Stockwell, Sarah, *The Business of Decolonization: British Business Strategies in the Gold Coast* (Clarendon Press, Oxford, 2000).

Stockwell, Sarah, 'Trade, Empire, and the Fiscal Context of Imperial Business During Decolonization', *Economic History Review,* LVII, no. 1 (2004), pp. 142–160.

Uche, Chibuike U., 'British Government, British Businesses, and the Indigenization Exercise in Post-independence Nigeria', *Business History Review,* 86 (2012), pp. 745–771.

Westcott, N.J., 'Closer Union and the future of East Africa, 1939–1948: A Case Study in the 'Official Mind of Imperialism'', *Journal of Imperial and Commonwealth History,* 10, no. 1 (1981), pp. 67–88.

White, Nicholas J., 'The Business and the Politics of Decolonization: The British Experience in the Twentieth Century', *Economic History Review,* 53, no. 3 (2000), pp. 544–564.

White, Nicholas J., 'The Survival, Revival and Decline of British Economic Influence in Malaysia, 1957–1970', *Twentieth Century British History,* 14, no. 3 (2003), pp. 222–242.

CHAPTER 4

Belgian Firms, Development Plans and the Independence of the Belgian Congo

Charlotte Strick
with Véronique Dimier

Dieu sait si l'Africain est soupçonneux d'un double jeu belge.[1]
[God knows the Africans suspect Belgium of playing a double game.]

In June 1960, just a few weeks before the formal independence of the Congo (30 June 1960), an in-situ study group sent by the Belgian government to the Congo to research the future development needs of the soon-to-be independent country met with distrust among the local elite. The Congolese feared that the Belgians were playing a double game. On the one hand, the old colonial masters offered development assistance and plans for the welfare of the Congolese people; on the other, they sought to maintain their companies' privileges and concessions. These concessions had a long history of facilitating the looting of Congolese resources, while impeding any local development. In this chapter we will show that the fears of the Congolese proved to be largely well grounded, as we examine the involvement of private companies in Belgian development strategies around independence. Drawing

C. Strick (✉)
Université Libre de Bruxelles, Bruxelles, Belgium

© The Author(s) 2020
V. Dimier, S. Stockwell (eds.), *The Business of Development in Post-Colonial Africa*, Cambridge Imperial and Post-Colonial Studies Series, https://doi.org/10.1007/978-3-030-51106-7_4

extensively on the private archives of Tractionel, the Belgian company, we investigate the creation of the Groupement international d'études pour le développement du Congo (GIDEC) by the Belgian government in May 1960. The main purpose of GIDEC was to conduct an in-situ study in the Congo and to propose a development programme for the new state. This study conformed to recommendations formulated by the social, financial and economic round table conference that was organised on decolonisation and was approved by the Executive Council of the governor general of the Congo on 4 May 1960, two months before the country gained its independence. The GIDEC study was formally independent of the Belgian government, or at least that was the initial intention; Brussels was keen to propose something acceptable to the government of the newly independent Congo. However, Belgian firms with a long history in the Congo, most notably Tractionel, a subsidiary firm of the famous Belgian company Société générale, did their utmost to secure a seat on GIDEC and thereby guarantee their interests into the future. Drawing on all their personal relationships, leveraging their long expertise in the development of the Congo, combined with rounds of intense lobbying, they eventually secured their place.

They were helped by the context of decolonisation. Two round table conferences were held in Brussels between Belgian and Congolese representatives: one in January-February 1960, to prepare the end of Belgian colonial domination, determine a date for independence, and set up future political institutions; the second, in April-May 1960, to find an agreement on social, economic and financial matters, including development aid, between the two countries.[2] This second conference discussed an inventory of Belgian-Congolese problems related to economic and financial matters. The main Congolese leaders, with the exception of the leaders of Katanga, were not represented at the economic conference, as they were preoccupied with the preparations for elections to be held in May. As noted by Michel Merlier, Belgium was hoping to negotiate technical aid and prevent likely conflict on the subject of colonial debt and the portfolio of holdings they continued to hold in the Congo.[3] The primary goal of the Belgian government was to guarantee Belgian economic interests and investments made during the colonial era and to maintain control, albeit limited, of the Congolese economy.[4] Referring to the catastrophic financial situation of the country, the Belgian government came up with the idea of establishing a Société de développement[5] that would be jointly funded by Belgium and the Congo. This company would be responsible for basic investment in infrastructure and would guarantee Congolese debts on the financial markets. The Brussels government also wanted to strengthen Belgium's authority over the future Congolese Central Bank in order to maintain its control of the Republic of Congo's monetary policy. In addition, Belgian ministers tried to secure formal guarantees for Belgian private investments, through a Traité d'amitié [Treaty of Friendship]; they sought to create clear conditions for the role and position of the private sector after independence and to introduce compensation measures for Belgian firms.[6]

During the conference, the Congolese delegation expressed concerns that Belgian private groups would interfere in the political sphere, as they had done during colonial times. Those private enterprises, indeed, had benefited from something akin to sovereign privilege. Hence, it was a bitter pill for the new leaders to swallow that even after independence, the Congolese state would be forced to deal with institutions and actors working under the influence and instructions of the former colonial power.[7] A Traité général d'amitié, d'assistance et de coopération was eventually signed on Independence Day, 30 June 1960. The treaty speaks in general terms about the aid that will be delivered by Belgium. Such were the suspicions of the Congolese government that the treaty was a covert means of perpetuating Belgian imperial domination that it was never ratified by the new administration.[8] In addition, political events made any development cooperation even harder. One of the objectives of Auguste De Schryver, the Belgian minister of the Colonies, was to create a pro-Belgian, moderate majority in the Congolese government. In this he failed, as the success of the nationalist parties, and most notably the party of Patrice Lumumba, during the first elections in May 1960 led to a more radical outcome: Lumumba was chosen as prime minister and Joseph Kasa-vubu as president. On 5 July a revolt broke out, led by frustrated Congolese soldiers. The ensuing massacres resulted not just in the hasty departure of Belgian executives but also the secession of the Katanga Province and the death of Lumumba—both backed by Belgium—and led to a state of civil war in the newly independent state. It was not until 1963 that the first development convention, which dealt mainly with education and technical assistance, was signed between the two countries.[9]

This context may account for the consistent contradiction in the relationship between the Belgian government and the private companies that is highlighted in the first section of this chapter: on one hand, the government tried as much as possible to be an autonomous actor in its dealings with the new African elite, setting up development plans that could benefit the Congolese people and not just Belgian firms. On the other, it did not succeed in freeing itself from the influence of the big actors whose interests were involved in the Congo. The second point developed in this chapter concerns the strategies adopted by Belgian firms that sought to be part of the future development plan of the Congo (GIDEC), without being too visible. This was a strategy they continued to follow long after decolonisation. It involved the creation of, or participation in, consortiums of consultancy firms to further their interests. The third key point here is the difficulties that Belgian actors encountered in acknowledging the political reality of the soon-to-be independent Congo: this was evident in their inability to fully involve Congolese partners in GIDEC. Whatever claims it may have made to the contrary, GIDEC remained de facto a paternalistic institution that was viewed with suspicion, no less by the Congolese elite than by the local Belgian administration.

TRACTIONEL AS A COLONIAL ECONOMIC ACTOR

As a private company, Tractionel was founded on 28 September 1895 by the Belgian engineer Charles Charlier and the Russian engineer Ivan Likhatschev under the name La Compagnie mutuelle des tramways.[10] The purpose of Tractionel was to create and run public transportation systems in Belgium and abroad. Within a few years, it had invested in more than fifty enterprises around the world. Faced with financial difficulties in 1910, however, Tractionel sought the help of Société générale de Belgique, and became a de facto subsidiary company of the most important Belgian holding and investment firm involved in the Congo. As a bank, created in 1822 by William I of the Netherlands and Luxembourg, Société générale became a major financial actor in the industrialisation and infrastructure development of Belgium in the nineteenth century. In 1906, at a time when the Congo was still the personal possession of Leopold II of Belgium, the King asked Société générale to become involved in the mise en valeur (development) of Central African territories. In collaboration with US and

UK consortiums, it created three companies which occupied a key role in the exploitation of Congolese resources. These were the Union minière du Haut Katanga, whose aim was to mine copper, gold and cobalt; the Société internationale forestière et minière du Congo, also known as Forminière, specialising in diamond mining; and the Compagnie du chemin de fer du Bas Congo au Katanga, which was responsible for building a national railway covering the entire Congo state, linking the mines to the ports. When the Congo was transferred to the Belgian state in 1908, Société générale became one of the main investors in the Belgian colony. The holding company had a huge political and social influence in Belgium and the Congo, controlling not just the production of copper and other ores, along with the transportation sector, but also the portfolios of over 800 Belgian enterprises which were located in the Congo, including Tractionel. All in all, their interests in the Congo corresponded to 40% of Belgian industrial assets.

As part of the Société générale group, Tractionel came to provide assistance to the Union minière du Haut Katanga in the 1920s. The two companies created Sogefor, a company which owned a mining concession on the waterfalls of Katanga, with Tractionel being involved in studies for the construction of hydro-electric power stations. These studies constitute the first instance of Tractionel operating as a consultancy firm, specialising in electricity production. As Tractionel benefited from a significant increase in its capital in 1929 (rising from 32 million to 96 million Belgian Francs), it was reorganised and transformed into a sub-holding, thereafter operating as the company of Traction et électricite (T.E). Despite this reorganisation, Tractionel continued to enjoy considerable managerial autonomy. The decision-making process was mainly in the hands of an executive committee, formed by the president of the company, a representative of Société générale, and three delegate administrators. Its growth continued through the 1930s, with an increase in capital from 120 million to 190 million Belgian Francs. In the 1950s, the management of the group sought to mitigate the perceived danger of the nationalisation of the Belgian electricity sector by branching out into new areas, like chemistry and oil. The company was also active in the steel industry, as well as in the smelting of non-ferrous metals and aluminium.[11] In 1960, it was active in the construction of power plants, tram and gas networks. In the Congo, it was able to make a huge profit in the aluminium, petroleum and power sectors. Most importantly, Tractionel was the leading consultancy firm involved in the Inga Dam Project.[12]

In July 1956, the Belgian minister of the colonies, De Schryver, had decided to relaunch the idea of developing a big hydroelectric station at Inga, on the Congo river. Belgian ambitions were huge: thanks to its enormous electricity production potential, Inga was considered the key element in the industrial development of the country, as envisaged in the 1950s by the long-term development plan of the Belgian government (Plan décennal de développement économique et social du Congo belge).[13] More specifically, it would contribute to the production of aluminium to be exported to the future EEC. Not only would it be a commercial success, however; it could be held up as an example of a successful project, showcasing not just the Congo itself but also, by association, Belgium's colonial mission there.[14] When the Belgian government set about looking for foreign investors, several consultancy firms, both from Belgium and abroad, competed for the contract to develop the preliminary study for the project. In the event, the Belgian government decided to create Abelinga, a national consortium which brought together a group of consultancy firms under the leadership of Tractionel. The firm could now legitimately leverage its expertise to secure its place as a key player in the future development plans of the Congo.

This was all the more important because decolonisation was an important challenge, if not a direct threat, to Tractionel's autonomy and interests. Like other Belgian firms in the Congo, it had benefited from very advantageous tax conditions and had operated almost entirely without governmental intervention during the colonial era. To secure business interests in the Congo the Belgian government adopted a new law thirteen days before independence:[15] henceforth, Belgian firms in the soon-to-be ex-colony would be free to choose the location of their registered offices. Their options were either to continue their business under Congolese law or to change the company's legal status to that of a company incorporated under Belgian law. Most firms opted for the second solution, as they feared the potential fiscal instability of the Republic of the Congo, or, even worse, the nationalisation of their company.[16] Against this background, Belgian companies, among them the influential Société générale, deployed several strategies to maintain their power and influence over the future Congolese economy. As noted by Jean Stengers, one tactic was to offer generous bribes to all Congolese political parties in order to establish some goodwill among the future Congolese political elite.[17] Another stratagem was to control the future Société de développement envisaged by the Belgian government during the Round Table conference. It was assumed that the future Congolese government would be unable to meet its financial obligations and, having posted its stock as collateral, would have little choice but to hand over its shares in the many Belgian Congo companies (in the areas of transport and mining, among others) that had previously been the property of the colonial-era state. This would effectively close the 'expropriation loop', leaving the Republic of Congo's former masters holding the deeds for the newly independent state's infrastructure and natural resources (through the Société de développement).

Meanwhile, lands and mining rights were conceded to the Congo state as financial compensation. The capital portfolios of the Union minière du Haut Katanga was split between the new state and the Companie du Katanga, controlled by Société générale. The Republic of Congo received two-thirds and Société générale, one. A similar arrangement was concluded for other similar firms. Following independence, long negotiations ensued between the Belgian government and Prime Minister Lumumba and President Kasa-vubu on these issues. The problem was partly solved, albeit not to the satisfaction of the Republic of Congo, by the secession of the Katanga, one of the richest regions in the country. This secession was largely supported by Société générale, and it allowed Belgian companies to keep the entirety of their assets, rather than just one-third, as previously agreed.[18] Within this context, it came as no surprise that Tractionel, and behind it, Société générale, did their utmost to play an active role in the work of GIDEC.

GIDEC as a Trojan Horse

The Groupement international d'études pour le développement du Congo was created on 4 May 1960.[19] The idea of drawing up a general study of the development of the Congo was launched in March 1960 by Raymond Scheyven, the minister in charge of economic and financial affairs of the Belgian Congo and Ruanda-Urundi. It was backed by the Congolese members of the round table conference in April-May 1960. They asked that an inventory of the resources and needs of the Congo be made, in preparation for the setting up, in the future Congolese government, of a programming office for the development of the country.[20] Hence, Scheyven commissioned the study, to be paid for by the Belgian government,[21] subject to the approval of the Executive Council of the governor general of the Belgian Congo.[22] GIDEC would conduct a general study in the Congo with the aim of producing an integrated, coordinated and flex-ible economic and social development plan for the future independent Congolese state: this plan would allow for the mise en valeur ('develop-ment') of Congolese resources, the improvement of the standard of living of the population, while reducing the dependency of the Congolese econ-omy on external aid.[23] Its main objective would be to benefit the 'com-munity of the people'.

Such a plan could be seen as the continuation of the ten-year plans adopted in the 1950s, whose aim was to ensure the development and wel-fare of the Congolese people. As Guy Vanthemsche has noted, the first plan, drawn up in 1949 by the Belgian government and supported by progressive elements of the Belgian political elite, recognised the necessity of important changes in the colonial economy and society:[24] previously, the exploitation of the Congolese resources had only benefited foreign companies, swelling their profits while impoverishing the local population, a situation that needed to be transformed through long-term structural changes. The welfare of the 'native' (to use the language of the time) could no longer be subordinated to the welfare of companies whose prof-its were siphoned off to Belgium. A home-based economy, relying on Congolese production and the local market, had to be created, along with the transformation of the agricultural sector and the development of small-scale industries.

In practice, those objectives and priorities were abandoned during the implementation phase of the plan: the money (coming mainly from pri-vate investment and external loans) was largely spent on the construction of infrastructure projects, which, unsurprisingly, benefited large Belgian construction companies. However, the same ideas and ambitions were to resurface at GIDEC: the idea was to foster development 'from below' in order to increase the standard of living of the Congolese people. This development would be based on an 'autonomous' process towards prog-ress.[25] What 'progress' meant was not specified, even though this progress, it was said, had to be human progress (whether moral or material) and had to be achieved while respecting the native human values and the knowl-edge of the local population. It had to conform to the 'aspirations of individuals and of the nation'. This was seen as the only way to ensure the 'collaboration of the population', to create in them the 'mystique of prog-ress' and to spark their 'enthusiasm' to carry out the tasks that were allot-ted to them.[26]

In the meantime, the study conducted by GIDEC would be limited to an analysis of the present economic and social situation of the Congo and its possible evolution over ten years. After analysing and synthesising its development problems, gathering all the necessary elements for the preparation of a working programme of development for the future state, it would devise the priorities and major lines of this development plan. This meant evaluating the needs for manpower, training facilities and investment in the Congo and the scale of technical and financial assistance required for the agreed development purpose. It also meant identifying human, monetary and technical obstacles to this development plan and the different possible ways of overcoming them, the potential improvements in terms of social and economic infrastructure necessary to sustain the development efforts of the country and the national production necessary to satisfy the needs of the population, be that in the field of agriculture or industry. For agriculture, it would focus on the past experience of paysannat indigène (subsistence farmers) and cooperatives.[27] For industrial development, it would consider the development of small local firms. Last but not least, it would recommend all measures, administrative, economic and social, that might be deemed necessary for the future development effort and would evaluate the degree of improvement in the quality of life of the population that could be achieved as a result.

A working plan was to be presented to the future government of the Congo, who would find in it an objective picture of the economic and social situation of the country on the eve of independence. It would lay out the prospects for improvement, the lines of action to be envisaged and the priorities to be adopted: in sum, an 'instrument of government'. This could also be useful to experts, entrepreneurs and prospective investors, who would draw on it when planning their initiatives. The study would be guided and coordinated by the Belgian and Congolese authorities and incorporated into the diverse economic and social sectors of the Congo. The first phase of the study (the fact-finding mission, mission de reconnaissance or preliminary in-situ study) was meant to gather information and establish useful contacts in the Congo, to lay out the precise aims of the study, mobilise any collaboration and create a working plan for the next phase. The second phase would consist of an 'in-situ study proper', gathering and analysing documents, consulting the public and private sectors involved in development projects, launching a discussion of the particular problems of development and writing a final report, to be submitted to the Congolese authorities. The members of the in-situ study (working party) would be selected according to their competence and with an eye to the international aspect of the study. Originally, it was proposed that a well-qualified Congolese economics expert should join the study team and serve as a mediator between the study and the Congolese authorities. It was also suggested that Congolese experts should be seconded to the study's various working groups.[28] Under these proposals, the Congolese government would be the general contractor and could decide the conditions under which the studies would be carried out.[29] The crux of all this, of course, was the composition of the working party, a point 'which led to long negotiations'.[30]

Building Independence from Private Actors

For Scheyven, the most important condition for the establishment of this study, and the only way for it to be accepted by the Congolese leaders, was for it to be indisputably independent; hence, the participation of Belgian firms had to be limited.[31] This demonstrated the will of the Ministry of the Colonies to assert its own autonomy vis-à-vis the interests of private companies. As shown by Guy Vanthemsche, the development plan launched in 1949 by the minister of the colonies, the Christian Democrat Pierre Wigny, was drawn up without the involvement of the major Belgian companies and purported not only to serve the interests and welfare of the Congolese people but also to control the private sector. A Société d'expansion coloniale, a semi-state body, created on the model of the British Colonial Development Corporation, was even envisaged at that time. While embodying the autonomous action of the colonial state, it would finance or create small 'native' firms in the industrial and agricultural sectors which were considered essential to local development. This idea was eventually abandoned, however. With its excessively interventionist character, the plan had little chance of succeeding in enrolling private sector actors, whose collaboration and investment were necessary. Indeed, the autonomy of the Belgian Ministry of the Colonies was limited by the fact that the Belgian state was not willing to pay for the development of its colonies.[32] It was also limited by the tremendous power that a small number of holdings had over the Belgian government and politics in Belgium. This was confirmed by the discussions on the composition of the GIDEC in-situ study.

Two consultancy firms approached the ministry to conduct the study: one was EUROPREDE (Groupement européen de programmation et d'études générales de développement),[33] a European consortium of consultancy firms sponsored by Société générale and including, among other Belgian firms, Tractionel. The other was the Association belge de sociétés d'études pour le développement, linked to the Coppée group.[34] The Coppée family had played an important role in the development of Belgian coal policy in collaboration with the governor of Société générale and formed part of several other holdings in Belgium and the Congo.[35] Baron Albert Coppée was also part of the executive committee of the Association belge de sociétés d'études pour le développement. Both Coppée and Edgar Van der Straeten, the vice-governor of Société générale, contacted Scheyven personally to propose their services—each hoping to get an exclusive contract for 'his' consultants.

When Van der Straeten asked for an appointment to discuss the development study of the Congo, Scheyven made it clear that 'from a political point of view, it was necessary to avoid too visible a presence on the part of the Société générale in the organisation of the study'.[36] In the event, Société générale's proposal to have EUROPREDE involved in the study was not accepted by the ministry. Indeed, their participation would raise conflict-of-interest issues with the Congolese. Hence, the minister at first insisted on working with a group that had no experience in the Congo, preferring to call on Italconsult (an Italian-led group) or US consultancy firms. This was unacceptable to the representative of Société générale, who 'reacted sharply and grew indignant at such a strange notion, inspired by groundless mistrust toward those who have created prosperity in the Congo'. Hence, he wondered 'why the government would consider Société générale unqualified to conduct the study and abandon this task to an organisation [the future GIDEC] with no experience in the country and whose main actors would be Italian industrial groups', groups that could hardly be considered neutral, of course.[37] Hence, he clearly objected to the participation of Italconsult, considered an offshoot of Italian construction companies.[38] Firms in the Société générale group, most notably Tractionel, 'were proud and aware of the preeminent role they had played over 50 years in the attainment of the industrial and social prosperity of the Congo. If the Belgian government was suffering from a guilt complex vis-à-vis the Congolese people, this feeling was not shared by the enterprises of the group, which had earned many times over the confidence, esteem and recognition of the Congolese people'.[39]

Likewise, Baron Coppée 'insisted that the preliminary study be granted to his association. He argued that it was preferable, both for the Belgian administration and the Congolese, that the firms of the Société générale group interested in these questions should remain outside the main study, whose impartiality might otherwise be impugned. Baron Coppée declared that he could arrange matters in such a manner that Italconsult would not intervene in the study'.[40] Rather, he proposed to include in the study a US firm, Lilienthal (Development and Resources),[41] and create an ad hoc council in the form of a technical committee with a strictly consultative mandate, in which firms like Tractionel could participate.[42] Tractionel, for its part, complained that Coppée's proposal would see responsibility for the tasks shared unfairly between the participants.[43] It disagreed with his stance that his proposed composition of GIDEC was the only one that could guarantee the impartiality and efficiency of the study.[44] Tractionel representatives continued to lobby the minister, seeking a place in the in-situ study and stressing their long experience and long-standing expertise.[45]

Eventually, in order to convince the Belgian government to accept the involvement of EUROPREDE in GIDEC, the director of Tractionel, Mr Smits, tried to find some compromise, a gentleman's agreement with Baron Coppée:[46] both EUROPREDE and the Association belge de sociétés d'études pour le développement would participate in GIDEC, alongside other international consultancy firms. The idea was to include as many actors as possible, thereby stressing the importance of having an independent study, while at the same time legitimising their own participation.[47] Eventually, because the governor general did not want to have any French participants in the study (and EUROPREDE included a French contingent), Société générale, through Tractionel, came up with a proposal that included two German consultancy firms, Kocks and Lahmeyer (one of which was already part of EUROPREDE), four Belgian firms, Electrobel, Sofina, Tractionel and the CCCI (Compagnie du Congo pour le commerce et l'industrie), another subsidiary company of Société générale and part of EUROPREDE, as well as two American firms, Lilienthal and the Stanford Research Institute.[48] However, this proposal could hardly hide the clear imbalance in favour of the Société générale group.

Given the stated opposition of the minister, a new, more subtle and less visible approach would be required. The solution found by Société générale and Tractionel was to create a new consortium of consultancy firms, the Groupement belge pour les études de développement en Afrique (GETAF).[49] GETAF was the result of an agreement between three Belgian private enterprises that were part of EUROPREDE, namely, Electrobel,

Sofina and Tractionel.[50] This group promised to keep EUROPREDE informed and to consult them on technical questions, when necessary.[51] Its objective was to carry out general development studies for Africa. GETAF negotiated an agreement with the Association belge de sociétés d'études pour le développement that would allow it not only to join the working party of GIDEC, but also to be part of its Management Committee (conseil de gestion).[52] It put itself forward as possessing expertise that was essential at every level from the good management of the study to the gathering and collation of the results. It was 'the only one' in the Committee who could bring a detailed knowledge of Congolese development problems to the table. Hence its participation could not be objected to.[53] Tractionel asserted that one or two of its representatives on the Management Committee would not give it anything like a dominant influence; it would, however, help with suggestions and appropriate solutions to problems that could arise during the work. The need to take a stance that was 'strictly disinterested' was seen as impossible and leading to an unbearable situation…a situation without Tractionel.[54] 'By wanting to appear neutral, one may just become incompetent'. 'Should we eliminate Tractionel because they have the necessary knowledge?'[55] As a consultancy firm, Tractionel had shown its independence. 'The development problems to be studied were so immense, that not bringing our collaboration to this study would compromise the chances of its success'.[56]

The protocol for the constitution and the organisation of an in-situ study in the Congo was eventually adopted by the Belgian government on 4 May 1960.[57] The study included experts from each of the following: Belgian experts from l'Association belge de sociétés d'études pour le développement and GETAF; foreign experts from the Stanford Research Institute (SRI), from Italconsult, and from Kocks and Lahmeyer, two German consultancy firms (with the latter being originally part, like Tractionel, of EUROPREDE). The Management Committee (whose aim was to develop the working party plans and take any necessary decisions regarding the running of the study) included a representative from each of these groups, one representative from the Belgian government, one from the Congolese government, one from the Executive Council of the governor general and, surprisingly, one representative listed simply as 'Investment'. The committee chairman came from GETAF: Neirynck, director of Tractionel, was chosen for the job.[58] The Management Committee (conseil de gestion) would nominate an Executive Committee (comité de direction) consisting of representatives of each consultancy firm, with the president of this Executive Committee being chosen by the Association belge de sociétés d'études pour le développement (M. Gracco). His function would be to keep the Management Committee informed of the practical implementation of the study.

In fact, the composition of GIDEC largely reflected the original proposal made by Société générale, with only a few changes: Italconsult was kept as a partner, while the Companie du Congo pour le commerce et l'industrie, a subsidiary company of Société générale, was dropped from the team, at least officially. In fact, the idea of creating a delegate called 'Investment', a rather broad term, came mostly from the Société générale management, who convinced the minister to appoint someone representing the interests of the investors.[59] Mr Lippens, a representative of Companie du Congo pour le commerce et l'industrie, was chosen for this task. His role was to keep abreast of the work of the in-situ study and to contribute to the orientation of the project. For Société générale, there was no doubt that 'through him, the GIDEC would benefit from the experience of the Congolese firms of the group [Société générale], as well as from their collaboration and that of their technicians'.[60] Tractionel and Société générale would eventually boast that their manoeuvering had been a notable success. 'Our action towards the constitution of the GIDEC and its first in-situ study was conceived and conducted with a single aim in mind: ensuring the influence of Société générale, and most notably of its Congolese firms, in this organisation. I think the efforts of Mr Neirynck can be considered as satisfactory, given the initial unfavourable conditions we encountered (opposition from the ministry, the unjustified wariness of certain Congolese politicians regarding the group, manoeuvering by Baron Coppée). The prestige of Société générale has been guaranteed and the influence of the group on the future orientation of the work has been safeguarded to a reasonable degree'.[61]

This was even clearer if one considers that the Stanford Research Institute was to be responsible for the in-situ study, that is, for the coordination of the resources, as well as the choice of the head of the study.[62] James Moran, director of the African Department of the SRI, was chosen by the Management Committee to be the head of the in-situ study in the Congo.[63] The fact that the coordination of the study was given to the SRI was no random stroke of luck, however. As a representative of Société générale noted: 'At Mr Van der Straeten's request, an action was undertaken to change the composition of the group [GIDEC] and ensure the reasonable participation of Société générale in it. For this purpose, we relied on the SRI, whose participation in the study significantly changed the structure of the in-situ study'.[64] Even though the SRI was quite reluctant to be part of it, given the 'resistance' of the ministry to the participation of Société générale, they eventually accepted.[65] The SRI had a 'solid reputation everywhere in the world and the US and was well connected to political and business circles'.[66]

Tractionel and Société générale were already well acquainted with the SRI and their work, as they had previously worked in partnership with them.[67] During a trip to the US in December 1959, Director Roger Neirynck of Tractionel had met with members of the SRI. Their discussions centred on a proposal to cooperate on an African development study that would bring together the US and Europe and would be supported by the Bank of America and other leading US companies. It was the SRI that had first approached Tractionel to participate in the African development study and they met with an enthusiastic response.[68] Later on, Société générale, l'Union minière du Haut Katanga, la Compagnie du Congo pour le commerce et l'industrie and the Companie du chemin de fer du Bas Congo in Katanga also lent their support, along with others such as Deutsche Bank, the Lever Group and firms involved in aluminium production.[69] Whether GETAF would participate remained a matter of discussion. But Tractionel even seconded an economist (M. Haine) to the SRI to learn their methods of analysis and participate in the study.[70] It was noted that such a study could not itself guide private firms in their investment plans. But it could help these firms to better understand the context they faced in Africa and help them to interact with African governments in ways that would allow those governments to take decisions that would facilitate private initiatives in the long term. Given the new African states' great need for capital, European firms would increasingly have to seek investment collaboration with US firms. This meant that an association with the US in the framework of the African development study was an attractive proposition on many levels.[71] In fact, Société générale managed to become a full partner and sponsor of the SRI's African development study, a study which was conceived as being for US investors, as Société générale recognised.[72] Including such a renowned institution in GIDEC gave the latter scientific credibility and a façade of autonomy. It also gave even more 'indirect' influence to Tractionel and Société générale. The problem, of course, was that, despite their best efforts to attain invisibility, both became all too visible to the Congolese elite and even to the last Belgian governor general.

AND WHAT ABOUT THE CONGOLESE?

It is interesting to note how the rapid political evolution of the Congo was presented as a justification for the urgency of GIDEC's mission,[73] but at the same time how little mention was made of the desires, needs and plans of the future Congolese elite. Letters from Van der Straeten, vice-governor of Société générale, or Scheyven, for example, stressed the importance of involving other actors like the International bank for reconstruction and development (IBRD) in GIDEC and, thus, in the future economic and social development of the country: it was essential for Belgium that the western nations jointly solve the problems of development aid.[74] Indeed, it was recognised that aid had previously been provided in a unilateral manner and, in spite of all the resources committed, had not produced satisfactory results. The lack of coordination, it was said, might lead to conflicts among western countries.

But what about involving the Congolese? In all their negotiations, Coppée, Neirynck and Van der Straeten made only passing reference to the possibility of including them. It came to Moran, the head of the study and a US citizen, to underline the importance of consulting the future Congolese government and integrating them into the study in order to add credibility to the final report.[75] His idea was to involve one or two suitably qualified Congolese officials in the work of the in-situ study. This could be a high-ranking civil servant, with expertise in economic affairs and chosen by the Congolese authorities, to ensure a good relationship between the head of the study and the Congolese administration. This idea was entertained in the first documents related to the organisation of GIDEC, but not discussed in later drafts. In the event, the protocol listing the make-up of GIDEC only mentions a representative of the Congolese government on the Management Committee.

In the end, there was no direct collaboration with the Congolese leaders for the preliminary study which took place between 28 May and 18 June. The future Congolese government would receive a proposition with the working plan and a detailed budget for the study, but no provision was made for them to be involved.[76] True, as one of the members of GIDEC remarked: 'we had to be very careful because to designate a direct Congolese partner before a Congolese government was formed could be counter-productive if that government did not consider this delegate as persona grata'.[77] Finding economic experts among the Congolese might also have been difficult given how few possibilities of training were available to Congolese during colonial rule. As David Van Reybrouck remarked, the future Republic of Congo was represented by students with little experience in economics at the round table conference.[78] Hence the preliminary GIDEC in-situ study (mission de reconnaissance) of May-June 1960 included no Congolese representatives. Its members were William Moran (SRI), François Gracco (Association belge de sociétés d'études pour le développement), Raimondo Craveri (Italconsult), Charles Desclée de Maredsous (GETAF), Mr Muller (Lahmeyer and Co.) and Philippe de Scot (Secretary).

The members of the study quickly discovered that they were unable to find or contact the relevant Congolese officials until the new government had been formed. However, as the working party had to change their schedule due to the limited transportation facilities, they were given more time to spend in Léopoldville. Finally, they had a chance to meet with President Kasa-vubu, who received them in the name of the General Executive College (the government-in-waiting) and assured them of his cooperation. '[He] looked like an honest man, even though strongly affected by mysticism', noted GIDEC member, Mr Muller.[79] He promised that he would publish an announcement in the press and on the radio to facilitate the work of the in-situ study, allowing them to gather information and make contacts in the country.[80] The working party also had a short interview with future Prime Minister Lumumba, 'too short, however, to make a clear opinion on this "character"'.[81] Mr Muller, the German expert of the working party, underlined that 'too many contacts with Belgians were avoided. The team chose to have direct contact with the Congolese', at both the central and provincial level.[82] Eventually, the team could boast of having met many different actors, especially among the future provincial governments. To Desclée de Maredsous, the expert representing GETAF, it was clear that the social and economic study they envisaged was greatly desired by this elite.[83]

The other problem the working party encountered was the lack of competent officials with whom they interacted. This, according to Desclée de Maredsous, was the direct result of Belgian colonisation, or lack of preparation for independence.[84] 'Against my expectations, I realised that "africanisation" had not made any headway. While in most other African countries, natives had been involved in shared responsibilities and had been trained as an elite, on the ground or in the home country, the Belgian Congo is lagging behind. (…) During these last years, an administration lacking character and firms of a certain type too well known in Belgium, have missed the opportunity to approach and negotiate with the future Congolese leaders. With a paternalism which has not gone beyond the relation between masters and servants, the administration and the firms have tried to distort social and political movements'.[85] 'The Russians, on the other hand, are cleverer as they are offering potential leaders accelerated training. Fifteen days ago, a plane took the young mentees of Lumumba to Moscow in order to offer them the training that Belgium has refused to provide. The Belgian government persists in choosing Congolese leaders, while the only leaders who can raise the mass of the people, the "goupils" (the foxes) of the place, are ignored'. Desclée de Maredsous further refers to the growing role of Lumumba: 'Tomorrow he will have raised the most active African circles and a chasm will widen between him and the Belgians. He is the one to come to power who knows the modern techniques of government'. Only a dialogue with Lumumba could help in saving the most important thing: 'the future relations between Belgium and the coming Congo, or more simply between the West and emancipated Africa'.[86] If the Bas Congo and the province of Katanga, which were the wealthiest in natural resources, were quite immune to the influence of Lumumba, the centre of the Congo was a tinderbox, awaiting only the Lumumba spark. These conditions seemed to make the Congo the perfect place for communism in the eyes of the members of the working party.[87]

Clearly such a conclusion could not lead to successful dialogue with a government led by Lumumba. Besides, their contacts in the Congo could not guarantee the continuation of GIDEC's work. 'We have multiplied our contacts with black leaders and prominent citizens. They seem interested in the study, but any decision is now dependent on the solution of the political problem'.[88] The typical response of the leaders they met was that 'the government of tomorrow will make the decision'.[89] They all agreed, however, upon one point: that Belgium had to be replaced in the different regions by Africans.[90] In these circumstances, any colonial, paternalistic reflex had to be avoided, not an easy task for some Belgian experts of the in-situ study. For example, Gracco, the expert representing the Association belge de sociétés d'études pour le développement, a person close to Baron Coppée, went far beyond the 'neutral' position that an international expert should have adopted in such circumstances, according to Desclée de Maredsous, the other Belgian expert of the working party and a representative of the GETAF: 'During the first days of the study, Mr Gracco was able to rein in his enthusiasm, but yesterday evening, in presence of the main leaders from Katanga, he allowed himself to give the conversion the character of a defence, and, what is even more serious, to modify the terms of reference of our study by proposing an emergency plan, followed by a long study programme. Mr Moran expressed some reservations in a friendly manner, but Mr Gracco tackled him in the strongest terms, declaring that *he* was the president of the Executive Committee. In these circumstances, Mr Moran was obliged to leave the meeting'. This incident inflicted great damage, according to Desclée de Maredsous: 'It is no secret that the contacts we make at present are highly risky: turning one's coat is frequent here and the people we talk to sometimes hide their anti-Belgian feelings or their real intentions. In such circumstances, we must listen rather than teach, record what they say rather than debate. This is a job for a diplomat: it requires a certain passivity, great diplomatic skills and particularly, strict discipline. We have to avoid excessively strong views'.[91]

Congolese distrust may well have been fuelled by the dissentions that occurred among members of the working party, and all the more so because of the involvement of international (US) experts who might have been be too critical of Belgian colonisation. The German expert of GIDEC (Mr Muller) remarked that 'ironically, many experts and international VIPs, who have just landed in the Congo, begin to utter radical points of view as to what is right and what is wrong about the work done by the Belgians in the Congo. They are all very critical of the Belgian mission'.[92] This was especially true for Moran, the US head of the working party, who did not miss an opportunity to question Belgian work in the Congo, a stance that Muller did not share. Hence, there was a fear 'that tensions in the working party had the potential to be highly damaging, especially in Stanleyville, where the population was anti-Belgium, and Léopoldville, where they would meet members of the future Congolese government'.[93] It seems also that the composition of the working party remained a matter of debate for those they met: some were reluctant to accept the fact that it included three Belgians and three foreigners. Ironically, Belgian officials from the governor general's office, especially Mr Carbonnel, said, 'it would have been much better to have only one Belgian and five foreigners'.[94] As for the Governor General Cornelis, 'we [the working team] could make nothing at all of the opinions he expressed. Mr Muller said of the governor general that "this fellow is so pro-Congolese as to render his opinions almost incomprehensible"'.[95] This may reflect once again the ambivalent position of the colonial administration and government vis-à-vis other, specifically economic, actors. This ambivalence is not exclusive to Belgium. Fred Cooper shows how the French and British colonial administrations were split between, on one hand, the necessity to protect the interests of colonial companies (whose help was indispensable for managing the colony), and, on the other hand, the need to protect the local population from the greed of these companies in order to garner some legitimacy and ensure the collaboration of the 'natives' in their ostensible civilising missions.[96] Trained in schools where they were taught to ensure the welfare of native people, they became, over the years, more and more reluctant to serve the interests of private companies (as also shown by Sarah Stockwell),[97] in terms of forced labour, for example. One may speculate that around decolonisation, freed from the constraints of the colonial state and its exploitative policies, colonial governors and administrators may have favoured those with whom they had worked for extended periods: the local elite.

However, the most problematic aspect of the in-situ study was flagged by a communication coming from an anonymous individual in Léopoldville on 20 June 1960. As the Belgian Desclée de Maredsous describes: 'One of my friends in Léopoldville, who is independent from any political movement, has given me some contradictory information about rumours that are doing the rounds in that big village that is the capital of the Congo'.[98] He could not locate the precise origin of the rumour, but 'he heard that GIDEC was an organisation of colonial firms that felt threatened and wished to pursue their own interests'. It was clear that 'if this rumour was anything other than gossip, it could undermine the success of the in-situ study'. However, 'I do not think that we must worry before having appreciated the importance and origin of this "*racontar*" (gossip). Many people are ill-intentioned or just thoughtless. I hope that my investigations will lead me to the conclusion that they were merely inconsistent statements to which we must not attach too much importance'.[99] Desclée de Maredsous ends his correspondence with the following statement: 'God knows the Africans suspect Belgium of playing a double game' [Dieu sait si l'Africain est soupçonneux d'un double jeu belge].[100]

Conclusion

Considering the intense efforts made by Tractionel to be part of GIDEC, this distrust may have been legitimate. More generally, the intentions of the experts involved in GIDEC were not disinterested. As one of them clearly stated: 'When we came back to Léopoldville yesterday [the 19th] we felt drowned by the political problem. We hope that the government will be formed and that we will be able to "sell" our studies'.[101] Indeed, selling development studies to the newly independent African states became a lucrative proposition, not only for consultancy firms or institutes like the SRI, but also for companies like Tractionel, who were involved in consultancy firms or consortiums like GETAF. Helping African states to draft development projects that served the interests of a certain company was the best way for the company to get new contracts, as Véronique Dimier will show in her chapter. As also remarked by Guy Vanthemsche, Belgian companies, through the national employers' association (Fédération des industries belges) continued to lobby the Belgian government to establish a commission for development cooperation.[102] In this new strategy, however, Belgian firms, notably Tractionel, were soon confronted with serious competitors. For example, despite the interest and experience of Tractionel in the Inga Dam project and lobbying efforts targeting the newly formed Congolese government, the project draft study was finally awarded to an Italian consortium of consultancy firms. Thanks to the funding of the EEC's European Development Fund and after a call for tenders, the first Inga dam was built by French, Italian and German companies.[103]

GIDEC was undoubtedly successful in convincing the new Congolese government that development—be it through Inga or other plans—was necessary. Its preliminary report gave some vague assessment of the current economic, financial and social situation of the Congo and called for a more thorough examination of the problem.[104] It concluded that a general study for the development of the Congo, as envisaged by Mr Scheyven and as planned by GIDEC, was badly needed. The US coordinator, Mr Moran, noted that the in-situ study was well received by the new Congolese leaders at both the central and provincial level. They were all interested in the general study proposed by GIDEC and particularly appreciated the international character of the team. They also wished that a Congolese member be included in the team charged with carrying out the proposed future study.[105] Given the dramatic events of July 1960, GIDEC could not pursue its mission, however.[106] It fell to the SRI to continue the work some months later through its own African development study.[107]

In this chapter, we have tried to show how Raymond Scheyven sought to ensure the autonomy of GIDEC from economic actors (more specifically, from Société générale and its subsidiary companies). For that purpose, his strategy was to involve international experts and as many consultancy firms as possible. We demonstrate, however, that through subtle manoeuvring, Société générale, and more precisely Tractionel, succeeded in being part of GIDEC. One of their strategies—to avoid any accusation of dominating the study—was also to involve international experts and institutes like the SRI. As a conclusion one may wonder whether these strategies did not lead to an outcome which may not have been envisaged by the Belgian government or Tractionel: to facilitate the opening of the Congolese market to US, German and Italian firms which could then bypass Belgian businesses, having fostered close relations with the African leaders. This was hinted at by Tractionel's Belgian representative, reviewing the first draft of the parallel joint study on African development envisaged by the SRI: 'On several occasions, you present yourself—unjustly, it seems to me—as the prosecuting counsel to the work accomplished by Europeans in Africa, and this, perhaps with the aim of making your country appear more friendly to Africans. This tone is not appropriate if a closer collaboration between Europe, Africa and the USA is what is sought. Honestly, you sometimes give the distinct impression of wishing to put Europeans out of the game'.[108]

Notes

1. Private archives of Tractionel, *Groupe compagnie mutuelle des tramways*, alias *Traction et électricité alias* Tractionel (AT), box 6335, Desclée de Maredsous (economic expert for the *Groupement belge pour les études de développement en Afrique*) to Neirynck (president of the board of management of the GIDEC), 20 June 1960.
2. David Van Reybrouck, *Congo, une histoire* (Actes Sud, 2011), pp. 278–279; Jacque Brassinne de la Buissière and Georges Henri Dumont, *Les autorités belges et la décolonisation du Congo*, Courrier hebdomadaire du CRISP, no. 2063-64, pp. 95–109.
3. In order to pay for the first development plan of the Republic of Congo, Belgium drew on private funds and external credit. This debt was passed on to the Congolese state after independence.

4. Michel Merlier, *Le Congo: de la colonisation belge à l'indépendance* ("Cahiers Libres" no. 32–33, Paris, 1962), pp. 291–292.
5. What the Belgian government meant by 'société'—a private company, public agency or semi-state body—is not clear.
6. 'Dossier de l'économie et des finances congolaises à la veille de le table ronde économique', *Courrier hebdomadaire du CRISP* 1960/15 (n 61), 5.
7. 'La Table ronde économique belgo-congolaise', *Courrier hebdomadaire du CRISP* 1960/20 (No. 66), 17.
8. Michel Merlier, *Le Congo*, pp. 291–292; Guy Vanthemsche, *Belgium and the Congo, 1885–1980* (Cambridge, 2012) p. 254.
9. Patrick Develtere and Aristide Michel, *Chronique d'un demi-siècle de coopération belge au développement* (Brussel, SPF Affaires étrangères, commerce extérieur et Coopération au Développement), p. 19.
10. AT: introduction to the archives, pp. 37–39.
11. In 1970, its administrative committee decided to merge with the Electrobel group to create Tractebel (Compagnies Réunies Electrobel et Tractionel).
12. Jean Claude Willame, *Zaïre. L'épopée d'Inga. Chronique d'une prédation industrielle* (Paris, 1986), pp. 33–34.
13. Guy Vanthemsche, *Genèse et portée du plan décennal du Congo belge (1949–1959)* (Bruxelles, 1994).
14. Etienne Deschamps, 'L'Eurafrique à l'épreuve des faits: la Belgique, la France et les projets de barrages hydro-électriques en Afrique (1954–1958), in Marie Thérèse Bitsch and Gérard Bossuat (eds.), *L'Europe Unie et l'Afrique* (Bruxelles, 2005), p. 173.
15. Frans Beulens, *Congo 1885–1960. Een financieel-economische geschiedenis* (Epo, 2007), pp. 327–425.
16. Van Reybrouck, *Congo, une histoire*, pp. 278–279.
17. Jean Stengers, *Congo, Mythes et réalités* (Racine, 2005), p. 282. A strategy also used in British colonies. See Sarah Stockwell, *The Business of Decolonization. British business strategies in the Gold Coast* (Oxford, 2000).
18. Ibid.
19. AT, box 6335, protocole relatif à la constitution et à l'organisation d'une mission d'études au Congo (protocol concerning the constitution and organisation of an in situ study in the Congo), annex 1, 4 May 1960.
20. AT, box 6604, Gracco to Neirynck (both members of GIDEC), 27 July 1960, including the report of the preliminary GIDEC.
21. The budget available for GIDEC was to be shared equally among the actors (consultancy firms) that were chosen to undertake the study: AT, box 6335, protocole relatif à la constitution et à l'organisation d'une mission d'études au Congo (protocol concerning the constitution and organisation of an in situ study in the Congo), 4 May 1960.

22. AT, box 6604, Dubois (EUROPREDE) to Lavianne (Administrateur-délégué, études et recherches industrielles), 29 July 1960. This consultative body comprising the governor and a college of six Congolese representatives was created at the Round Table in February 1960 as a temporary form of government before independence. See: Brassinne de la Buissière and Dumont, *Les autorités*, p. 104.

23. AT, box 6335, note on the organisation of the first GIDEC mission to Congo, 20 May 1960.

24. Vanthemsche, *Genèse et portée*.

25. AT, box 6335, note on the organisation of the first GIDEC mission to Congo, 20 May 1960.

26. AT, box 6335, plan de Développement du Congo, Etude Globale de Développement, p. 4, included in the 'protocole relatif à la constitution d'une mission d'étude au Congo' (protocol concerning the constitution and organisation of an in situ study in the Congo), 4 May 1960.

27. On the similar experience of paysannat indigène in the French colonies see: Véronique Dimier, *Le gouvernement des colonies: regards croisés franco-britanniques* (Bruxelles, 2014).

28. AT, box 6335, note on the organisation of the first GIDEC mission to Congo, 20 May 1960.

29. AT, box 6335, plan de développement du Congo, Etude globale de développement, p. 11, included in the 'protocole relatif à la constitution d'une mission d'étude au Congo' (protocol concerning the constitution and organisation of an in situ study in the Congo), 4 May 1960.

30. AT, box 6604, folder 2, Dubois to Lavianne, 29 July 1960. This letter summarised all of the negotiations.

31. Ibid.

32. Vanthemsche, *Genèse et portée*.

33. Whose headquarters and Secretary General were in Tractionel. AT, box 5488: EUROPREDE, protocol constitutif, 9 March 1960. EUROPREDE included on the Belgian side: Electrobel, Tractionel, Etude et Recherche Industrielles, Société belge de recherche minière en Afrique, CCCI (Compagnie du Congo pour le commerce et l'industrie), SOFINA, Société financière de transport et entreprises industrielles.

34. AT, box 5488, Smits (president of the Société de Traction et d'Electricité) to Scheyven, 15 March 1960, proposing EUROPREDE for the study and referring to the Association belge de sociétés d'études pour le développement; box 6603, Dubois (EUROPREDE) to Scheyven, 5 April 1960.

35. Ginette Kurgan-Van Hentenryk and Jean Puissant, *Dictionnaire des Patrons en Belgique: Les Hommes, les Entreprises, les Réseaux* (Bruxelles, 1996), p. 124.

36. AT, box 6335, note for M. Van der Straeten (vice-governor of the Société générale) relating an interview with Minister Scheyven, unsigned, 24 March 1960.
37. Ibid.
38. AT, box 5488, note from Tractionel, including proposals as to the composition of GIDEC, 14 April 1960.
39. AT, box 6335, note to Van der Straeten, relating an interview with Baron Coppée, 23 March 1960.
40. Ibid.
41. AT, box 5488, Smits to Scheyven, 15 March 1960, proposing EUROPREDE for the study and referring to the Association belge de bociétés d'études pour le développement; AT box 6603, Dubois (EUROPREDE) to Scheyven, 5 April 1960.
42. AT, box 6604, folder 6, Baron Coppée to Scheyven, 11 April 1960.
43. AT, box 5488, Smits to Baron Coppée, 8 April 1960.
44. Ibid.
45. AT, box 6604, folder 6, Neirynck (director of Tractionel) and Smits (president of Tractionel) to Scheyven, 12 April 1960.
46. AT, box 6604, folder 6, Baron Coppée to Smits, 7April 1960; box 5488, Coppée to Smits, 29 March 1960; letter Smits to Coppée, 4 April 1960.
47. AT, box 6604, Baron Coppée to Smits, 7 April 1960.
48. AT, box 6604, proposal as to the composition of GIDEC, 14 April, included in a letter to Van der Straeten, 24 May 1960.
49. AT, box 5488, protocol of the constitution of the GETAF, 20 May 1960.
50. AT, box 6604, document: 'Entre la Compagnie générale d'entreprises électriques et industrielles—"ELECTROBEL", Société financière de transports et d'entreprises industrielles—"SOFINA", Société de traction et d'électricité—"T.E" pour créer le Groupement belge pour les études de développement en Afrique—GETAF'; Annex 5: Composition of GETAF, 11 May1960.
51. AT, box 6604, Dubois to Lavianne, 29 July 1960.
52. AT, box 2345, document: Etudes de Développement et de Programmation au Congo, from M. Dubois (administrateur-directeur of the Société de Traction et d'électricité) and G. Landsberg (*administrateur-délégué* of the Société de Traction et d'électricité) to A. Thys (administrateur-directeur of Société de Traction et d'électricité), 17 May 1960.
53. AT, box 5488, note from Tractionel, including proposals as to the composition of GIDEC, 14 April 1960.
54. Ibid.
55. Ibid.
56. Ibid.

57. AT, box 6335, protocole relatif à la constitution d'une mission d'étude au Congo (protocol concerning the constitution and organisation of an in situ study in the Congo), 4 May 1960.

58. Ibid.

59. AT, box 5488, note (unsigned) to Mr Van der Straeten, 1 June 1960.

60. AT, box 5488, Van der Straeten to Smits, 30 May 1960.

61. AT, box 5488, note to Van der Straeten (unsigned), 24 May 1960.

62. AT, box 6335, protocole relatif à la constitution et à l'organisation d'une mission d'études au Congo (protocol concerning the constitution and organisation of an in situ study in the Congo), 4 May 1960.

63. Proposed by the SRI and chosen by the management committee of GIDEC: AT, box 6335, protocole relatif à la constitution et à l'organisation d'une mission d'études au Congo (protocol concerning the constitution and organisation of an in situ study in the Congo), 4 May 1960.

64. AT, box 5488, note to Smits (without signature), 23 May 1960.

65. Ibid.

66. AT, box 6603, note Van Straeten to Smits, 4 April 1960; draft of a letter from the management of Tractionel to Aba (Deusche Bank), without date.

67. AT, box 5488, note to Van der Straeten (without signature), 18 May 1960.

68. AT, box 6603, Van der Straeten to Smits (president of Tractionel), 26 May 1960; Prentice (director of Research at SRI) to Neirynck, 11 April 1960; Benedict (SRI) to Neirynck, 23 December 1959.

69. AT, box 6603, note to R. Neirynck, without signature, concerning the details of the study, 5 July 1960; note to Sterkendries, 18 August 1960; letter Moran (SRI) to Neirynck, 7 February 1961.

70. AT, box 6603, note for Sterkendries, concerning Haine's US trip, 18 August 1960.

71. AT, box 6603, note to Neirynck, 31 May 1960.

72. AT, box 5488, note to Van der Straeten (not signed), 24 May 1960.

73. AT, box 6603, Prentice (Director of the international program for the Stanford Research Institute and working party meetings in Brussels) to Mayer (US representative in the Société générale), 22 March 1960.

74. AT, box 5488, Van Der Straeten to Smits, 4 April 1960; box 6335, Scheyven to Neirynck (director of Tractionel and president of GIDEC), 10 June 1960. See also box 6335, Conseil de Gestion GIDEC, 27 May 1960, report by Mr Moran on his discussion with international organisations in New York and Washington.

75. AT, box 6603, Moran to Mayer, 9 February 1960.

76. AT, box 6335, Scheyven to Neirynck, 23 May 1960.

77. AT, box 6604, meeting of the Management Committee, 27 May 1960.

78. Van Reybrouck, *Congo, une histoire*, pp. 278–279

79. AT, box 6335, discussion with M. Muller, member of GIDEC (and hydrology and agricultural science expert, seconded to Elektrisitats-Actien-Gesellschaft vorm. W. Lahmeyer & Co.) 30 June 1960.
80. AT, box 6604, Moran to Neirynck, 5 June 1960.
81. AT, box 6335, discussion with M. Muller, 30 June 1960.
82. Ibid.
83. AT, box 6335, Desclée de Maredsous (economic expert from the Groupement Belge pour les Etudes de Développement en Afrique) to Neirynck, 20 June 1960.
84. Belgium refused during its colonisation to establish secondary and higher education or to allow Congolese students to study at Belgian universities. Belgium feared that Congolese intellectuals would become rebels, politicians, nationalists or, even worse, that they would apply for leading positions that were reserved for Belgians. The Congo, at the time of independence, had no more than a thin scattering of university students, most of whom had not even completed their studies. Clergymen, both Protestant and Catholic, made up the largest single group of intellectuals in the Congo at independence: Jef Van Bilsen, *Congo, 1945–1965: la fin d'une colonie* (Davidsfonds, 1993), p. 351.
85. AT, box 6604, Desclée de Maredsous to M. Thys (administrateur-directeur of Société de Traction et d'Electricité), 6 June 1960.
86. Ibid.
87. AT, box 6604, Desclée de Maredsous to Thys, 11 June 1960.
88. Ibid.
89. Ibid.
90. Ibid.
91. AT, box 6335, Desclée to Neirynck, 12 June 1960.
92. AT, box 6335, discussion with Muller, 30 June 1960.
93. AT, box 6335, Desclée to Neirynck, 12 June 1960.
94. AT, box 6335, discussion with Muller, 30 June 1960.
95. Ibid.
96. Frederick Cooper, *Decolonization and African Society, the labour question in French and British Africa* (Cambridge, 1996).
97. Stockwell, *Business of Decolonization*.
98. AT, box 6335, Desclée de Maredsous to Neirynck, 20 June 1960.
99. Ibid.
100. Ibid.
101. Ibid.
102. Vanthemsche, *Belgium and the Congo*, p. 256.
103. Willame, *Zaïre. L'épopée d'Inga*.
104. AT, box 6604, members of GIDEC to Scheyven, 18 July 1960; 6604, Gracco to Neirynck, 27 July 1960. These letters include the report of the preliminary mission

105. AT, box 6604, Moran to Prentice, SRI, 18 June 1960.
106. AT, box 6604, Gracco to Neirynck, 27 July 1960.
107. AT, box 6603, letter from Moran to Neirynck, 7 February 1961.
108. AT, box 6603, Haine to Benveniste (representative of the SRI), 25 July 1960.

REFERENCES

Beulens, Frans, *Congo 1885–1960. Een financieel-economische geschiedenis* (Epo, Anvers, 2007).
Brassinne de la Buissière, Jacques, and Georges Henri Dumont, *Les autorités belges et la décolonisation du Congo* (Courrier hebdomadaire du CRISP, no. 2063-64, 2010).
Cooper, Frederick, Decolonization and African Society, the Labour Question in French and British Africa (Cambridge University Press, Cambridge, 1996).
Deschamps, Etienne, 'L'Eurafrique à l'épreuve des faits: la Belgique, la France et les projets de barrages hydro-électriques en Afrique (1954–1958)', in Marie Thérèse Bitsch and Gérard Bossuat (eds.), *L'Europe Unie et l'Afrique* (Bruylant, Bruxelles, 2005), pp. 165–184.
Develtere, Patrick, and Michel Aristide, Chronique d'une demi-siècle de coopération belge au développement (Brussel, SPF Affaires Etrangères, Commerce Extérieure et Coopération au Développement), https://diplomatie.belgium.be/sites/default/files/downloads/chronique_demi-siecle_cooperation_belge.pdf
Dimier, Véronique, *Le gouvernement des colonies: regards croisés franco-britanniques* (Palgrave Macmillan, Basingstoke, 2014).
Merlier, Michel, *Le Congo: de la colonistion belge à l'indépendance* ("Cahiers Libres" no. 32–33, François Maspero, Paris, 1962).
Stengers, Jean, *Congo, Mythes et réalités* (Racine, Bruxelles, 2005).
Stockwell, Sarah, *The Business of Decolonization. British Business Strategies in the Gold Coast* (Oxford University Press, Oxford, 2000).
Van Bilsen, Jef, *Congo, 1945–1965: la fin d'une colonie* (Davidsfonds, Leuven, 1993).
Van Reybrouck, David, *Congo, une histoire* (Actes Sud, Paris, 2011).
Vanthemsche, Guy, *Genèse et portée du plan décennal du Congo belge (1949–1959)* (Acadamie Royale de sciences d'outre-mer, Bruxelles, 1994).
Vanthemsche, Guy, *Belgium and the Congo, 1885–1980* (Cambridge University Press, Cambridge, 2012).
Willame, Jean Claude, *Zaïre. L'épopée d'Inga. Chronique d'une prédation industrielle* (Harmattan, Paris, 1986).

CHAPTER 5

Oil Companies as Agents of Post-Colonial Relations: France, Algeria, and Italy in the Sahara

Marta Musso

The 'oil curse' and the 'Dutch disease' are well-known expressions used in modern development studies to indicate the negative economic and social impact that hydrocarbon production can have on a country. However, this use reflects fairly recent theories, developed since the late 1970s. In previous decades, and particularly in the years of the decolonisation process, oil was considered a blessing, the best opportunity for newly-independent countries to develop and to obtain economic as well as constitutional independence. European countries also needed access to a resource that after 1945 fuelled the global economy; as the largest importing area in the world, Europe became particularly dependent on producer countries, but also on the decisions of the international oil industry, which controlled oil supplies in Europe. In the EEC-6 area, this created a split between the Netherlands and Germany on one side, which preferred to leave oil

M. Musso (✉)
King's College London, London, UK
e-mail: marta.musso@kcl.ac.uk

© The Author(s) 2020
V. Dimier, S. Stockwell (eds.), *The Business of Development in Post-Colonial Africa*, Cambridge Imperial and Post-Colonial Studies Series, https://doi.org/10.1007/978-3-030-51106-7_5

127

supplies to the control of the Dutch-based Shell and the US majors, and Italy and France on the other, which preferred to establish a strong state-owned oil industry. This chapter analyses the role of the oil industry in the negotiations between France and Algeria during the decolonisation period, and assesses the importance attached to the oil industry as a means of facilitating Algerian development and independence.

In France, the problem of energy supplies went hand in hand with the redefinition of the country's position in the world during decolonisation. A strong national oil industry, with control over resources, technology, and distribution, was considered an important aspect of international power, as well as economic development. Furthermore, it was believed that the development of a French-controlled oil industry would provide the means to launch serious development projects in Algeria, much needed to legitimise France's presence in the territory. The French government was willing to invest a great deal in the newly-discovered Saharan hydrocarbon reserves. However, the independence war in Algeria forced the French government and French companies to reconsider how best to exploit the resources of territories they no longer had sovereignty over.

At the opposite end of the Mediterranean, the new Algerian establishment considered it paramount for the independence of the country that it distance itself from French businesses and bring its oil reserves under full state control. Much like the French establishment, the Algerian independence fighters wanted control over the oil industry as a way to boost the economic development of the country, the one tool needed to collect the capital and energy sources required for the industrialisation process. As this chapter shows, in their negotiations with both France and Algeria, oil companies strongly promoted themselves as agents of development, the actors capable of transforming hydrocarbon resources into important revenues for the country—as long as governments in producer countries limited their role to facilitating the presence of companies in a territory. For a newly-independent Algeria, however, control over oil did not just mean the right to give out concessions to foreign companies and collect revenue. Like the French, the Algerian government aimed to have direct control over the technology, the processing industry, and, most importantly, the capability of influencing the prices at which the resources were sold. The international oil industry was unsurprisingly against any form of nationalisation, and, traditionally, had been successful in ousting countries that had tried to nationalise their oil industry from the international market.

While France was able to impose a deal by which Algeria would gain sovereignty over the Sahara, and French companies would maintain their rights to exploit the area, two factors helped Algeria to reach its goals. The first was the rise of the Organisation of Petroleum Exporting Countries (OPEC), as a body that allowed producer countries to negotiate as one bloc with the oil majors and coordinate the imposition of prices; and the second was the presence of the Italian state company Ente Nazionale Idrocarburi (ENI) and other independent oil companies that provided an alternative to French outlets. In particular, during the years of the Algerian independence war, the Italian company promoted nationalisation in producer countries as a way of reducing the power of private oil majors and of allowing the producer governments to deal directly with governments from consumer countries, making oil revenues part of a larger plan for international development programmes. This chapter first presents the French and Algerian interests in the Sahara during the independence war with regard to the newly-discovered reserves; then it introduces the role of the Italian company ENI in the Évian peace negotiations, and introduces the idea of state-state negotiations and oil nationalisations. It then shows how oil absorbed the majority of the post-independence negotiations between France and Algeria, and describes how Algeria was able to nationalise its oil industry by steps, over a decade. Overall, this chapter shows that oil was an important part of the decolonisation process, perceived as a tool for independence and economic development, and that in this process, the problem of ownership of the oil reserves and the oil industry became an important issue, not only for producer countries, but for importers as well.

FRENCH OIL IN THE SAHARA

After the two world wars had exposed the geostrategic importance of oil reserves, several countries in Europe started to adopt a national policy for the research and supply of hydrocarbons—a phenomenon known since the interwar years as 'oil nationalism'.[1] With the Middle East and Latin America largely controlled by international (mostly US-based) oil majors, a notorious cartel nicknamed 'The Seven Sisters', French efforts focused mostly on the Sahara. However, it was only in 1956, almost 30 years after the launch of the first research programme, that the probes of the Société Nationale de Recherche et d'Exploitation de Pétrole en Algérie (SN REPAL), a state company formed by the French Algerian Directorate, found the vast reserves of Hassi R'Mel and Hassi Messaoud, deep in the Saharan desert. The discovery was hailed as a revolution for the French economy, both in the metropole and in Algeria. In French politics and the media, the discoveries came as manna that would solve a set of fundamental problems. First, it would alleviate the excessive dependence on Middle East supplies: even with uncertain numbers, the quantity of oil seemed to be enough to cover an important part of the French energy deficit. Second, the Sahara allowed for the establishment of a crude market trade in francs, rather than in US dollars. The government calculated that the Saharan fields could allow savings of more than 200 million dollars per year.[2] Third, and most importantly, the oil discoveries and wealth they promised were a powerful tool for France to re-launch a development model for Algeria that would reiterate the legitimacy of French interests over the territory, in a period of strong centrifugal forces: 1956 was also the year in which Morocco and Tunisia gained independence, while the battle of Algiers marked the descent of the Algerian rebellion into open war. Instead of paying exorbitant sums of money to the Seven Sisters and increasing its dollar deficit, through state oil revenues, France could re-circulate a large part of the money spent on energy in development projects.

Hydrocarbons were considered a powerful agent of economic growth: as raw material for the growing petrochemical industry, as a source of cheap energy for industrialisation, and, most importantly, as a source of capital formation. The international oil companies were very careful to promote themselves as a fundamental instrument with which to fight poverty, particularly after the Suez crisis, when nationalisation was hailed by newly-independent countries as the solution to their economic problems. In the *Petroleum Press Service*, a specialised journal on the oil industry co-owned by BP and Shell, several articles were dedicated to the relevant role that the oil industry could play in the fight against global poverty: 'One of the features of the modern world is that it has poverty on its conscience and wants to remove it—an article stated in May 1961—[...] all the advanced countries accept that they have to do something to help to overcome the problems of under-development in the less advanced countries of the free world where acute poverty still exists'.[3]

How to fill the gap between developed and under-developed countries was a hot topic for the Western oil industry at the time. First, the development of a nation was calculated through its energy consumption, especially of oil: its consumption was connected to transportation, mass motorisation, house heating, and the usage of plastics and other petrochemical products, namely fertilisers, for industrial agriculture. The higher the consumption of oil, the higher the level of a country's economic development—and the larger the market for the oil industry, especially at a time when companies were looking for new markets in which to place their overproduction. Under-developed countries were the fastest-growing market for the oil industry, albeit tiny compared to the US and Europe.[4] Second, and most importantly from the point of view of the oil industry, companies did not want to be associated with imperialism and foreign powers—and they wanted to discourage any attempt towards nationalisation, or towards the imposition of tougher rules on the part of producer countries. The Suez Canal incident had been an alarming sign for the oil industry and its freedom to operate in producer countries; companies needed to remind producer countries that the oil industry could successfully solve the problem of capital formation in under-developed countries, and that companies were a benign and much needed presence—as long as they were left free to operate. Demand for investment capital was greater than ever, and poor countries were scrambling to obtain it: the oil industry could provide a large amount of capital, both through direct investment and through the large sums it paid in royalties to the governments of producer countries. Indeed, in 1957 alone the oil industry had poured $2200 million into the Venezuelan and Middle Eastern treasuries, without counting the income those treasuries received from further oil revenues. International organisations and governments from the free world had raised $4000 million in development funds for developing countries since the end of the war—less than $400 million a year, a quarter of the capital raised by the oil industry.[5] The *Petroleum Press Service* commented that 'The whole prospects of future peace and economic growth in all parts of the world would be seriously affected if the under-developed countries as a group were to fail to attain significantly higher standards of living within a reasonable time'[6]; however, it also warned that the 'generosity' of the oil industry and its capability for providing a beneficial input to the development of producer countries was dependent on 'a more enlightened attitude towards private capital'.[7]

In France, oil was one of the fundamental features of de Gaulle's ambitious Plan de Constantine, the development programme that aimed to weaken the Algerian nationalist political party, the Front de Libération Nationale (FLN); it was the last effort made by the French establishment before giving in to independence. One of the main points of the plan was the establishment of a heavy industry with metallurgic and chemical factories, to be carried out through a five-year industrialisation plan that aimed at achieving a growth in industrial production of 73%, from 499 billion francs in 1959 to 861 in 1963: a 7.5% growth rate per year. This economic miracle, that would have established a new world record, was to be achieved mainly thanks to low-price oil and gas.[8] The importance of the Saharan hydrocarbons for the development of the area was reiterated in the new Petroleum Code passed by French president, Charles de Gaulle, in 1958, which stated: 'The oil revenue will be dedicated to the development of the Sahara, but also to the social advancement of the population; we don't want the Sahara to offer the spectacle of certain Middle Eastern countries: enormous profits on the one side, deep misery on the other'.[9] Furthermore, at least 50% of the investments for the implementation of the other points of the Constantine plan (wider industrial developments, construction, schooling for Muslim children) would be paid with oil revenues from production, which was planned to start in 1960.[10] The plan was welcomed as part of the new wave of French policy in Algeria, and it was considered different from the previous failed development plans because of the new discoveries of oil and gas. In fact, one of the main reasons for the failure to industrialise Algeria was traditionally indicated to be the scarcity of cheap energy sources.[11]

Another important aspect of the development of the Saharan hydrocarbons was the debate on the possible presence of non-French companies in the area. In Paris, the Parliament was divided between those in favour of finding a way to develop the oil industry in the Sahara without opening to foreign capital, and those in favour of adopting a more liberal policy. The issues on either side were both economic and geopolitical in nature. Allowing the entry of foreign companies mostly meant American companies: either the cartel, or the so-called independents, that mostly operated within the US borders but were looking for new production areas in the world that were not yet controlled by the majors. On the one hand, France feared that the majors would seek to get concessions in the Sahara, but then leave production lagging, as Saharan oil represented competition from their main areas of production in the Middle East. France also feared that the presence of foreign capital would worsen the Algerian crisis, especially because the cartel could adopt a pro-independence stance to avoid possible tensions with the Middle East, and also because of the attitude of the US government towards Algeria, which oscillated between ambiguity, under President Eisenhower, and an openly pro-independence stance under the then presidential candidate J.F. Kennedy.[12] France feared that foreign companies could negotiate with the FLN in exchange for future concessions after independence; indeed, since the discoveries, rumours about negotiations between the FLN and oil companies had grown.

On the other hand, by allowing the presence of American companies under the 'watchful' eye of French partners, Paris hoped that the US would adopt a clearer pro-French view in the Algerian war. Moreover, de Gaulle's new petroleum code rigidly regulated the presence of foreign companies in the Sahara, which could only enter through a joint venture with a French company that would control at least 50% of shares, while the foreign partner would provide transfers of technologies and training by highly-skilled French personnel. Furthermore, the distribution network in France was partly nationalised to ensure that Saharan resources—hence French—would be given priority on the domestic market. A series of public French bodies, such as the Bureau de recherche de pétrole (BRP) were set up to form these joint ventures and were mostly run by technocrats. In exchange for such strong government control, the petroleum code instituted an extremely advantageous fiscal regime that attracted capital and promoted long-term investment.[13] In this way France sacrificed the financial aspect of revenue in order to allow the absorption of technology and training from the leading American industry; as a developed 'oil producer' country, it could forgo immediate revenues to focus on control. The new petroleum code perfectly centred the objectives set by the French government in attracting foreign capital, technology, and market outlets, while maintaining full state control over the reserves. However, it was a complete failure with regard to pushing the US government to adopt a pro-French stance in Algeria. If anything, the presence of US oil companies in the Sahara gave the FLN an extra talking point in the secret negotiations carried out by FLN representatives in various parts of the world. In February 1959, France complained to the US government about the activities of M'hamed Yazid, the FLN United Nations representative, who was accused of approaching the American companies present in the Sahara. The government threatened to revoke any concession to any company that was caught secretly negotiating with him. The Department of State replied that Yazid was a regularly registered foreigner in the US, and that he was free to talk to any oil company whenever he wished to do so. The US government emphasised that France had no proof that any American company had ever made secret deals with the FLN and that, in any case, the official government position was that US companies were going to the Sahara at their own risk.[14]

SAHARAN OIL TO THE ALGERIANS

The fact that the US government refused to check on the activities of American companies in relation to the Algerian fighters did not make France wrong. In the same way in which France was trying to use the oil industry as a proxy in the Algerian war, the FLN was also extremely active on the diplomatic side: in the US, in Europe, and elsewhere. An important part of this diplomacy consisted in following closely what happened in the oil industry, and contacting the companies themselves. The pages of *El Moudjahid*, the newspaper of the FLN, which started to circulate from 1954, dedicated more and more space to the problems of the development of the Sahara, with at least one or two articles for every issue. Its information on the activities of the oil companies, the concessions, and the infrastructure plans was sharply accurate, sometimes more than the bulletins from the single oil companies. At the same time most companies, at least according to the oral sources available,[15] kept their discussions open to both sides, to make sure that they would be on friendly terms with whoever eventually 'won' the Sahara. Just like France, the FLN was firmly convinced that control over the oil industry would bring economic independence, prosperity, and power. Also, just like France, the acquisition of expertise in the management and the technology of the oil and gas industry became an absolute priority for the FLN.

Through *El Moudjahid*, the FLN denounced the colonial attitude shown by France in starting the oil exploitation before coming to a peace agreement, and warned that it would consider any contract signed with France as an act of aggression against Algeria. In 1959 the Armée de Libération Nationale, the armed wing of the FLN, set up a special task force with the objective to attack the economic potential of French Algeria: the infrastructure set up by the Constantine Plan, the oil-related facilities, and all lines of communication.[16] The industry was forced to take extra safety measures and allegedly paid protection money,[17] but the attacks were not strong enough to undermine productivity, only resulting in extra costs for the companies. For the FLN, the main gain was to be able to keep open channels of communications with the companies. In general, threats and offers for collaboration on better terms than those offered by France were carefully mixed. The FLN did not consider the foreign oil companies an enemy; it just wanted to make clear that the FLN was the legitimate owner of the Saharan resources. 'We understand that the development of such an immense territory requires technical and financial means that not even France can provide, let alone a nation subject to foreign domination for more than 125 years', wrote *El Moudjahid* in November 1957. 'However the Algerians intend to determine by themselves the conditions of these indispensable foreign contributions'.[18] The professional training of Algerian oil workers was also an important aspect of the strategy of the FLN, one of the main points of the secret negotiations with other countries. In July 1961, for example, 1991 grants had been offered to enable Algerians to study in 20 countries: 947 for secondary education, 847 for the equivalent of high school and college, and 197 for engineers.[19] Most of the future Algerian ruling class around the Ministry of Energy were beneficiaries of this type of experience, studying in France, the UK, or the US, or doing internships—sometimes under a false identity—for oil companies in the US, Europe, and Russia.[20]

For their part, oil companies, including the largest French Company, the Compagnie française de pétrole (CFP), did not worry excessively about the problem of sovereignty. More realistically than the French government, they thought that eventually Algeria would obtain sovereignty over the Sahara. Whatever the end of the war in Algeria would bring, companies were confident that the Saharan resources could not be exploited without their technology and specialised workforce: 'Sooner or later, the political problems will have to give way to the economic imperatives—declared a French banker—and the priority of the French rights on the Sahara will not be contested by anyone, not even by the Algerian nationalists'.[21] The French establishment was sure that even if France lost formal sovereignty over the Sahara, once the drill had started to pump, the pipelines were laid out, and revenues started to come in, no one would put a stop to the oil flow to change the concessions. For this reason, in spite of the Algerian threats, most companies entered the desert in joint venture with CFP and the French bodies, while keeping a communication channel open with the FLN. Only one company followed a different plan: the ENI, the Italian State body with which France hoped to collaborate closely, but that instead openly endorsed the Algerian side.

Rogue Oil: Enrico Mattei and Oil Development Projects

In the postwar period, the other European country that took action to avoid energy dependence on hydrocarbon supplies managed by American companies was Italy. In 1953, the Ente Nationale Idrocarburi (State Hydrocarbon Company) was funded by law as a wholly state-owned company, controlled by the Ministry of Economics. The company was originally created to manage some gas reserves that were discovered in the north of the country at the end of the war, and for which several oil majors had bid to obtain concessions. Its first president and main promoter was Christian Democrat MP Enrico Mattei, who had fought to keep the gas reserves under state monopoly, and who was leading an aggressive energy policy for Italy to develop a state oil industry—an energy strategy that also became an aggressive foreign policy, particularly in the Sahara. Just like the French government, Mattei wanted to establish a strong national oil industry in charge of both extraction and distribution, in order to limit the control of the US majors on the European energy market. However, Italy did not have colonial territories in which to invest in research, having been stripped of its colonies in the war. Mattei decided to use the country's status of failed colonial empire to promote the company (somewhat paradoxically) as a champion of decolonisation, proposing Italy as an alternative economic partner to the former colonisers. He presented Italy, which had nationalised its gas reserves, as an example for oil producer countries, against the international oil majors that were exploiting producers' resources. He caused a stir in the international oil industry because his strategy was based on a new contractual formula that let control over extraction rest with the producer country, and openly endorsed the nationalisation of the oil industry as a way to lead state-state negotiations. In a way, he anticipated and promoted the policies of OPEC, in which Algeria would become one of the hawks in the build-up to the 1973 oil crisis. Particularly in Algeria, this strategy was destined to cause strong diplomatic tensions with France.

Initially, France looked at ENI as a possible partner for the Sahara, considering it a valid alternative to US companies: the Italian company controlled a growing domestic market, was eager to invest and had accumulated strong technical expertise. In January 1957, ENI was one of the first companies contacted by France. The state-owned Compagnie d'exploitation pétrolière (CEP) proposed the formation of a consortium for new concessions, in which the French would be the sole owners of mining rights, and ENI would participate in the consortium's capital up to a maximum of 30% shares. The negotiations focused on the relationship between capital investment and machinery employed: France wanted ENI to invest financially but leave the CEP free to choose the machinery and personnel, effectively asking Italy to simply provide a market and capital for France to develop the fields. The Italian company rejected the offer, claiming that it wanted shared management, and dismissed the French nationalist approach to the Sahara as 'ridiculous'.[22]

In reality, Mattei was not sure that the French would be the best interlocutors for the Sahara; his loud rejection of the offer was in preparation for the negotiations with the FLN. A large part of the Italian establishment looked favourably on Algerian independence, and as a businessman, although a state businessman, Mattei had more freedom of action than any politician in Italy. While maintaining a formal pro-French attitude, the Italian governments, particularly those headed by Mattei's ally Amintore Fanfani (July 1958-February 1959 and July 1960-June 1963), were happy to let him conduct a parallel secret diplomacy in Algeria. ENI's diplomatic activities were sufficiently developed that Pietro Quaroni, the Italian ambassador to France until 1958, declared that 'for years, real Italian foreign policy has been carried out by Enrico Mattei'.[23] Quaroni insisted that ENI should accept the French proposal and get concessions in the Sahara under French rules; he agreed with Mattei that eventually France was going to lose the war, but he feared that the concessions, once assigned, would not be re-assigned after the Algerians took control of the territory.[24] Mattei was aware that the future Algerian state would have neither the capability nor the interest to withdraw the concessions in the Sahara assigned by France. However, at the same time, ENI was negotiating in Morocco, Tunisia, and other newly-independent countries, as an anti-colonial company: Mattei knew that while France offered breadcrumbs, openly backing Algerian independence could provide great reputational capital for the future.

In July 1958, a new French company, the Compagnie raffinage Afrique Nord, proposed again to ENI participation in the creation of a refinery in Hassi Messaoud, this time on more generous terms; Mattei still refused, and *Il Giorno*, the Italian newspaper owned by ENI, explained this refusal by questioning the juridical validity of the French concessions over the Sahara, as it was a contested territory.[25] Mattei, however, took the occasion to counter-propose to France a much bigger plan of investments for the whole of the Maghreb. He suggested the creation of a new joint venture in Morocco, in which the Moroccan government held 50%, ENI 35%, and France 15%. In Tunisia, where negotiations between ENI and the government were also ongoing, a similar tripartite joint venture would be formed, in which the Tunisian government would hold 50%, and ENI and France the same percentages in reverse: 15% for ENI, 35% for France. Finally, Mattei suggested the establishment of a third tripartite company in Algeria with similar percentages of control, leaving himself to negotiate with the independence fighters an agreement over the Saharan resources. In the document presented to France, Mattei wrote that the ultimate goal was 'to reach the objective for Europe and France to preserve access to the Sahara, without the unsustainable burden for France to continue the subjugation of Algeria'.[26] Mattei made explicit reference to a project advanced by Italy within the Organisation for Economic Co-operation and Development (OECD) for a 'Marshall Plan' of the Middle East and North Africa. After the Suez crisis, and ten years after the European Recovery Programme, the minister for foreign affairs Giuseppe Pella had proposed to the Department of State the creation of a new development fund within the OECD, in which European countries would deposit part of the restitution instalments due to the US Treasury from the Marshall Plan loans, together with a fee for each OECD country. Middle East countries would be able to have access to this fund, as long as they remained in the Western orbit. Though the 'piano Pella' never went past the stage of an official memo presented by the Italian Ministry of Foreign Affairs to the Department of State, at the time of its release both the US and several European countries looked at it favourably.[27] In particular, France wanted to push for a Marshall Plan for the MENA area (Middle East and North Africa) that would be preparatory to a 'Mediterranean Pact'. Mattei's proposal was inspired by the Pella plan, but focused specifically on North Africa, and was centred around the oil industry. Mattei suggested that European countries (initially Italy, France, and Spain) should make North Africa their main hub for energy supplies, and that a percentage of their payments to producer countries for oil supplies should be placed into a special fund that would be used for larger development projects. This would be a way to re-channel part of the oil revenues towards larger development projects. Rather than being France-based, these development plans would be discussed by North Africa and at an OECD (or European) level. If France agreed to this proposal, ENI would immediately cede to France 15% shares of its joint ventures in Morocco and Tunisia, and it would start parallel negotiations with Algeria.[28] This extremely ambitious proposal, which openly welded oil politics not only to the end of the Algerian war but to future relations between Europe and North Africa, might have been endorsed by the Fourth Republic of Félix Gaillard, who in March 1958 proposed a coastal pact between Mediterranean countries under British and American supervision as a possible solution to the Algerian war.[29] However, in de Gaulle's France, such a multilateral proposal in which ENI and Italy would have most of the agency, was simply not acceptable.

After France's rejection of the offer to act as an intermediary, Mattei simply continued negotiating with the Algerians only, and in secret. Mario Pirani, a former journalist of the Italian communist newspaper *L'Unità*, was hired to conduct the negotiations. ENI offered logistical help to the FLN, and professional training for Algerian personnel, with about a dozen students sent to the ENI's School of Hydrocarbons near Milan under false identities, for a course on oil management, between 1960 and 1962.[30] ENI also put his engineers at the disposal of the Algerian delegation to act as consultants in the negotiations in Évian.[31] Pirani presents ENI's personnel at Évian as the inspiration behind Algeria's stance in the negotiations: he claims that it was the company's secret consultants who suggested that Algeria should never give up on the claim of sovereignty over the Sahara, but should be open to discuss a collaboration with France for the shared development of the resources. These claims were probably highly exaggerated: Yves Roland-Billecart, one of the negotiators on the French side, remembers that other than the problem of sovereignty, the Algerian delegation was not prepared to discuss in more detail the problems of the oil industry.[32] However, recent work on ENI in Algeria confirms the Italian company had a pivotal role in providing data to the Algerian delegation during the Évian negotiations.[33] Moreover, different sources confirm that during the last phase of the negotiations, both in Tunis and at Évian, there was a proliferation of technical experts, lawyers, and engineers from different companies, who acted as generic consultants, maintaining contacts with the Algerian delegation.[34] Indeed, while reports on potential energy sources were restricted to a limited circle of French civil servants, at Évian the FLN was very well informed not only on new concessions and infrastructure, but also on geodata, the most secret type of information in the oil industry: information that the Algerian delegation could only have acquired through leaks by the partner companies of France.[35]

The final months of the French-Algerian negotiations were occupied by the problem of sovereignty over the Sahara in Algeria's southern territories. France agreed to concede independence to the north of the country, but claimed that the idea that the desert part belonged to Algeria was purely arbitrary, a French decision taken in 1848 that had nothing to do with the cultural and economic reality of the territory. It proposed instead to transform the Algerian Sahara into a 'mer riveraine' managed by Algeria together with its neighbours (Morocco, Tunisia, and Chad), under the supervision of France. The Algerians, however, did not concede, stalling the negotiations for months until, in September 1961, France gave up. Immediately before the announcement, de Gaulle made a change in the petroleum code, introducing a new clause giving the holders of concessions the right to freely organise the transport of the oil and gas they extracted. Previously, France wanted to preserve the right to decide upon the export of the hydrocarbons extracted; now the lack of this clause could be used against French companies, which were about to become foreign companies in the Sahara.[36]

After France had made this concession, the peace negotiations proceeded fast. The French conditions sine quibus non were that none of the agreements already signed between the French government and the oil companies would be changed; that the technical control and the security of the infrastructure remained under the direct control of France; and that France would maintain military bases in the Sahara.[37] In exchange, the FLN asked that the Algerian state be allowed to retain 60% of the oil revenues, and that companies operating in the Sahara commit to facilitating the creation of an Algerian oil industry—requests inspired by the 'innovative ideas that independent companies such as ENI are starting to spread'.[38]

The Évian accords, signed on 18 March 1962, envisaged an entire chapter dedicated to the future management of the Saharan hydrocarbons, based on two principles. First, while recognising Algeria's sovereignty over the area, the hydrocarbon resources of the Sahara would be 'co-managed' through a shared technical body called Organisme mixte technique de coopération saharienne with representatives from both France and Algeria. Second, Algeria would replace France in the rights to grant future concessions, while respecting all previous rights and laws established for the Sahara by France before independence (and allowing French companies to have priority over new bids), which meant that the French petroleum code had to remain not only untouched but untouchable—any change would be considered a breach of the peace agreement.[39]

Towards an Algerian Oil Industry

In September 1962, after months of civil unrest, the first government of independent Algeria, headed by the FLN nationalist politician Ahmed Ben Bella, took office. Very few of the men who had conducted the peace negotiations were still part of the Algerian establishment at that point, and Ben Bella was strongly critical of the Évian agreements, considered a betrayal of the socialist outlook of the country, which aimed to nationalise all industries. The French and the other companies carefully monitored the evolving situation. Jean Loyrette, a prominent French jurist and one of the writers of the Saharan Petroleum Code, wrote in a report for the CFP in October 1962 that it was probable that Algeria, eventually, would follow the model of complete nationalisation rather than the French model of mixed capital; for this reason, he advised the companies to be very careful in considering further investments.[40] Between 1962 and 1964, various companies commissioned reports on the legal instruments that they could use in case of breach of the Évian agreements, to defend themselves against nationalisation, but they remained confident that the Évian accords would be respected. Sid Ahmed Ghozali, one of the Algerian members of the Organisme mixte, remembers that in 1962 'we did not even know what it was, this oil so important […] I did not know how an oilfield looked like, what it actually was'.[41]

At independence Algeria had a much worse starting economic and social situation than Morocco or Tunisia.[42] Capital fled the country by 400 million dollars, and between November 1961 and July 1962 private deposits dropped to 300 million dollars; the national debt was placed at 1.7 billion dollars;[43] the oil revenues represented the only income for the state. As it had been for France, the Algerian oil industry was an essential source of foreign currency, a way to balance the Algerian tax system, and a way to invest in the agricultural and industrial sector.

Algeria was also heavily dependent upon foreign help, namely French.[44] As the French economist Pierre Courant wrote, 'Algeria hopes to cover the gap through the Sahara, but the fields were not very profitable in direct revenues [because of the 1958 Petroleum Code] and Algeria cannot confiscate these companies without offending an important part of the world'.[45] Furthermore, France was buying Saharan oil at a very high price, $2.30–$2.40 per barrel against the $1.80 from Libya; on the international market, Algerian oil would not be competitive.[46] Algerian engineers were so rare that they were renowned figures in the country, and were all immediately contacted by the Organisme mixte and by the Algerian government.[47] One of them, Laroussi Khalifa, was nominated minister of energy, and he immediately issued an appeal to all Algerian engineers and economics graduates working abroad to contact the Ministry and to come back and serve in the public administration. He also commissioned the Institut français du pétrole to write a report on how to train specialised workforce in the oil industry. Algeria was in no position to negotiate anything more than what it had obtained in Évian. Apart from the Organisme mixte, the only Algerian presence in the Saharan fields was through SN REPAL, the joint venture in which the Algerian Governorate owned 40% of shares, which had now been inherited by the Algerian state.[48]

It was clear that the companies in the Sahara considered their presence safe. However, at the same time, the new Algerian establishment immediately focused a large part of its nation-building efforts on the establishment of a national oil industry. In only nine years Algeria was able not only to gain control over the Saharan concessions, but to nationalise its oil industry—the first producer country to successfully do so.[49] Oil immediately became the centre of Algerian post-independence discussions with France and with the rest of the world; in and out of the country, everyone agreed that the Saharan oil and gas reserves would make Algeria's fortune.[50]

While repeatedly providing reassurances about the validity of the Évian accords, the government started a process of 'Algerianisation' of the Saharan oil industry, which remained at the top of their agenda for the years to come. Immediately after the government was formed, the Direction de l'Énergie et des Carburants (DEC) and the Bureau Algérien des Pétroles (BAP, equivalent to the French BRP) were established to manage the participation of the Algerian state in SN REPAL, and to promote domestic production, refining, and distribution. In practice, these two bodies were a way to set up new direction centres that were Algerian only, against the Organisme mixte. The government's strategy was based on three main points: the establishment of training exchanges with other countries outside France; having Algerian personnel replacing French and Americans in the field; and progressive government intervention in the industry, with the final goal of complete control.

The government immediately sought the opportunity to intervene directly in the Saharan fields. The first occasion arose because a new pipeline to connect the field of Hassi Messaoud to the new refinery in Arzew was urgently needed to allow production from the operative fields to reach full capacity. Early in 1963, the Trapal consortium, established amongst the sixteen companies operating in the Sahara, presented the project to the Algerian government. Thanks to the last-minute changes before the Évian agreements, the petroleum code gave the companies the right to build transport infrastructure, but it did not explicitly state that they also had the right to ownership over these structures. The government seized the opportunity to declare that it would only endorse the project if SN

REPAL could control 51% of its shares. The companies refused, as owner-ship of the pipelines entailed the right to decide upon transportation fees, an important aspect of revenues and production costs. Negotiations con-tinued for most of 1963; meanwhile, Khalifa set up a team of experts from BAP and DEC to study the feasibility of a project that did not include the consortium at all, looking for investors elsewhere thanks to the mediation of the Arab Bank in Switzerland. No one from the Organisme mixte was involved in this operation, for fear that the French would discover the parallel project.[51] Initially, the Algerians turned to the US; however, high-ranking officers in the US administration tried to dissuade the government for fear of worsening the relations with France.[52] The US construction companies also refused as they were not willing to alienate the interna-tional companies operating in the Sahara, their most important clients. Thyssen, a German company, also expressed its perplexity in going against the companies and France.[53] In the end, it was several British banks that offered a loan, and the Scottish construction company John Brown agreed to build the pipeline.[54] In order to supervise the project, Ben Bella announced in December 1963 the establishment of the Société nationale pour le transport des hydrocarbures, or SONATRACH, a state company modelled on French law, entirely owned by the state and with headquar-ters in an office confiscated from the Organisme mixte. Unsurprisingly, the other companies and the French government protested vehemently against the decision, claiming that not having control over the pipeline was a very serious breach of the Évian accords, and the consortium turned to international arbitration in The Hague. However, the Algerian govern-ment simply ignored the arbitration, refusing to appoint a third party and stating that it would not give validity to any verdict. While the trial went on as a pantomime, in the absence of the Algerian government, the works in the desert proceeded under the supervision of Aït Sid Mohamed, an Algerian engineer who had graduated from the Yugoslav University of Ljubljana.[55] The establishment of SONATRACH and the construction of the third pipeline represented a milestone in the history of the Algerian oil industry; not only had the state established its own company to engage in negotiations, but SONATRACH found the credibility to attract funds and technical partnerships to work in the Sahara. The ultimate goal of the company was to acquire concessions to extract oil in the Sahara; for this reason, the government blocked the release of all new concessions until French companies agreed to allow SONATRACH to enter into a joint venture with 50% of shares. However, France refused anything that would not give French companies majority control, in line with the Évian agreements.[56]

While the situation stalled, SONATRACH focused on the downstream sector (refining and marketing), implementing another of the main objectives of the Algerian government: the differentiation of the oil and gas markets outside of France. The main ally, in this respect, was again ENI, with which the negotiations for the import of oil and gas to Italy and future concessions had never stopped, and resumed immediately after Évian, this time as official talks. SONATRACH tried for months to claim 50% shares of the Société de la raffinerie d'Alger, the consortium for the Algiers refinery set up by French and American companies, with no success. In the end, in July 1963, it instead signed an agreement with ENI on the creation of another refinery in Arzew, with limited production of 1.25 million tons a year, in which the Algerian government would sell 50% of the total market of petroleum and 100% of the bitumen products.[57] The project worried France and the companies of the cartel, as the Arzew refinery would obviously have the support of the Algerian government, unlike their refinery in Algiers. Still, they refused to offer more than 30% to SONATRACH to enter the consortium.[58]

The ENI-SONATRACH refinery, with its limited production, was meant for the domestic market rather than for exports, but the Algerian government wanted to enter the international market rather than restrict SONATRACH to the limited domestic market. For this reason, initially the talks with ENI included the construction of a second, larger, refinery for massive exports, as a way to help SONATRACH to become an exporter of refined products. But from the end of 1963, the company went through a drastic change of course, caused by the sudden death of its president, Enrico Mattei, who died in a bomb attack while travelling from Sicily to Milan. While the instigators are to this day unknown, for years rumours spread about the involvement of the Organisation de l'Armée Secrète or the French secret service. In any case, the sudden death of its energetic president, and the financial exposure of the company after a series of large investments (£700 billion debt to Italian and European banks in 1963),[59] caused the company to withdraw from many of the upstream projects it had in newly-independent countries, which were often more politically oriented than economically viable.[60] ENI's withdrawal from the plan for a second refinery was a big blow to Algerian-Italian relations. A second blow came in 1965, when ENI announced that it had signed a large contract with a US major to deliver Libyan gas to Italy, rather than continuing the negotiations with SONATRACH for the import of gas from Algeria. At the time, the Algerian government had just reviewed the Évian agreements with France to allow SONATRACH to start production in the Sahara. The move was treated as a stab in the back and incompatible with the anti-colonialism professed by the Italian company the previous year: instead of signing an agreement with a local company, ENI preferred to do business with an 'imperialist' oil major, an American company that controlled Libyan oil. In fact, after the death of Mattei, the Italian government had cut credit to the company and its 'rogue' projects, focusing on the more modest aim of providing energy supplies to the country without defying the structure of the world energy business. While ENI continued to use a narrative of development, like all other oil companies, it no longer promoted the establishment of local national oil companies for the direct control of extraction and sales.

Mattei's legacy in Algeria was nonetheless detectable in the debate over the revision of the Évian agreements, which occupied France and Algeria from 1963 until 1971. In 1965, the new Ascoop (Association coopérative) accords allowed SONATRACH to expand in the Sahara. Both France and Algeria defined it as a revolutionary agreement, a new era in relations between the two countries. The agreement created a new body replacing the Organisme mixte, represented by the French state company ERAP, which was created for the occasion with the merger of the BRP and other institutions, and SONATRACH. This new Association coopérative would manage all new research permits in the Sahara, but it was not a joint venture. Rather, it was a convoluted system by which ERAP and SONATRACH could form joint ventures with other companies independently, or delegate the works to other companies of the same nationality, as long as the total participation in the new concessions and total revenues amounted to a fifty-fifty division between France and Algeria. The crude extracted would be independently sold by ERAP or SONATRACH, but they would buy each other's surpluses—which meant in practice that France committed to sell the oil that SONATRACH was not able to place in its limited domestic market. The Ascoop accords also included the creation of an Institut algérien du pétrole, the first Algerian school for hydrocarbons. Finally, the accords allowed SONATRACH to acquire 50% shares in SN REPAL, so that the company could have direct access to current production. SONATRACH's extended name was changed to Société nationale pour la recherche, la production, le transport, la transformation, et la commercialisation des hydrocarbures.[61] In practice, the Ascoop agreement created a quasi-state monopoly, but one shared between two states, France and Algeria. It was a way for France to retain rights over the territory, in exchange for allowing Algeria to enter the upstream sector.

Another interesting aspect of the Ascoop agreement was that it envisaged French-Algerian collaboration in other industries apart from oil, in order to help Algeria to differentiate its economy rather than relying on hydrocarbon exports only. In theory, this could have been a way to put oil revenues back into the economic circle towards different industries, similar to the oil-based Marshall Plan for North Africa that Mattei had suggested.[62] In reality, the agreement remained idle because it started with the wrong premise: for France it was a new type of cooperation based on some of Mattei's theories of state-state negotiations and the reduction of companies to contractors as a way to consolidate its presence in the Sahara. For Algeria, it was the first step towards acquiring full control over the reserves, completing the process of nationalisation of the oil industry. Neither country saw it as a genuine cooperation model to develop the overall Algerian economy, but rather as a tool to gain more control over the oil industry.

In fact, the Ascoop agreement was mostly used by the Algerian government to oust France from the Sahara. SONATRACH proceeded with the creation of a series of joint ventures with independent US companies for the research of new fields. Whenever France tried to veto a project, the Algerian government answered with an indefinite blockade of all work. At the same time, talks about the nationalisation of the oil industry started to be an important part of the government's rhetoric. In March 1966, the inauguration of the pipeline built by SONATRACH was turned into a power showdown: a solemn ceremony in the presence of several heads of state was held and it was said that the 'first 100% Algerian pipeline' should be celebrated as 'a new 1st November'.[63] By the end of the year, it became obvious that Algeria was only waiting for a new opportunity to nationalise; it was no longer a matter of *if*, but of *when*. The first occasion came with the Six-Day War, in June 1967—Algeria urged all Arab countries to place an embargo on Israel's supporters, namely the US and the UK. In order to enforce the embargo, the Ministry of Energy declared that all Anglo-Saxon companies present in Algeria would be nationalised. The directors of Shell-Algérie, Unilever-Algérie, Sinclair Mediterranean, Mobil, Phillips, Esso, El Paso, Tidewater, and Getty, among others, were summoned to the Ministry, while the police sealed their offices and confiscated the establishments.[64] These measures, however, did not concern the joint-ventures in which Algeria already had more than 50% shares; the government did not want to expel foreign investment, but to acquire majority control over companies.[65] In January 1969, the Algerian government announced the nationalisation of the domestic distribution network, which forced CFP to sell its stakes to SONATRACH. The French press protested this covert nationalisation, defining it as 'a dispossession that is new and shocking because of its level of injustice and brutality'.[66]

That same year, the financial aspects of the Ascoop agreement had to be renegotiated. In October, a new contract with an American independent company put France in a very weak position: the American independent Getty Oil agreed to establish a joint venture in Algeria in which SONATRACH controlled 51% of the shares. Paul Getty, the company president, had already signed other types of agreements that were very convenient for producer countries, based on the model made famous by Mattei. This agreement established a new benchmark for the Algerian government, which expected all other companies to adopt a similar agreement, including the French ones. In 1969, Algeria formally joined OPEC, and started to pressure its members to adopt a revision of oil prices on a global scale, as well as to nationalise their oil resources. In May 1970, a break in the Syrian section of the Tapline, a vital nerve of oil supplies to Europe with 875,000 barrels per day transported from Saudi Arabia to the Mediterranean Sea, caused an interruption in energy provision. In normal circumstances, only 24 hours would have been required to fix the break, but the Syrian government refused to allow the technicians to enter the area unless the companies operating the Tapline agreed to give Syria a much higher transit fee. The *bras-de-fer* was only concluded in January 1971. When the country was granted its request, the pipeline was fixed overnight.[67] Meanwhile, Libya followed Algeria in demanding higher percentages on revenues, and cut production until an agreement was reached. After more than two decades of low oil prices, within a system where the market was controlled by Western multinationals, crude prices started to rise. In Libya, as in Algeria, it was an American independent company that accepted the deal, causing a domino effect for other companies operating in the country: Armand Hammer of Occidental Petroleum agreed to raise prices for Libyan oil by 30%, an unprecedented move that left 55% of profits to Libya.[68] Algeria immediately followed: in July 1970, it announced a unilateral rise in the taxation system, which an indignant Georges

Pompidou, the French president, described to the Algerian ambassador as a 'Hitlerian' diktat.

While negotiations with France continued, on 23 February 1971 all of the OPEC countries signed an agreement in Teheran in which they demanded an immediate raise from $1.79 to $2.17 per barrel on crude— an increase of approximately 11% per year.[69] Against the threat of a general embargo, the companies of the cartel decided to sign the deal. Two months later, a new agreement in Tripoli imposed a further rise in crude prices to $3.45 per barrel and also required companies to invest in research.[70] When French companies in Algeria protested and refused to comply with this agreement, the government answered with a nationalisation decree that unilaterally ended all concessions for hydrocarbons, even those protected by the Évian agreement, and took possession of 51% of all oil activities, in both the downstream and upstream sectors, as well as 100% of the gas industry. For France, despite the warning signs, it was a shock. While CFP decided that it was pointless to proceed with further negotiation and was able to close a deal with the Algerian government within two months, the French government considered the event treason, and a big blow to future relations between the two countries. Negotiations with ERAP dragged on for months, until the state company decided to simply quit the country. A senior Algerian representative commented that 'Because CFP worked in the Middle East it had understood that the times were changing', and 'that the Bedouins had now become oil executives and...wanted to be in control of their own resources'.[71] In contrast, the French government 'had lost the occasion of placing France on the world scene as a forerunner with a progressive view of the future and of the economic relations with the peoples of the Third World'.[72] However, it should be noted that the French Ministry of Finance had repeatedly asked Algiers to start talks for investment projects in other sectors related to the Ascoop agreement, but these requests were simply ignored by its Algerian counterpart.

With the nationalisations, the Algerian government declared complete the process of independence, a second revolution that was as important as the first one, because it would guarantee real economic independence to Algeria. France, on the other hand, had to accept that the Évian era was over, and that Algeria was entirely a foreign country.

CONCLUSION

The development of the hydrocarbon reserves in the Algerian Sahara in the 1950s and 1960s shows the vital importance of the industry for governments not only in producer countries, but in developed countries such as France and Italy. The obsession with control over the Saharan resources affected Algeria and France in similar ways and for similar reasons, though the two countries were at opposite ends of the spectrum of development. The oil industry was a very important part of the Algerian decolonisation process, and remained at the heart of the relationship between the two countries thereafter, though after 1971 French companies had lost much of their position in the Sahara.

Companies traditionally expressed the positive aspects of their presence in a country, as long as they were left free to operate. Decolonisation also gave producer countries the means to exercise actual power over the management of their resources and of the revenues from these resources. In this sense, even 'enlightened' plans like the unrealised Pella plan, or the failed Ascoop agreement, could still be interpreted as patronising efforts by Western countries and Western companies to take charge of economic development in former colonies. Enrico Mattei, with his insistence on recognising and promoting producer countries as partners in the management of the international oil market, placing negotiations on an international level, was better at capturing the spirit of decolonisation, anticipating the moves of OPEC.

The Algerian example is also interesting for what it tells us of the role of state companies and the oil industry in development. The nationalisation process and the establishment of a strong state company that became one of the most important clusters of power in Algeria is sometimes indicated as one of the reasons why the country failed to democratise and develop. However, there are no indications that a counter-history of Algeria, in which oil and gas reserves were left to foreign companies, or never developed, would have brought about a better economic or political system. On the contrary, the literature on Algerian economic history suggests that the country could have remained an agricultural society based on exports from large properties, and that even though there was mismanagement and corruption, the oil and gas sector did allow capital to be raised that would have otherwise never been at Algeria's disposal. It is impossible to know whether this capital would have been better spent through international institutions that channelled them towards development projects;

however, perhaps most importantly, it raises important questions about the patronage of development projects and, ultimately, again, about sovereignty—the struggle of the Algerian government was precisely to have full control over resources, and to influence revenues as much as possible. The Saharan negotiations allow us to explore the relations between the formal aspects of sovereignty over a territory and the reality of control over the systems that allow for its exploitation—which goes to the heart of the problem of decolonisation. In this sense, the actions of the Algerian establishment in the final years of the war and the first years of independence are an interesting example of the leveraging of formal sovereignty to gain actual control. While the foreign companies in the Sahara and France considered the actions of the Algerian government disgraceful, and the Algerian government sought to project itself as being truly revolutionary, in reality it simply sought a situation similar to what France had established with the petroleum code: a mixed system with the largest possible participation of the state, control over the actions of companies, and a massive effort to develop local technology and competencies. Its success was in large part due to its ability to coordinate with other producer countries through OPEC, and to find alternatives to French investments.

It is clear then that the oil industry played an important role in the process of decolonisation, in both its economic and cultural aspects. While companies did not act as direct agents of economic development, they did play an active role as both formal and informal mediators in the negotiations, as they represented interests that always intersected, and often overcame, those of institutional powers. More importantly, they were symbols of modernity, of technological and financial power—a 'Western' tool that a proud representative of the developing world such as Algeria wanted to reclaim.

NOTES

1. P.R. Odell, *Oil and World Power: Background to the Oil Crisis* (Baltimore, 1974).
2. Archives Total, Paris, Centre de Documentation et de Synthese (CDS), note, 21 March 1957.
3. Petroleum Press Service [hereafter PPS], "Fresh Attack on Under-Development", May 1961. London edition.
4. PPS, "Mobilizing capital", November 1958, London edition.
5. Ibid.
6. Ibid.

7. Ibid.
8. Daniel Lefeuvre, 'Les Réactions Patronales Au Plan de Constantine', *Revue Historique*, 1986, pp. 167–189.
9. Archives Total, Paris, *Principes du code pétrolièr*, 10 October 1958.
10. US National Archives and Records Administration [hereafter NARA]. General Records of the Departments of State—France. *Report on Constantine plan*, 1959.
11. Olivier Dard and Daniel Lefeuvre, *L'Europe Face à Son Passé Colonial* (Paris, 2008).
12. For the bibliography on US-French relations, see: Arthur M. Schlesinger, *A Thousand Days. John F. Kennedy in the White House* (Boston, 1965).; Bruna Bagnato, *L'Italia e La Guerra d'Algeria (1954–1962)*, vol. 32, Storia Politica (Soveria Mannelli, 2012); Philippe Bourdrel, *La dernière chance de l'Algérie française. Du gouvernement socialiste au retour de De Gaulle, 1956–1958* (Paris, 1996); Irwin M. Wall, *France, the United States, and the Algerian War* (Berkeley, 2001); Roberto Cantoni, *Oil Exploration, Diplomacy, and Security in the Early Cold War: The Enemy Underground* (New York, 2017).
13. PPS, "50:50 for the Sahara", November 1958, London edition.
14. NARA. General Records of the Departments of State—France. *FLN relations with US companies*, 6 February 1959
15. Interviews conducted by the author with Mario Pirani, Nordine Aït-Laoussine, Yves Roland-Billecart; Interview to Paul Delouvrier conducted by Daniel Lefeuvre and cited in Dard and Lefeuvre, *L'Europe Face à Son Passé Colonial*.
16. Redha Malek, *L'Algérie à Évian: Histoire Des Négociations Secrètes, 1956–1962, L'épreuve Des Faits* (Paris, 1995).
17. Interview by Daniel Lefeuvre cited in Dard and Lefeuvre, *L'Europe Face à Son Passé Colonial*.
18. *El Moudjahid*,'Les Illusions Sahariennes de La France et Ses Ayants-Droit', 15 November 1957.
19. Abdelatif Rebah, *Sonatrach: Une Entreprise Pas Comme Les Autres* (Alger, 2006).
20. See M. Pirani, *Poteva andare peggio* (Milano, 2012); Rebah, *Sonatrach*.
21. Archives Diplomatiques France [hereafter ADF], Secrétariat d'Etat aux affaires algériennes. Press releases.
22. Archivio Storico ENI [hereafter AS ENI]. *Report on to the exploitation of oil in the Sahara*, 16 January 1958.
23. Ambasciata d'Italia a Parigi, 1951–1958, b. 81 (Algeria '58), telesp. N. Ris. 851, Quaroni to MAEI, "I rapporti italo-francesi", 14 March 1958. In Bruna Bagnato, *Petrolio e politica: Mattei in Marocco* (Firenze, 2004).
24. Ibid.

25. Archives Total. CDS. Association France Presse, *L'exploitation des ressources pétrolieres du Sahara vue par M. Mattei, president de l'office national italien des hydrocarbures*, 8 November 1957.
26. AS ENI. *Report on the Italian participation to the exploitation of the Sahara*, November 1958.
27. Consiglio, G., 'Il piano Pella e l'Africa', *Africa: Rivista trimestrale di studi e documentazione dell'Istituto italiano per l'Africa e l'Oriente*, May–June 1958, 13 (3), 119–120.
28. Ibid.
29. Jean Baptiste Duroselle and Enrico Serra (eds.) *Italia, Francia e Mediterraneo* (Milano, 1990).
30. Interview conducted by the author to Mario Pirani.
31. Ibid.
32. Interview conducted by the author with Yves-Roland Billecart.
33. See Malek, *L'Algérie à Évian.*; Ambasciata d'Italia ad Algeri, *Il Contributo Dell'Italia Alla Costruzione Dell'Algeria Indipendente* (Milano, 2010); Pirani, *Poteva andare peggio*; Bagnato, *L'Italia e La Guerra d'Algeria (1954–1962).*
34. Interview conducted by the author with Mario Pirani and Nordine Ait-Laoussine. See also Malek, *L'Algérie à Évian.*
35. See Pirani, *Poteva andare peggio*; Cantoni, *Oil Exploration, Diplomacy, and Security in the Early Cold War.*
36. Mario Brogini, *L'exploitation Des Hydrocarbures En Algérie de 1956 à 1971* (Nice, 1973).
37. Interview conducted by the author with Yves Roland-Billecart
38. Malek, *L'Algérie à Évian.*
39. Archives Total, Direction Générale Et Directions Centrales. Accords et contracts—Algérie, *Cessez le feu. Declaration Des Principes Relative A La Coopération Economique Et Financiers*, 1962.
40. Archives Total, Direction Générale, Loyrette, J., *Remarques sur l'organisation pétrolière en Algérie et au Sahara*, 12 October 1962.
41. Rebah, *Sonatrach.*
42. NARA, General Records of the Departments of State, Central Decimal Files, 1960–1963, Economic. Economic Affairs French Africa. *Views of Pierre Courant on Post War Economy of Algeria*, 21 February 1962.
43. NARA, General Records of the Departments of State. Central Decimal Files, 1960–1963. Economic. Economic Affairs French Africa NARA RG—2569 "Algerian industrial prospects problems—view of a French businessman" (November 1962).
44. John Douglas Ruedy, *Modern Algeria: The Origins and Development of a Nation* (Indianapolis, 1992).
45. NARA, *Views of Pierre Courant*, 21 February 1962.
46. Ibid.

47. Interview conducted by the author with Nordine Aït-Laoussine.
48. Archives Total. Accords et contracts—Algérie. Journal Officielle de la République Française. *Accords entre l' Exécutif Provisoire et le gouvernement Français*, 28 August 1962.
49. After the failed experiments of Latin America in the 1940s. See Daniel Yergin, *The Prize: The Epic Quest for Oil, Money, & Power* (New York, 2008); Leonardo, 2006).
50. Robert Fosset, 'Pétrole et Gaz Naturel Au Sahara', *Annales de Géographie* 71, no. 385 (1 May 1962): 279–308, http://www.jstor.org/stable/23445027.
51. Rebah, *Sonatrach*.
52. Archives Total. *Note de La Villerabel*, 13 January 1964.
53. Interview with Djaâfer Eskenazen. In Rebah, *Sonatrach*.
54. Archives Total. *Note de La Villerabel*, 13 January 1964.
55. Rebah, *Sonatrach*.
56. PPS, 3 March 1964.
57. Ibid.
58. BP Archives, North Africa—*Algeria. Finance, Loans, Credit Facilities, Capital Expenditure.*
59. Paul H. Frankel, *Mattei: Oil and Power Politics*, 1st Edition (Londra, 1966).
60. Franco Briatico, *Ascesa e Declino Del Capitale Pubblico in Italia: Vicende e Protagonisti*, Storia/Memoria (Bologna, 2004).
61. Henry Cattan, *The Law of Oil Concessons in the Middle East and North Africa* (Dobbs Ferry, New York, 1967).
62. Centre des Archives Économiques et Financières. Trésor. Action régionale. Outre-mer. *Aide libre financière de la France à l'équipement et au développement économique et social de l'Algérie (1965–1972)*.
63. A national holiday in Algeria, the day that celebrated the start of the Algerian insurrection against France in 1954.
64. Archives Total. Archives de Vincent Labouret. *Rapport*, 15 February 1966.
65. Ibid.
66. Archives Total. Archives de Vincent Labouret. "Une spoliation nouvelle et surprenante par son injustice et son brutalité".
67. M. A. Adelman, *The Economics of Petroleum Supply: Papers by M.A. Adelman, 1962–1993* (Cambridge, 1993).
68. Daniel Yergin, *The Prize: The Epic Quest for Oil, Money, & Power* (New York, 2008).
69. For crude from the Persian Gulf (34°API). In Adelman, *The Economics of Petroleum Supply*.
70. For the 40° API. In ibid.
71. Belaid Abdesselam, *Le Pétrole et Le Gaz Naturel En Algérie* (Algiers, 2012).
72. Ibid.

REFERENCES

50:50 for the Sahara (Petroleum Press Service, November 1958).

Abdesselam, Belaïd, *Le Pétrole et Le Gaz Naturel En Algérie* (Editions ANEP, Algiers, 2012).

Adelman, M.A., *The Genie out of the Bottle: World Oil since 1970* (MIT Press, Cambridge, MA , 1995).

Ambasciata d'Italia ad Algeri, *Il Contributo Dell'Italia Alla Costruzione Dell'Algeria Indipendente* (Roma, 2010).

Bagnato, Bruna, *Petrolio e politica: Mattei in Marocco* (Polistampa, Firenze, 2004).

Bagnato, Bruna, *L'Italia e La Guerra d'Algeria (1954–1962)*. Vol. 32, Storia Politica (Soveria Mannelli, Rubbettino, 2012).

Bourdrel, Philippe, *La dernière chance de l'Algérie française. Du gouvernement socialiste au retour de Gaulle, 1956–1958* (Albin Michel, Paris, 1996).

Brault, Julien, *Les Transactions Internationales de La France Des Années 1920 Aux Années 1970* (Graduate Institute of International and Development Studies, 2013).

Briatico, Franco, *Ascesa e Declino Del Capitale Pubblico in Italia: Vicende e Protagonisti*. Storia/Memoria (Il Mulino, Bologna, 2004).

Brogini, Mario, *L'exploitation Des Hydrocarbures En Algérie de 1956 à 1971* (Université de Nice Sophia Antipolis, 1973).

Cantoni, Roberto, *Oil Exploration, Diplomacy, and Security in the Early Cold War: The Enemy Underground* (Routledge, New York, 2017).

Cattan, Henry, *The Law of Oil Concessions in the Middle East and North Africa* (Dobbs Ferry, NY, published for the Parker School of Foreign and Comparative Law by Oceana Publications, 1967).

Dard, Olivier, and Daniel Lefeuvre, *L'Europe Face à Son Passé Colonial. Actes Académiques* (Riveneuve, Paris, 2008).

Duroselle, Jean Baptiste, and Enrico Serra (eds.). *Italia, Francia e Mediterraneo* (Franco Angeli, Milano, 1990).

Fossel, Robert, 'Pétrole et Gaz Naturel Au Sahara', *Annales de Géographie* 71, no. 385 (1 May 1962), pp. 279–308. http://www.jstor.org/stable/23445027.

Frankel, Paul H., *Mattei: Oil and Power Politics*, 1st Edition (Faber & Faber, London, 1966).

'Les Illusions Sahariennes de La France et Ses Ayants-Droit', *El Moudjahid*, 15 November 1957.

Malek, Redha, *L'Algérie à Évian: Histoire Des Négociations Secrètes, 1956–1962* L'épreuve Des Faits (Éditions du Seuil, Paris. 1995).

Maugeri, Leonardo, *The Age of Oil* (Greenwood Publishing Group, Westport, 2006).

Mobilising Capital (Petroleum Press Service, November 1958).

Odell, Peter R., *Oil and World Power: Background to the Oil Crisi* (Penguin, Baltimore, 1974).

Pirani, Mario, *Poteva andare peggio* (Edizioni Mondadori, Milano, 2012).

Rebah, Abdelatif, *Sonatrach: Une Entreprise Pas Comme Les Autres* (Casbah editions, Algiers, 2006).

Ruedy, John Douglas, *Modern Algeria: The Origins and Development of a Nation* (Indiana University Press, Indianapolis, 1992).

Schlesinger, Arthur M., *A Thousand Days. John F. Kennedy in the White House* (Houghton Mifflin Company, Boston, 2002).

Tramerye, Pierre L. de, *La Lutte Mondiale Pour Le Pétrole* (Éditions de la Vie universitaire, Paris, 1921).

United Nations Human Rights Office of the High Commissioner (OHCHR), 'General Assembly Resolution 1803 (XVII) of 14 December 1962, "Permanent Sovereignty over Natural Resources"'. Accessed 15 March 2019. https://www.ohchr.org/Documents/ProfessionalInterest/resources.pdf.

Wall, Irwin M., *France, the United States, and the Algerian War* (University of California Press, Berkeley, 2001).

Yergin, Daniel, *The Prize: The Epic Quest for Oil, Money, & Power* (Free Press, New York, 2008).

CHAPTER 6

A Partner in Progress? Shell-BP's Development Role in Nigeria During the Transition to Independence

Chris Minton

Shell-BP is growing with Nigeria and is her partner in progress.
(Shell-BP promotional pamphlet, 1965)[1]

The history of modern Nigeria is intimately connected to the growth of the country's oil industry. The leading firm in that growth, Shell-BP, was

I would like to express my appreciation to the BP Archive Manager, Peter Housego, and BP plc for granting me permission to cite materials researched at the BP Archive. Thanks to Peter and his colleagues, particularly Joanne Burman, for their help during my many visits between 2013 and 2017. Special thanks to Dr Spencer Mawby, the supervisor of my doctoral thesis, whose skilful advice and guidance again proved essential in this project. Thanks also to my second supervisor, Dr Anna Greenwood, for her insightful comments on the elements of my thesis that informed this chapter. I am particularly indebted to Sarah Stockwell and Véronique Dimier for the opportunity to join this project at a late stage. Finally, love and thanks to Vega and Astrid, to whom I dedicate this chapter.

C. Minton (✉)
University of Nottingham, Nottingham, UK

© The Author(s) 2020
V. Dimier, S. Stockwell (eds.), *The Business of Development in Post-Colonial Africa*, Cambridge Imperial and Post-Colonial Studies Series, https://doi.org/10.1007/978-3-030-51106-7_6

committed to achieving long-term commercial success in Nigeria by out-lasting the Empire and maintaining its dominant position as industry leader. For imperial businesses (in this context British businesses operating overseas in colonies and ex-colonies) like Shell-BP, nationalism and decol-onisation raised the issue of legitimacy: the degree of popular consent that companies could command, not in the sense of the ballot box, but rather, as Stephanie Decker has interpreted it, in the form of 'local goodwill'.[2] This chapter shows how Shell-BP devised and implemented strategies for independence to justify its continued presence in the country and entrench its position by building up 'local goodwill' with nationalist politicians and the Nigerian public. It focused on constructing a positive local image of itself as, for instance, a model employer, a modernising and industrialising force, and a source of development finance.

Shell-BP sought to express its legitimacy by adopting a term first used by the British government in 1942 to describe its new development rela-tionship with the colonies: 'partnership'.[3] As David Fleming, Shell-BP's General Manager, explained ahead of independence in 1960, 'Nigeria and ourselves are in business together. We are partners'.[4] Nationalist politicians adopted similar terminology when describing their country's relationship with the company.[5] From the British government's perspective, partner-ship meant that colonial peoples would now share responsibility for devel-oping their own countries. In this sense, partnership was distinct from the earlier concept of trusteeship, which denoted a measure of subordination and had informed British colonial development policy for much of the inter-war period. But for the company, partnership was about securing nationalist political backing for the development of the oil industry and, importantly, guaranteeing its own dominant role in this process. Partnering the independent Nigerian government was a means of securing commer-cial primacy during a period in which Shell-BP's colonial monopoly was being eroded by an influx of new competitors from the United States and Europe. For nationalists, partnership was about stabilising the economy and financing development using revenues from oil by achieving an equal share in Shell-BP's profits. Compared to the price fluctuations on the world market which affected Nigeria's cash-crop staple exports such as cocoa, between the early 1950s and mid-1960s the price of crude oil, though on a slight downward trend in the wake of the Suez Crisis (1956), appeared relatively dependable and the revenue from it consequently more predictable.[6] As Nigeria was a sterling area country, oil exports also had the potential to earn much-needed dollars which Nigeria could use to purchase goods and services from the dollar area—especially since Nigeria's sterling assets were not easily available for spending on development.[7]

In seeking to present itself as a partner in development, Shell-BP benefited in the 1950s and 1960s from the commitment of many West African politicians to post-war orthodox development theory that not only validated the intervention by Western governments in African economies, but also envisaged a key role for foreign business as sources of capital and expertise.[8] At the same time, Shell-BP elected to fuel the optimism shared by most Nigerians and departing British colonial administrators regarding Nigeria's prospects of achieving rapid development.[9] In November 1959, for example, the company expressed its 'absolute confidence' that Nigeria would become an oil-producing country of 'some size'.[10] To this end, the *West African Pilot* had earlier pointed out, Nigeria was 'pin[ning its] hopes' on Shell-BP.[11] By fulfilling these hopes and partnering the Nigerian government to achieve the country's development potential, the company looked to guarantee its longevity by attaining legitimacy in its ultimate form: 'citizenship'. To be considered a 'good citizen of Nigeria' by nationalists was an objective the company first outlined publicly and began to promote in the late 1950s.[12] Citizenship implied that Shell-BP might enjoy a new status as a 'naturalised' entity, or in other words be accepted locally as a Nigerian firm associated with the country's future instead of an imperial business intimately connected with its colonial past. As with real citizenship, while inferring duties and obligations on the company, for example to pay taxes, this new status would, crucially, afford Shell-BP rights and protections, further entrenching its position.

Shell-BP and the Nigerian oil industry have been overlooked in the literature on oil and imperial business and, as a result, the firm's development role during the transition to independence has not been explored fully. What follows is a new analysis which, contrary to conventional wisdom, demonstrates the significance of Shell-BP and the oil industry in Nigeria's modern history prior to the massive revenues accrued in the 1970s. The chapter shows that Shell-BP was able to use the language of development and partnership, and play off the Nigerian federal government's development ambitions, to protect and advance the company's own interests. In 1964, this strategy even saw Shell-BP become a source of development finance to the federal government under the terms of a new £15 million advance/loan deal. While this strategy in many ways served the company's interests, it also carried risks as well, with the result that Shell-BP had to manage Nigerian expectations carefully.

The chapter begins by introducing the concept of 'black gold hype', which explains how nationalist expectations regarding the company's role in development became inflated as a result of the intense excitement surrounding the prospects of Nigerian oil. This section also details how Shell-BP implemented a new public relations strategy to manage these inflated expectations and encourage a tone of 'cautious optimism' among its stakeholder groups. This is followed by an overview of the company's independence settlement with the federal government in 1958–1959, which addressed two key issues relating to development: education and federal revenues. The final section discusses how Shell-BP's advance/loan deal of 1964 helped to make up for a shortfall in Nigerian development finance caused in part by the refusal of the British Treasury to write Nigeria a blank cheque (which also thereby demonstrates how the British government had a significant impact on the company's development role). Crucially this deal shored up the firm's position as Nigeria's 'partner in progress' and heralded a new era of Nigerian economic dependence on oil revenues.

'BLACK GOLD HYPE' AND MANAGING EXPECTATIONS

Shell-BP had begun exploring for oil in Nigeria as early as 1937, but it was 1958 before the company was able to export its first oil shipment following its initial discovery of oil in commercially exploitable quantities at Oloibiri in 1956. This development fuelled nationalist expectations regarding Shell-BP's capacity to enrich an independent Nigerian state. In January 1958, a series of positive articles about oil appeared in the *West African Pilot* which emphasised 'the vital role of the oil industry in the Nigerian economy'.[13] In fact, despite the *Pilot*'s enthusiasm, it was predicted that the federal government could hope for no more than £60,000 in royalties from Shell-BP in 1958. Royalties nearly quadrupled in 1959 to £206,369 and more than doubled again in 1960 to £434,045,[14] but the actual contribution of oil to federal revenue during this period was relatively small, representing only 0.1% of total revenue in 1958, 1.8% in 1959, and 1.1% in 1960.[15] Nevertheless, optimism regarding the potential of oil to bring about rapid development was encapsulated in the notion, popular with the press, that Nigerian oil was 'black gold' or 'liquid gold'. In a newspaper article from February 1958, for example, a *Daily Times* journalist visiting Shell-BP's operations at Oloibiri in a helicopter described his urge to shout down to some Nigerian fishermen in the mangrove swamps below, 'Do you know? You are standing on LIQUID GOLD'.[16] Using a different metaphor to similar effect, the *Pilot* argued in May 1959 that 'oil is the bloodstream of our modern economy, and pipelines are the arteries not merely of the petroleum industry but of the world itself'.[17]

Such powerful imagery encouraged nationalists to expect that Shell-BP and other foreign oil companies would play a part in enabling Nigeria to keep this vital 'bloodstream' flowing, for which the country would be handsomely rewarded. As the *Pilot* described in January 1958, 'oil means wealth and power, it rules the world'.[18] Plans put forward by Shell and BP in consultation with the British Ministry of Fuel and Power in 1950, to build a local refinery 'when the annual production of crude oil reaches 500,000 tons and adequate reserves have been established to maintain such production over a substantial period of years', appeared to present an opportunity for Nigeria to achieve its development aims.[19] By refining its own oil for domestic consumption and export Nigeria could take advantage of the added economic benefit of manufacturing, and in the words of Muhammadu Ribadu, Federal Minister of Lagos Affairs, Mines and Power, 'add to the country's importance to the outside world'.[20] Such possibilities, as conjured up through this 'black gold hype', created a feeling of intense excitement about the oil industry which infected nationalist politicians, company leaders, and British governmental officials alike, even if each mobilised their enthusiasm differently to support their own group's visions of a way forward.

Shell-BP attempted to harness 'black gold hype' to strengthen its position in the public eye but it proved difficult to control effectively, particularly after the advances made by the company at Oloibiri in 1956 widened interest in oil matters among ordinary Nigerians. 'Black gold hype' was fuelled in part by media reports of positive developments in the Nigerian oil industry, including minor newsworthy instances of everyday progress as promoted by the company through its press releases, and more genuinely momentous events, for example Shell-BP's initial discovery of oil in commercially exploitable quantities. A prominent Oloibiri local, Chief Sunday Inengite, remembered how after the discoveries there was 'jubilation' among expatriate members of Shell-BP's exploration team, who threw a party at their houseboat to which everyone in the nearby village was invited and given the opportunity to view samples of the oil.[21] This feeling of jubilation was reported in the *Daily Times*, along with the idea that members of the public should see the oil discovered for themselves. 'Oloibiri is likely to feature in the news regularly', the paper enthused, 'and it is desirable as many people as possible should visit this isle of hope where [Shell-BP] has established the industry of industries in this country'.[22]

'Black gold hype' had a more significant effect on nationalist perceptions of Shell-BP than it did on its competitors, Gulf Oil, Tennessee Gas Transmission, the Italian firm ENI, and the Société anonyme française des recherches et d'exploration de pétroles, which had all been granted licences to explore for oil between 1960 and 1962.[23] John McVean Luard, a director at BP, argued that Shell-BP was a victim of its own hyperbole. In a confidential memorandum dated 30 July 1964, he complained that

> The impression has grown in recent years that Shell-BP is in a position to influence the progress of the Nigerian economy at innumerable points outside its main commercial tasks. [...] I recommend that the new representative's [i.e. the new Lagos director's] "brief" include a positive direction to dissipate any such impression; and this would include both conscious abstention from excessive activity, and absence of visible display or any suggestion that Shell-BP is, as it were, the doyen of the Nigerian oil producing companies.[24]

The company's image as industry leader was so firmly established, however, that its impression as an influential actor in the Nigerian economy and, therefore, as a potential source of development finance was already fixed in the minds of nationalists. Because of its 'first mover advantage', Shell-BP had by the early 1960s asserted its dominion over all of Nigeria's most promising onshore concessions, developing at significant and well-publicised cost an impressive oil infrastructure, including a giant network of pipelines and a crude oil terminal at Bonny, to secure its position as the country's leading exporter of crude oil.[25] A combination of 'black gold hype' and Shell-BP's perceived status as 'the doyen of the Nigerian oil producing companies' served to disproportionately inflate nationalist expectations regarding the firm's role in development compared to more recent entrants.[26] Crucially, this occurred at a time when Shell-BP was under growing pressure to prove its commitment to Nigerian development.

Beginning in the 1950s, managing expectations to mitigate this pressure and exert control over the parameters of its commitment became a central aspect of Shell-BP's public relations operations. In articles examining the prospects of Nigerian oil published by the press in Nigeria and Britain in the mid- to late 1950s, the oil-producing states of the Middle

East were often used as benchmarks for comparison. The production output of Kuwait, for instance, was considered by some industry commentators and professionals to be so great as to be unobtainable for Nigeria. In May 1959, *West Africa*, the London-based weekly news magazine, described how 'comparisons with Kuwait are clearly fantastic'.[27] In November of the same year, Shell-BP's Lagos director David Fleming concurred, noting that Kuwait was producing two million barrels a day from one well alone, whereas Nigeria could never hope to produce more than one million barrels a day 'from the whole country'.[28] Nevertheless, the proven economic impact of oil revenues on the oil-producing states of the Middle East served to inspire optimism regarding Nigeria's relative prospects. In 1958, the *Times* (UK) explained how

> The example of the Middle Eastern oil states, and particularly of the fabulous splendours that oil is reported to have brought to Kuwait and Saudi Arabia, raises great hopes in all the countries where no oil has been found, and even greater ones in those countries where the search for oil shows prospect of success. Nigeria is already enjoying some financial benefits from the search for oil.[29]

In February 1958, the *Pilot* discussed the 'hope that small [oil] revenues will become large', with 'hope thence of the economic development of a new Nigeria, taking her place among the oil producing nations of the world'.[30] In March 1960, Shell-BP's Managing Director, R. P. R. McGlashan, announced at a press conference that 'Nigeria may become one of the world's major crude petroleum producers... perhaps in ten years time'.[31] This inflated forecast contrasted sharply with Fleming's sober comparison between Kuwait and Nigeria in November 1959. However, it was qualified with the reminder 'that there was no certainty in oil prospection', an example of the company's policy of managed expectations.[32]

The responsibility for 'managing expectations' rested with Shell-BP's Public Relations Department, the formation of which in March 1955 marked a new era of professionalisation of the company's public relations operations in Nigeria. Previously this aspect of the business had been managed by the company's Land and Legal Department.[33] Professionalisation was necessitated by the increased levels and complexity of resources involved in implementing a new policy of managed expectations alongside the company's original public relations policy of 'managed transparency'.

Formulated in response to anti-Shell-BP protests during 1948–1949, managed transparency involved the firm being ostensibly more open with nationalists and local communities in oil-producing areas. The company shared carefully selected and presented information on certain aspects of planned operations both face-to-face and through the media.[34]

With managed expectations, Shell-BP sought to strike a balance between caution and optimism in its 'transparent' official statements, progress reports, and public relations materials, to encourage a tone of 'cautious optimism' among its stakeholder groups.[35] While emphasising its achievements and potential role in development to attain legitimacy, the company also downplayed the chances of achieving commercial success as a strategy to counter 'black gold hype' and limit nationalist expectations regarding Shell-BP's assumed role in development. Both these aspects of the policy in combination—and seemingly without too much internal tension, despite their contradictory central messages—formed Shell-BP's core public relations strategy heading into the independent period. The company's policy of managed expectations conforms to Decker's assertion that all companies 'emphasised to a greater or lesser degree their own role in the seminal process of developing West Africa and this became one of the dominant tropes in companies' advertising and public relations'.[36] Nationalists were provided with updates, published regularly in the press, overloaded with technical information, including, as oil output increased, quantitative data on the company's progress in the search for and production of oil. If progress was being made nationalists were placated and expectations, as well as bad news, could be managed more easily.

Managed expectations centred around nationalists' and the Nigerian public's perceptions of the company's progress in the search for oil. In September 1955, for instance, the company lamented that 'the majority of Nigerians are genuinely puzzled that we do not produce the shows of oil we have found, small as they are'.[37] Shell-BP used the rhetoric of positive and negative progress reports to inflate and deflate expectations in turn, alternately encouraging optimism and promoting caution to achieve both contradictory public relations objectives at once. For example, two press releases were issued by the company in March 1957. The first, an example of a negative update, was entitled 'Oloibiri appraisal well proves dry', while the second, 'Two new Drilvo rigs on order', expressed positivity and implied an overall trend of progress despite the failure at Oloibiri.[38] Negative updates were always tempered by descriptions of the next steps to be taken in the search for oil. In other words, failures were just a step in what the *Pilot* described in July 1957 as the 'onward march' of progress in the Nigerian oil industry.[39] While downplaying its chances of commercial success and trying to give an impression of overall progress, Shell-BP emphasised the expense incurred during the search for and production of oil in Nigeria's 'difficult' terrain.[40] This strategy, which evidenced the company's fear that nationalists might regard it as 'a philanthropic society with inexhaustible funds' instead of 'a commercial concern', endured even after the company's first export shipment of oil in 1958.[41] Writing in *The Shell-BP Story* in March 1965, the company's Managing Director Stanley Gray stated, 'a long drawn out effort it has been, pioneered by Shell-BP, in the face of the difficult country of the Niger Delta'.[42]

In the second half of the 1950s, Shell-BP's sequence of positive and negative updates on progress caused confusion and created suspicion among some nationalists who started to question whether accurate information regarding the quantities of oil discovered was being withheld by the company. In July 1955, for example, Chike Ekwuyasi, national publicity secretary for the National Council of Nigeria and the Cameroons, stated that he was 'inclined to believe that oil has been found in economic quantities in many parts of the country', but that Shell-BP was concealing this to 'discover all possible oil deposits in Nigeria and thus establish a monopoly... or withdraw announcing failure... and send out a subsidiary firm'.[43] A similar idea took hold in December 1956, following remarks made in the British House of Commons by the MP Sir Albert Braithwaite regarding a discovery of 'oil in quantity' by Shell-BP.[44] In June 1957, a critical editorial appeared in the *Pilot* arguing that Shell-BP was 'gradually creating the impression that it is determined to fool the country over the issue of having struck oil in commercial quantity'.[45] Sometimes it benefited the company to present a mostly positive outlook and at other times a more negative one. By this point, however, the company was beginning to doubt the wisdom of this sort of flexible management of expectations, explaining in August 1957 that 'we have not reported the results of the last appraisal wells at Oloibiri and Afam to the press as previous experience has shown that appraisal drilling results can give rise to misinterpretations which we are anxious to avoid at this present stage when the public seem quite happy at the way things are going and are looking forward to the commencement of production next January'.[46]

In February 1958, after the ceremony held in Port Harcourt marking Shell-BP's first export shipment of crude oil, Shell-BP noted that its public relations campaign had 'produced results'. This was indicated, the company explained, by 'the general tone of...cautious optimism' displayed in the remarks of the principal Nigerian speakers at the ceremony and in editorial comments from various newspapers, both Nigerian and British.[47] The achievement of this desired tone indicated that the contradictory objectives of managed expectations had been achieved as planned, and that a tangible marker of significant progress, such as Nigeria's first export shipment of oil, could be fitted into Shell-BP's favoured narrative about the hazards and benefits of oil production. The eventual success of managed expectations created an environment in the late 1950s in which the company could exert control over the parameters of its commitment to Nigerian development by making a measured contribution to the national budget, as it did when it concluded an independence settlement with the federal government in 1958–1959.

SHELL-BP'S INDEPENDENCE SETTLEMENT WITH THE FEDERAL GOVERNMENT

A white paper published by the Commonwealth Relations Office (CRO) in 1957 outlined the vital role to be played in economic development by the private sector, both local and foreign.[48] While the CRO intimated that the onus was largely on countries such as Nigeria to attract development finance from foreign companies like Shell-BP, an editorial in the *Pilot* in March 1958 pointed out that it was in oil companies' 'own interest[s]' to conclude a 'wise settlement' with the federal government on issues such as profit sharing.[49] Seeking to strengthen its position by building up 'local goodwill', in 1958–1959 Shell-BP seized the initiative and concluded a two-part independence settlement with the federal government. Addressing two issues connected to development, education and federal revenues, the first part comprised a one-off gift of £500,000 for improvements to technical education and the second a 50/50 profit-sharing agreement with the federal government. Both parts helped Shell-BP demonstrate its role as a partner in Nigeria's development.

The £500,000 gift awarded in January 1958 should be viewed to some degree as an attempt to attain legitimacy by distracting nationalists from their growing impatience for more significant oil revenues at a time when these were still relatively small. It also addressed Shell-BP's poor record on Nigerianisation of technical roles at the company which compared unfavourably with its progress in replacing expatriates in non-technical or managerial roles. From the nationalist perspective the importance of Nigerianisation derived from the nationalist vision of colonial development which prioritised attaining economic independence as soon as possible.[50] Achieving this outcome depended on the expedient appointment of Nigerians to positions of power and responsibility in both the public and private sector. Improvements to technical education had the potential to boost the pace of Nigerianisation of technical roles both at Shell-BP and throughout the wider oil industry.

As Toyin Falola has described, the gift of £500,000 was used for the construction of two new teaching buildings at Yaba Technical Institute in Lagos, while Peter Kilby has noted how a portion was also used to purchase sophisticated equipment for training purposes.[51] Kenneth Younger pointed out that Shell-BP already operated its own trade school in Port Harcourt, covering five trades and enrolling fifty students per year on the three-year City and Guilds accredited course.[52] Shell-BP's decision to fund improvements to technical education in the federally administered national capital, Lagos, was an attempt to balance the bestowal of its favours between the federal and Eastern Region governments, due to the need to attain legitimacy at both the national and regional level. Through its diverse contributions to academic and technical education at different levels, the company protected its entrenched interests. Shell-BP sought to demonstrate that it was attuned and receptive to the development ambitions of ordinary Nigerians and not just the elites and this conveyed the important message that the company was committed to moulding Nigeria's future through funding postcolonial education.

Not only was Shell-BP able to neatly define the parameters of its own commitment to development with this gift, but it was also able to oversee how the money was spent.[53] The *Daily Times* quoted Prime Minister Abubakar Tafawa Balewa, who noted that a condition attached to the gift by Shell-BP was 'that it should be utilised for training Nigerians in those intermediate technical grades which are as essential for economic development as are sergeants and corporals to an army'.[54] While it is not clear if the military metaphor came from Balewa or Shell-BP, this condition stipulated by the company highlighted its belief that Nigerians should resign themselves to being middle-ranking 'officers' in the development of their own country. The implication of this was that expatriates, who made up the vast majority of all the senior technical and management roles in Shell-BP, would continue to operate as high-ranking 'officers' with control over the direction of Nigerian development after independence.

According to the company, the gift was 'a gesture to mark Nigeria's approaching independence', and was received positively by much of the Nigerian media, striking national newspaper headlines and featuring prominently in bulletins aired by the Nigerian Broadcasting Service.[55] Shell-BP recorded editorial tributes from both the *Pilot* and the *Daily Times* which, it stated, complimented the company 'not only for the gift, but for the part which Shell-BP is playing towards the economic, social and educational development of the country'.[56] These tributes linked the gift directly to Nigerian development and there can be little doubt that support from some sections of the media proved immediately useful, serving to dampen the effect of 'an attack on the company' published in the *Eastern Nigeria Guardian* which dealt with the questionable award of transport contracts in Port Harcourt.[57] As reported in the *Pilot*, Prime Minister Balewa explained that an expansion of 'facilities for training Nigerian technicians' was necessary 'as there was evidence of a growing shortage of sub-professional grades which', according to Shell-BP, 'was likely to be a grave handicap to economic development in the future'. He 'welcomed the gift wholeheartedly' and expressed his government's gratitude to Shell-BP. The gift, he explained, was comprised of two £250,000 contributions from Shell-BP's parent companies.[58] He reminded members of the House of Representatives that this was made in addition to the approximately £20,000 per year that Shell and BP had already spent on scholarships for Nigerians.[59] Balewa's response demonstrated how upon making the gift the company attained legitimacy from the prime minister who, in his enthusiastic display of public thanks to Shell-BP and its parent companies, appeared genuinely grateful for the sum. The focus of Balewa's comments, however, particularly his emphasis on Shell's and BP's existing expenditure on education and Nigeria's technical shortcomings, indicate that he was proceeding from notes prepared by Shell-BP, perhaps even as a condition for awarding the gift in the first place. This suggests that the company was concerned that it still had some way to go to attain legitimacy from most of the ordinary members of the House of Representatives. Any genuine dissatisfaction from nationalist politicians at this stage can be attributed, at least in part, to the fact that at this point discussions for a 50/50 profit sharing arrangement between Shell-BP and the federal government were yet to be concluded.

The 50/50 profit sharing arrangement with the federal government, the second part of the independence settlement, was finalised in June 1959. It promised Nigeria an equal share in Shell-BP's profits 'over the long-term'.[60] Although in the short-term the arrangement was largely symbolic, it nevertheless served to inspire hope for the future. Federal Minister of Finance Festus Okotie-Eboh's concluding remark at the signing ceremony was that 50/50 was a 'significant [step] towards achieving economic independence on which... plans for political and social advances greatly depended'. According to the minister, the deal marked 'the beginning of what all hoped would be a "highly profitable partnership" between the federal government and Shell-BP'. Managing Director McGlashan echoed this sentiment, commenting that the arrangement was 'the start of a partnership which all hoped would become increasingly fruitful for Nigeria'. With independence only months away, McGlashan added that 'he and his colleagues would like to be considered as good citizens of Nigeria to be intimately identified with the future of Nigeria which... would follow the "great and historic events of 1960"'.[61] These comments evidenced the two key aims at the centre of Shell-BP's policy on Nigerian development, first to secure a 'partnership' with the federal government, and second to secure 'citizenship' of Nigeria. The achievement of these aims would, it was hoped, help to shore up the company's position both ahead of and after independence.

The idea of a 'partnership' between Shell-BP and Nigeria implied a business relationship mutually beneficial to both parties. In theory 50/50 offered fairer terms to the federal government. Under a revenue sharing formula devised by the Raisman-Tress Commission in 1958, the Nigerian share was to be split between the federal government (20%) and the producing region (50%), with a distributable pool for all regions based on need (30%).[62] In the long term, 50/50 was useful to both federal and regional government development planners as it allowed them to 'plan for future investment on the basis of a stable taxation system' for the oil industry.[63] But in practice in the short term the 50/50 arrangement proved more beneficial to Shell-BP, as it significantly strengthened the company's position ahead of independence with no immediate financial cost. The arrangement bolstered Shell-BP's position by legally binding the federal government in its support for the development of the oil industry and enabled the expansion of the company's interests and operations in the pursuit of greater profits. As detailed in the *Daily Times*, for example, one object of the bill to provide for the 50/50 arrangement, voted on by the House of Representatives in February 1959, was 'to ensure that the development of a flourishing oil industry [would] be facilitated by a realistic fiscal policy'. What's more, if Shell-BP could cast off its colonial identity, changing its image from that of an imperial business to a local Nigerian company that 'intimately identified', as McGlashan hoped in June 1959, 'with the future of Nigeria', then it would have attained legitimacy in its ultimate form.[64] By 1959, the company had already been trying to achieve this outcome for the best part of a decade. Its local incorporation as the Shell D'Arcy Petroleum Development Company of Nigeria Limited in September 1951 (renamed Shell-BP in 1954), followed by the implementation of a limited policy of Nigerianisation, were both efforts aimed at achieving this outcome.[65] Similarly, the company's commitment to purchasing Nigerian goods and materials should be seen as a carefully considered exercise in legitimation. The *Pilot* reported that in the year leading up to independence Shell-BP's 'local purchasing more than trebled in value— from £74,000 to £261,000 a quarter—reaching a grand total of £1,070,401'.[66]

The notion of a 50/50 split in oil profits between Shell-BP and the federal government was based on internationally accepted principles already adhered to by foreign oil companies in many other major oil-producing nation states since the early 1950s.[67] In Nigeria it came about as the result of new local legislation governing income tax for oil companies called the Petroleum Profits Tax Ordinance 1959.[68] Following what had been from the nationalist perspective 'three years of detailed and exacting negotiations', contractual agreements were signed at a ceremony held at the Federal Ministry of Finance on 1 June 1959.[69] In 1952, to incentivise foreign investment in Nigeria, a change had been made in federal income tax law which introduced capital allowances to enable companies to write off their capital costs against taxable profits.[70] After one year the initial rate was given only on further expenditure incurred and the allowance diminished rapidly if no additional expenditure was made.[71] Because of its sustained high levels of capital expenditure over a long period, this formula worked to Shell-BP's advantage. The company's capital allowances had accumulated to £15 million even prior to the discovery of oil in commercially exploitable quantities in 1956, with a further £10 million added before payment was received for its first shipment of oil to Europe in 1958.[72]

The outlook in 1959 was that the reduction in profits tax brought about by capital allowances meant that the government's take would remain 'considerably below' that of Shell-BP's, with full 50/50 profit sharing not expected to be achieved until 1968.[73] Indeed, Shell-BP paid no profits tax at all until 1964. As capital allowances so greatly minimised the short-term impact of the 50/50 deal on the company's finances, the arrangement should be considered a means by which Shell-BP maintained access to independent Nigeria on the cheap. The company was aware of the 'ill effects of capital allowances' on the country, and the impatience that it could give rise to among nationalists, but was careful to divert nationalist attention away from these by emphasising 'the sharp increase in government revenues' which would follow once all capital allowances had finally been absorbed.[74] Profits tax would, the company explained in 1965, eventually make up the biggest share of its future payments to government. Until then, royalties, including a fee for each barrel of oil produced, licence and lease fees, concessional rentals and premiums, and harbour and port dues, would make up the bulk of government oil revenues. These totalled approximately £18 million (gross) up to end of 1964.[75]

The notion of gaining 'citizenship' implied that Shell-BP might enjoy a new status as a naturalised entity. In short, the 50/50 arrangement was Shell-BP's passport to 'citizenship' of an independent Nigeria. Furthermore, just as with actual citizenship, the arrangement did provide Shell-BP with certain rights and protections. For instance, as the *Daily Times* explained, the arrangement 'provide[d] that except for royalties and rents payable under the terms of any licence or leases and except for the tax payable under the ordinance no tax … shall be imposed on profits under any other ordinance or law in Nigeria'.[76] Shell-BP was protected against the 'disproportionate imposition… [by] any government or… district or local government authority in Nigeria' of any tax, duty, or rate which might discriminate against it, either directly or indirectly. In other words, the company was shielded by the federal government against the levying of extra taxes by the governments of the regions in which it operated. In addition to the terms of the 50/50 arrangement, 'the company had also volunteered to pay royalty at 12½ per cent on the value of oil won instead of the flat rate of 4s. per ton which has been payable to date'.[77] This gesture also fitted in with the notion of actual citizenship, specifically the duty or obligation to serve the interests of one's country. In this case, Shell-BP served Nigerian interests by modernising an outdated and exploitative agreement. The new terms provided for a relatively small but ready source of income with the potential to increase if oil values rose. This came at a time when, as noted in the *Manchester Guardian*, 'any additional source of revenue [was] welcome to Nigeria as a whole […]'.[78] In the *Pilot*, it was noted that this voluntary agreement was made 'in order that enhanced benefits might be seen by Nigerians to flow from the increasing volume of oil now being won'.[79] It promised to help alleviate nationalist impatience to stabilise the economy and finance development using more predictable revenues from oil. Increased royalty payments, along with regular rent payments, customs and harbour dues, were, Okotie-Eboh argued, 'substantial advantages for Nigeria'. The finance minister asserted that they 'enable[d] Nigeria to plan for increasing revenues steadily in the coming years against the uncertainty of being left in hope of a sudden windfall at some future date which "cannot at present be forecast"'.[80] However, despite the additional voluntary agreements concluded by Shell-BP, the firm's capital allowances continued to pose problems for Nigeria by reducing government revenues at a time when the country was struggling to raise the necessary levels of finance to fund its first post-independence development programme.

SHELL-BP's ADVANCE/LOAN DEAL WITH THE FEDERAL GOVERNMENT

Having strengthened its position through its independence settlement with the federal government in 1958–1959, Shell-BP's susceptibility to nationalist pressure increased throughout the early and mid-1960s, first as competition in the Nigerian oil industry grew, and second as the federal government struggled to raise the finance needed for its Six-Year Development Plan. But in both cases Shell-BP was ultimately able to manage this pressure to its own advantage.

Regardless of the benefits accruing to the company through its 'first mover advantage', the influx of multiple foreign competitors between 1960 and 1962 had ended the effective monopoly enjoyed by Shell-BP throughout the colonial period and made it much less sure-footed.[81] According to Roland Ubogu, the increasing number of concession holders 'improved the negotiating position of the federal government with the oil companies, placing the former in a position where it c[ould] more or less dictate its terms'.[82] In August 1964, Federal Minister of Finance Okotie-Eboh announced an export duty on crude oil and demanded an extra £15 million from the oil industry over the next two and a half years (i.e. in addition to expected revenues).[83] Nevertheless, along with other members of the Nigerian oil industry, Shell-BP was able to convince the federal government to abandon its proposals for an export duty, forcing it to recognise that it would be a 'dis-incentive to the growth of industry and would thus not be in the best interests of Nigeria'.[84]

The Six-Year Development Plan had been introduced in 1964. To finance it, Nigeria aimed to raise a total of £1.2 billion, with half coming from the federal and regional governments and half from overseas contributions. In addition to a £10 million loan for projects agreed in the first two years, the British government committed to a £1.5 million loan for steel rails, a pledge of up to £5 million for the Niger Dam, 'a £5 million grant for capital expenditure on institutions of higher education', and technical assistance estimated to cost £500,000 a year.[85] Falola has argued that the intellectual and technical foundations for development planning in Nigeria in the 1960s were provided by the development plans of the 1940s and 1950s, with post-independence plans borrowing extensively from colonial ones.[86] The British Treasury's initial backing for Nigeria's Six-Year Development Plan seems to support this model of continuity. At first the Treasury complimented Nigeria on a 'well-conceived and... not wildly optimistic' plan which, with its emphasis on agriculture, productive industry, and technical education, was, in its emulation of previous colonial development plans, 'sound'.[87] By 1964, however, when the Treasury believed that Federal Minister of Finance Okotie-Eboh was seeking a British guarantee for a further £40 million between 1964 and 1968, it was less supportive. Treasury officials complained that federal government proposals to invest more in infrastructure and less in agriculture and education had 'distorted' the plan.[88] The Treasury was expressing its displeasure that Nigeria had deviated from colonial precedents to pursue its own development priorities instead of those prescribed by the metropole. It also noted how progress with raising external funding during the first two years had been slow.[89]

In July 1964, the British government refused to commit further funds to the development plan except for a tentative £15 million loan for a telecommunications scheme. This decision came down to British self-interest and the desire for control. The telecommunications scheme was deemed worthy of investment only because 'British industry [was] well placed to bid for the business' and plans had been 'fully worked out' and could, therefore, be appraised by the British in advance.[90] Additional reasons against further commitments included the slow pace at which Nigeria had disbursed previous British aid and Britain's own balance of payments which the Treasury asserted meant that it could not, despite Nigerian protestations, make any loans to cover the local costs of development.[91] As already indicated, capital allowances had also prevented the federal and regional governments from benefiting as much as they had hoped from Shell-BP's investment during the crucial financing stage of the Six-Year Development Plan.

In these circumstances the federal government was faced with an 'extreme shortage of funds'. Okotie-Eboh informed Shell-BP that a shortfall in development finance was 'compelling the country to draw heavily on its reserves'.[92] The reserves of the regions' agricultural marketing boards, for instance, had been swiftly drained by several early post-independence capital projects, while their surpluses had ceased as early as 1962–1963.[93] The British Treasury blamed the shortfall on lower than anticipated rates of investment from the federal and regional governments. To explain this the Treasury cited a number of factors, including a 'sharp decline in executive capacity in the Nigerian administration' due to the departure of expatriates, 'the inefficiency and venality of ministers', rising external debt, and increased government costs due to the wage awards conceded following the 1964 Morgan Report.[94] Released on 27 May 1964, the Morgan Report evaluated and made recommendations on wages/salaries and other conditions of service for workers in the public and private sectors.[95] In the Treasury's opinion, then, Nigeria was characterised as suffering from a lack of British oversight following decolonisation. Shell-BP similarly suspected that the wage awards had had an impact on available finance, a point firmly denied by Okotie-Eboh. Instead, the minister claimed that the shortfall had arisen due to the federal government's inability to raise half of the total costs of the plan from overseas contributions.[96] Ultimately it was lower than anticipated rates of investment from the federal and regional governments *and* from external sources that contributed to the shortfall. According to the British Treasury, Okotie-Eboh's claim was inevitable as the Nigerians were 'inclined… to attribute the disappointing progress of the plan' not only 'to a shortfall in foreign aid', but also to 'the difficulty of obtaining it on suitable terms (by which [Nigeria] will mean, in this context untied)'.[97] The issue of untied or unconditional aid was a sore point for the Treasury, which, in aiming to maintain British influence and protect the large British export trade, wanted to determine exactly which projects British finance would be used for and what role British firms would be able to play in them.[98] The Treasury's insistence on tied or conditional aid demonstrated how imperial businesses like Shell-BP were set to benefit financially from post-independence British influence purchased in this way.

Less than a month after Chancellor of the Exchequer Reginald Maudling's refusal to inject more British cash into the current plan, the federal government turned directly, for the first time, to the oil industry for financial assistance. Maudling and the British Treasury inadvertently played a significant role, therefore, in reducing the British government's direct influence over Nigerian economic affairs while increasing that wielded by Shell-BP. The company committed to an advance/loan deal of £15 million, paying out its first of three scheduled instalments of £5 million in 1964. This conveyed to nationalists the company's preparedness to immediately co-operate with and assist the country's development by providing a more stable and predictable income. Lagos director Fleming argued that Shell-BP's commitment 'enable[d] oil companies and particularly ourselves to be seen to be helpful in a very difficult stage of Nigeria's development'.[99] Managing Director Gray understood the importance to the federal government of the advance/loan deal as a means for bridging the gap in finance for the Six-Year Development Plan.[100] Compared to the 50/50 arrangement agreed in 1959, which promised the federal government and, after the redistribution of cash through the revenue sharing formula, the regional governments, an eventual equal share of the company's profits sometime in the future, the advance/loan deal provided a more immediate cash-injection exclusively for the federal government. Gray explained that this was because while Shell-BP's 'regular payments tend to get siphoned off in recurrent expenditures either regional or federal', the £15 million advance/loan 'contributes directly to [the] federal capital development fund'.[101]

Okotie-Eboh's demand for more money had initially been levelled at the whole oil industry. However, 'black gold hype' combined with nationalist perceptions of Shell-BP as the 'doyen of the Nigerian oil producing companies', and the supposed inability of its less well-established competitors to contribute at this time (Shell-BP was the only company producing oil) focused pressure for an advance/loan specifically on Shell-BP.[102] In August 1964, T. R. Grieve, Shell's regional co-ordinator (oil) for the UK and Eire, described how he was 'disappointed to see' that Shell-BP was being disproportionately affected by the federal government's demands. This, he asserted, 'constitute[d] a penalty on the pioneers'.[103] However, Shell-BP's monopolisation of specialist knowledge gave it some room for manoeuvre. For example, the company was in possession of data which suggested that the federal government could expect to receive a further £16.09 million in oil revenues over the next three years compared to earlier lower figures forecast by Shell-BP. By concealing this new data, Shell-BP could avoid committing the company 'to maximum envisaged potential' and push through its preferred option of providing advances on oil revenues to the federal government under the terms of the new £15 million advance/loan deal.[104]

Moreover, the advance/loan route was preferable for Shell-BP, as central to the £15 million deal was the re-assertion of the partnership between Shell-BP and the federal government, first introduced with the 50/50 arrangement, and the guarantee that government would do all within its power to assist the expansion of the oil industry.[105] The company could now confidently refer to itself not only as a development partner of government but 'Nigeria's partner in progress', stating that what was in the best interests of Shell-BP was also in the best interests of the country.[106] Shell-BP was promulgating the idea that Nigeria's economic development was pegged principally to the fortunes of the oil industry, an idea later lent credence by a report on Nigeria's economic prospects published by the World Bank in 1966. The report's balance of payments section detailed 'high and low estimates of gross proceeds from oil exports', concluding that the Nigerian oil industry's prospects were 'phenomenal'.[107] This assessment provided a degree of justification both for the 'black gold hype' that had enveloped the Nigerian oil industry for the past decade and for Shell-BP's optimistic forecasts as part of its public relations policy of managed expectations.[108] More significantly, it justified the pressure applied to Shell-BP by nationalists for a greater commitment to development. The *Pilot* had seemingly been correct in January 1958, when it had stated that 'the vital role of the oil industry [and, therefore, of Shell-BP] in the Nigerian economy steadily increases in importance as the country's development progresses'.[109] With this new, stronger relationship, Shell-BP could secure its own future by continuing to foster Nigerian economic dependence on oil as a means to stabilise the economy and finance development.

CONCLUSIONS

In the transitional period before and after decolonisation, Shell-BP sought to consolidate its position in Nigeria and achieve some 'legitimacy' in the newly independent state. It was able to use Nigerian hopes that oil revenues would help fund the country's economic development to promote itself as a 'partner' in development, even though, for much of the period,

Shell-BP's level of economic activity was relatively small. Even in the mid-1960s, after oil production began to take off in both the Eastern and Mid-Western Regions, revenues remained relatively low. Prior to independence in the absence of significant income, the company looked to strengthen its position through its independence settlement with the federal government. This included a gift of £500,000 for the improvement of technical education and a new 50/50 profit-sharing arrangement. The latter laid the foundations for a 'partnership in progress' between Shell-BP and the federal government.[110] While the federal government had its say, the company was very influential in deciding the details of this settlement—and in many ways it played to its advantage. Throughout, Shell-BP consistently emphasised its commitment and contribution to development. But defining the parameters of its own commitment to development was a process over which the company tried to exert as much control as possible. Shell-BP was set to benefit from post-independence British government influence over Nigerian economic affairs. However, the company gained more influence of its own in 1964 when the British Treasury refused to commit itself to additional aid. At the federal government's insistence, Shell-BP filled the development finance void left by the British government by agreeing an advance/loan deal against future oil revenues. For a time, Federal Minister of Finance Okotie-Eboh increased nationalists' power to determine the company's level of commitment to development, and to make oil revenues more predictable. Shell-BP used the 1964 advance/loan deal to its own advantage, however, by casting itself in the role of 'Nigeria's partner in progress'. The firm convincingly argued that what was in the best interests of the company was in the best interests of the country, thus promulgating the idea that the pace and progress of Nigerian economic development was dependent on the fortunes of the oil industry and its own continued success.[111] This legitimised Shell-BP but marked the beginning of Nigeria's economic dependence on oil, the detrimental effects of which are still felt to this day.

NOTES

1. *The Shell-BP Story* (1965), p. 7, BP 106485, BP Archive, University of Warwick, Coventry (hereafter BPA).
2. Stephanie Decker, 'Building Up Goodwill: British Business, Development and Economic Nationalism in Ghana and Nigeria, 1945–1977' (unpublished PhD thesis, University of Liverpool, 2006), p. 3.

3. For example, see: HL Deb (6 May 1942), vol. 122, cc885–943, https://api.parliament.uk/historic-hansard/lords/1942/may/06/colonial-administration (accessed 27 May 2019); HC Deb (26 Nov. 1942), vol. 385, cc905–976, https://api.parliament.uk/historic-hansard/commons/1942/nov/26/colonial-development (accessed 27 May 2019).
4. *Daily Times* (Lagos), 16007 (7 Nov. 1959), p. 2, British Library, London (hereafter BL).
5. *West African Pilot* (Lagos), XXII/6593 (2 Jun. 1959), p. 1, BL.
6. https://www.winton.com/longer-view/cocoas-bittersweet-bounty (accessed 27 May 2019); https://www.macrotrends.net/1369/crude-oil-price-history-chart (accessed 27 May 2019); Daniel Yergin, *The Prize: The Epic Quest for Oil, Money and Power* (Simon & Schuster: London, 1991), p. 529.
7. Requests for Financial Aid from Nigeria (undated, c. Oct. 1957), CO 554/1794, The National Archives, London (hereafter TNA).
8. Decker, 'Building Up Goodwill' (PhD), p. 16.
9. Toyin Falola, *Development Planning and Decolonization in Nigeria* (Gainesville, FL, 1996), p. 177.
10. *Daily Times*, 16007 (7 Nov. 1959), p. 1, BL.
11. *West African Pilot*, XXI/6227 (31 Jan. 1958), p. 2, BL.
12. *West African Pilot*, XXII/6593 (2 Jun. 1959), p. 1, BL.
13. *West African Pilot*, XXI/6205 (6 Jan. 1958), p. 2, BL; XXI/6221 (24 Jan. 1958), p. 2; XXI/6227 (31 Jan. 1958), p. 2.
14. Shell-BP press cutting, *Manchester Guardian* (18 Feb. 1958), BP 18273, BPA; Shell-BP Annual Report 1960, Profit & Loss Account, BP 101686, BPA.
15. T. Falola, *The History of Nigeria* (Westport, CT, 1999), p. 134.
16. Capitalisation appears in original source. *Daily Times*, 14390 (18 Feb. 1958), p. 5, BL.
17. *West African Pilot*, XXII/6584 (22 May 1959), p. 2, BL.
18. *West African Pilot*, XXI/6227 (31 Jan. 1958), p. 2, BL.
19. Nuttall (Ministry of Fuel and Power) to Stokes (Shell) (27 Sep. 1950), BP 60555, BPA. Construction of the refinery was completed in 1965.
20. *West African Pilot*, XXII/6586 (25 May 1959), p. 1, BL.
21. Andrew Walker, 'The day oil was discovered in Nigeria', http://news.bbc.co.uk/1/hi/world/africa/7840310.stm (accessed 18 Sept. 2017). Oil workers used houseboats to explore the Delta.
22. *Daily Times*, 14265 (24 Sep. 1957), p. 5, BL.
23. Jêdrzej George Frynas, Matthias P. Beck & Kamel Mellahi, 'Maintaining Corporate Dominance: the 'first mover advantage' of Shell-BP in Nigeria', *Review of African Political Economy*, vol. 27, no 85 (2000), pp. 407–425, esp. 408, 409; Phia Steyn, 'Oil Exploration in Colonial Nigeria, c.

1903–1958', *The Journal of Imperial and Commonwealth History*, 37/2 (2009), pp. 249–274, p. 267.

24. John McVean Luard, Memorandum (30 July 1964), BP 125318, BPA.

25. 'On the most basic level, [the] concept [of the first mover advantage] suggests that pioneering firms are able to obtain positive economic profits as the consequence of early market entry, that means profits in excess of the cost of capital'. Frynas *et al*, 'Maintaining Corporate Dominance After Decolonisation', pp. 407–408.

26. J. McVean Luard, Memorandum (30 Jul. 1964), BP 125318, BPA.

27. CO press cutting, *West Africa* (London), 2195 (9 May 1959), CO 1029/255, TNA.

28. *Daily Times*, 16007 (7 Nov. 1959), pp. 1–2, BL.

29. Shell-BP press cutting, *The Times* (London), 'British Colonies Review First Quarter 1958', BP 18273, BPA.

30. *West African Pilot*, XXI/6244 (20 Feb. 1958), p. 2, BL.

31. *West African Pilot*, XXIII/6834 (12 Mar. 1960), p. 8, BL.

32. *The Shell-BP Story* (1965), p. 3, BP 106485, BPA; ibid.

33. General Monthly Progress Report (Mar. 1955), p. 1, BP 44655, BPA.

34. General Monthly Progress Report (Nov. 1957), p. 2, BP 44724, BPA; Steyn, 'Oil Exploration in Colonial Nigeria', p. 264.

35. General Monthly Progress Report (Feb. 1958), BP 44723, BPA.

36. Decker, 'Building Up Goodwill' (PhD), p. 93.

37. General Monthly Progress Report (Sep. 1955), p. 1, BP 44655, BPA.

38. General Monthly Progress Report (Mar. 1957), p. 2, BP 44653, BPA.

39. *West African Pilot*, XX/6067 (29 Jul. 1957), p. 2, BL.

40. The difficulty of Nigeria's terrain, particularly of the swampy Niger Delta, was mentioned often by Shell-BP. See, for example, *West African Pilot*, XXII/6685 (19 Sep. 1959), p. 8, BL; Shell-BP press cutting, *Daily Telegraph* (UK) (24 Sep. 1959), BP 18273, BPA.

41. General Monthly Progress Report (May 1959), p. 1, BP 44720, BPA.

42. *The Shell-BP Story* (1965), p. 3, BP 106485, BPA.

43. *West African Pilot*, XVIII/5430 (12 Jul. 1955), p. 2, BL.

44. General Monthly Progress Report (Dec. 1956), p. 2, BP 44654, BPA.

45. *West African Pilot*, XX/6019 (3 Jun. 1957), p. 2, BL.

46. General Monthly Progress Report (Aug. 1957), p. 2, BP 44653, BPA.

47. General Monthly Progress Report (Feb. 1958), BP 44723, BPA.

48. Barrie Ireton, *Britain's International Development Policies: A History of DFID and Overseas Aid* (Basingstoke, 2013), p. 21.

49. *West African Pilot*, XXI/6271 (24 Mar. 1958), p. 2, BL.

50. Decker, 'Building Up Goodwill' (PhD), p. 238.

51. Falola, *Development Planning*, p. 150; Peter Kilby, *Industrialization in an Open Economy: Nigeria, 1945–1960* (London, 1969), p. 261.

52. Kenneth Younger, *The Public Service in New States* (London, 1960), p. 48.
53. *West African Pilot*, XXI/6383 (5 Aug. 1958), p. 1, BL.
54. *Daily Times*, 14533 (7 Aug. 1958), p. 1, BL.
55. *West African Pilot*, XXI/6383 (5 Aug. 1958), p. 1, BL; General Monthly Progress Report (Aug. 1958), p. 1, BP 44722, BPA.
56. General Monthly Progress Report, ibid.
57. *West African Pilot*, XXI/6383 (5 Aug. 1958), p. 1, BL; *Daily Times*, 14533 (7 Aug. 1958), p. 1, BL; ibid.
58. *West African Pilot*, ibid.
59. Ibid.; *Daily Times*, 14533 (7 Aug. 1958), p. 1, BL.
60. *West African Pilot*, XXII/6593 (2 Jun. 1959), p. 1, BL.
61. Ibid.
62. Shell-BP press cutting, *Petroleum Press Service* (Apr. 1959), BP 18273, BPA.
63. *West African Pilot*, XXII/6593 (2 Jun. 1959), p. 1, BL.
64. *Daily Times*, 14693 (24 Feb. 1959), p. 1, BL.
65. Steyn, 'Oil Exploration in Colonial Nigeria', p. 265.
66. *West African Pilot*, XXIII/6928 (2 Jul. 1960), p. 5, BL.
67. Venezuela was the first country to adopt 50/50 profit sharing with foreign oil companies, in 1948. The arrangement spread to the Middle East in the 1950s, beginning with Saudi Arabia (1950), and then Kuwait (1951), Iraq and Qatar (1952), and Iran (1954). Marius S. Vassiliou, *Historical Dictionary of the Petroleum Industry* (Lanham, MD, 2009), p. xxxvi; James H. Bamberg, *The History of the British Petroleum Company: British Petroleum and Global Oil, 1950–1975: The Challenge of Nationalism* (Cambridge, 2000), p. 38.
68. Income Tax—the 50/50 Principle in Nigeria (Oct. 1963), p. 1, BP 51907, BPA.
69. *West African Pilot*, XXII/6593 (2 Jun. 1959), p. 1, BL.
70. T. Falola, *Economic Reforms and Modernization in Nigeria, 1945–1965* (Kent, OH, 2004), p. 84.
71. Report of Investigation made by the Oil Taxation Study Group (1958), CO 1029/257, TNA.
72. *The Shell-BP Story* (1965), pp. 37, 38, BP 106485, BPA.
73. Parry to Easton (18 Nov. 1965), BP 51935, BPA; Davies to Steel (3 Dec. 1965), BP 51935, BPA.
74. Text of message from Shell, London to Shell-BP, Port Harcourt (30 Sep. 1965), BP 42028, BPA.
75. *The Shell-BP Story* (1965), pp. 31, 35–36, BP 106485, BPA.
76. *Daily Times*, 14774 (2 Jun. 1959), p. 3, BL.
77. Ibid.

78. Shell-BP press cutting, *Manchester Guardian* (18 Feb. 1958), BP 18273, BPA.
79. *West African Pilot*, XXII/6593 (2 Jun. 1959), p. 1, BL.
80. Ibid.
81. Frynas *et al*, 'Maintaining Corporate Dominance After Decolonisation', pp. 407–425.
82. Roland Ubogu, 'Mining and Quarrying', in Olaloku (ed.), *Structure of the Nigerian Economy*, p. 56.
83. Watson to Banks (19 Aug. 1964), BP 125318, BPA.
84. Fleming (Shell-BP) to Grieve (Shell) (20 Aug. 1964), BP 125318, BPA.
85. Nigeria: Future Aid Brief (6 Jul. 1964), p. 6, T 317/424, TNA.
86. Falola, *Development Planning*, p. xxii.
87. Aid to Nigeria—Brief (Jul. 1964), I—The Development Plan, 1962–1968, T 317/424, TNA.
88. Nigeria: Future Aid Brief (6 Jul. 1964), p. 6, T 317/424, TNA.
89. Aid to Nigeria—Brief (Jul. 1964), I—The Development Plan, 1962–1968, T 317/424, TNA.
90. Watson to Banks (19 Aug. 1964), BP 125318, BPA.
91. Nigeria: Future Aid Brief (6 Jul. 1964), p. 6, T 317/424, TNA; Maudling to Okotie-Eboh, ibid.
92. Watson to Banks (19 Aug. 1964), BP 125318, BPA.
93. Siyanbola Tomori, 'Agriculture, Forestry and Fishing', in F. Akin Olaloku (ed.), *Structure of the Nigerian Economy* (The Macmillan Press Ltd: London & Basingstoke, 1979), pp. 16–17.
94. Aid to Nigeria—Brief (Jul. 1964), I—The Development Plan, 1962–1968, T 317/424, TNA.
95. *Report of the Commission on the Review of Wages, Salaries and Conditions of Service of the Junior Employees of the Governments of the Federation and in Private Establishments, 1963–1964* (Federal Ministry of Information: Lagos, 1964).
96. Milne (Shell-BP) to Robertson (5 Aug. 1964), BP 125318, BPA.
97. Nigeria: Future Aid Brief (6 Jul. 1964), p. 2, T 317/424, TNA; Okotie-Eboh told Shell-BP that funds had been diverted to the defence budget, although this was not mentioned in the Treasury's brief. Telegram, Milne (Shell-BP) to Robertson (5 Aug. 1964), BP 125318, BPA.
98. Maudling to Okotie-Eboh (22 Jul. 1964), T 317/424, TNA.
99. Fleming (Shell-BP) to Grieve (Shell) (20 Aug. 1964), BP 125318, BPA.
100. Copy of a cable received [by BP] from Gray (Shell-BP) on the question of bridging finance (undated, 1966), BP 42028, BPA.
101. Ibid.
102. J. McVean Luard, Memorandum (30 July 1964), BP 125318, BPA; Fleming (Shell-BP) to Grieve (Shell) (20 Aug. 1964), BP 125318, BPA.

103. Grieve (Shell) to Fleming (Shell-BP) (13 Aug. 1964), BP 125318, BPA.
104. Fleming (Shell-BP) to Grieve (Shell) (7 Aug. 1964), BP 125318, BPA.
105. Fleming (Shell-BP) to Grieve (Shell) (20 Aug. 1964), BP 125318, BPA.
106. *The Shell-BP Story* (1965), p. 5, BP 106485, BPA.
107. World Bank report discussed in Parry to Gamble (BP) (12 Jan. 1966), BP 42028, BPA.
108. *The Shell-BP Story* (1965), p. 3, BP 106485, BPA.
109. *West African Pilot*, XXI/6221 (24 Jan. 1958), p. 2, BL.
110. *The Shell-BP Story* (1965), p. 5, BP 106485, BPA.
111. Ibid.

REFERENCES

Bamberg, James H., *The History of the British Petroleum Company: British Petroleum and Global Oil, 1950–1975: The Challenge of Nationalism* (Cambridge University Press, Cambridge, 2000).

Decker, Stephanie, 'Building Up Goodwill: British Business, Development and Economic Nationalism in Ghana and Nigeria, 1945–1977' (unpublished PhD thesis, the University of Liverpool, 2006).

Falola, Toyin, *Development Planning and Decolonization in Nigeria* (University Press of Florida, Gainesville, FL, 1996).

Falola, Toyin, *The History of Nigeria* (Greenwood Press, Westport, CT, 1999).

Frynas, Jêdrzej George, Matthias P. Beck, and Kamel Mellahi, 'Maintaining Corporate Dominance: The 'First Mover Advantage' of Shell-BP in Nigeria", *Review of African Political Economy*, 27, no. 85 (2000), pp. 407–425.

Ireton, Barry, *Britain's International Development Policies: A History of DFID and Overseas Aid* (Palgrave Macmillan, Basingstoke, 2013).

Kilby, Peter, *Industrialization in an Open Economy: Nigeria, 1945–1960* (The Syndics of the Cambridge University Press, London, 1969).

Steyn, Phia, 'Oil Exploration in Colonial Nigeria, c.1903–1958', *The Journal of Imperial and Commonwealth History*, 37, no. 2 (2009), pp. 249–274.

Tomori, Siyanbola, 'Agriculture, Forestry and Fishing', in F. Akin Olaloku (ed.), *Structure of the Nigerian Economy* (The Macmillan Press Ltd., London and Basingstoke, 1979).

Ubogu, Roland, 'Mining and Quarrying', in F. Akin Olaloku (ed.), *Structure of the Nigerian Economy* (The Macmillan Press Ltd., London and Basingstoke, 1979).

Vassiliou, Marius S., *Historical Dictionary of the Petroleum Industry* (The Scarecrow Press, Inc., Lanham, MD, 2009).

Yergin, Daniel, *The Prize: The Epic Quest for Oil, Money and Power* (Simon & Schuster, London, 1991).

Younger, Kenneth, *The Public Service in New States* (Oxford University Press, London, 1960).

CHAPTER 7

The 'Know-How of the World is Mainly with Private Companies': The Commonwealth Development Corporation and British Business in Post-Colonial Africa

Sarah Stockwell

The connections between British overseas development aid and business in the post-colonial era have primarily been considered in relation to 'tied aid',[1] and mostly with reference to the later 1970s and the 1980s when British governments sought to make British aid work more closely in support of British commercial, as well as political, interests.[2] But an equally intimate association between British governmental aid and British business existed in relation to the activities of the Commonwealth Development Corporation (CDC).

Formed in 1948 as the Colonial Development Corporation, the Corporation was established in the context of the severe post-war 'dollar gap' to facilitate the development of colonial resources. Although initially

S. Stockwell (✉)
King's College London, London, UK
e-mail: sarah.stockwell@kcl.ac.uk

© The Author(s) 2020
V. Dimier, S. Stockwell (eds.), *The Business of Development in Post-Colonial Africa*, Cambridge Imperial and Post-Colonial Studies Series, https://doi.org/10.1007/978-3-030-51106-7_7

prevented from taking on new projects in countries once they became independent, in 1963 the Colonial Development Corporation was restyled the Commonwealth Development Corporation and its geographical field of operation extended to most independent Commonwealth states. In 1969 this was further widened to include other developing countries. By then CDC had acquired an extensive and varied portfolio of investments, ranging from smallholder agricultural schemes to housing finance, and had created a cadre of territorially based development companies to promote new industries in developing countries.[3] It was part of the UK's aid programme, but operated on a semi-commercial basis, being required to break even or better. By the early 1990s its annual operating surplus was nearly £100 million, and its commercial nature was recognised in 1999 when it became the CDC Group plc, wholly owned by the British government. This chapter, however, focuses not on the Corporation's hybrid character, but on its association with the British private sector, which saw it partner overseas with some of the most familiar British firms of the colonial era. The chapter principally discusses the 1960s, when Africa (continuing a trajectory from the 1950s) constituted CDC's most important geographical region of operation, and investment in projects in collaboration with the private sector became an increasingly significant part of CDC's portfolio.

CDC has received surprisingly little attention from historians, with most historical analysis concentrated on the Corporation's chequered early years in the late 1940s and very early 1950s when project failures and management problems nearly led to its demise.[4] Three institutional histories, however, are valuable for understanding CDC's subsequent evolution.[5] Of these, Michael McWilliams' account in particular discusses contemporary debates about the Corporation's semi-commercial nature. But CDC's partnership with British firms remains largely below the scholarly radar—probably because projects involving British private enterprise were always a minority element in the Corporation's overall portfolio and were not among those areas (like smallholder schemes) with which its reputation became most bound up.

This chapter shows that in its choice of private sector partners the CDC was not required to favour British firms over other foreign businesses: indeed CDC was quite promiscuous in the variety and national origin of organisations with which it partnered. Moreover, in contrast to its French equivalent, the Caisse centrale de coopération économique, CDC's funds were not tied to the purchase of metropolitan goods or services.[6] CDC's priority was to promote economic development in recipient countries while ensuring its own investments were commercially sound. Nevertheless, there was a broad understanding that British aid should, where possible, benefit British trade and industry, and CDC itself instrumentalised claims that it could assist British exports in ongoing struggles with the Treasury to secure its own financial base. Analysing the relationship between CDC and British business also highlights underlying structural factors that, as we shall see, worked in favour of British companies when the funding organisation in question was British. The nexus between CDC and British private enterprise illustrates one hitherto under-recognised way in which, in a globalising world where companies no longer had all the privileges they had previously enjoyed under colonialism, British overseas aid could (intentionally or otherwise) advance the position of British business interests in colonies and former colonies.

CDC and the Benefits of Partnership with Private Enterprise

That CDC should come to work so closely with business (whether British or of other national origin) might have surprised some observers of its early history. CDC was the initiative of the post-war Labour government. It was intended to supplement rather than replace the private sector, investing in projects where business was reluctant to do so. But such was the initial concern in the City that CDC represented an intrusion by a public body into a sphere that was properly the preserve of private enterprise that the Colonial Office (CO) sent its financial adviser to reassure business leaders at a meeting at Unilever House. Problems encountered early in the Corporation's history encouraged a shift towards more extensive collaboration with the private sector. In its first three years CDC's board of directors approved investment in 50 projects in 20 colonies, stretching the Corporation's resources beyond capacity. Begun in haste, too many of these projects were (like the notorious Tanganyika groundnut scheme of CDC's sister organisation, the Overseas Food Corporation) ill-conceived and poorly managed. By the end of 1950 only eight projects were making a profit, and CDC's losses amounted to £1.7 million. This disastrous record led to the departure of the Corporation's first chair. CDC itself secured a reprieve under a new chairman, Lord Reith, best known as the first director-general of the BBC. Reith reviewed the

Corporation's project portfolio and streamlined the Corporation's structures, establishing a small executive management board as well as a chain of regional controllers resident overseas who would be responsible for projects in their regions.[7]

Most importantly, it was apparent that CDC could not continue to manage so many projects itself: it needed to operate more in partnership with others. The CDC Board decided that where possible it should 'look for experienced private enterprise partners' to invest in and share management of its projects.[8] 'Experienced management was to be an essential requirement [of future projects]', write Brain and Cable in their official history of CDC, and 'in practice, this normally meant going to the private sector, those involved being encouraged to take a small stake in ownership as a demonstration of their commitment'.[9] The election in October 1951 of a Conservative government gave greater impetus to this new direction.[10] As a result, in the 1950s CDC increasingly shifted the model under which it provided capital from equity investment to loans, a development that prompted criticism from Labour politicians, and led to an unsuccessful attempt to amend the 1956 Overseas Resources Development Bill to try to get CDC to limit its business to enterprises under its own control.[11]

During the years that followed CDC's reorientation under Reith it entered into partnership with an array of companies. Capital invested in the form of loans or shares in associated companies consequently came to represent a higher proportion of CDC's total investment, rising from approximately 33% of CDC's existing investments in 1959 to around 40% in 1971. At the same time, the proportion of capital invested in CDC's directly managed projects and subsidiaries contracted, while that loaned to government and public authorities declined slightly.[12] By 1975 more than one third of CDC's projects—some 90 of 240—involved association with the private sector.[13]

For CDC, the strategy proved commercially sound. The Corporation returned a profit for the first time in 1955 and continued to do so thereafter. As projects became established and began generating a return, income increased; at the same time, the Corporation began receiving the return on loans it had advanced, often under terms that allowed for an initial deferral of repayment to permit projects to begin generating income. Through the 1960s its net remittances of funds back to the UK balanced its award of funds to new projects or further investment in those already established.[14] In 1965 CDC averaged a rate of return of between 6.5 and 7.0 % on capital invested in Africa.[15] This compares not unfavourably with the average real rate of return on European investment in Africa, recently calculated to have been around 10% in the 1960s.[16] Between 1968 and 1972 interest profits and dividends on CDC investments (after interest had been deducted on the advances CDC had received from the UK Exchequer) rose nearly five-fold from £1.1 to £5.3 million.[17]

It was by no means the case that partnership with the private sector guaranteed success. CDC sustained some significant losses, but there were notable successes as projects previously struggling were quickly turned around. East Africa Industries Ltd. (EAI) provides one illustration. This had been one of CDC's first ventures, acquired in 1949 after the Kenyan government approached CDC with a request that it take over the struggling EAI, a collection of state-owned import-substituting industries begun during the Second World War. Under CDC EAI was refocused around the production of vegetable oils. In 1952 EAI's enterprises were still struggling. In that year, after the disposal and re-evaluation of some assets, CDC made a loss on EAI of over £31,000, and it began entering into 'partnership talks'.[18] Sir William Rendell, who became General Manager of CDC, notes in his history of the Corporation that at this point EAI 'had the good fortune' to prove attractive to the Anglo-Dutch combine, Unilever.[19] It was also to Unilever's good fortune, although David Fieldhouse observes that when Unilever was first approached to assess the prospects for the local manufacture of margarine, it was 'anything but enthusiastic'. However, as he also shows, Unilever had already explored possibilities for manufacturing in East Africa and, once it became evident that CDC was willing to partner with commercial firms, Unilever was able to propose an arrangement by which it would be able to operate a plant under its own management.[20] A Unilever executive visited EAI in October 1952 to assess the potential of the East African market. He calculated that by manufacturing locally, Unilever could price its products more competitively, and, by extending EAI's existing operations from the manufacture of edible oils to soap, could generate healthy profits.[21]

In 1953 Unilever took a 50% equity share in EAI and assumed managerial responsibility from CDC. The original owners, CDC and the Industrial Management Corporation (owned by the Kenyan government), retained a third and a sixth respectively of the remaining equity. EAI also had a £35,000 loan from CDC. Under Unilever's management, EAI at once embarked on the construction of a margarine factory, followed by a new soap and glycerine plant to manufacture Unilever brands including Blue Band margarine (introduced in 1956), Lux soap (1958), and Omo washing powder (1967) to sell throughout East Africa.[22] The company's net profits immediately began to rise, and, as anticipated, its entry into soap manufacturing proved particularly lucrative, boosting EAI's annual profits from £34,000 after tax in 1958 to £126,000 the following year.[23] Thereafter, with little local competition, and a substantial tariff levied on comparable imported products, EAI flourished.[24]

As the EAI example indicates, one of the principal attractions of partnership with the private sector was the access it gave CDC to the sector's expertise. The role of scientific, economic, and similar experts in the history of British development is widely acknowledged.[25] But less commonly recognised is the role also of private-sector expertise. Sir Evelyn Baring, created Lord Howick and appointed chair of CDC in 1960, even claimed that the 'know-how of the world is mainly with private companies'.[26] CDC employed its own experts on a permanent basis in its own directly managed projects. But the independence of African states probably had the effect of increasing the importance of private-sector expertise. In the new environment of the 1960s CDC found that conditions in independent states made expatriate recruitment more difficult.[27] At the same time, the greater emphasis placed on manufacturing in post-colonial states made co-operation with the private sector more important, enhancing the value of industry-specific technical expertise.

As well as its importance for successful project management, expertise was essential to CDC's claims to offer local employees on-the-job training—the context in which Howick made his observation about private-sector know-how. In private correspondence with the Anglican priest Trevor Huddleston, a close family friend, Howick claimed that this was more important than the provision of financial aid. African states needed 'know-how and organisations which can train Africans as the managers of productive enterprises', a 'far more difficult' task than training them to be professionals.[28] CDC took this task seriously, in the 1960s producing annual surveys of 'indigenous' senior appointments, as well as funding scholarships. But the rate of Africanisation was slow, especially outside West Africa. Moreover, while CDC representatives on company boards 'invariably' encouraged 'training indigenous staff for senior positions', CDC had much less control over appointments in those projects where CDC's involvement was restricted to share or loan capital.[29] In the case of EAI, there was still no African employed at managerial level in 1965 some ten years after the venture had been restructured under Unilever's management.[30]

PRIVATE ENTERPRISE AND THE BENEFITS
OF PARTNERSHIP WITH CDC

While some of CDC's partnerships with business were (like EAI) initiated by CDC, others were the result of proposals put to the Corporation. The 1960s especially saw a surge in the number of applications for CDC funding from private-sector companies. At this time the extension of the Corporation's geographical field of operation to independent Commonwealth states and its rebranding as the *Commonwealth Development Corporation* made CDC a potentially useful resource for companies navigating both the opportunities and the challenges consequent upon decolonisation.

Many of the proposals CDC now received from companies related to manufacturing. The 1960s have been described as the 'golden age' of manufacturing in Africa.[31] Local conditions which had previously discouraged firms from moving into manufacturing now looked more favourable: not only did the absence of prior industrial development mean there were unexploited opportunities for manufacturing, but surging agricultural export earnings fuelled growth in local markets, and independent governments, committed to rapid economic diversification, now adopted policies favouring industrialisation. At the same time for expatriate companies hitherto dominant in the import sector, diversification was also defensive since independent governments were willing to protect nascent industries through concessionary taxation regimes and increased duties on imported products.[32]

As a result (although there was a shift back towards agriculture in the mid-1970s)[33] in the 1960s industry came to represent a slightly increased share of investments within CDC's portfolio.[34] This was most marked in the case of Nigeria.[35] With a population almost twice as great as that of any other sub-Saharan African state, and little previous industrialisation, Nigeria offered considerable market opportunities, and both its federal and regional governments were committed to the development of industries and welcoming to foreign direct investment. Although CDC did not have explicit country strategies or quotas, its regional controller was aware that the stakes were high for British interests in the country. 'Foreign trade delegations...[are] still pouring into Nigeria', the controller reported in late 1961, although at this juncture the UK was 'still ahead of any other country'.[36]

The case of two British companies which each sponsored funding applications to CDC in the 1960s provide examples of these trends: the United Africa Company Ltd (UAC) and Thomas De La Rue and Company Ltd. (DLR), a wholly owned subsidiary of the De La Rue Company Ltd.

UAC was a giant of the colonial scene. A subsidiary of Unilever, UAC's business revolved around the export of agricultural produce, including palm-oil products destined for Unilever's European factories, and the import of European manufactured goods. It was the archetypal colonial merchant firm and one which exemplified the near monopolistic hold that a small number of European enterprises had exercised over European colonies in the colonial era. In the early 1950s it controlled between 35 and 40% of the import market in Ghana and Nigeria.[37] Its interests not only sprawled throughout Africa, but extended back into Britain, as it acted as agent for a variety of British manufacturing companies which relied on the company's local expertise to manage the import and sale of their brands in Africa.

From the late 1950s UAC found itself under both commercial and political pressure to diversify its activities into local manufacturing. As a market leader, local politicians looked to it for technical and financial assistance. In Ghana, UAC experienced behind-the-scenes pressure from the country's first prime minister, and then president, Kwame Nkrumah, whose public rhetoric against 'neo-colonialism' belied the tenor of some of his private interactions with one of UAC's directors, Frederick Pedler.[38] More generally in West Africa UAC faced competition from new entrants to the import trade and new difficulties in its traditional produce-buying business. In this context a shift towards manufacturing looked the most promising avenue open to the company.[39] Trading would remain UAC's most important activity, but by the end of the 1950s it had nonetheless embarked on new enterprises while also beginning its withdrawal from produce buying.[40]

It is, then, perhaps no surprise that in 1963 UAC sponsored several Nigerian-based import-substituting schemes that sought funding from CDC and its subsidiary and associated development companies. One initiative was the Textile Printers of Nigeria Ltd. (TPN), which aimed to produce 20 million square yards of printed cloth a year. TPN was a joint venture between the [Nigerian] Eastern Regional Government, the Industrial and Agricultural Co Ltd. (INDAG), a development corporation in which CDC had a leading role, and Adatig, a textile consortium in which UAC was the largest shareholder and exercised overall control.[41]

For UAC the venture was defensive as much as expansionary. It was worried that if it did not act, the Eastern Regional Government's determination to encourage local manufacturing might lead it to enter into partnership with other textile printers and impose protective tariffs against imported products, damaging UAC's existing interest in the extensive textile import trade. To avoid this scenario the Adatig consortium had already signed an agreement with the Eastern Regional Government in 1961.[42] But the entry of the CDC into the Commonwealth sphere raised new funding options. In 1964 CDC was asked to make a financial commitment to TPN, thought to be the first occasion on which CDC had invested in a project alongside one of its development corporations.[43] CDC loaned the company £200,000.[44]

UAC's other Nigerian manufacturing applications to CDC and its subsidiaries at this time also followed the same import-substituting pattern. They included the establishment of a factory to manufacture fibre bags; the construction of a cigarette manufacturing factory, Kwara Tobacco Co Ltd.; Norspin Ltd. (a venture in partnership with Dunlop Rubber Co. and the English Sewing Cotton Co. to supply yarn to UAC and tyre cores and fabric to Dunlop); and a company for the production of bicycles in Nigeria in conjunction with Raleigh. UAC's wholly owned subsidiary G.B. Ollivants was the sponsor of a further two Nigerian schemes being considered by CDC.[45]

Unlike UAC, DLR had not had its own premises or businesses in Africa in the colonial period. British colonies had nevertheless been a significant market for its security print and note products, procured through the British Crown Agents.[46] For DLR the changes associated with decolonisation threatened that part of its business concerned with manufacturing banknotes and other products for colonial markets. On the other hand, the adoption by new states of their own national currencies also offered significant opportunities to pick up new business, contributing to a process of worldwide expansion. In 1963 the company marked its 150th anniversary by producing a world atlas for its shareholders and employees, an unsubtle statement of its international influence.[47]

As recalled by Alexis Napier, who travelled extensively not least in West Africa as a DLR salesman in the 1950s and 60s, DLR's management realised that Nigeria's population and location made it a 'suitable place' to set up a local security printing works.[48] DLR entered into partnership with the Nigerian Federal Government to establish the Nigerian Security Printing and Minting Company Ltd. (NSPMC) to supply all the Nigerian government's and central bank's requirements for security material, including banknotes, coins, and postage stamps. DLR held 40% of the shares, the Government 55%, and the Nigerian central bank 5%.[49] The Nigerian president, Nnamdi Azikiwe, who opened the new facility, hailed the venture as 'a milestone in our country's evolution towards economic prosperity'; DLR's chairman, Sir Arthur Norman, declared that it showed DLR's belief 'in the future of this country'.[50] The investment carried very little short-term risk for DLR itself because its own financial stake in the company took the form of credit to be used against purchases from DLR of equipment to instal in the new facility.[51] The arrangements also gave DLR sweeping powers over the management of the new company.[52] CDC's participation in NSPMC was first sought in summer 1963. In July 1964 it agreed to contribute to the new Nigerian venture, in the form of a loan of £500,000 offered at 2% interest above the rate at which the Corporation received money from the Treasury and repayable over eight years in sterling.[53]

From a business perspective, public-private partnership might not be unproblematic. For example, UAC was reluctant to share control of TPN with CDC. TPN had a board of six. UAC, its British partner in Adatig, Calico Printers Association, and the Eastern Regional Government each nominated two members. While they solicited CDC financial support, neither UAC nor the Calico Printers Association was willing to increase the size of the company's board to permit either CDC or INDAG (the local development corporation in which CDC played a leading part) to be represented, although they proposed that INDAG might nominate one of the members allocated to the Regional Government.[54]

UAC's parent company, Unilever, also showed some frustration that, some years after it had acquired managerial control of EAI, it was still forced to share equity in the business with CDC. Unilever found that 'whatever we may think…C.D.C.'s policy ought to be', CDC was unwilling to dispose of its EAI shareholding.[55] Fieldhouse suggested that the reason Unilever disliked sharing equity with external partners like CDC was that these partners expected to receive profits, whereas Unilever preferred these to be ploughed back into the business.[56] But an exchange from 1963 shows that this was not necessarily the case. In that year EAI's pre-tax profits climbed to £477,000, and, combined with further profits carried over from the previous year, this enabled £500,000 to be distributed in dividend payments, of which over 80% went to UK shareholders.[57] In October EAI's local management warned that Unilever's 'partners' would not stand for another dividend distribution, and proposed instead that some of the company's profits should be retained to finance the construction of a new non-soapy (laundry) detergent plant which the company proposed to build in Tanzania. Unilever responded that CDC's views, at least, were 'clear and definite'. The Corporation (which needed income to repay the Treasury loans it had received and fund new investment) liked dividends ('the larger…and the sooner the better'). CDC and Unilever were 'in complete agreement' that another 20% dividend should be paid before the end of the year.[58]

If some firms had misgivings about sharing equity and control, association with CDC offered private-sector firms several possible advantages. Most straightforwardly, CDC served as a source of expertise and capital. CDC's accumulated local knowledge was probably especially useful for foreign industrial concerns launching new manufacturing enterprises in countries in which they had little prior experience.[59] Through its loan or equity investment, CDC also carried some of the risk of new enterprises in challenging environments: indeed, this had been a principal rationale for CDC's creation in the first instance since businesses had proven reluctant to invest in some British colonies. In the 1960s, for all the opportunities available, investment in some African enterprises remained commercially and politically risky. CDC claimed in 1975 that in all cases where CDC loan finance contributed to a project in which there were private enterprise partners, its loan terms were fully commercial.[60] But where CDC had a significant equity or some other financial interest—as it often did—or where the drawdown period was short, it was willing to adjust its standard interest formula.[61] Since CDC required 'special treatment' from host governments for its projects in terms of taxation and other matters that were 'essential to the Corporation on account of the way it is financed',[62] concerns might also benefit from the concessionary terms of operation, although of course this was by no means dependent on partnership with CDC.

Not all applicants for CDC funding were dependent on CDC money, however, and the reasons for seeking support were more complex than simply financial. In some instances, including the TPN and the NSPMC, CDC represented an additional source of funding for projects that companies had already determined to embark upon. In the case of the NSPMC, CDC did not in the event invest: although the NSPMC was listed as one of several new projects in CDC's 1964 annual report, the NSPMC varied the terms for securing the loan in ways unacceptable to CDC.[63] NSPMC therefore went ahead without CDC support, securing significant influence for DLR,[64] which continued to hold a substantial stake until the early 2000s.[65]

The example of EAI provides a different perspective on why some companies might seek CDC funding. When in 1965 EAI sought money to proceed with its new detergent plant, although in Kenya rather than Tanzania, Unilever (despite its reservations about CDC's ongoing role within EAI) successfully applied to CDC to assist with the costs. CDC noted that Unilever hoped that 'if it could be shown' that to provide for the new plant EAI had to obtain further capital from CDC, as well as from Unilever and the other shareholder, the Kenyan Industrial Development [formerly, Management] Corporation, 'there would be a greater chance of avoiding restriction in future payment of dividends by the company'.[66] CDC's expertise proved helpful for EAI too when it prepared for certification as an approved enterprise under the new Foreign Investments Protection Act introduced by the Kenyan government in 1964 to guarantee foreign investment against nationalisation.[67]

More generally, and perhaps most significantly, partnership with CDC may also have reinforced a perception that the expatriate firms' activities constituted a form of 'development' and have increased the acceptability of new ventures locally. Whereas CDC found that overseas governments were frequently suspicious of expatriate plantation and manufacturing firms, the Corporation had generally been 'free from this' suspicion.[68] In private correspondence Howick noted, 'No one calls us neo-colonial'.[69] A few years before he argued that CDC's investment in smallholder agriculture and training had generated local trust, and that CDC benefited from association with the World Bank and International Finance Corporation with which it was in partnership in agricultural schemes in Kenya and Zambia.[70] CDC also took steps to curate its own image, producing a film, *Partners in Development*, first screened in 1968 and thereafter distributed widely in Britain and abroad.[71] Most importantly, in the years immediately prior to independence of some African states CDC had associated itself explicitly with public authorities in ways that enhanced its standing overseas—and, by extension, its value to its private sector partners. It established a series of wholly owned CDC subsidiaries which operated under a local name. It also invested in overseas development corporations (including INDAG in Nigeria). CDC had assumed a leading role in establishing most of these corporations. They operated independently of CDC and had their own locally recruited boards of directors, but CDC was the principal shareholder and manager. In a context of anticolonialism and suspicion of foreign business Michael McWilliam argues that this strategy helped make CDC the acceptable face of foreign capitalism and contributed to a sense of the CDC 'being [morally] better than many private investors'.[72] Writing in the mid-1960s, CDC's general manager, Rendell, claimed that Commonwealth governments appreciated CDC for its ability to act as 'honest broker' in dealings with overseas contractors and industrialists. Conversely, 'Private enterprise of *any* nationality [my emphasis] presses for CDC participation partly at least because of CDC's standing with Commonwealth Governments'.[73]

THINKING BRITISH? CDC AND BRITISH BUSINESS

If CDC was indeed perceived as 'honest broker', it may in large part have been because CDC money was *not* tied to partnership with British firms *or* to UK procurement. Instead CDC's terms of reference gave it the freedom to associate with nationals of any origin, and CDC aimed as a matter of policy to encourage participation by local investors. For CDC the priority was to engage in projects that looked commercially sound by whatever means possible.

We can see this in relation to discussion of the policy to be adopted towards American capital. Early on in CDC's existence it had been agreed that it was desirable for CDC to co-operate with American business so long as this brought the prospect of a net return of hard currency earnings or savings.[74] The issue was revisited in 1964 in response to correspondence from the British high commissioner to Trinidad, when it seemed likely that further CDC funding might be sought for an existing American-owned business in which CDC had already invested, Federal Chemicals Ltd. Although Federal Chemicals had proved profitable, the commissioner thought CDC should concentrate its funding on British companies. He pointed out that neither the Trinidadian company nor its American parent firm, W.R. Grace & Co, had done much to publicise CDC's past contribution, and that, since Federal Chemicals had purchased all its machinery and equipment in the US, 'British money has been used to promote American exports'.[75] Officials at the Commonwealth Relations Office (CRO) and the CO agreed that it was important to showcase Britain's development contribution in the Caribbean,[76] but they had less sympathy for the commissioner's concern with British exports. It was curious, one CO official remarked, to see the '"buy British" drum being beaten so hard in this context'. He thought that if CDC was only to invest in British firms, CDC would dry up as there was 'just not enough British money'.[77] In a draft letter to the CRO, he observed that 'it was in no way our [British] policy to discourage the CDC from investing along with foreign investors'; to do so could prevent the establishment of worthwhile enterprises in developing countries. Insisting on CDC 'being British only would in the end produce little net help for anybody'.[78]

Even so, many of the firms with which CDC associated *were* British. In 1975 British firms, including British banks and their own development bodies, constituted about one half of the private investors with whom CDC associated.[79] While there was no deliberate policy to seek British partners, it is evident that British firms enjoyed certain structural advantages over other private-sector actors that influenced official decisions.[80]

One structural advantage concerned the sterling area. In the era of exchange control, colonial and Commonwealth members of the sterling area were unable to freely procure imports from beyond the sterling area, increasing their dependency on sterling-area sources: in practice this was likely to mean procurement from Britain. Even after the relaxation of exchange control, Commonwealth states' continued membership of the sterling area facilitated trade with other sterling countries.

British firms were also known to CDC and in Whitehall. For example, among the factors that contributed to CDC's support for TPN was that UAC and Calico Printers Association were 'probably unsurpassed in their respective fields'. While CDC anticipated that unforeseen problems might arise, 'it would be difficult to pick partners better qualified to deal with any difficulties'.[81] The NSPMC principally commended itself to UK civil servants for political rather than economic reasons. The CDC had noted that the company was virtually 'a Government sponsored scheme',[82] and within the CRO officials were cognisant of the importance attached by Nigerian ministers to a venture which would see Nigeria become the first country in sub-Saharan Africa to have its own security printing facility and mint.[83] Nevertheless, CDC noted the 'high standing' of DLR among several reasons for supporting the NSPMC's application to the UK government for approval for CDC participation.[84] It was agreed that CDC's participation would be conditional upon DLR's continued involvement: CDC could call for the immediate repayment if the technical and management agreement was terminated by default of DLR.[85]

It was essential to CDC's own viability that it invest in sound enterprises with reputable partners, and the Corporation sometimes commented in similarly approving terms on the reputation and standing of prospective private-sector partners that were *not* British. A 'reputation' nevertheless reflects the geographical and cultural situation of individuals and institutions.

The diaspora of British officials who in some locations remained in senior positions in public administration in Commonwealth countries in the early years of independence could also be important.[86] For example, that the NSPMC got off the ground in the first instance owed much to a British permanent secretary in one Nigerian government department, who together with 'his Minister' became a 'prime mover' behind the project.[87] CDC's own expatriate overseas managers represented an additional resource of this kind. The Corporation noted that *British* managers were important in a world 'where, for good or ill, financial aid is used as a way to further the interests of national industries', and could constitute 'the most effective and cheapest way of maintaining expatriate national influence in politically independent but economically underdeveloped countries'.[88] The role of representing CDC and British industry was sometimes even elided. This was the case in Malaya, where CDC's regional controller was also employed as a part-time regional representative for the Federation of British Industries. In 1963 the FBI approached William Rendell to suggest that the arrangement be extended to East Africa and the Caribbean. While Rendell worried that the arrangement might carry greater risks in East Africa, generating suspicions, 'however unjustifiably', that CDC gave preferential treatment to British interests, he broadly commended the proposal to CDC's East African controller,[89] although no evidence has been found to indicate that in the end anything came of the FBI's proposal.[90]

As noted earlier, the award of CDC funds was not tied to British procurement. Ironically, in the 1960s CDC only departed from its policy of untied aid not to link aid to British exports, but rather to American exports: the condition of receipt from the US Agency for International Development of a £2 million line of credit in 1966, which CDC would have been 'reluctant' to accept were it not that it needed to raise additional capital to be able to undertake new projects. CDC tried to get the Americans to drop this condition. Although CDC did not succeed, it hoped to mitigate the potentially disadvantageous effects of the requirement by ensuring that the relatively small sum involved might be employed in projects in which some measure of USA procurement 'was already justified on price/quality grounds'.[91] This discussion indicates that the commitment to the principle of untied aid was genuine; at the same time, the comments about CDC as 'honest broker' show awareness of the advantages to be had from eschewing an overtly commercial policy.

But while CDC money was not formally tied to British trade, CDC operated in a context in which there was a general understanding that, where possible, aid should benefit British exports. Since British sponsors of overseas projects were more likely to procure UK plants than foreign companies, this presumption was another factor which could work in the interests of British firms overseas. Shortly after the conversion of the Colonial into the Commonwealth Development Corporation, the Board of Trade sought reassurance from the CRO that British interests would 'receive at least an equal chance to compete for any business', noting that 'ideally we would like some preference'.[92] The CO (which the CRO consulted) advised that when CDC was involved in procurement, and where the Corporation had a free hand to ensure it, 'preference is given to British goods and services'. Moreover, the Corporation 'prides itself on the degree to which its activities generally lead to British exports'. CDC could consequently be 'trusted to "Buy British" whenever it can', and although it had a statutory obligation to operate on a commercial basis, 'wherever British goods are competitive (and perhaps even where in strict terms they are not)', CDC acted in support of British interests.[93] For its part the CRO routinely asked UK high commissions to comment on the general political and economic desirability of applications it received from CDC in order to establish whether there was any 'special British interest in the proposal'.[94] Overseas British trade commissioners advised on the potential benefits of projects to UK exports, and their judgement could reflect whether or not the applicant was British. For example, within the CRO file on CDC in Nigeria, the acting British trade commissioner in Lagos observed in the case of several applications relating to textile manufacturing submitted by non-British firms that the Corporation's participation was of relatively little benefit to British exports.[95]

CDC itself used the justification that it could support British trade and industry to promote itself to the British government. Howick made this case when arguing that CDC be allowed to embark on new projects in independent Commonwealth countries. Thereafter similar arguments were used by CDC in its ongoing battles with the Treasury. CDC was funded by advances from the British Exchequer on which interest was charged at the prevailing rate. Although before privatisation in 1999 various adjustments were made to the funding formula, there were longstanding concerns within CDC that the Treasury's terms were both restrictive and insufficiently generous.[96] In 1972, the Corporation's chair noted that CDC's French counterpart, the Caisse, received its money at a significantly lower rate of interest.[97]

Particular difficulties arose in 1966 when in the context of the growing sterling crisis the Treasury raised rates of interest and proposed a new ceiling on the sum CDC could borrow. In response CDC's general manager, William Rendell, sought to demonstrate CDC's value to Britain as well as its use as a development agency. Where it supplied the bulk of funding he claimed that British firms would in the majority of cases receive contracts for the supply of goods. But where it had only a minority interest, British interests were still more likely to 'get a look in' when they would not otherwise have done so. He cited one case (the Tana River Development Co. Ltd., Kenya) where the contracts would have gone to the 'Germans or the East Europeans' had CDC not provided the funds to cover local costs. In contrast, he noted that while CDC investment and management could assist British interests, international agencies had to deal with suppliers and contractors on an even-handed basis. If, he said, given *'merely* a fair field' [my emphasis] it could not be assumed that British contractors would prevail over other foreign enterprises for the award of contracts arising as a result of aid channelled through these multilateral bodies.[98]

Such arguments were sharpened as the features of development aid in the post-colonial landscape took shape and it became evident that other donor countries were using aid to promote their own commercial interests. At the end of the decade Rendell noted that it not only tried to give British manufacturers a 'fair chance' in competition for the award of contracts, but was 'not sympathetic' to proposals involving projects where 'suppliers from other established industrial countries have established a position, either by favour of tied aid or other less reputable means'. CDC's geographical field had just been extended beyond the Commonwealth, and, in an interesting comment, Rendell drew a distinction between the Commonwealth and the non-Commonwealth. He suggested that within the Commonwealth promoting British business interests was secondary to the Corporation's foremost priority to act in the interests of the developing country. But in *non*-Commonwealth countries he thought there might be some modification of the established position that CDC funds be 'untied'.[99] It is unclear whether this was because Rendell believed that Britain should support the economic development of Commonwealth countries without there necessarily being any expectation of return, or, alternatively (or additionally) recognised that underlying structural factors that tended to work in favour of British interests within the Commonwealth would not apply in non-Commonwealth countries.

The claim that it supported British commercial and manufacturing interests was a useful weapon in CDC's armoury. But it does not necessarily mean that this translated into practice—as implicit in Rendell's observation that within the Commonwealth the promotion of British interests was secondary to CDC's primary objective: economic development. One regional manager working in Africa in the 1970s does not recall receiving any specific instruction to think British.[100] Even so, other evidence cited above suggests that the issue weighed with CDC, and the possibility that projects might generate exports was certainly sometimes cited by CDC when evaluating requests for investment.[101] In the early 1960s, in line with the argument Howick had made in support of the case that CDC be allowed to embark on new projects in independent Commonwealth countries, CDC's annual reports began to record CDC's impact on the UK's visible export earnings. The Corporation estimated that its contribution rose from £9.3 million to £13.7 million between 1963 and 1968.[102] In a different context CDC claimed that its projects in 1975 had procured an estimated £35 million in orders for British machinery. How far they also benefited the recipient countries lies beyond the scope of this chapter, but, as well as generating local employment and training, CDC estimated in the same year that they had contributed £150 million to the balance of payments of overseas countries.[103]

CDC's performance drew favourable comment in a parliamentary select committee report on overseas aid published in 1971. That year the British government not only increased the scale of public lending to the Corporation but recommended in a white paper on British private investment in developing countries that CDC enter into more joint ventures with British firms to encourage more private investment.[104] A few years later the Confederation of British Industry was similarly positive about CDC's contribution—not just in terms of export stimulation, but because CDC gave British firms opportunities to tender for, and take equity in, CDC's projects. It judged that CDC was one form of British governmental aid to the developing world that brought 'home bacon to the British private sector'.[105]

CONCLUSION

In the early 1960s Africa continued to be CDC's most important region of operations, accounting for approximately two thirds of CDC's investment.[106] While CDC still operated principally within the public sector, a growing proportion of its investments were in association with the private sector. It provides an illustration of what Emanuele Fantini and Luca Puddu identify in relation to Ethiopia as the 'internal plurality' within the international development community, in which private companies constituted one kind of 'development broker' alongside an array of other actors.[107] As Howick put it, CDC was a 'laboratory for experiments in co-operation between state-owned agencies and private firms'.[108]

The importance of this co-operation to business success should not be overstated. Consideration of the fate of UAC's new Nigerian enterprises that we encountered earlier in this chapter indicates that private-public sector collaboration was insufficient to ensure new industries would prosper in challenging political and economic environments. Located in the country's Eastern Region, TPN sustained irreparable damage during the Biafran war. It was dissolved in 1971. UAC repaid CDC's share of investment when, together with a Hong Kong-based firm, it acquired TPN's assets to form a new concern, General Cotton Mills Limited. A 'phoenix arising from the ashes', the new company was generating a profit by 1975.[109] Other than its purchase of TPN's assets, in the 1970s UAC did not invest in other new industries in Nigeria, and the company directed some of its activities towards (a largely unsuccessful) diversification away from Africa. In retrospect it is apparent that the early 1960s had constituted a distinctively favourable period for foreign direct investment in manufacturing that was not continued into the following decade. Moreover, several of the other new industries for which UAC had sought assistance from CDC or its associated local development corporations fared worse. Kwara Tobacco struggled to break into the Nigerian market, accruing significant debt within its first couple of years. Norspin suffered as a result of technical problems as well as new federal excise duties that effectively cancelled out a protective tariff sheltering the new enterprise.[110] UAC eventually disposed of the tobacco concern in 1978 and Norspin was liquidated in 1984. While the Nigerian boom helped sustain UAC's fortunes in the 1970s, by the end of the decade the impact of the two Nigerian Enterprise Promotion Decrees of 1972 and 1977, which compelled foreign-owned businesses to sell a proportion of equity to Nigerians, and an economic downturn in Nigeria in the 1980s, contributed significantly to a poor performance by UAC. The company ceased to operate as an independent company within Unilever and was merged into its parent company's new Africa and Middle East Group.[111]

However, public-private partnership could be mutually beneficial (as the example of UAC's parent company, Unilever, and EAI, shows). The Corporation benefited from private-sector expertise. The private sector could profit from CDC's financial capital invested in the form of loans or equity in new or established enterprises, its local knowledge, and the cultural and political capital derived from its development record and association with overseas public authorities. In a variety of ways, CDC could ease the path of private investment in Anglophone African states as firms sought new opportunities in rapidly changing, and potentially challenging, environments.

Where this was the case, this chapter argues that—as senior figures within the Corporation themselves claimed—these benefits accrued particularly to British business. But this was not because CDC aimed straightforwardly at benefiting the British private sector. Rather, from the 1950s, after the Corporation ceased to function principally as an instrument for the development of resources to assist British post-war economic recovery, CDC's objectives coalesced around the development of infrastructure and resources in recipient countries while also ensuring that it broke even itself. Despite a broad British commitment to the promotion of British trade and industry, CDC worked with a wide array of different partners, including local public authorities, non-British firms, and local entrepreneurs—although it was only in the 1980s that CDC's distinctive value within the British aid programme came to be seen as a vehicle for the development of the private sector overseas. Nor were CDC's priorities and those of British government departments the same as those of British firms; equally, the interests and objectives of British firms were distinct from those of the local authorities with which they partnered. Each adopted the idioms and language of development to serve their own interests.

Yet, that CDC funds were *not* formally tied to projects that privileged British over other companies or to British procurement probably enhanced CDC's reputation and its worth as a vehicle of British soft power, and thereby also its value to British firms. Moreover, while distinct, the interests of different British actors—CDC, business, and government—were aligned, and could be mutually reinforcing. That local authorities sponsored or supported some projects helped secure the British government's willingness to agree to CDC investment in them. In some parts of the British government, such as the CRO, the political dividends to be gained from supporting projects adopted by local elites were as important as, if not more important than, any potential financial return to the British Exchequer or to British companies. But the participation of a British firm could also enhance the chances of projects succeeding in obtaining CDC funding. British firms were not only important sources of expertise but known quantities to those making funding decisions. Moreover, the involvement of British firms meant that projects would address British interests and might benefit British exports. For reasons that were structural or circumstantial as much as deliberate, CDC could indeed work in the interests of British companies.

Acknowledgement I am most grateful to CDC Group plc for permission to cite from their records and for hosting me in their offices, and, especially, to Christopher Brain for facilitating access. CDC's records are currently warehoused and there is no guarantee that the records consulted will remain in their current boxes. Since the papers consulted are organised in files according to the dates of meetings of the Executive Management Board, I have chosen to reference papers by the Board meeting date. My thanks also to Lord Howick for permission to quote from his father's correspondence; to Unilever plc for permission to quote from their records, and, especially, to the staff at the Unilever Archives & Records Management Department for their assistance; to staff at Special Collections Reading (which has some De La Rue papers), and to a member of De La Rue Ltd. for trying to locate further archival material; to the Modern Records Centre, University of Warwick; and to the Bodleian Library, Oxford. My thanks also to Christopher Brain and Andrew Dilley for their insights and helpful comments on a draft of the chapter. The views presented here, and any errors, are of course my own.

NOTES

1. Aid linked to the purchase of donor nation exports or services.
2. The 1977 Aid and Trade Provision introduced aid-related subsidies for UK exports; aid policy was subsequently commercialised to a much greater extent under the Conservative government of Margaret Thatcher. See John Toye, 'The Aid and Trade Provision of the British Overseas Aid Programme' in Anuradha Bose and Peter Burnell (eds.), *Britain's Overseas Aid Since 1979. Between Idealism and Self-Interest* (Manchester, 1991), pp. 97–124; Oliver Morrissey, 'Commercialization of British Aid:

Business Interests and the UK Aid Budget 1978–1988', *Development Policy Review*, 8, no. 3 (1990), pp. 301–322; Barry Ireton, *Britain's International Development Policies. A History of DfID and Overseas Aid* (Basingstoke, 2013), pp. 23, 185–210; Gordon Cummings, *Aid to Africa. French and British policies from the Cold War to the New Millennium* (Aldershot, 2001), pp. 74–77.

3. PP 1968–1969, XVIII, *Commonwealth Development Corporation. Annual Report and Statement of Accounts, 1968* (HMSO, 1969), p. 2.

4. One exception is D.J. Morgan, *The Official History of Colonial Development. Volume Four. Changes in British Aid Policy, 1951–1970* (Basingstoke, 1980), which includes an extended discussion focused on Whitehall's dealings with the Corporation and CDC's place in British aid policy. On the early years, see as well as the institutional histories, *inter alia*, Mike Cowen, 'Early Years of the Colonial Development Corporation: British State Enterprise Overseas During Late Colonialism', *African Affairs*, 84, No. 330 (1984), pp. 63–75; Michael Havinden and David Meredith, *Colonialism and Development. Britain and its Tropical Colonies 1850–1960* (London, 1993); Charlotte Riley, 'Monstrous predatory vampires and beneficent fairy-godmothers: British post-war colonial development in Africa' (PhD. Thesis, University College London, 2013), pp. 92–108, 186–190.

5. Sir William Rendell, *The History of the Commonwealth Development Corporation, 1948–1972* (London, 1976); Michael McWilliam, *The Development Business. A History of the Commonwealth Development Corporation* (Basingstoke, 2001); Christopher Brain and Michael Cable, *Pioneering Development* (2nd edn., CDC Group PLC, London, 2018).

6. See the discussion of the Caisse and French business in Véronique Dimier and Sarah Stockwell, 'Introduction', 13 in this volume.

7. McWilliam, *Development Business*, pp. 5–6, 15–19, 26–27, 37–38; Havinden and Meredith, *Colonialism and Development*, p. 285.

8. PP 1951–1952, IX, *CDC. Annual Report and Statement of Accounts, 1951* (HMSO, 1952), p. 5.

9. CDC, *Pioneering Development*, p. 41.

10. The UK National Archives [TNA], CO 537/7848, no 38, note of a meeting 19 May 1952.

11. McWilliam, *Development Business*, p. 41.

12. Calculated from PP 1971–1972, XIII, *CDC. Annual Report and Statement of Accounts, 1971* (HMSO, 1972), fig. 2, p. 14.

13. PP 1975–1976, XXXVII, *Second Report from the Select Committee on Overseas Development together with the proceedings of the committee, part of the minutes of evidence and appendices. The relationship between UK invest-*

ment and trading patterns and development with reference to the specific problems of small developing economies, CDC memo., paras. 2–3.

14. Details *CDC. Annual Reports and Statements of Accounts,* 1963–1969.
15. CDC [Group plc], Executive Management Board papers [EMB] 14 July 1966, 'CDC's place in UK Aid Programme', Rendell, 8 July 1966, pp. 4–5.
16. Klas Rönnbäck and Oskar Broberg, *Capital and Colonialism. The Return on British Investments in Africa, 1869–1969* (Basingstoke, 2019), pp. 109–110.
17. *British Aid Statistics, 1968–1972* (HMSO, London, 1973), pp. 12–13, Tables II and III.
18. PP 1952–1953, VIII, *CDC. Annual Report and Statement of Accounts,* 1952 (HMS0, 1953), pp. 40–41.
19. Rendell, *Commonwealth Development Corporation,* p. 37.
20. D.K. Fieldhouse, *Unilever Overseas. The Anatomy of a Multinational 1895–1965* (London, 1978), pp. 391–399.
21. Unilever [PLC, Unilever Art, Archives and Records Management, Port Sunlight], GB 1752. Uni/RM/OC/2/2/57/5, 'Mr. E.C. Cook's Report on his Visit to East African Market—Kenya, Uganda, and Tanganyika, Oct. 1952', incorporating 'Report on Project for Local Manufacture at the Plant of EAI, Nairobi'.
22. PP 1954–1955, IV, *CDC. Annual Report and Statement of Accounts,* 1954 (HMSO, 1955), p. 36. CDC, *Pioneering Development,* p. 18.
23. Unilever, GB 1752.UNI/GF/LG/1/4/21, 'Profits 1956–1965' (in note, R.W. Archer to Sec., Capital Issues Committee, 20 June 1966).
24. Fieldhouse, *Unilever Overseas,* pp. 402–403. The tariff rose from 20 to 37% under the independent Kenyan government.
25. See Joseph Hodge, *Triumph of the Expert. Agrarian Doctrines of Development and the Legacies of British Colonialism* (Athens, OH, 2007).
26. Bodleian Library, Oxford [hereafter Bod.], Mss Huddleston 15, Baring to Huddleston, 29 October 1970.
27. It called for recipient governments to provide more by way of inducements to expatriates: PP 1967–1968, XVIII, *CDC. Annual Report and Statement of Accounts, 1967* (HMSO, 1968), pp. 1–3.
28. Bod., Mss Huddleston 15, Baring to Huddleston, 29 October 1970.
29. CDC, EMB 14 Jan. 1965, BP 8/65, 'Indigenous Senior Staff', Rendell paper, 7 January 1965.
30. Fieldhouse, *Unilever Overseas,* p. 404.
31. David Fieldhouse, *Merchant Capital and Economic Decolonization. The United Africa Company 1929–1989* (Oxford, 1994), p. 494.

32. Ibid.; Peter Kilby, 'Manufacturing in Colonial Africa' in Peter Duignan and L.H. Gann, *Colonialism in Africa 1870–1960. Volume 4. The Economics of Colonialism* (Cambridge, 1975), pp. 470–520, esp. 499.

33. As a result of an adjustment in CDC's own funding model, and in line with the priorities of the Labour government elected in 1974 which saw CDC agree to prioritise projects in poorer developing countries involving renewable natural resources that would benefit those living in rural areas: *Second Report from the Select Committee on Overseas Development*, CDC memo., para.6.

34. See tables on 'Functional Distribution of Continuing Projects' in *CDC. Annual Reports*, 1962–1969; however, much of the change indicated by the tables is accounted for by the reclassification of the processing of raw materials as 'industry': Rendell, *Commonwealth Development Corporation*, pp. 223–224.

35. McWilliam, *Development Business*, pp. 82, 91.

36. CDC, EMB, 11 January 1962, inc. EMB 6/62, and 21/62, Extracts from RC's confidential reports for November and December 1961.

37. Kilby, 'Manufacturing', p. 491.

38. See, for example, Bod., Mss Afr. s 1814, Pedler papers, FP 50, 95, August 1963.

39. Bod., Mss Afr. s 1814, FP 50, 22–23, Pedler memo. industrial development in Ghana, 8 August 1958.

40. Fieldhouse, *Merchant Capital*, pp. 425, 497

41. Of a total equity of £N1.25m, Adatig subscribed £N.1.25m, of which UAC held £N0.625m. TNA, DO 221/107, no. 74, John Sadler (Lagos) to J.M.A. Herdman (CRO), 19 September 1964; no. 89, G.W. Totman (CDC) to J.D. Hennings (CRO), 13 Nov. 1964, and enclosure. The other members of Adatig were two Dutch companies and the Manchester firm, Calico Printers Association Ltd.

42. Fieldhouse, *Merchant Capital*, pp. 512–513.

43. TNA, DO 221/107, no. 89, Totman to Hennings (CRO), 13 Nov. 1964, and enclosure.

44. *CDC. Annual Report 1965*, p. 89.

45. TNA, CO 852/2202, Reports of schemes under investigation by CDC, and by subsidiary and associated development companies, 31.12.62, 31.3.63, 30.6.63, 30.9.63.

46. University of Reading Special Collections, Papers of De La Rue [DLR], Ms 937/28/133, Security Production Department, paper stock book: crown agents, 1942–1947.

47. Ibid., Ms 937/4/10, *The De La Rue Journal*, no 46, quotation in article '50 Years On'.

48. Cited Peter Pugh, *De La Rue. The Highest Perfection. A History of De La Rue* (London, 2011), pp. 179–180. Napier had recorded his memories in 1980.

49. PP 1963–1964, X, *CDC. Annual Report and Statement of Accounts, 1963* (HMSO, 1964) p. 1; *CDC. Annual Report 1965*, p. 95.

50. DLR, Ms 937/32/14, *The De La Rue Journal*, no 47, Nov. 1964, 'New Jobs for Nigerians', p. 33.

51. TNA, DO 221/107, minute, Mr Long [?], 20 July 1964.

52. Under a ten-year agreement, DLR was to act as technical adviser and purchasing agent, manufacturing and procuring all equipment to be used in the new facility as well as arranging for the design and construction of the buildings and the appointment and training of staff. DLR had responsibility for general management, and would also appoint the new company's managing director, as well as one other director. TNA, CO 852/2198, E/171 (ii), copy CDC application for capital for NSPMC Ltd., paras. 2–12.

53. TNA, DO 221/107, no 72, annex 3 (extract from document not on file) on CDC loan to NSPMC.

54. CDC, EMB 11 March 1965, EMB 101/65, 'Textile Printers of Nigeria Ltd.', 2 March 1965.

55. Unilever, GB 1752.UNI/GF/LG/1/4/21, 'East Africa', N.P. Stubbs (Unilever Legal Dept.) to D.A, Orr (Unilever Overseas Dept.) 8 August 1963.

56. Fieldhouse, *Unilever*, p. 594.

57. Unilever, GB 1752.UNI/GF/LG/1/4/21, 'Profits 1956–1965' (in note, R.W. Archer to Sec., Capital Issues Committee, 20 June 1966).

58. Ibid., A.B. Butler (Unilever) to W.H. Chester-Jones (EAI), 18 October 1963.

59. CDC, EMB 14 July 1966, 'CDC's place in UK Aid Programme', Rendell, 8 July 1966, p. 4.

60. *Second Report from the Select Committee on Overseas Development*, CDC memo., para. 2.

61. CDC, EMB 12 December 1968, BP 111/68, 'Terms of CDC lending', 23 November 1968.

62. *CDC. Annual Report, 1970*, p. 2.

63. CDC, EMB 11 November 1965, BP 118/65, 'Schemes lapsed during quarter ended 30.9.65'.

64. Sarah Stockwell, *The British End of the British Empire* (Cambridge, 2018), pp. 198–202. At the time this was written, I was unaware that CDC did not eventually invest in the Nigerian mint.

65. The Nigerian company is still listed as an associate in DLR's annual report 2002, but not in 2003, though no details of the disposal are given:

https://www.delarue.com/investors/results-reports-and-presentations/reports/archive, accessed 17 September 2019.

66. CDC, EMB 11 February 1965, 'East Africa Industries', 15 January 1965. IDC (now Industrial and Commercial Development Corporation) stipulated that its share of the loan should be raised by retention of its dividend payments: Unilever, GB 1752.UNI/GF/LG/1/4/21, G.H. Williamson (EAI) to Unilever, 3 May 1966.

67. Unilever, GB 1752.UNI/GF/LG/1/4/21, H.L. Parsons (EAI) to Boyd (Unilever), 22 December 1965.

68. CDC, EMB 14 July 1966, Howick to Sir Andrew Cohen (ODM), 10 June 1966.

69. Bod., Mss Huddleston 15, Baring to Huddleston, 29 October 1970.

70. CDC, EMB 14 July 1966, Howick to Cohen (ODM), 10 June 1966. On relations with the IBRD, see Christopher Brain, 'Pioneering Development? The Colonial/Commonwealth Development Corporation and the World Bank, 1948–1972' (MRes., King's College London, 2012).

71. CDC, EMB 11 September 1969, EMB 238/69, 'Public relations for August 1969'.

72. *CDC. Annual Report, 1963*, pp. 4–5; McWilliam, *Development Business*, pp. 42, 78, 107–112.

73. CDC, EMB 14 July 1966, 'CDC's place in UK Aid Programme', paper by Rendell, 8 July 1966, p. 1.

74. TNA, CO 852/840/1, no 24, minutes meeting CO-CDC, 20 September 1948.

75. TNA, CO 852/2198, no 204/E(ii), N.E Costar to E. Skyes (CRO), 22 July 1964.

76. Ibid., E/189-1, 'CDC. Note of Talks' G. Booth, 10 August 1964.

77. Ibid., minute on 204/E(ii), E.C. Burr (CRO), 7 October 1964.

78. Ibid., draft letter to J.D. Hennings (CRO), October 1964. The exchange proved academic since no more CDC money was in fact sought.

79. *Second Report from the Select Committee*, CDC memo. paras. 2–3.

80. See also research by development economists that shows in relation to British multilateral aid in a later period that British interests tended to secure a higher proportion of aid-generated business in Commonwealth Africa and Asia than in non-Commonwealth regions, indicating the importance of historic connections: Ranald S. May, Dieter Schumacher, and Mohammed H. Malek, *Overseas Aid. The Impact on Britain and Germany* (Hemel Hempstead, 1989), pp. 52–61.

81. CDC, EMB 11 March 1965, EMB101/65, 'Textile Printers of Nigeria Ltd.', report by Totman, 1.3.65.

82. TNA, CO 852/2198, E/171 (ii), copy of CDC application for capital for the NSPMC Ltd., para. 3.

83. TNA, CO 852/2197, 3/E2, H.E. Davies (CRO) to John Sadler (British High Commission, Lagos), 14 August 1963.

84. TNA, CO 852/2198, E/171 (ii), copy of CDC application for capital for the NSPMC Ltd., para. 4.

85. TNA, DO 221/107, no. 72, annex 3 (extract from document not on file) on CDC loan to NSPMC.

86. On which see, Stockwell, *British End*, pp. 78–80.

87. Pugh, *De La Rue*, pp. 179–180.

88. CDC, EMB 14 July 1966, 'CDC's place in UK Aid Programme', paper by Rendell, 8 July 1966, pp. 1, 3.

89. Ibid., EMB 19 April 1963, Rendell to regional controller, East Africa, 15 March 1963.

90. No further details were found in CDC papers I was able to consult or in the archive of the FBI, Modern Records Centre, University of Warwick.

91. CDC, EMB 14 July 1966, EMB 12 May 1966, minutes and EMB 139/66, 'CDC/AID co-operation', 3.5.66. The extension of AID money to CDC arose from UK-US governmental discussions about compensating the UK government for an increase in its subscription to the East Asia Development Bank: EMB, 10 February 1966, EMB 42/66.

92. TNA, CO 852/2158, E/1, Philip Ridley (BoT) to Harold Davies (CRO), 11 November 1963.

93. Ibid., E.C. Burr (CO) to G.R. Lee (CRO), 6 December 1963.

94. Details from TNA, CO 852/2197, E.34, H.E. Davies (CRO) to Deputy British High Commissioners in 8 Commonwealth countries, 30 October 1963.

95. TNA, DO 221/107, no. 74, John Sadler to J.M.A. Herdman (CRO), 19 September 1964, and enclosures, including G.J. Swaffield (Ibadan) to Sadler, 15 September 1964.

96. McWilliam, *Development Business*, pp. 9–14.

97. *CDC. Annual Report 1971*, p. 4.

98. CDC, EMB 14 July 1966, 'CDC's place in UK Aid Programme', paper by Rendell, 8 July 1966, pp. 2–3, 5, 8.

99. Ibid., EMB 11 September 1969, EMB 213/69, 5.8.69, 'Finance for new projects and selection criteria', Rendell paper, 4 August 1969, p. 6.

100. Anonymous source.

101. For example, this was the case with another textile printing scheme, Afprint (Nigeria) Ltd., which proposed using UK spinning equipment: CDC, EMB 12 June 1969, paper re. Afprint.

102. Based on figures reported in *CDC Annual Reports*, 1963–1969.

103. *Second Report from the Select Committee*, CDC memo., para. 3.

104. Bruce Dinwiddy (ed.), *Aid Performance and Development Policies of Western Countries. Studies in US, UK, EEC and Dutch Programs* (New York and London, 1973), pp. 38–40, 50.

105. Modern Records Centre, University of Warwick, Archive of the Confederation of British Industry, Mss 200/c/Jan1998/8079, 'Commonwealth Development Corporation', memo. 31 March 1981.

106. The proportion had risen from approximately 49% in 1951, to approximately 58% in 1955, to about two thirds in 1961. Africa's share declined in the later 1960s: calculated from *CDC. Annual Reports*, 1951–1969.

107. Emanuele Fantini and Luca Puddu, 'Ethiopia and international aid: development between high modernism and exceptional measures', in Tobias Hagmann and Filip Reyntjens (eds.), *Aid and authoritarianism in Africa. Development without Democracy* (London, 2016), pp. 91–108. Fantini and Puddu in turn draw on others' work in using the term 'development brokers'.

108. CDC, EMB 14 July 1966, Howick to Sir Andrew Cohen (ODM), 10 June 1966.

109. Unilever, GB 1752.UAC/2/12/2/E/1/4/4/1, 'General Cotton Mill Limited', attached to note, D.E. Barter, and GB 1752. UAC/2/12/2/E/2/1/1, GCM Ltd. Annual accounts & reports; PP 1969–1970, XIII, *CDC. Annual Report and Statement of Accounts, 1969* (HMSO, 1970), p. 99; Fieldhouse, *Merchant Capital*, p. 515.

110. CDC, EMB 13 August 1964, EMB 207/64, 'General Manager's Tour of West African Region', 23. 7. 1964; Unilever, GB 1752.UNI/PLC/ BM/1/17, Board minutes, 14 October 1966; GB 1752. UAC/2/12/2/1/5/3, 'Textile Division and Industrial Development in Nigeria', 15 November 1968.

111. Fieldhouse, Merchant Capital, pp. 6–9, 46, 71, 77, 515–516, and esp. chs. 14–15.

REFERENCES

Brain, Christopher, and Michael Cable, *Pioneering Development*, 2nd Edition (CDC Group PLC, London, 2018).

Brain, Christopher, 'Pioneering Development? The Colonial/Commonwealth Development Corporation and the World Bank, 1948–1972' (MRes. thesis, King's College London, 2012).

British Aid Statistics, 1968–1972 (HMSO, London, 1973).

Colonial/Commonwealth Development Corporation. Annual Report and Statement of Accounts (HMSO, London, 1951–1972).

Cowen, Mike, 'Early Years of the Colonial Development Corporation: British State Enterprise Overseas During Late Colonialism', *African Affairs*, 84, no. 330 (1984), pp. 63–75.

Cummings, Gordon, *Aid to Africa. French and British Policies from the Cold War to the New Millennium* (Ashgate, Aldershot, 2001).

Dinwiddy, Bruce (ed.), *Aid Performance and Development Policies of Western Countries. Studies in US, UK, EEC and Dutch Programs* (Overseas Development Institute, Praeger Publishers, New York and London, 1973).

Fantini, Emanuele, and Luca Puddu, 'Ethiopia and International Aid: Development between High Modernism and Exceptional Measures', in Tobias Hagmann and Filip Reyntjens (eds.), *Aid and Authoritarianism in Africa. Development Without Democracy* (Zed Books, London, 2016), pp. 91–108.

Fieldhouse, David K., *Merchant Capital and Economic Decolonization. The United Africa Company 1929–1989* (Oxford University Press, Oxford, 1994).

Fieldhouse, David K., *Unilever Overseas. The Anatomy of a Multinational 1895–1965* (Croon Helm, London, 1978).

Havinden, Michael, and David Meredith, *Colonialism and Development. Britain and Its Tropical Colonies 1850–1960* (Routledge, London, 1993).

Hodge, Joseph, *Triumph of the Expert. Agrarian Doctrines of Development and the Legacies of British Colonialism* (Ohio University Press, Athens, OH, 2007).

Ireton, Barry, *Britain's International Development Policies. A History of DfID and Overseas Aid* (Palgrave Macmillan, Basingstoke, 2013).

Kilby, Peter, 'Manufacturing in Colonial Africa', in Peter Duignan and L.H. Gann, *Colonialism in Africa 1870–1960. Volume 4. The Economics of Colonialism* (Cambridge University Press, Cambridge, 1975), pp. 470–520.

May, Ranald S., Dieter Schumacher, and Mohammed H. Malek, *Overseas Aid. The Impact on Britain and Germany* (Harvester Wheatsheaf, Hemel Hempstead, 1989).

McWilliam, Michael, *The Development Business. A History of the Commonwealth Development Corporation* (Palgrave Macmillan, Basingstoke, 2001).

Morgan, D.J., *The Official History of Colonial Development. Volume Four. Changes in British Aid Policy, 1951–1970* (Macmillan, Basingstoke, 1980).

Morrissey, Oliver, 'Commercialization of British Aid: Business Interests and the UK Aid Budget 1978–1988', *Development Policy Review*, 8, no. 3 (1990), pp. 301–322.

Pugh, Peter, *De La Rue. The Highest Perfection. A History of De La Rue* (Icon Books, London, 2011).

Rendell, Sir William, *The History of the Commonwealth Development Corporation, 1948–1972* (Heinemann Educational Books, London, 1976).

Rönnbäck, Klas, and Oskar Broberg, *Capital and Colonialism. The Return on British Investments in Africa, 1869–1969* (Palgrave Macmillan, Basingstoke, 2019).

Riley, Charlotte, 'Monstrous Predatory Vampires and Beneficent Fairy-Godmothers: British Post-war Colonial Development in Africa' (PhD. Thesis, University College London, 2013).

Stockwell, Sarah, *The British End of the British Empire* (Cambridge University Press, Cambridge, 2018).

Toye, John, 'The Aid and Trade Provision of the British Overseas Aid Programme', in Anuradha Bose and Peter Burnell (eds.), *Britain's Overseas Aid Since 1979. Between Idealism and Self-Interest* (Manchester University Press, Manchester, 1991), pp. 97–124.

CHAPTER 8

Decolonising Finance, Africanising Banking

François Pacquement

INTRODUCTION

Based on Agence française de développement (AFD) archives, this chapter analyses, from the perspective of development officials, Africanisation in the banking sector of former French African colonies, from the 1950s to the 1980s. Africanisation (or 'indigenisation')[1] refers to the transfer of responsibilities from colonial to local interests or persons.[2] But Africanisation was also associated with the creation of a new activity, since until the 1940s the banking sector within these territories had been largely dedicated to the needs of colonisers. This study shows how in French African colonies the Caisse centrale, the forerunner of the present day

The opinions expressed in this chapter are those of the author and do not necessarily reflect the position of AFD. It is therefore published under the sole responsibility of its author. This work owes very much to Véronique Dimier and Sarah Stockwell. Special thanks to Gordon Cumming for rereading this chapter. Pascale Gruson kindly allowed me to consult archives of former deputy secretary general of the UN Philippe de Seynes.

F. Pacquement (✉)
Agence Française de Développement, Paris, France
e-mail: pacquementf@afd.fr

© The Author(s) 2020   213
V. Dimier, S. Stockwell (eds.), *The Business of Development in Post-Colonial Africa*, Cambridge Imperial and Post-Colonial Studies Series, https://doi.org/10.1007/978-3-030-51106-7_8

AFD, initially contributed, in ways that aimed to serve African interests, to the diversification of a financial sector originally dedicated to colonial activities. Subsequently, after the independence of African colonies, the Caisse centrale as an operator for the new Ministry of Cooperation fostered development through the advancement of the private sector in Africa, and supported the Africanisation of banks as part of its mission of promoting development in African independent countries. In order to help African small businessmen and artisans, the Caisse centrale first created credit institutions which became development banks, then operated a single subsidiary, Proparco. However, as the process of Africanisation, both of personnel and ownership, met considerable obstacles, the idea of development through the private sector came to have a different meaning and reality, with French companies receiving many of the benefits from the Caisse's credit, as exemplified by a debate about Proparco. To what extent the economies of former French colonies became really 'decolonised' remains an open question. This chapter hence shows how difficult economic independence could be in a context where French colonial banking institutions and French business interests still prevailed.

In French colonies the so-called colonial banks were created as a response solely to the needs of colonisers. These banks' activities (which included central banking as well as commercial banking) have been traced back to the nineteenth century and been subject to detailed analysis.[3] The principal colonial bank was originally the Banque du Sénégal,[4] which became the Banque de l'Afrique Occidentale (BAO) in 1901.[5] It expanded quickly thereafter, extending its services to most of French West Africa, then to French Equatorial Africa, Togo, and Cameroun, establishing offices across a broad range of territories. After the First World War, the BAO's transformation, together with the limited scope of its activities, increased its financial vulnerability, especially when depositors withdrew their assets during the Great Depression.[6] A restructuring in 1931 failed to solve the problems of the bank itself, and to attract possible competitors to the bank, although metropolitan banks had growing interest in financing operations in Africa.[7] This history explains the creation, during the Second World War, of the banking and monetary institution of Free France, the Caisse centrale, which would ultimately develop into today's French official development assistance provider, the AFD.[8] There are some existing scholarly accounts of the Caisse and banking. A symposium in 2016 offered contextual details on the activities of the institution as well as its banking subsidiaries (listed in an annex to this chapter).[9] These subsidiaries were first studied in Robert Badouin's work on development banks.[10] Cissé Moussa's dissertation on the Banque nationale de développement du Sénégal also offered an extensive case study.[11] But the historiography of banking in the former French colonies of Africa is not exhaustive, probably because development scholars focus on either foreign development finance or sector approaches.[12]

Africanisation first became a preoccupation for a broad range of actors, from nationalists to colonial administrators to representatives of international institutions, around the time of the preparations for the independence of France's African colonies. It remained an issue after independence, not only in the 1960s but also later, during structural adjustment processes of the 1980s.[13] Africanisation as a process would involve customers,[14] staff,[15] and equity ownership, and seems to have been undertaken in that order. For political reasons, nonetheless, the Africanisation of staff, and then of ownership, was particularly contentious.

However, after the War, the focus in central banking was more on nationalisation than on Africanisation. Regarding the commercial banking sector, the shift was more towards 'localisation' since the sector was heavily centralised, concentrated in Paris and/or Dakar. This banking activity is difficult to analyse separately from industrial development,[16] since this is both the prerequisite and the outcome of banking.

Just as the banking sector generally has not attracted significant attention, so the literature on Africanisation in relation to banking is rather limited. For the most part, Africanisation is discussed in general in papers on nationalisation or foreign direct investment. One author observes that the perception of Africans in the eyes of the bankers was 'often evidently negative'.[17] In relation to Nigeria and Ghana respectively, Stephanie Decker and Sarah Stockwell each discuss how Africanisation became an issue for British banks as they approached independence.[18] Decker also shows how lending to Africans became a key part in Barclay's decolonisation strategy in Nigeria, although it ultimately failed. As she notes, the issue of Africanisation adds a further layer of complexity to the issue of decolonisation, begging the question as to 'whether the indigenisation of staff is a reasonably good indicator for the extent to which a business can be considered decolonized'.[19]

This chapter aims to contribute new insights and findings on Africanisation in the banking sector. It follows a broadly chronological approach, first showing how, in French colonies the development of banking was an answer to colonial trade needs and the monetary consequences of a divided colonial empire during the second World War. It then accounts for the beginning of

French development assistance and the emergence of a new financial infrastructure. The next section focuses on the independence process and subsequent delays to the Africanisation both of personnel and ownership.

From the Origins of the Caisse Centrale to the First Steps of French Development Assistance

After the German invasion of France, de Gaulle established 'la France Libre' (Free France) in London. Equatorial Africa pledged its support as early as August 1940. However, French West Africa remained under the control of the Vichy government, which suppressed the BAO privilege of banknote issuance in French Equatorial Africa. In March 1941, the United Kingdom guaranteed a fixed parity with the pound for the 'Free France' Franc, while Vichy's currency depreciated continuously. Since BAO banknotes continued to circulate in Free France Equatorial Africa, it became necessary to distinguish the two monetary zones, Vichy's and that of Free France, in order to ensure a smooth flow of trade within Central Africa. At the same time, to prevent monetary speculation, de Gaulle's financial attaché, Pierre Denis,[20] suggested the creation of the Caisse centrale de la France libre (CCFL). With the assistance of the Bank of England, this occurred on 2 December 1941. On the 24 July 1942, a Free France order enabled the CCFL to issue banknotes from the 1 August 1942. Pierre Denis was joined by a small team, including, from autumn 1942, André Postel-Vinay, a young Treasury auditor (inspecteur des finances)[21] and resistance fighter. In 1944, he succeeded Pierre Denis.

The Caisse should have disappeared at the end of the war,[22] but as it happened it took on a new role, brought about by the principles outlined at Brazzaville, in January-February 1944, where de Gaulle held a meeting of the French colonial governors to present his vision of peace. The 'spirit of Brazzaville' promised new French investment in colonial economic development. Delivering on this vision required adequate resources. A special financial institution was therefore necessary, and this would be the new role for the Caisse, which changed its name from Caisse centrale de la France libre to Caisse centrale de la France d'Outre-mer (overseas France). The Caisse's close association to the Bank of England contributed to the banking culture or 'world view' of Postel-Vinay, preparing him to undertake important measures such as the separation of central banking from commercial functions. This was not an obvious step for any French professional to take at this time, when the so-called colonial banks still had central and commercial banking responsibilities.[23]

After the war, independence for France's African colonies was not yet on the agenda: France had to rebuild itself materially in order to regain its ability to act as a world power. The Law of 30 April 1946, provided a basis for the creation of local semi-public companies which would enjoy the financial support of local authorities.[24] It established an Investment Fund for Economic and Social Development (IFESD—FIDES in French), which broke new ground by providing subsidies to support colonial development. Until then colonies had only been eligible for loans and had to be self-sufficient.[25] The Caisse was tasked with helping to address the basic needs of African citizens at a time of reconstruction and economic reorganisation in France as well as fostering colonial economic development. The effect of these reforms was an increase in net public expenditure in the French colonies. In French West Africa this rose from around 10 francs per head in 1945 to 35–40 francs in the 1950s.[26] This level was maintained after African independence. The system followed a liberal approach that aimed at promoting favourable development conditions for the private sector, the support of public capital being considered transitory.[27] As Louis Rey, another Treasury auditor, observed, 'At no time was IFESD or the Caisse or its subsidiaries intended to replace private initiative: their aim was to trigger it'.[28] The 1946 law strived to attract private investors, and, albeit cautiously, French banks sought to increase their exposure to African risk. Some of them held significant shares in the BAO. In the 1950s, once the idea of independence seemed inevitable, these banks had to start building an African network of branches. But Africa was still considered a continent with limited economic prospects, and one in which development was likely to occur mainly in the rural sector. Bankers were reluctant to take on African customers, who were considered riskier, and preferred to limit their exposure in Africa to the activities of their metropolitan customers.

The Law of 1946 was intended to provide help for urban executives, farmers, craftsmen, and small entrepreneurs. In the context of the reluctance of the commercial banks to extend credit to African customers, the Caisse aimed to help African customers carry out their housing projects or professional activities. Access to housing was difficult after the war, both in metropolitan France and in colonial cities, where investment did not keep pace with population growth. Therefore, allowing 'new' citizens to access housing was among the first goals of development. To do this, the Caisse was to set up a network of banks, electricity, and local housing companies, all activities likely to achieve financial returns, while remaining in line with the 'spirit of Brazzaville'.[29] This network targeted people, at the heart of the economic fabric, in territories where the few large companies that existed were metropolitan. It signaled a shift away from the former French colonial system which offered no incentives to Africans to conduct their own agricultural or artisanal projects, or indeed to create small businesses. To increase the banking sector's coverage, the solution was to create a local 'reference offer', in order to create a competitive incentive to improve the terms of, and access to, credit. The Caisse funded housing companies' programmes, which produced flats that could be bought by urban dwellers, with credit granted by the banking subsidiary. This banking subsidiary was also to finance tenants who needed equipment and furniture. Through this distribution of credit to individuals or small businesses, the Caisse launched a process of Africanisation of customers, a shift followed by major French banks, which began opening branches or subsidiaries on the continent, in anticipation of independence and emerging African demand.

This provision of a form of 'social credit' represented a new approach to banking for Africans. Cissé Moussa summarises the logic that led to the creation of 'social credit companies' (SCC) as specialised credit granting institutions, adapted, on the one hand, to the multiple tasks that economic expansion provides and, on the other hand, to solving the problems raised by the complexity of local economic structures.[30] Thus, the creation of such institutions was part of a general framework, a policy aimed at 'increasing economic development and globalising the improvement of the standard of living of African populations'. These institutions were to be managed according to the flexible methods of the private sector. The mission was not to make a profit, but to contribute to creating and promoting private companies, and conducting development experiments. Subsidiaries of the Caisse, created in each territory, were able to make decisions that took account of local conditions, without having to wait for a decision from Paris. The organisation of SCCs was based on an Executive Council, led by a director general. Representatives of the colonial administration, as well as the Caisse and the issuing institution sat on the Board of Directors alongside others, including representatives of local assemblies who provided 'at the indigenous level the means of the institution's policy'.[31] In addition to their share capital, the resources of these companies included public funds from the Caisse and the issuing institution (which could offer favourable terms for specific activities). The advances and credit facilities granted by the Caisse centrale or the issuing institution were accompanied by other special conditions, such as a lower interest rate and a significant repayment period. In this way these credit institutions were able to act in the interests of borrowers who, at that time, were not otherwise accommodated within the standard channels of bank credit.[32] Claude Panouillot, the newly appointed head of the Institut d'émission d'Afrique Équatoriale et du Cameroun (IEAEC), the new public central bank for the region, explained that the rationale of the system was to stimulate the savings of Africans, or to offer a substitute where these were insufficient. He observed there was no desire to prioritise metropolitan over local investment: the provisions were targeted at all local businesses, regardless of their origin or ownership (French or national). Indeed, the Caisse wanted to promote local initiative, whether it was French or African, even if, in the post-war period, it was difficult to have a clear vision of 'African' affairs.

THE FIRST STEP TOWARDS AFRICANISATION: THE AFRICANISATION OF PERSONNEL

Prior to the independence process, France had tried by all means possible to promote its main interests by controlling currency, maintaining or establishing military bases, and providing bilateral aid essential to states unable to meet their operating expenses and the costs of their administrators.[33] Hence, 'everything was in place to continue a policy based on the connivance between the first generation elites now in power and the metropolitan authorities' to ensure the continuation in other forms of the 'colonial project'.[34] Following the independence of French African colonies, the Ministry of Overseas France was replaced in 1961 by the Ministry of Cooperation,[35] the FIDES becoming the 'Aid and Cooperation Fund' (ACF—FAC in French). The FAC was now managed by the French Ministry of Cooperation, which carried on supplying grants, while the Caisse provided loans and equity investments (both could be combined to fund the same project). French major banks were represented on the Board of Directors of the Caisse, whose loans sought to avoid competing with other banks resources, in design or in practice. The Caisse changed its name from de la France d'Outre-mer to de Coopération économique (of Economic Cooperation). The Ministry of Cooperation chose from the outset to keep the local missions of its predecessor independent from

France's diplomatic missions. The Caisse already had its own network of local offices, allowing for an everyday relationship with local administrations or subsidiaries. These were often still being managed by expatriate staff, some of them belonging to the Caisse itself.

Inevitably, Africanisation became a challenge to this cooperative approach to state building after independence. It was recognised as a crucial issue by French senior civil servants—including in relation to banking. In 1955, Claude Panouillot, suggested,

> on the one hand to amplify the effort of intellectual formation, and on the other hand to give it a new orientation. Why? Because it has become clear that everything must be done to ensure that Africans are able, as quickly as possible, to take over the administration of their country. This is a problem that is frequently referred to today as the "Africanisation of executives" (…). This evolutionary policy is difficult to carry out because it tends not only to introduce all Africans to our intellectual concepts, but also to build the frameworks that the overseas populations need.[36]

The Caisse being then the parent company of IEAEC, the views of its director reveal the more general preoccupation of preparing the field for development after independence.

The Africanisation of personnel was rendered difficult, however, by chronic underfunding of education in colonial times. For example, a sectoral breakdown of French development expenditure after the war shows that only a limited share was dedicated to education.[37] After independence, this resulted in a lack of African professionals and a need for technical assistance to replace expatriates in unfilled posts. In these circumstances the new Ministry of Cooperation sought to contribute to creating and developing capacities, and, to this end, financed French executives and teachers to carry out their mission. The latter simply changed into 'technical assistants'.[38] Their numbers kept growing,[39] France's increasing technical assistance being financed on the basis of sharing costs increasingly with the beneficiary. Moreover, the effect of huge sector-wide programmes by the World Bank was to create an inflow of experts, which helped to raise the prospect of exposing African executives to responsibilities.

The goals of French development assistance policy were set out in several reports, produced on an almost annual basis. The 1962 report stated that

> the ultimate goal is the Africanisation of positions, Africanisation that France must promote, particularly through its training actions; but in the mean-

time, French technical assistance staff can play a vital role in ensuring the efficient functioning of the administrative and technical services in the least developed countries (…) Specialised middle managers (accountants, technicians, tax or customs officials, etc.) will have to be maintained for a long period of time because of the difficulty for states to replace them and the essential nature of their activities. If the maintenance of these personnel does not appear to be of primary interest from the French point of view, it is so if we want to avoid the almost total paralysis of the administrative and technical services of the least developed states, because it is paradoxically these average and subordinate jobs that are currently the most difficult to Africanize. It is also necessary to encourage local governments to make a greater effort to train these middle managers because it is not normal to keep these jobs held indefinitely by French staff.[40]

Two years later the 1963 report, coordinated by de Gaulle's former minister of Trade and Industry,[41] observed that

African leaders fear that an adaptation will tend towards "Africanisation on the cheap". (…) The need for senior executives pushes states to direct their graduates to study to the detriment of middle management training. Finally, as no training plan exists, teaching takes place independently of training needs.

'Africanisation on the cheap' referred to another part of the report where the authors stated that French teaching was too abstract and modelled on methods relevant more for metropolitan areas than rural African communities. The approach risked hindering development, uprooting rural students, pushing them towards office jobs, instead of moving towards the training of intermediary technicians and executives.

Aficanisation was, of course, not just an issue for the public sector since in the early 1960s, most companies in the formal sector were owned and staffed by French citizens. Although the 1950s saw investment in training, change took time. As a result, although independence should logically have led to Africanisation, at first it was slow, and only became more intensive in the 1970s, with the increase in the number of graduates. In the Ivory Coast, for example, there were only around 500 graduates per year in the late 1960s; the number then tripled to more than 1600 in 1973. Here, a national commission was set up under the aegis of the leading party, to encourage companies to adopt plans to facilitate Africanisation. The Ivorian government set as its aim an increase in 'Ivorian participation in the modern sectors of the economy'. 'In industry, participation was low on three levels: there was a lack of Ivorian entrepreneurs, an absence of Ivorian executives and also a lack of Ivorian financial participation. To overcome the first difficulty, the government created in 1968 the 'Promotion Office of the Ivorian Company' which provided technical assistance to Ivorians wishing to engage in business. To address the second difficulty, more training was required to enable young Ivorians to access senior technical or managing positions.'[42]

In the banking sector, the Caisse centrale played an important part in attempting to facilitate Africanisation. It opened its own internship service to national executives working within banking and credit institutions whose management and supervision were provided by agents of the Caisse centrale. This was a way 'to take into account the importance that developing countries attach to the training of their elites'.[43] It became the Center of Economic, Financial and Banking Studies (CEFBS—CEFEB in French) at the Paris headquarters of the Caisse centrale. Candidates were proposed by their home institutions and had to be on course to be part of the management of the bank as well as either hold a diploma of higher education or have at least two years' professional experience. They also had to be under thirty-five. Admission was determined by a selection panel. The internship session lasted approximately nine months and comprised two successive stages: the first in which all trainees participated, devoted to 'refreshing basic knowledge' of areas such as accounting, financial mathematics, corporate and projects financial analysis, banking techniques and credit mechanisms, cost accounting and business management, statistics and tools for decision-making, and economic analysis of development projects; the second part being devoted to specialised options (development banking, business management, analysis of development projects). From its creation until September 1981, 2225 trainees from 52 countries benefited from the training given by the CEFBS. This comprised 1213 annual internship sessions, 203 short-term specialised courses, 135 development seminars, and 674 on-site training sessions.[44]

In 1966, the French UN under-secretary for Economic and Social Affairs, Philippe de Seynes[45] elaborated on the issues surrounding Africanisation in an address at New York University, stressing the differences between Africa and Asia, which makes 'Africanisation' a specific concept:

> the lack of high level and middle level skills—which incidentally are far scarcer than they were in Asia at the time or independence—does not permit these small markets to produce the economic activity of a contemporary

European town of 100,000 inhabitants. Moreover, with such small national communities, the burden of administrative expenditures is disproportionate. (…) One of the big problems is to Africanize business. Too often such industries as have been created, are manned by expatriates from the top management down to the last accountant. This means high emoluments, long paid vacations abroad, and, consequently, sometimes fantastically high costs. This in turn makes it more difficult to overcome the handicap of small markets. (…) What is lacking are the necessary skills, the chance to acquire management experience and access to capital.[46]

THE AFRICANISATION OF OWNERSHIP: THE MULTIPLICATION OF DEVELOPMENT BANKS

For the Caisse centrale, independence impacted two categories of actors: governments, which became fully sovereign states, and companies, which could become partly or fully African. Fostering economic independence followed three possible approaches: reliance on foreign capital, nationalisation, or the development of private capitalism at the national level. From the very early 1960s, the role of the private sector in development was identified as an important issue by the OECD Development Assistance Committee.[47] Caisse centrale funding was directed at developing the private sector and was designed to be accessible to local initiatives, whatever the nationality. Developing private capitalism at the national level required the financing of infrastructure projects, technical assistance for management (expertise or training schemes), and specific resources for investment promotion (funding of studies, appropriate technology transfers), or insurance. Between 1961 and 1964, Caisse centrale activities focused on the private sector, accounting for 41% of financial commitment, and almost the same share in the form of credit to its subsidiaries. This was far ahead of lending to states.[48]

In line with this approach the contribution of the Caisse centrale to its African banking subsidiaries combined financing and technical assistance. As their capital increased, the Caisse centrale gradually diluted its nominal share to the benefit of the new government, Caisse centrale loans funding the share of the state when necessary. Social Credit Companies were turned into 'development banks',[49] which followed the same operating principles. The Caisse centrale carried on using development banks as a privileged channel for reaching people and businesses, its credit lines following a wholesaler/retailer scheme, with Caisse centrale as wholesaler and the development banks as retailers.

Development banks seemed a good way to stimulate the emergence of a grassroots private sector, and France was soon followed in this approach by other donors that progressively extended their funding to former French colonies, and financed these banks so that they could distribute credit along with a number of development objectives, and with a leverage effect. Development banking had the effect of influencing commercial banks to improve their offer. In addition to its share of capital, the Caisse centrale also contributed to its subsidiary Crédit du Sénégal through the secondment of managers and the attribution of financial resources (credit lines). In 1960, another bank, the Senegalese Development Bank was created with a mission to collect aid from the Aid and Cooperation Fund and the European Development Fund (created when the Treaty of Rome came into force) or other donors. To reach a critical mass and given its complementarity with the Crédit du Sénégal, the two institutions were merged in 1964 into the Senegal National Bank of Development, the Caisse remaining a major contributor to its mid- and long-term resources. In the Ivory Coast, the Crédit of Côte d'Ivoire (CREDICODI), created in 1955 with the same contribution as the Senegal subsidiary had received, quickly offered a range of services including short-and medium-term credits for farms, cooperatives, agricultural associations, and craft enterprises. These extended to short-term loans for the purchase of semi-durable goods (with easier access for products sold by craftsmen already financed by CREDICODI). Other short-term credits were granted for seasonal needs, such as financing the crop cycle in rural zones. Medium-term credit was primarily intended for farming cooperatives and housing investment. Long-term loans were less common and focused on real estate acquisition or housing improvement, with easier access for residents of the housing company, SICOGI, another subsidiary, created by the Caisse centrale in 1952. In addition to CREDICODI, the Ivorian government established the Ivorian Industrial Development Bank (BIDI) in 1964, with a contribution of the Caisse equity (10.7%) as well as credit lines and technical assistance. Although 'Ivorisation' was a political priority—not only in terms of employment, but also of business ownership—the bank was created with the assistance of major foreign shareholders, including the Chase International Investment Corporation and Lazard Frères.[50] In fact, the Ivorian government wanted to legitimise this new African bank through association with prominent international partners. Its role in the finance industry promptly made the BIDI a point of reference.

Developing an African banking sector required action in relation to commercial banking as well as central banking. According to Guy Vallet,[51] a Caisse centrale agent seconded as top-ranking executive of the National Bank of Madagascar, Africanisation of staff had been a concern mostly in development banks, but not in commercial banks, which consequently had difficulties catching up.

In this early phase, the Ivorian state made subscribing to the capital of banks an instrument of its economic policy, with direct state involvement in five commercial banks ranging from 8.5% to 35%. In Senegal, the government also directly held a substantial share of three commercial banks (from 35% to 62.24%).[52] Conversely, Cissé shows that there was also a significant participation of commercial banks in the capital of development banks. But this Africanisation was mostly in terms of ownership, rather than of personnel. As regards central banking, a new Western Africa Monetary Union (WAMU) treaty was signed in 1973, replacing that of 1962, accompanied by new statutes for the Central Bank (Banque Centrale des Etats de l'Afrique de l'Ouest—BCEAO) which allowed the Africanisation of the Central Bank. According to Jeanneney, 'Its seat was transferred from Paris to Dakar, the role of the purely African authorities was strengthened, notably through the allocations given to the council of ministers of the WAMU, and the place of the representatives of the French government in the Executive Board of the BCEAO has gone from one third of the members to one seventh'.[53]

Many African executives in countries with small urban populations and new 'elites' were probably ambivalent about Africanisation. There were also tensions between professional criteria and social capital strategies. Appointing a French executive may have been a convenient way of circumventing requests from relatives or acquaintances that they be appointed to key posts. In 1974, when the Central African governments of the Franc Zone were given the opportunity to select the manager of their Central Bank (Banque Centrale des Etats d'Afrique Centrale), they faced a tricky situation and handled it in a way that suggests how difficult this period may have been. Instead of the candidate from the very influential French Treasury, the 'banker' of the Franc zone, African administrators decided in favour of a candidate of their own. Was this Africanisation? In fact, their candidate ended up being Christian Joudiou, not an African, but an expatriate Caisse executive, who had been working for twenty years in the institution. The candidate was selected without even being informed of his candidacy by his African colleagues.[54] He ceded his position to his African deputy director five years later. This story is an exception, and Africanisation, even in central banks, accelerated in the 1970s.

Was Africanisation too quick? The new bank executives, although still assisted by experts, proved unable to resist state pressure to politically instrumentalise the distribution of credit. Therefore, the situation of these banks made the Caisse more reluctant to use them as reliable intermediaries, and, from the mid-1970s, it chose to increase its direct exposure to the private sector. The first step, in 1975, was to provide loans at market conditions, although still on tied terms.[55] The second step, in 1977, was to create a subsidiary, Proparco, whose aim was to take shares in the capital of African companies.

There was controversy, however, over whether Proparco should prioritise local firms, and the Africanisation of the economy, or French interests and French firms. Since tied aid already favoured French exports, and the industrial prospects of Africa were still limited at that time, restricting the benefit of Proparco to a category of businesses would produce limited development impact. Officially, Proparco was not to prioritise French investments. However, given the context, the reality was different. In former French colonies, French companies still represented more than half of the formal sector economy, as stated in a report on industrial cooperation:

> in most French-speaking African countries these African potential partners do not exist. Also, the projects assisted by the Caisse in Côte d'Ivoire, directly or through Proparco, were in fact pushed by French companies associated with a national notable, which for the most part does not promote the training of Ivorian executives. With the emergence of a new generation of local entrepreneurs, these "joint ventures" openly appeared as majority French companies that compete with Ivorian entrepreneurs while they use loans from other sources (Canadians for example). On the other hand, the acquisition of experience and technological skills by the Ivorians followed different paths: a professional experience in a foreign company, the constitution of a network of relations, the recourse to permanent training and professional development institutions, the establishment of links with preferred suppliers, the direct recruitment of expatriate technicians, etc.[56]

Whatever the nationality of a company's ownership, there were still two difficulties to address: lack of equity and credit. Lack of equity was due to a general reluctance of investors vis-à-vis what were generally thought to be risky countries, with an evolving business climate and unclear economic policy choices. Lack of credit was still attributed to insufficient savings, as it had been in the 1950s. Finally, Stéphane Hessel, a retired diplomat, observed that

> The mechanisms necessary to encourage companies to invest more, in the psychological as well as in the financial sense, should include repayable study funds, possibly temporary participation in the capital of joint companies to be created, the financing of audit bodies having the expected capacity and reliability. It seems important, in the context of the creation of venture capital companies, to find formulas mixing public and private capital (…) in the light of the experiences acquired in this field.[57]

In a succession of reports published in 1989 and 1990 officials discussed what objectives Proparco should have.[58] These reports aimed at a reshaping of aid, and the end of the Cold War made them more insistent on the promotion of the private sector. The Thill report, focused entirely on Proparco, recommended allowing subsidiaries to use their full range of instruments. A Treasury report (by Samuel-Lajeunesse) agreed: 'the expertise acquired by the Caisse centrale in the private sector financing, especially through Proparco, is certainly very rich. But it is necessary to boost even more the range of its instruments in this field. The question of Proparco's means and the opening of its capital to industrial and banking partners should be studied'. Later, Member of Parliament Alain Vivien submitted a report to the prime minister on the renewal of cooperation. He proposed that

> A tool or a complete sequence of instruments should comprise different components: a technical assistance instrument (technical and economic training, technological research, support for the creation of enterprises), one or more preliminary study funds, a mechanism for venture capital to participate (temporarily) in the capital of mixed companies, public (Proparco type) or private, a banking instrument for medium or long-term loans, one or more guarantee funds open to SMEs (like ARIA, a prototype created by Caisse centrale to support Proparco), and finally a mobilisation and animation unit in the French industrial sector. Of course, some elements already exist for limited areas or with precarious status.

Eventually, this debate resulted in the transfer of the Caisse's private sector funding to Proparco, and this subsidiary company secured the right to provide loans in 1991.[59] Gradually Proparco made its way into the Caisse centrale group and the project financing landscape in Africa, where it became more and more autonomous in the management of its agents and their movements. However, its very existence showed how difficult Africanisation was.

CONCLUSION

Through its actions, the Caisse helped to improve and diversify the financial sector in Africa. The process of Africanisation probably took longer than the promoters of the banking sector had originally anticipated in the 1950s. In the first years of independence, Africanisation was twofold: dilution of the share of the Caisse in the capital of banks and progressive withdrawal from top management responsibilities, although promoting African staff and managers proved challenging because of the lack of skilled personnel. The creation of Proparco was meant to address this issue. In fact, although there were a growing number of African bankers, the model did not significantly change until the time of structural adjustment. But thereafter the transformation of the banking sector was more likely to be controlled by the Bretton Woods institutions than African governments or bankers.

Then came the difficult period of general debt crises in most African countries. Originally tempted to reject the structural adjustment processes,[60] which France saw as multilateral intrusion into the 'Franc zone', the French Treasury was forced not only to acknowledge the pressure that deficits of the Franc zone countries exerted on its own budgetary situation but also to endorse multilateral financial solutions. It rallied around the consensus and contributed to the process through debt rescheduling in the framework of the Paris Club, and provided additional funding with Caisse centrale's structural adjustment loans. During the adjustment period, development banks faced increasing criticism. Whereas they were able to provide medium-term finance where only short-term operations and documentary credit were available from commercial banks, their very survival was compromised by their management difficulties and the challenges of state intervention that were deemed excessive and clientelistic. If banks reflected the economic situation in their country, African public development banks reflected neo-patrimonialistic state practices under budgetary constraints, leading them to accumulate more and more suspicious credits.[61] Thus, the model of national development banks came face to face with its own limitations and stirred up growing criticism. Logically, aid providers progressively withdrew from financing development banks, preferring 'apex facilities', making their funds available to the entire banking sector via central banks, in order to avoid skewing competition. In the Ivory Coast the reform resulted in bank restructuring, without, avoiding in the end, their disappearance.[62] Finally, from 1988 to 1989, all development banks closed, including the BIDI, the CREDICODI, and the BNDA. In Senegal, the World Bank considered that the financial system was inadequate as a whole and called, in 1989, for banking reform. This resulted in massive restructuring. It follows that the final stage of the Africanisation process examined in this chapter was accompanied by important institutional changes across the entire African banking sector.

NOTES

1. Josephine Lucy Fisher *Pioneers, Settlers, Aliens, Exiles—The decolonization of white identity in Zimbabwe*. Chapter Title: The mobilisation of indigeneity (Canberra, 2010).

2. See, for instance, Donald Rothchild, *Kenya's Africanisation Program: Priorities of Development and Equity* (Cambridge, 1970); Van Der Laan H. Laurens, *Modern Inland Transport and the European Trading Firms in Colonial West Africa* (Paris, 1981); Stephanie Decker, 'Decolonizing Barclays Bank DCO? Corporate Africanisation in Nigeria, 1945–69', *The Journal of Imperial and Commonwealth History*, 33, no. 3 (2005), pp. 419–440; Andrea Cornwall, 'Historical perspectives on participation in development', *Commonwealth & Comparative Politics*, 44, no. 1 (2006), pp. 62–83; Miatta Fahnbulleh, *In Search of Economic Development in Kenya: Colonial Legacies & Post-Independence Realities* (Abingdon, 2006); Gareth Austin and Chibuike Ugochukwu Uche, 'Collusion and Competition in Colonial Economies: Banking in British West Africa, 1916–1960', *The business History Review*, 81, no. 1 (2007), pp. 1–26; Edward A. N. Dakora, Andrew J. Bytheway and André Slabbert, *The Africanisation of South African retailing: A review* (Cape Town, 2010); Fisher, *Pioneers, Settlers, Aliens, Exiles*. The approach of this paper does not extend to a later understanding of Africanisation as internationalisation of one African country to neighbouring countries or the whole continent (such as for instance Dakora).

3. Dissertations of Pierre Denizet, *Essai sur les banques coloniales* (Paris, 1899) and E. Renaud, *Les Banques Coloniales* (Poitiers, 1899) and the book of André Goumain-Cornille, *Les Banques Coloniales* (Paris, 1903). Later work provided contextual elements with a presentation of colonial economic management: R. Vally, *Les Banques Coloniales Françaises d'émission: un point de vue historique et critique* (Paris, 1924); Albert Duchêne, *Histoire*

des finances coloniales de la France (Paris, 1938) and Jean Dufour, *La monnaie* (Paris, 1943).

4. The central colonial government for French Africa was established in Senegal; this bank could operate in all territories of this jurisdiction. The end of slavery had the unexpected side-effect of promoting the banking system in French colonies, with the creation of so-called 'colonial banks'; in Africa the colonial bank was originally named Banque du Sénégal. Ghislaine Lydon elaborates on the specificities of the Banque du Sénégal vs other colonial banks in the West Indies or the Indian Ocean (Lydon, Ghislaine, *Les Péripéties d'une Institution Financière: La Banque du Sénégal 1844–1901* (Dakar, 1997)).

5. A symposium of the French history department of the Ministry of Economy and Finance dedicated to the financial issues of overseas territories included a communication on colonial banks (Lara Oruno, Inez Fisher-Blanchet, Nelly Schmidt, *Les banques coloniales de la Guadeloupe et de la Martinique pendant la deuxième moitié du XIXe siècle* (Paris, 1998)). Regarding banking more generally, Bonin, showed the prominent role of metropolitan banks before the Second World War and the central role of Colonial banks; he deplored a very limited and fragmented historiography (Hubert Bonin, *L'outre-mer, marché pour la banque commerciale (1876–1985)?* (Paris, 1998)). Some studies focused on Overseas French departments, dealing but marginally with African colonies. A paper described the case of Martinique from 1848 to 1871 (Agnès Festré, Alain Raybaut, *Banques coloniales, crédit et circulation: l'exemple de la Martinique 1848–1871* (Nice, 2009)). Only more recent work included a political economy analysis of the creation of these banks (Ines Fisher-Blanchet, *L'indemnisation des propriétaires d'esclaves dans les colonies françaises des Amériques, 1848–1855* (Paris, 1980) and Yves Ekoué Amaïzo, *Naissance d'une banque de la zone franc—1848–1901: Priorité aux propriétaires d'esclaves* (Paris, 2001)). A later compilation was published in 2011 by a former director of the Banque de France (Didier Bruneel, *Des banques coloniales à l'IEDOM* (Basse-Terre, 2011)).

6. Lionel Zinsou-Derlin, *La Banque de l'Afrique occidentale dans la crise, Revue française d'histoire d'outre-mer*, tome 63, no. 232–233 (Paris, 1976).

7. Jacques Alibert, *De la vie coloniale au défi international. Banque du Sénégal, BAO, BIAO, 130 ans de banque en Afrique* (Paris, 1983).

8. The founder of the institution, Pierre Denis (1883–1951), originally a prominent geographer, joined the League of Nations as of its creation, as advisor to Jean Monnet, and was in charge of economic and financial activities. A couple of years after the end of Jean Monnet's mandate, Pierre Denis joined the bank of the Monnet family; his banking and international experience were an asset for General de Gaulle's Free France (Philippe Oulmont, Pierre Denis, Free Frenchman and Citizen of the World (Paris,

2013). Alix Le Masson wrote two studies on the *Caisse centrale de la France d'Outremer* (CCFOM): *Le financement des investissements publics Outre-mer sous la 4ᵉᵐᵉ République* (Paris, 1994), and *La CCFOM et le financement public des investissements dans la France d'outre-mer, 1944–1958* (Paris, 1996). Sophie Dulucq analysed urban development and the financial contribution of CCFOM in *La France et les villes d'Afrique noire francophone: quarante ans d'intervention, 1945–1985; approche générale et études de cas: Niamey, Ouagadougou et Bamako* (Paris, 1997) and *Les investissements publics urbains de la France en Afrique subsaharienne: la nouvelle donne des années cinquante ?* (Paris, 1997). I published studies about the history of AFD and its subsidiaries in Côte d'Ivoire (François Pacquement, *Histoire de l'Agence française de développement en Côte d'Ivoire* (Paris, 2015)) and AFD in Haïti (François Pacquement, Margaux Lombard, *Histoire de l'AFD en Haïti—à la recherche de la juste distance* (Paris, 2018)) and about its private sector subsidiary, Proparco: *Dans les laboratoires du développement—Proparco et le secteur privé—40 ans d'histoire* (Paris, 2017).

9. The publication that followed is: *Actes du colloque d'Histoire de l'Agence Française de Développement (30 novembre 2016)* (Paris, September 2017).
10. Robert Badouin, 'Les Banques de développement en Afrique noire francophone', *Revue Tiers-Monde*, 6, no. 21, (Paris, 1965) pp. 265–271.
11. Cissé Moussa, *Les banques nationales de développement en Afrique Noire* (Paris, 1986).
12. For instance, such an in-depth analysis as Abou Bamba on Côte d'Ivoire does not dwell on banking: Bamba, Abou, African Miracle, African Mirage: Transnational Politics and the Paradox of Modernisation in Ivory Coast (Athens, OH, 2016).
13. Fisher, *Pioneers, Settlers, Aliens, Exiles.*
14. It may have been a result of a change from a vision of Africa as mostly rural—see Frederick Cooper, *Decolonization and African Society: The Labor Question in French and British Africa* (New York, 1996). The apparently technical notion of creditworthiness fuelled distrust between Africans and Europeans. In addition, such technical determinants of securities, for instance (such as land rights), made it difficult in Africa for local owners to mortgage their land or property to a foreign bank. Hence, Africans had difficulty providing security for loans. See Gareth Austin, *Land, Labour and Capital in Ghana: From Slavery to Free Labour in Asante, 1807–1956* (Rochester, New York, 2005).
15. Although the emotive charge associated with money issues should have been an incentive for banks to use national rather than foreign staff, there was a strong representation of foreigners associated to 'know-how'.
16. In this respect: see analysis of Kenya's Africanisation program in terms of priorities of development and equity (Rothchild, 1970), and Africanisation

in mining (Philip Daniel, *Africanisation, nationalisation and inequality: Mining labour and the Copperbelt in Zambian development* (Cambridge, 1979)).

17. Joseph Hodge, Gerald Hödl, Martina Kopf, *Developing Africa: Concepts and Practices in Twentieth-Century Colonialism* (Manchester, 2014).

18. Decker, 'Decolonising Barclays'; Sarah Stockwell, *The business of decolonization: British business strategies in the Gold Coast* (Oxford, 2000).

19. Decker, 'Decolonising Barclays', p. 422.

20. Oulmont, *Pierre Denis, Free Frenchman and Citizen of the World*.

21. Fabien Cardoni, Nathalie Carré de Malberg, Michel Margairaz (dir.) *Dictionnaire historique des Inspecteurs des Finances: 1801–2009* (Paris, 2012).

22. André Postel Vinay, *La passion du développement - 32 ans de Caisse centrale* (Paris 2019).

23. On the Bank of England doctrine and agenda, see Sarah Stockwell, *The British end of the British Empire* (Cambridge, 2018), pp. 142–190.

24. Postel-Vinay, André *Pierre Denis, Free Frenchman and Citizen of the World*.

25. According to Denis Cogneau, Yannick Dupraz and Sandrine Mesplé-Somps, 'between 1920 and 1944, the colonial empire was almost self-financed. Cumulated French grants represented 1.2% of cumulated expenditure only, and 0.03% of French GDP. The visible exception is Central Africa (AEF), where grants represented up to 6.6% of expenditure. Yet, the cost to Metropolitan France was negligible, and ten times compensated by grants from Indochina. (…) In the 1930s, some colonial infrastructure projects were financed by state-guaranteed loans': Denis Cogneau, Yannick Dupraz and Sandrine Mesplé-Somps 'African states and development in historical perspective: Colonial public finances in British and French West Africa', *PSE Working Papers* no. 2018–29 (2018).

26. Ibid., pp. 19, 27.

27. Louis Rey, *L'aide de la France à l'Afrique noire et à Madagascar depuis 1946*, Conférence faite à l'Université de Bâle le 26 janvier 1961.

28. Ibid., p. 6.

29. Pacquement, *Histoire de l'Agence française de développement en Côte d'Ivoire*.

30. Cissé, *Les banques nationales de développement en Afrique Noire*; Guy Rosier, *Essai sur les Sociétés de crédit social en Afrique noire*, Thèse (Paris, 1962), p. 42; Gaston Leduc, 'L'expérience française des "Crédits sociaux" en Afrique noire', *Revue internationale du travail*, no. 1 (1958).

31. Cissé, *Les banques nationales de développement en Afrique Noire*, pp. 12–13.

32. Ibid., p. 14.

33. Nicolas Bancel, *La voie étroite: la sélection des dirigeants africains lors de la transition vers la décolonisation* (Paris, 2002).

34. Ibid.

35. About the recycling of French colonial administrators, see Véronique Dimier, 'From Dakar to Brussels: Passing on Colonial Methods to the Heart of European Development Policies', in Gérard Bossuat and Gordon D. Cumming (dir.), *France, Europe and Development Aid. From the Treaties of Rome to the Present Day* (Paris, 2013).

36. Claude Panouillaud, *Le développement des territoires français d'Afrique au Sud du Sahara—Cours commun technique à l'École Nationale d'Administration* (Paris, 1955), p. 185.

37. According to Denis Cogneau, Yannick Dupraz and Sandrine Mesplé-Somps, in West and Central Africa, the share of education in public expenditure and development outcomes was 3.6% in 1925 and 7.8% in 1955. Denis Cogneau, Yannick Dupraz and Sandrine Mesplé-Somps 'African states and development in historical perspective: Colonial public finances in British and French West Africa', p. 29.

38. Julien Meimon, *En quête de légitimité. Le ministère de la Coopération (1959–1999)* (Lille, 2005), pp. 113–114.

39. The annex provides data for Senegal and Côte d'Ivoire.

40. Pignon and Solal, *Commission chargée de la réorganisation des structures de l'aide et de la coopération aux pays en voie de développement* (Paris, 1962), pp. 26–27.

41. Jean-Marcel Jeanneney, *La politique de coopération avec les pays en voie de développement* – annexe by Bandet and Creyssel (Paris, 1963), p. 203.

42. Banque Mondiale, *Croissance et perspectives économiques de la Côte d'Ivoire* (four volumes) December 1971, p. 52.

43. André Postel-Vinay, *La Caisse Centrale de Coopération Économique* (Paris, 1964), p. 9.

44. Cissé, *Les banques nationales de développement en Afrique Noire*, pp. 200–202; Caisse centrale, Annual Report (Paris, 1984), p. 51.

45. Although he served in the UN since 1954, he maintained closed relations with former colleagues of the Finance Inspection Service, one of which, Claude Gruson, was a contributor to the Jeanneney report.

46. International Law Societies of Columbia and New York Universities Conference on legal problems of investment and development in Africa - Address by Mr. Philippe de Seynes at New York University, on 3 March 1966 Outlook for African Development.

47. OECD, Development assistance efforts and policies in 1961 of the members of the Development Assistance committee (Paris, September 1962).

48. Postel-Vinay, *Pierre Denis, Free Frenchman and Citizen of the World*, pp. 203–213.

49. Two families of institutions can be called development banks, international banks (such as the World Bank, regional or bilateral banks) and domestic banks. According to Cissé (op.cit.), the latter appeared in the 1930s in Latin America. There does not seem to be a specific legal basis for defining

this category, which is rather based on the specific provision of long-term finance. William Diamond already observes that such institutions 'have taken forms so diverse that, despite frequent similarity of formal title, they often have little resemblance to each other and often have little in common'. William Diamond, *Development Banks* (Baltimore and London, 1957). Development banks may have sometimes limited or no access to short term resources such as deposits, but they rather rely on specific long-term finance (which often multilateral banks provide, such as the IFC, according to Kapur Devesh, *World Bank—Its First Half Century* (Washington, DC, 1997). There is only a semantic difference between SCCs and their successor in the newly independent states, the development banks.

50. Badouin, *Les banques de développement*.
51. Interview of Guy Vallet by the author, 17 December 2018.
52. Cissé, *Les banques nationales de développement en Afrique Noire*, p. 65.
53. Sylvianne Jeanneney, Patrick Guillaumont, *La Zone franc en perspective* (Clermont-Ferrand, 2017).
54. Source: interview by the author, November 2016.
55. With conditions of procurement tied to French exports.
56. Gilles Duruflé, Jean Hubert Moulignat, Ivana Fornesi, *Bilan et perspectives d'évolution de la coopération française en Afrique noire francophone* (Paris, 1986).
57. Stéphane Hessel, Les Relations de la France avec les pays en développement. Rapport à Monsieur le Premier ministre Paris: Premier ministre, 02/1991.
58. Jean Thill (dir.), *La Coopération française et les entreprises en Afrique subsaharienne* (Paris, 1989); Denis Samuel-Lajeunesse (dir.) *Rapport sur les orientations à moyen terme de notre politique d'aide au développement* (Paris, 1989); Stéphane Hessel, *Les Relations de la France avec les pays en développement. Rapport à Monsieur le Premier ministre* Premier ministre, pp. 56–57 (Paris, 1991); Alain Vivien, *La Rénovation de la coopération française. Rapport au Premier ministre* (Paris, 1990).
59. Pacquement, *Dans les laboratoires du développement*, pp. 93–95.
60. Carol Lancaster (in Kapur, vol 2, p. 166) assigned the designation 'structural adjustment' to the approach by the World Bank of non-oil producing countries' economic difficulties. They had to adjust their economies to export more and import less in order to be able to cover the deficit of the balance of payments. At the end of the 1980s, the recommended measures were stylised by Williamson, who described them under the term 'Washington Consensus' as primarily resulting from an agreement between the IMF, the World Bank, and the Inter-American Development Bank, on the one hand, and the US Treasury on the other.

61. For neopatrimonialistic practices of State in Africa, see Jean-François Bayart, *L'État en Afrique*. *La politique du ventre* (Paris, 1989); in the banking sector, see Béatrice Hibou, *La force de l'obéissance—économie Politique de la répression en Tunisie* (Paris, 2006).

62. This process followed different steps: the sale of state shares or the capping of state participation, the withdrawal of the state from the credit distribution process, and the removal of its safeguards borrowing by public enterprises—see Demirgüç-Kunt, Asli, Levine, Ross, The Financial System and Public Enterprise Reform Concepts and Cases The World Bank Policy and Research Department Finance and Private Sector Development Division—p. 38. (Washington, July 1994).

TABLES

Côte d'Ivoire and Senegal: French Technical assistants (including in education) in 1962 and 1963

	1962	*1965*
Côte d'Ivoire	1333 (755)	1389 (834)
Sénégal	1404 (819)	1485 (1080)

Data: rapport Jeanneney—annexe sur ' l'aide en personnel de la France aux pays en voie de développement'—Rapport particulier établi par MM. Bandet et Creyssel, Paris, 1963

Côte d'Ivoire: French Technical assistants from 1960–1965 to 1969

	1960–1965	*1966*	*1967*	*1968*	*1969*
Technical assistants	1.346	1.579	1.715	2.102	2.252
total cost (mds de FCFA)	3.5	3.5	4.8	5.6	6
Contributions France	2.2	2.1	2.1	2.1	2.1
Contributions Côte d'Ivoire	1.3	1.4	2.7	3.5	3.9
	1970	1971	1972	1973	1974
Nombre d'assistants techniques	2.476	3.034	3.115	3.250	3.390
Coût total (mds de FCFA)	7.9	9.6	10.8	12.8	14.8
Contributions France	2.1	2.4	2.6	2.8	2.8
Contributions Côte d'Ivoire	5.8	7.2	8.2	10	12

Data: Ivory Coast—The challenge of success—A World Bank Country Economic Report 1978 Table SA25 p. 353

REFERENCES

Alibert, Jacques, *De la vie coloniale au défi international. Banque du Sénégal, BAO, BIAO, 130 ans de banque en Afrique* (Chotard et associés éditeurs, Paris, 1983).

Austin, Gareth, *Land, Labour and Capital in Ghana: From Slavery to Free Labour in Asante, 1807–1956* (Rochester, New York, 2005).

Austin, Gareth, and Chibuike Ugochukwu Uche, 'Collusion and Competition in Colonial Economies: Banking in British West Africa, 1916–1960', *The Business History Review*, 81, no. 1 (2007), pp. 1–26.

Badouin, Robert, 'Les Banques de développement en Afrique noire francophone', *Revue Tiers-Monde*, 6, no. 21 (1965), pp. 265–271.

Bamba, Abou, *African Miracle, African Mirage: Transnational Politics and the Paradox of Modernisation in Ivory Coast* (Ohio University Press, Athens, OH, 2016).

Bancel, Nicolas, 'La voie étroite: la sélection des dirigeants africains lors de la transition vers la décolonisation', *Mouvements* no. 21–22, mai-juin-juillet-août (La Découverte, Paris, 2002).

Bauduin, Philippe, 'Communication sur les banques de développement', in *Actes du colloque d'Histoire de l'Agence Française de Développement—De 1941 à 2016: 75 ans d'engagement—L'Agence, ses origines, ses partenaires et ses terrains d'action* (AFD éditions, Paris, Septembre 2017), pp. 93–105.

Bayart, Jean-François, *L'État en Afrique. La politique du ventre* (Fayard, L'espace du politique, Paris, 1989).

Bonin, Hubert, 'L'outre-mer, marché pour la banque commerciale (1876–1985)?', in Jacques Marseille (dir.), *La France & l'outre-mer, Actes du colloque de novembre 1996; Les relations économiques & financières entre la France & la France d'outre-mer* (Comité pour l'histoire économique & financière de la France, Paris, 1998), pp. 437–483.

Bruneel, Didier, *Des banques coloniales à l'IEDOM (Institut d'émission des départements d'Outre-mer)* (Société d'histoire de la Guadeloupe, Basse-Terre, 2011).

Cardoni, Fabien, Nathalie Carré de Malberg, and Michel Margairaz (dir.), *Dictionnaire historique des Inspecteurs des Finances: 1801–2009* (IGPDE, Paris, 2012).

Cissé, Moussa, *Les banques nationales de développement en Afrique Noire (avec référence plus spéciale à la Banque nationale de développement du Sénégal)—Thèse pour le doctorat de l'Université de Paris l en Droit* (Université de Paris l, Paris, 1986).

Cogneau, Denis, Yannick Dupraz, and Sandrine Mesplé-Somps, 'African States and Development in Historical Perspective: Colonial Public Finances in British and French West Africa', *PSE Working Papers* no. 2018-29 (2018).

Colin, Roland, et al., 'Alors, tu ne m'embrasses plus Léopold ? Mamadou Dia et Léopold S. Senghor', *Afrique contemporaine*, no. 233 (2010), pp. 111–132.

Cooper, Frederick, *Decolonization and African Society: The Labor Question in French and British Africa* (Cambridge University Press, Cambridge, 1996).

Cornwall, Andrea, 'Historical Perspectives on Participation in Development', *Commonwealth & Comparative Politics*, 44, no. 1 (2006), pp. 62–83.

Cumming, Gordon, *Aid to Africa: French and British Policies from the Cold War to the New Millennium* (Ashgate, Aldershot, 2001).

Dakora, Edward A.N., Andrew J. Bytheway, and André Slabbert, 'The Africanisation of South African Retailing: A Review', *African Journal of Business Management*, 4, no. 5 (May 2010), pp. 748–754.

Daniel, Philip, *Africanisation, nationalisation and inequality: Mining labour and the Copperbelt in Zambian development* (Cambridge University Press, Cambridge, 1979).

Decker, Stephanie, 'Decolonizing Barclays Bank DCO? Corporate Africanisation in Nigeria, 1945–1969', *The Journal of Imperial and Commonwealth History*, 33, no. 3 (2005), pp. 419–440.

Demirgüç-Kunt, Asli, and Ross Levine, *The Financial System and Public Enterprise Reform Concepts and Cases* (The World Bank Policy and Research Department Finance and Private Sector Development Division, Washington, DC, July 1994).

Denizet, Pierre, *Essai sur les banques coloniales* (Pedone, Paris, 1899).

Dimier, Véronique, 'From Dakar to Brussels: Passing on Colonial Methods to the Heart of European Development Policies', in Gérard Bossuat and Gordon D. Cumming (dir.), *France, Europe and Development Aid. From the Treaties of Rome to the Present Day* (IGPDE, Paris, 2013), pp. 31–48.

Duchaussoy, Vincent, 'Les filiales bancaires loi de 1946 de la Caisse centrale en Afrique', in *Actes du colloque d'Histoire de l'Agence Française de Développement* (AFD éditions, Paris, 2017), pp. 83–91.

Duchêne, Albert, *Histoire des finances coloniales de la France* (Payot, Paris, 1938).

Dufour, Jean, 'La monnaie', in René Maunier (dir.), *Éléments d'économie coloniale* (Sirey, Paris, 1943).

Dulucq, Sophie, *La France et les villes d'Afrique noire francophone: quarante ans d'intervention, 1945–1985: approche générale et études de cas: Niamey, Ouagadougou et Bamako* (L'Harmattan, Paris, 1997).

Ekoué Amaïzo, Yves, *Naissance d'une banque de la zone franc—1848–1901: Priorité aux propriétaires d'esclaves* (Études africaines, L'Harmattan, Paris, 2001).

Fahnbulleh, Miatta, 'In Search of Economic Development in Kenya: Colonial Legacies & Post-Independence Realities', *Review of African Political Economy*, 33, no. 107 (2006), pp. 33–47.

Festré, Agnès, and Alain Raybaut, *Banques coloniales, crédit et circulation: l'exemple de la Martinique 1848–1871* (DEMOS—GREDEG/CNRS et Université de Nice—Sophia Antipolis, Nice, 2009).

Fisher-Blanchet, Inez, *L'indemnisation des propriétaires d'esclaves dans les colonies françaises des Amériques, 1848–1855* (EHESS, Paris, 1980).

Fisher, Lucy Josephine, *Pioneers, Settlers, Aliens, Exiles—The Decolonization of White Identity in Zimbabwe* (ANU Press, Canberra, 2010).

Goumain-Cornille, André, *Les Banques Coloniales* (J.-B. Sirey, Paris, 1903).

Guillaumont Jeanneney, Sylviane, and Patrick Guillaumont, 'La Zone franc en perspective', *Revue d'économie du développement*, 25, no. 2 (2017), pp. 5–40.

Hibou, Béatrice, *La force de l'obéissance—économie politique de la répression en Tunisie* (La Découverte, Paris, 2006).

Hodge, Joseph M., Gerald Hödl, and Martina Kopf, *Developing Africa: Concepts and Practices in Twentieth-Century Colonialism* (Manchester University Press, 2014).

Kapur, Devesh, John Prior Lewis, and Richard Charles Webb, *World Bank—Its First Half Century* (Brookings Press, Washington, DC, 1997).

Lancaster, Carol, 'The World Bank in Africa since 1980: The Politics of Structural Adjustment Lending', in Devesh Kapur, John Prior Lewis, and Richard Charles Webb, *World Bank—Its First Half Century*, Vol. 2 (Brookings Press, Washington, DC, 1997).

'Les investissements publics urbains de la France en Afrique subsaharienne: la nouvelle donne des années cinquante?', in *Actes du colloque La France et l'Outre-mer—un siècle de relations monétaires et financières* (IGPDE, Ministère de l'économie, Paris, 1997).

Le Masson, Alix, *Le financement des investissements publics Outre-mer sous la 4ème République* (Études et documents VI, CHEFF, Paris, 1994).

Le Masson, Alix, *La CCFOM et le financement public des investissements dans la France d'outre-mer, 1944–1958* (Thèse de doctorat, Université de Paris X-Nanterre, Paris, 1996).

Lydon, Ghislaine, 'Les Péripéties d'une Institution Financière: La Banque du Sénégal 1844–1901', in Saliou Mbaye, Ibrahima Thioub, and Charles Becker (eds.), *AOF: Réalités et Héritage. Sociétés Ouest-Africaines et Ordre Colonial 1895–1890* (Archives Nationales du Sénégal, Dakar, 1997), pp. 475–491.

Meimon, Julien, *En quête de légitimité. Le ministère de la Coopération (1959–1999)* (Université Lille 2, 2005).

Oruno, Lara, Inez Fisher-Blanchet, and Nelly Schmidt, 'Les banques coloniales de la Guadeloupe et de la Martinique pendant la deuxième moitié du XIXe siècle', in Jacques Marseille (dir.), *La France & l'outre-mer, Actes du colloque de novembre 1996: Les relations économiques & financières entre la France & la France d'outre-mer* (Comité pour l'histoire économique & financière de la France, Paris, 1998), pp. 365–374.

Oulmont, François, *Pierre Denis, Free Frenchman and Citizen of the World* (Nouveau Monde éditions, Paris, 2013).

Pacquement, François, *Building global policies: Development Assistance, a Source of Inspiration?* (IDGM-Sciences Po, Université d'Auvergne, Paris, October 2010a).

Pacquement, François, *Dans les laboratoires du développement—Proparco et le secteur privé—40 ans d'histoire* (Karthala, Paris, 2017).

Pacquement, François, *Histoire de l'Agence française de développement en Côte d'Ivoire* (Karthala, Paris, 2015).

Pacquement, François, 'How Development Assistance from France and the United Kingdom Has Evolved: Fifty Years on from Decolonization', (*Revue internationale de politique de développement*, no. 1) (Genève, 2010b), pp. 55–80.

Pacquement, François, and Margaux Lombard, *Histoire de l'AFD en Haïti—à la recherche de la juste distance* (Karthala, Paris, 2018).

Postel-Vinay, André, *La passion du développement—32 ans de Caisse centrale* (éditions AFD, Paris, 2019).

Renaud, E., *Les Banques Coloniales* (Thèse pour le Doctorat, Imprimerie Blais et Roy, Poitiers, 1899).

Rothchild, Donald, 'Kenya's Africanisation Program: Priorities of Development and Equity', *The American Political Science Review*, 64, no. 3 (1970), pp. 737–753.

Stockwell, Sarah, 'Exporting Britishness, Decolonization in Africa, the British State and Its Clients', in Miguel Bandeira Jerónimo and António Costa Pinto (eds.), *The Ends of European Colonial Empires. Cases and Comparisons* (Palgrave Macmillan, London, 2015), pp. 148–177.

Stockwell, Sarah, *The British End of the British Empire* (Cambridge University Press, Cambridge, 2018).

Stockwell, Sarah, *The Business of Decolonization: British Business Strategies in the Gold Coast* (Oxford University Press, Oxford, 2000).

Vally, R., *Les Banques Coloniales Françaises d'émission: un point de vue historique et critique* (Picart, Paris, 1924).

Van Der Laan, Laurens, 'Modern Inland Transport and the European Trading Firms in Colonial West Africa', *Cahiers d'études africaines*, 21, no. 84 (1981), pp. 547–575.

Williamson, John, 'What Washington Means by Policy Reform', in John Williamson (ed.), *Latin American Readjustment: How Much has Happened* (Institute for International Economics, Washington, DC, 1989).

Zinsou-Derlin, Lionel, 'La Banque de l'Afrique occidentale dans la crise', *L'Afrique et la crise de 1930 (1924–1938), Revue française d'histoire d'outre-mer*, 63, nos. 232–233 (Paris, 1976), pp. 506–518.

CHAPTER 9

The European Development Fund, a Dowry for French Companies?

Véronique Dimier

In 1952, while the Consultative Assembly of the Council of Europe and the member states of the newly created European Coal and Steel Community discussed their respective plans for the political future of Europe and how the French overseas territories could fit into them, French MP Paul Coste Floret wondered whether Africa would be willing to be offered as a 'dowry to the French European partners'.[1] Léopold Senghor, who, from 1952, took part in the work of the Consultative Assembly of the Council of Europe, shared this concern: 'we may agree in this marriage of convenience to be the servants who carried the veil of the bride, but we do not want to be the wedding gift'.[2] In 1957, after long negotiations during the preparation of the Treaty of Rome, a form of Association

This research was financed through the Gutenberg Chair, funded by the local councils of the Alsace Region and hosted by SAGE, the research Centre on Society, Stakeholders and Government in Europe, at the University of Strasbourg. I am grateful to Louis Bataille and Julia Mussig for their help in translating German documents.

V. Dimier (✉)
Université Libre de Bruxelles, Bruxelles, Belgium
e-mail: vdimier@ulb.ac.be

© The Author(s) 2020
V. Dimier, S. Stockwell (eds.), *The Business of Development in Post-Colonial Africa*, Cambridge Imperial and Post-Colonial Studies Series, https://doi.org/10.1007/978-3-030-51106-7_9

241

with overseas countries and territories was eventually agreed upon by the European Community member states, albeit without consulting the main territories concerned (mainly French and Belgian colonies in Sub-Saharan Africa).[3] Renamed the Yaoundé Convention (with the Associated African and Malagasy States, AAMS) after these territories became independent, it included trade agreements (the extension of the system of French colonial preferences to the EEC) and a financial aid instrument, the European Development Fund (EDF). In total, the fund amounted to 581.25 million ECU (EEC units of account), directly paid by the EEC member states. Its official aim was to ensure 'the development and welfare of the population' of overseas territories, but as we will see in this chapter, it proved to be a 'wedding gift' of sorts for European companies, or French ones at least.

This is certainly how it was perceived by the same European Commission civil servants who ran the fund, as exemplified by the sketch 'The metro-circulaire ou l'anti-FED', put on for the commissioner for development Henri Rochereau when he left the Commission in 1968, and a precious oral source. The piece, which was professionally recorded by the Commission unit in charge of communication, was a vivid caricature of the functioning of the EDF. All the actors were actual Commission civil servants playing their own roles. The whimsical 'metro-circulaire' was typical of the prestige projects that EDF Director Jacques Ferrandi was prone to negotiating with his 'African friends'. The idea was to build a subway system serving all of Africa, 'to enhance the grandeur and prestige of France by replicating the Paris underground system', and 'serve the particular and general interests of our associated states and member states, a project that reflected the main goal of the African people—meaning economic liberation'. The play opens with a young African ambassador coming to Brussels to present a project in the name of all the African associated countries. The young diplomat is dismissed in perfunctory style by Ferrandi: 'I know about this project. Eighteen African heads of state have already talked to me about it. (…) I've already given my agreement for this operation during my 18 missions in Africa. I have to do everything, I have to be everywhere. Everyone knows—even me—that without me the EDF would never be the EDF'. Having made the decision to fund the project, Ferrandi consults the departments of the Commission's Directorate General VIII (DG VIII) in charge of supervising EDF projects. He receives advice that includes the following:

Mr Auclert conveyed his concerns as to whether it was possible to respect the rules of competition with such a project. Indeed, if the radius of the circular metro is set in advance, this will determine the rail curve radius, which will give an advantage to the member state whose rolling mills have the same curve. On that basis, Mr Auclert painted a chilling picture to his terrified audience: it featured the UNICE [EEC business union] dragging the EDF through the dirt; the EDF Committee [representing the member states and whose approval was necessary for any project to be financed] reasserting that its main, if not unique preoccupation was that the money spent in Africa would rightly come back to Europe; and the permanent representatives of the member states complaining that the European Commission showed more interested in the development of the associated states than in the profits of European corporations. The dreaded word "discrimination" was even uttered (…). Mr Berrens, for his part, considered that the project was entirely ill-conceived. Being himself opposed to the project, he however thought necessary, were it to be accepted anyway, to launch a competition based on 27 separate calls for tenders, each split into some fifteen lots. In its great simplicity, this procedure would offset the dominant position of French firms in the associated states.[4]

Despite these objections, Ferrandi greenlights funding for the project and asks the few economists in DG VIII to provide a justification for the project before sending it to the EDF Committee for approval. Among these justifications were the following: 'this project fulfils all the requirements of Yaoundé II (…) It is a productive project, with an industrial impact because it will provide work for European industry which is very interested in supplying the track and rolling stock'. Then, each representative of a member state in the Committee seeks to have at least two metro stops bearing the name and the flag of his own country—a way to show how much they contributed financially to the project—and, of course, a share of the business for his country's firms. The project is finally accepted. After months of intrigue, a final call for tender is launched. Two big European firms compete: Vianini and Mannesmann. The Italian firm wins, in large part thanks to the Pope's benediction. The work is completed; the ribbon is cut as the music plays and the curtain falls.

The play is framed as a way to remember that the objective behind the project—and the Yaoundé Convention in general—was as much 'the development and welfare of the population' of the countries and territories associated with the EEC as the welfare, visibility, interests and prestige of its funders. The interests and priorities of the member states were already clear during the negotiations on the Treaty of Rome. Germany only agreed to participate in the future development fund (providing up to 200 million units of account, thereby matching France's contribution) for the sake of the EEC and after France had promised that German firms would get their fair share of contracts from the fund.[5] Hence, the treaty stipulated that all EDF-funded contracts should be open to all the firms in the member states and in the associated countries on equal terms. This applied equally to supply and work contracts (to implement the project) and to commissioned studies (for technical assistance and control). The European Commission, the supranational body of the EEC, had to see to it that fair terms of competition were respected. More generally, it was responsible for the administration of the EDF. The authorities of the associated countries (colonial bureaucracies and, subsequently, independent African administrations) were responsible for both presenting funding requests for suitable projects and subsequently implementing them (i.e., launching the call for tenders, choosing the winning firms and undertaking the necessary work). As they participated in the EDF Committee, EEC member states had the final say on all development projects to be financed. The Commission, through its dedicated service DG VIII, was in charge of appraising the projects proposed by the African administrations, forwarding them (along with a financial proposal) to the EDF Committee for approval, and supervising the implementation of the work undertaken by the recipient territories (including the call for tenders).[6]

As we will see in this chapter, administering the fund and enforcing free competition (one of the EEC's founding principles) proved difficult in post-colonial Africa. The difficulties came as much from the recipient states as the member states of the EEC, France especially. While I have elsewhere emphasised the direct link between former colonial officials in DG VIII and their African friends, and in particular the neo-patrimonial character of their relations,[7] in this chapter I will look more deeply at the relationships between European companies, African and EEC states, with the Commission being only one among several actors in a complex patron-client system. As discussed in the first section, France was keen to use development aid (more specifically tied aid) as a means to maintain the privileged position of its firms in its former colonies and secure its influence. However, as this strategy was shared by many donors at that time (such as the USSR, USA, Japan, China, Germany and the UK), it failed to keep competitors out of its African markets. Rather, it encouraged the local elite to take advantage of the competition between donors to get their development project approved. In the context of the neo-patrimonial state, where the legitimacy and authority of those in power depended on their capacity to distribute money to their clients, it allowed them to obtain more funding. In this sense, it would be wrong to describe the African elite as purely passive objects of domination by Western donors and their firms. However, within the framework of the EDF, this game became more complex. Indeed, access to the EDF funding was limited by clear rules (a fair competition for firms in European and associated states) supervised by a neutral entity (the European Commission). These rules had to be respected equally by the interested firms and by the African states that received funding and issued the calls for tenders. We will see here how, backed by the French state, French firms tried to distort competition in their favour at all costs, drawing on their networks in local administration and technical assistance and on dubious practices like bribery and corruption—staples of the neo-patrimonial administration. My main argument is that companies from other member states (most notably German) only acceded to EDF funding and succeeded in competing with French firms by adopting the same practices.

BUSINESS AS USUAL

As the quote by Michel Debré cited in the introduction of this book attests,[8] there is no doubt that the French government considered development aid as a means to promote its companies and economic interests in the world. The problem of course was that other countries adopted similar strategies, a competition which largely threatened the quasi monopoly of French firms in former French African colonies. As noted by Debré in the same letter: 'US aid and its procedures are a threat to our traditional exports'.[9] While Debré promised the French Fédération des industries mécaniques et transfrontalières de métaux that he would tie French aid, his administration was highly critical when the same practice was adopted by other countries. Discussing US aid and his experience with Senegal, Jean Vyau de Lagarde, the French Ambassador in Dakar, concluded: 'We may wonder why, after such a long experience in the provision of development aid to under-developed countries, the USA are still proceeding so tentatively. The reason for this is that they are bound to a moral, legal and mercantile system from which they cannot escape, because it reflects their worldview'.[10] US aid, it was noted, 'was far from free'.[11] 'Loans made in US dollars cannot be used freely. They are only granted on the condition that goods of the same value be bought in the USA'.[12] Upon first glance, it seems that President Senghor largely shared the French view of US aid: 'The head of state [of Senegal] compared French aid favourably [with US aid], deeming it more serious, more direct, simpler and much more disinterested. He underlined that this justified Senegal's preference for France, not to mention all the affective ties that link the two countries'.[13]

These 'preferential' connections could, however, easily be side-lined in favour of other friends. Japan's economic activism and attempts at 'helping' Africa were as 'warmly' welcomed by Senghor as French offers.[14] The experience of Japan, which had managed to keep its 'soul' intact as it embarked on the path to modernisation, appealed to Senghor because it resonated with his idea of 'negritude': it served as 'an example for Africa, which is pursuing both development and the conservation of its traditions'.[15] Japanese interests in Africa were manifold and largely similar to those of France at the time. One of them lay in securing a supply of raw materials and new markets; another was more political, consisting in 'expanding a base of political clients in the 50 states of the continent, whose vote in the international organisations could be useful to Japan down the line'.[16] 'We expect to see Japan and Africa develop closer economic ties and bonds of friendship. Admittedly, great powers like France have always tried to obstruct Japanese trade in Africa, but this cannot go on indefinitely'.[17] Hence, the most pressing need for Japan was to 'open African states to the Japanese economy, particularly the former French colonies, which, until now, were almost always closed for its business'.[18] One of the strategies to achieve this consisted in offering states credit (in the form of development aid) to buy Japanese products. For that purpose, Japanese official delegations, including business delegations and 'study missions', began touring around Africa.[19] They even began to inquire about the conditions and rules of call for tenders launched through the EDF and the FAC, only to realise that they were not open to outsiders.[20] These strategies worked quite well: from then on, Japanese products (textiles, cars, transistors) began pouring into the African market.[21] This invasion was a great source of concern for French firms in Africa: 'The Japanese, who, until recently were not very active in Mali, have shown a keen interest in this country, especially putting effort into looking for rare metals and selling car parts. (…) As far as the automobile sector is concerned, the Hino firm has recently made a spectacular break through in Mali. (…) The director of the Compagnie malienne des transports routiers reported that his company had offered to purchase nearly 480 additional vehicles from Hino, to be delivered within five years, and up to an amount of 4,800,000,000 Malian Francs (48 million French Francs). Reportedly, exceptional financial facilities have been offered to pay for the first tranche and the Japanese government has granted an additional supplier credit. In light of these projects, one may wonder whether the Japanese firm might be aiming to eliminate all its competitors by using unorthodox commercial methods'.[22] This was enough to worry the local representatives of French firms Berliet and Saviem. Commercial agreements between Senegal and Japan as well as Japanese development projects had serious consequences for French firms, resulting in the 'sharp decrease of European imports—especially from France. In particular, the French automobile industry, which is practically the sole supplier of cars on the Senegalese market, will have to face serious competition'.[23]

Similarly, serious competition also came from the USSR, Soviet satellite countries, China[24] and Europe itself: 'President Senghor has acknowledged that British investors were beginning to know the way to Dakar and he invited even more of them to come'.[25] As shown by Abou Bamba in this volume, the competition between donors was largely fuelled and used to their advantage by African leaders.[26] Disappointed by the outcome of the Yaoundé Convention, Senghor went so far as to conclude: 'With Europe failing us, we will turn to China as a last resort. I am not saying that I will proceed this way, but I am only one among 3,800,000 Senegalese'.[27] The message to the EEC was clear.

Lobbying the French government for funding and manoeuvring to influence the form taken by the calls for tenders issued by African administrations were the best ways to negotiate and secure future contracts for French firms. This is clear from the response of the French ambassador in Abidjan to a query by Alsthom (a French company that specialised in the electricity sector):

> Mr Diawara argued that the clause [required by Alsthom] stipulating that firms from Common Market countries must have at least 35 percent of French supplies, was doubly ill-advised: it projected a warped image of French-Ivorian cooperation by giving the impression that the project was somehow the preserve of French builders. The clause, discouraging EEC firms from taking an interest in the project, did not allow the Energie électrique de Côte d'Ivoire (EECI) [the government agency responsible for the call for tenders] to ensure that submitted proposals were competitive (…).

On the other hand, the Minister has reminded me that he did not allow Japanese firms to compete, because they would have constituted a real threat to French builders. I am convinced that Ivorian technicians, the EECI leadership and Minister of Planning want French builders to win the bid. But Mr Diawara also insisted that the competition should be open enough to avoid accusations that the EECI used Franco-Ivorian cooperation to issue an ostensibly open call for tenders that would be in practice reserved to French builders.[28]

As competition became compulsory within the framework of the European Development Fund, in the form of open calls for tenders, French firms were less free to act pre-emptively and their strategies had to be refined accordingly...precisely to avoid competition.

THE EDF: A PIGGY BANK FOR FRENCH FIRMS

In 1965, the German embassy in Senegal complained about the Senegalese government's proclivity for levying taxes on certain kinds of machines. This resulted in an increased cost for certain German firms, which became less competitive in their responses to EDF calls for tender. The embassy thus asked the German Ministry of Foreign Affairs to write to Brussels to demand that DG VIII add such practices to the discriminatory clause.[29] The 'discrimination' issue mentioned in the sketch discussed earlier attracted much criticism by German firms and their representatives, the Bundesverband der Deutschen Industrie (BDI), Afrika Verein and the Hauptverband der Deutschen Bauindustrie. Dr Walter Sheel, the German minister of cooperation, even bluntly declared that 'the money paid by Germany to the EDF goes directly to the French cashier'.[30]

Such criticisms were largely justified in light of the following figures: French companies were awarded over 40% of contracts for the first EDF (1958–1964), vs. 13.88% for Italy, 3.28% for Germany, 2.37% for Belgium, 4.48% for the Netherlands and 0.25% for Luxembourg, the rest (35.74%) being allocated to firms from the associated states, that is, indirectly to French firms.[31] Indeed, besides setting up subsidiary companies, one of the strategies employed by French firms to retain their monopoly in former colonies was to don 'false colours' in an effort to present themselves as local.[32] For example, at a time when President Senghor was calling for the 'Senegalisation' of the local economy, they became African. Their board would include one or two Senegalese members, usually influential political figures, but their capital would mainly come from abroad. As a German official noted, most associated states would tend to favour local firms, who themselves tended to make undervalued offers, even though these practices could not be proven legally.[33] This would indirectly favour French interests, most notably in the construction sector, which was largely put to work in the infrastructure projects favoured by the associated states and the EDF. The BDI[34] noted that this was a sector in which the gap between French and German shares of EDF contracts was the widest.[35] Not everyone was fooled by the strategy of French firms, however, and certainly not the Italian and German firms, who kept complaining about this state of affairs.[36] By contrast, a French official boasted: 'the EDF's intervention in Mauritania has so far had positive outcomes for the French economy, since all of the study contracts and calls for tenders have been won by firms from the Franc zone, to an extent that it is to be feared that France's partners in the EEC might take offence. To avoid future difficulties, French firms should progressively team up with firms from the other five member states'.[37]

Beyond this apparent good will, French firms kept on arguing that things were not as bad as other member states contended: 'It seems that the main reason for the intervention of our partners is a wrong interpretation of the outcomes of tenders. It is wrong to assume that France was awarded a range of supply contracts on the basis that the firm who won the bid was French'.[38] Indeed, taking its own example, the Société commerciale des potasses d'Alsace mentioned a call for tenders where its own subsidiary company, the Société d'engrais et de produits chimiques d'Afrique Equatoriale, in Douala, won the bid (for three fertiliser lots). This subsidiary, however, had to procure supplies from firms in a variety of member states (49% in France, 10.2% in Belgium, 16.6% in Germany, 5.5% in Holland, 18.4% in Italy). According to that firm: 'It is clear that if the EDF attributes this supply solely to France's credit again, it will result in a wrong interpretation from our partners, hence a perfectly sound reaction which could be detrimental to our interests (…). From our point of view, the nationality criterion is insufficient and should be complemented by taking into account the origin of the goods'.[39] Certainly, the numbers given above may be distorted by some misinterpretation. Still, the dominance of French firms in EDF contracts was undeniable. As a German construction firm, Strabag, concluded, the French government went to great lengths to protect the interests of the French companies in Africa.[40]

For the German Ministry of Foreign Affairs, there was no doubt that this French 'indulgence' and administrative influence were detrimental to German industry.[41]

Undeniably, firms from other member states encountered many obstacles compared to the French firms that were already established in Africa. The first of these obstacles was the right to establish an enterprise in an associated state. During the negotiations on the Treaty of Rome, Bonn had defended and eventually obtained from France equal rights for all European firms to establish themselves in French overseas territories. In practice, however, the French administration did nothing to facilitate the establishment of German or Italian enterprises or nationals in territories which were still under French sovereignty.[42] After decolonisation, the Yaoundé Convention bound each associated country to amend its laws and regulations to that effect within three years. However, it seems that German consultancy firms still faced many hurdles in the form of local regulations in trying to establish themselves in Africa.[43] Indeed, local rules and practices could easily make laws null and void, especially within the framework of the neo-patrimonial states. Administrative opacity and operating outside of the rules were constant features of the neo-patrimonial system. Above all, the system rested on the capacity of political leaders to 'nurture' clients by distributing sinecures and money taken from external aid and other sources. Hence, African administrations were prone to using a jungle of regulations and irregular practices, such as bribery and corruption, to protect their local interests against any kind of competition and maintain their patronage networks. Requests for access to official documents and exemptions from rules were excellent opportunities to extract money from the applicants, often firms looking to establish themselves or to consult documents related to a call for tenders. These 'administrative' expenses were variable and sizeable, as the Hauptverband der Deutschen Bauindustrie noted.[44]

French firms were used to this jungle of regulation and opaque rules. They were able to rely on highly personal and privileged relationships with the local elites, as German officials emphasised.[45] They were also used to bribing local administrations to secure a contract, a bid or some official documentation. Those practices were so common that the bribes given to obtain favours from African officials were tax-deductible in France and remained so until the 2000s—a boon for French firms, bolstering their advantage over their competitors.[46] This largely explains the many irregularities in the call for tenders launched by African administrations under the supervision of the Commission, irregularities that the European Court of Auditors later on highlighted: these bids only aimed to hide the fact that firms had been selected beforehand.[47] Such 'irregular' practices were largely criticised by French firms themselves when, in the case of Congo Brazzaville, they lost the bid against Belgian companies: being based in Leopoldville (current DRC), Belgian companies had facilities to produce materials (such as concrete) which proved less costly than those imported from France. To be able to export materials to Congo Brazzaville, they needed 'the preliminary agreement of the authorities in Leopoldville, as export of materials is subjected to payment in a hard currency or to a barter trade agreement. But given the current state of the Congo and given the irregular practices which are established in the administration of this state, we believe this is possible'.[48]

Such 'irregular' practices were more difficult to indulge in for firms which had never been in Africa before and lacked the knowledge and the networks necessary to obtain privileges.[49] The difficulty of creating personal contacts with African elites was more than clear to the German federation representing the construction companies (Hauptverband der Deutschen Bauindustrie): the participation of German firms in the EDF bids still suffered from 'the political weight of France in its former colonies'. 'Administrative hindrances', 'personal contacts, the French language, the fact that French firms had long been established in those countries', and, last but not least, 'the local preference in favour of firms from the former colonial power' were all seen as obstacles to the participation of German firms in the EDF bids.[50] Hence, as officials from the German Ministry of Foreign Affairs underlined, the necessity for German firms to develop informal ties with local administrations.[51] The reason why German firms were losing bids, according to one of them, was that compared to their Italian counterparts, they were not active enough on the ground (economically, but also and more specifically, politically).[52] This was a difficult task, however: in 1967, Ivory Coast president Houphouët-Boigny invited a German delegation to discuss future German investments in the country, but to the great disappointment of the Germans, he left the discussion to a French adviser. 'The German delegation was very angry. They wanted to talk with the Ivorians, not the French'.[53] This was also a risky game, as the German government became the target of the same blackmail as the French: as he was looking for funding for the creation of a free zone in Dakar, Senghor asked the German chancellor to react quickly in order for German firms to have their 'chance'. Indeed, the

USSR were interested in creating a tuna factory and the USA were competing with the member states to take their place—not to mention the Chinese. The German government was expected to encourage and give more money to large firms like Mannesmann to ensure their greater involvement in development projects.[54] The lesson, as we will see, was learned.

Another obstacle lay in the fact that the administrations of the associated states were responsible for drafting the tender documents, calling for tenders and then selecting the bids and granting the contracts. It was not just that procedures differed from one country to another; tenders, contract laws and technical specifications (cahier des charges) were most likely to be written in French and follow French procedures, themselves largely influenced by colonial ones, as the BDI pointed out.[55] Moreover, in former French colonial territories, because of the absence of local skilled personnel, most administrations needed technical assistance in order to conceive their own projects, write the preliminary studies included in the project proposals, draft the tender documents, supervise the bid, control the execution and so forth. In doing so, they were advised mostly by French technical staff, consultancy firms and former colonial officials who had stayed on after decolonisation.[56] This was one of the things German officials and firms kept complaining about: those who devised the project proposals, prepared the call for tenders and selected the bids were mostly former colonial personnel, who were prone to favouring French firms.[57] Indeed, through their work on the preliminary studies required to be included in all project proposals, these experts were in a position to influence them during the formulation phase.

This raised the issue of the difficulty of ensuring neutrality in the technical definition of the work covered by the project proposals and calls for tenders. Tender documents drafted by local administrations could include technical specifications and norms so detailed and specific (featuring, for instance, in an example denounced by a German firm, an avalanche of technical French terms and numbers that only the French could decipher) that they would favour some firms at the expense of others. In some cases, the safety standards specified in the call also required machines and products to be certified by a specific agency (e.g., the consultancy firm SOCOTEC). The problem was that German firms did not know anything about SOCOTEC's criteria, and there was no indication in the call for tenders as to the person who could provide that kind of information.[58] In sum, contract laws and technical specifications remained an 'enigma' for most German firms.[59]

The BDI, for its part, continued to complain about the 'hidden words' that implied French fabrication and products (especially in the pesticide sector), precluding firms which produced the same good with a different name from making an offer.[60] This was a direct reference to the experience of Bayer, who also complained to the Chamber of Commerce of Frankfurt. In 1966, Bayer tried to participate in all the EDF calls for tenders where pesticides were involved, but did not win any of these bids. Indeed, the technical specifications only allowed pesticides based on specific molecules (carbon and hydrogen). Bayer, who was producing pesticides with similar effects but with different molecules, could not participate in the bid, even though, according to its representative, the product was much less toxic for the local population. Indeed, the local administration—a Frenchman, the letter said—singlehandedly decided that the pesticide produced by Bayer was not equivalent to the one described in the technical specifications of the call for tenders. This was the last straw for Bayer, who made several proposals to the German government—most notably that the Commission should publish a list of all pesticides, set up an agency to test the products and prove their equivalence, as well as make these tests and the resulting list available to the public. In any case, leaving testing and the choice of equivalence in the hands of local administrations was hopeless: according to Bayer's representative, if one African state really wanted to favour the products of a specific firm, nothing could be done.[61] This was a clear recognition of the collusion between French firms and the local elites.

The problem was deftly summarised by a representative of the Bremen Chamber of Commerce: 'The conditions of the call for tenders are drafted in such way as to give a clear advantage to firms already established in the country, through local branches or representations. This is clear if we consider the supplementary agreements of the call for tenders (like added services) that only local firms can fulfil but that are not essential to the project's aim'. As the same person remarked, some of these requirements were not even included in the specifications of the call. 'Technical specifications linked to orders of works and services made by ACP states are often drafted with a certain type of products in mind. This is largely due to the action of consulting firms, which had influenced the project proposal beforehand, during its formulation'.[62] Of course, as a German consultant explained, consulting firms of a given country would tend to favour the norms and products of their country, which would then give a clear advantage to that country's firms once the call for tenders was launched. This national bias was further enabled by quick communication (with a shared language) and psychological factors (the tendency to favour nationals or have a national approach).[63] The representative of the BDI was even more categorical: in the associated states, there was abundant propaganda against German projects. This was largely due to the lack of neutrality among the French technicians and advisers within African administrations, who would openly give advantages to French firms.[64]

While having overly detailed technical specifications was problematic, an exceedingly broad description of a project could result in too much uncertainty for the firms concerned. This was also denounced by a representative of the Chamber of Commerce of Bremen: 'German firms interested in EDF bids complained that those bids were written in such a manner as to preclude the involvement of any specialised firm. They involve products or services so different from one another that no single firm can provide them'.[65] As the European Commission itself concluded, after recognising this problem: 'Finding a middle way between too vague a description and too precise specifications was the rule of the art in the working out of the tenders' documents'.[66]

In any case, as the BDI stressed, reinforcing the German presence in Brussels was necessary at the preparation level, within the departments in charge of supervising the preliminary studies,[67] but also on the ground, where the consultancy firms entrusted with these studies were operated. The weakness, it was recognised, lay in the lack of German consultancy firms in Africa: if they were involved in devising the preliminary studies and the calls for tenders, these could help German firms in the construction and supply sector to respond to calls. This collaboration between consultancy firms and construction companies was expected to allow the latter to avoid misinterpreting specifications in the bids.[68] Afrika Verein, another association representing the interests of German firms in Africa, even proposed sending its own technical advisers to Africa, using German bilateral aid, to help the African administrations write up project proposals and to remedy 'the discrimination' issue.[69] This is exactly what President Houphouët-Boigny replied to the German delegation who complained about having met only French advisers: 'in order to give advantage to German investments and avoid embarrassing mediation through French advisers', he needed to rely on German consultants.[70]

Having German consultants on the ground could provide the added advantage of providing quicker access to information. Otherwise, even though calls for tenders were published in the European Community's *Official Journal*, established French firms, thanks to their links with the local administration, generally received information earlier than their European competitors. As German firms had to have the documents translated, their chances of meeting deadlines were even slimmer, which in some instances led to discrimination. For example, in Senegal, German firms heard about a call for tenders, but never found information about it. When they asked the Senegalese administration for documents, they did not receive replies. They eventually received a small note about the call, but it was too late to make an offer. Similar experiences occurred in Madagascar, which led the representatives of the German construction firms to conclude that this was definitely a French business; hence, they insisted that the German government intervene at the European Commission level so that German firms could have a chance.[71] In Somalia, a German firm had to pay 200 DM to obtain a document in Italian from the local government. Despite this, they did not receive the document in time, as the local government argued that they had never received the money.[72]

This problem was largely outlined by the German Federal office for information about external trade (BfAI), which stressed that access to information was absolutely necessary to ensure fair competition and to fulfil the interests of the German industry. It noted, for instance, that the DG VIII's bulletin *Le Courrier* was only published in French.[73] This was also noted by a representative of the Bremen Chamber of Commerce: 'After numerous observations, we found that the following issue was problematic: deadlines concerning the calls for tender are too short, as calls for tenders are published late'. He added: 'German firms are not active and present enough on the ground to search for preparatory information that would allow them to be competitive'.[74] However, as the Hauptverband der Deutschen Bauindustrie noted, finding information in Africa could amount to an 'obstacle course':[75] not only did contract laws and technical specifications attached to EDF calls for tenders differ from one country to another, but these documents ordered the firms in question to comply with the laws and rules of the recipient country in the implementation of the works (and therefore in their bids). The problem was that these rules and laws were never attached to the documents. Finding them and getting them translated was a time-consuming process, which deterred many German firms from making offers. In addition, taxes and customs duties could vary so much from one country to the next, as well as in the same country from one day to the next, that making the estimate of costs required by the tender documents was almost impossible, as noted by a German firm which was asked to pay 53% additional taxes but never received a response as to whether this was right or not.[76] Hence, the German firms repeatedly demanded the exclusion of such costs (especially for supply contracts) from the bids, arguing that they should instead be paid directly by the EDF to the recipient state.[77] Overall, German representations in Africa (at the political level) needed to make a greater commitment not only to finding and circulating information, but also to defending the interests of German firms in the field and in Brussels.[78]

This was all the more necessary as the discrimination occurred not only at the adjudication stage, but also at the implementation stage. As a German firm noted, even when a German firm won a call for tenders, it would face many obstacles as a result of local rules, insufficient awareness of taxes and customs law, not to mention added 'administrative' expenses.[79] In addition, French firms had easy access to cheap supplies and machines that were already paid off and ready to be used on the spot, while their German counterparts had to import them and pay for transportation and taxes.[80] French firms (unlike German ones) could also obtain cheap credits from local banks, which were in fact subsidiary companies of French banks or banks with a significant French influence, as François Pacquement shows in this volume. This was all the more problematic as EDF payments to the firms involved in the implementation of projects were often delayed by the recipient states. These firms needed intermediary credits to honour their engagements. In addition, as the currency in use was the local currency, that is, Franc CFA for most states, French firms avoided the cost and risks of currency exchange and money transfers.[81] State guarantees in case of political upheavals were also more expansive for German companies: those looking to make an offer for a development project in an African country had to ask for a Hermes credit, granted by the German government to cover possible losses and risks inherent in these countries. But the firm had to pay a 20% deductible, much more than the 5 or 10% usually asked from French firms within the French system.[82] Only big German firms could afford these multiple costs and risks, but, as many German officials noted, the projects were not big enough to attract their interest,[83] or to encourage them to create subsidiary firms in Africa.[84] As a German firm concluded, given all the obstacles they faced, it was surprising that German firms even secured 4% of the EDF contracts at all.[85] Some

German firms did not hesitate to call the situation the 'biggest Panama since Panama', a scandal paid for by the German taxpayer.[86]

DEALING WITH THE 'DISCRIMINATION ISSUE'

The Commission and its officials were heavily criticised by German firms for giving advantages to French companies. French officials in DG VIII, it was believed, were more qualified than their German counterparts and had more contacts with the French administration in Paris, whereas German Commission officials had little contact with the German government.[87] True, until mid-1975, DG VIII was dominated by a small team of French colonial officials led by Jacques Ferrandi, who was recruited as the head of cabinet of the first commissioner for development, the French businessman Robert Lemaignen, and who became the EDF director from 1963 to 1975. Ferrandi's omnipotence, clientelistic practices and disregard for the rules in distributing the EDF money are highlighted in the 'metro-circulaire'.[88] In practice, shopping lists of projects were presented directly to Ferrandi by African heads of state and then appraised on an ad hoc basis. Criteria used for this appraisal were above all linked to Ferrandi's opaque bonds of loyalty with the heads of state in question, to French or European political and economic priorities in Africa, and to the 'political needs' of the emergent African elite.

It would, however, be wrong to conclude that Ferrandi was simply promoting French interests. Even though he had close ties to French business circles,[89] he had an interest in acting as the arbiter between the member states, in order to increase his own power within DG VIII and the credibility of the European Commission in running the EDF.[90] Ferrandi (a former colonial official) had been director general of the economic services of the French West African Federation in Dakar from 1953 to 1958, an important position which allowed him to build an extensive network among African political elites, as well as valuable experience with local French firms and technical assistance. However, when in 1960 France proposed to entrust control of the EDF projects and technical assistance to French firms, Ferrandi proposed to set up his own monitoring team instead. Thanks to German support, this system was eventually established in 1963.[91] These 'technical controllers', later renamed 'Commission delegates', were member states nationals hired under individual private contracts. As Ferrandi's permanent delegates on the ground they had several functions: assisting African administrations in devising their projects (technical assistance); supervising the calls for tenders launched by African administrations; and monitoring their implementation of the projects and their use of the allocated funds.[92]

In addition to introducing the technical controllers, Ferrandi tried hard to increase the transparency of the adjudication procedures and to make information available.[93] Calls for tenders were publicised in numerous specialist journals in member states and in several languages (in addition to the *Official Journal* of the EEC and of the AAMS country concerned). The Commission forwarded records for each project (including technical and financial details) to the Permanent Representations in Brussels and the information offices of the EEC in the member states. These records were also supposed to be circulated locally by the AAMS concerned among the relevant consulates. The results of the calls for tenders (the amount of the contract and name of the contractors) were published in the *Official Journal* under a special heading.

Following recurrent German criticisms and as negotiations for Yaoundé II in 1968 neared, a meeting was organised in July 1967 between the European Commission and German representatives to discuss a variety of measures (most notably those proposed by the BDI and the Hauptverband der Deutschen Bauindustrie) to improve the conditions of competition among the firms interested in the EDF bids: one of them was to write a general specifications document for all the EDF-funded contracts, to be translated into the Community's four languages.[94] This involved standardisation and modernisation of the relevant contract law and technical specifications to be applied in the associated countries. As the Commission representative noted, this was politically sensitive, as it could be considered a breach of sovereignty by the African states concerned: it was as if the Commission was making laws for the associated states.[95] Following these talks, a general specifications document was eventually drafted,[96] and a German official, Klaus Prange, was appointed to head the DG VIII department in charge of the calls for tenders.

Another measure, backed by France and Germany, was to encourage the creation of consortiums of firms from several member states. French representatives suggested that the French administration could act as an honest broker in these contacts and proposed setting up a working group for representatives from firms and administrations to exchange their experiences and find practical solutions to their problems. It was agreed that the Commission would organise contacts between French and German firms already established in Africa and between the business unions of both countries. In fact, in 1959, Robert Lemaignen and Helmut Allardt, respectively the French commissioner for development and the German director general of DG VIII, had already decided to support the formation of a joint French and German group of consultants, similar to that of the Société générale d'études et de planification in Paris, which brought together French, Belgian and Italian consulting firms.[97]

Ferrandi himself regularly travelled around Europe to meet business-men and representatives of the German, Dutch and Italian governments in order to encourage them to be more active in their efforts to bid and join consortiums with French firms.[98]As a representative of the Hauptverband der Deutschen Bauindustrie later remarked: 'German firms have been trying to work around the problems they encounter (relating to the privileged ties between France and its former colonies or language issues), by establishing working communities with French firms'.[99] However, these strategies had their limitations. The German minister of cooperation, after talking with French business representatives, recog-nised that many offers of cooperation by French firms were turned down by their German counterparts.[100] A representative of the BDI reported that many German firms resented working in collaboration with French ones, because they could not stand some of their habits. But the main obstacle came from local firms which were unequivocally against any cooperation. There were also anti-German feelings in most African states. In addition, France, thanks to its influence and hefty contributions to the budgets of many African states, was playing a double game: in some cases, German firms made tremendous efforts to provide studies and bid for a project, but in the end the EDF project was granted to a French firm. Indeed, French authorities declared to the African authorities concerned that if the firms selected were not French, they would stop contributing to their budget entirely.[101]

Last, but not least, EDF projects were split into several small shares, a strategy which was supposed to give more chances to firms from diverse member states, as the 'métro-circulaire' sketch noted. There were side effects to this strategy: one of them was that it discouraged large compa-nies, those who could have a chance to win a call, from making offers.[102] In 1966, President Houphouët-Boigny, for instance, wondered why so few German firms, especially major ones like Krupp, responded to a call concerning the construction of a paper mill.[103] The other side effect was the reinforcement of French dominance on the ground. An Italian docu-ment noted that with many EDF projects split into small shares, local or 'already established firms, most notably those of certain member states', tended to be favoured, clearly sparing the blushes of France.[104] This was also deplored by German officials and businesses.[105] The situation continued to puzzle EDF officials: in May 1962, the EEC representatives wondered why only already established firms, meaning French ones, had made an offer for a road project in the Casamance area of Senegal. They attributed this first to the multiple numbers of shares and to the high cost of applying, and second to the fear of coming up against local firms who had knowledge of the country and had materials available on the ground.[106]

In fact, despite the Commission's intensive efforts to solve 'the discrimination issue', companies regularly brought cases to the European Court of Justice, claiming that the Commission had failed to exercise its power of regulation in the context of tender procedures.[107] Yet, the Commission's powers in that area were actually limited. The German representative of the BDI argued that the problem of German firms in West Africa was not linked to EDF rules, but to the countries themselves and their tax and customs systems and regulations on construction—aspects over which the European Commission had no control. The real problem, he said, was that administrations in these countries worked hand in hand with local firms, and this problem could not be solved by adapting the EDF rules. Likewise, modifying the rules would do nothing to change the fact that long-established firms resented the idea of German firms coming and investing in Africa, and openly displayed their resentment. As the German representative of the BDI concluded, the main obstacle for German firms looking to do business in Africa was 'psychological'.[108] The German minister of the economy came to the same conclusion: things could not be changed by merely using administrative rules.[109]

Being aware of this state of affairs, the Commission eventually decided to resort to psychology, meaning here 'disloyal practices'. It intervened on the ground and tried to 'influence' local administrations in the way they dealt with calls for tenders. This kind of intervention came to annoy the French authorities: in Senegal (Casamance), where a German firm specialising in road construction won the EDF bid (being the lowest bidder, according to the European Commission), the French clearly thought that 'the argument put forward by the Commission was not at all convincing and could not hide the fact that Brussels had decided, well before the results of the call for tenders were known, to give its preference to the firm Sotrapom Hotzman [a German firm already established in Senegal, where it had already participated in German-funded development projects]'.[110]

The Commission's efforts were not always rewarded, however, as the Strabag affair exemplifies. One of the few construction firms interested in EDF projects, Strabag tirelessly lobbied the German government, the Bundestag and the European Commission, complaining about its lack of success in responding to the EDF's calls for tenders. In 1962, after Strabag lost yet another bid for an EDF road project in Somalia (eventually granted to an Italian firm), the Commission decided to talk to the Somalian government and convinced them to launch a new call for tenders (without the participation of the Italian firms). However, Strabag never made an offer, which led enraged Commission officials to conclude that the 'discrimination issue' was not so much due to discriminatory practices or rules as to the lack of interest of German firms in EDF contracts.[111] The same situation irritated the EDF controller in Niger, who noted that: 'German firms did not even participate in the bids (and make an offer). This is also the case for construction companies, who do not waste an opportunity to complain to the German government about their non-participation in the EDF projects'.[112] The German director general, Heinrich Hendus, himself deplored that German firms, although they kept complaining, did not play the game and made no effort to bid for EDF contracts.[113] Even the representative of the Hauptverband der Deutschen Bauindustrie began to suspect that these complaints might be exaggerated.[114]

Turning Local

Eventually, discrimination among European companies let up to some extent: in 1980, German firms obtained 12.52% of all EDF contracts, compared to 22.71% for France, 7.01% for the UK, 6.10% for Belgium, 13.61% for Italy, 0.38% for Luxembourg, 5.13% for the Netherlands, 0.85% for Denmark, 0.32% for Ireland, 1.32% for third countries and 30.05% for the ACP.[115] However, it appears that this was due equally to the adaptation of German and Italian enterprises to local practices and to the European Commission's efforts to set up more transparent and clearer rules. The complaints of French firms regarding the practices of other European firms make this clear. In 1965, the dubious practices of an Italian enterprise 'deeply affected' the French companies that lost the bid.[116] According to the French official who wrote the letter, the firm in question 'had a permanent representative in Brussels and many contacts in EEC circles (…) The owners of the firm are on personal terms with certain European Commission civil servants, most remarkably Berrens, an engineer from Luxembourg tasked with supervising the works done by the EDF in the Indian Ocean area'. According to him, the Italian firm was able to make a much cheaper offer than competitors (French ones included) because it had cheated. There was no doubt indeed that the firm 'intended to, and eventually succeeded in, getting the EDF authorities to accept technical solutions which were not in accordance with the initial call for tenders, but which proved, in the end better, and obviously, less costly that those envisaged by the call'. To be able to do this, the French official argued, 'the firm had benefited from some favours on the part of EEC authorities in general and from Berrens in particular'. 'If French firms had, during the adjudication, the certainty that they could have used techniques that differed from those specified in the call for tenders for some parts of the work, they too would have been able to propose more competitive offers'. Hence, the letter asked whether (within the EDF framework) 'there was a possibility for firms who won a bid, to receive exemptions from the technical specifications of the call for tenders during the execution of the work, allowing them to use cheaper material than initially envisaged. French firms should be informed of this possibility in order to take this into account when making offers'.[117] The French official concluded: 'One of the EDF's basic rules consists in dealing with firms from all over the EEC on an equal footing. We are under the impression this is not always the case when some foreign controllers are involved'.[118]

'Turning native' was no easy task. Some German firms faced a steep learning curve. For example, the firm Gauff Consultants, a consulting firm specialising in infrastructure and water projects, had the unfortunate idea of handing a bribe directly to a Commission civil servant, who gave it to an African minister (in 1968). When the incident came to light (in 1974), the civil servant was fired and the firm banned from competing in subsequent EDF calls for tenders. The firm brought a case to the European Court of Justice to complain about this state of affairs, arguing that the incident had a damaging effect on its reputation and its ability to compete for tenders on a broader market, and even sought damages. Their lawyer claimed that, under Belgian and German law, only the civil servant was at fault. They also pressured the German Permanent Representation in Brussels to intercede on their behalf with the German Director General of DG VIII, Karl Meyer.[119]

The 'Mannesmann affair' was another case in point.[120] Mannesmann, a giant in the German steel industry, convinced Léopold Senghor, the president of Senegal, to build a 300km-long water pipe from Guiers Lake to

Dakar. The project was first presented to the French government for funding, but was rejected by the French Ministry of Cooperation and the Ministry of Foreign Affairs. The truth was that the project, in its original form, would benefit a German firm at the expense of French companies. While it had secured some funding from the German Ministry of Cooperation, the Senegalese government sought EDF support and submitted a first proposal in 1964. The proposal was soon opposed by Ferrandi, who deemed the project both technically flawed and too expensive, as it would have absorbed the entirety of the EDF funds allocated to Senegal. In addition, the technical specifications of the project were so detailed that they prevented all other firms, most notably French ones, from competing.[121] His view was shared by the French Ministry of Cooperation.[122] Their complaints about the 'dubious' practices of Mannesmann and Senghor (meaning here, bribery) speak volumes about the whole 'affair'.[123] When Senghor proposed the project a second time, Ferrandi's team, in collaboration with a consultancy firm, the French Bureau des recherches géologiques et minières, provided a competing plan (a project meant to desalinate salt water), which was much less costly.[124] To avoid any criticism as to a possible bias in favour of French companies, Ferrandi's plan envisaged that the project would be carried out by another giant of German industry, Krupp, in collaboration with other (most notably French) firms.[125] The issue then became a German-German issue as Senghor accused Krupp of torpedoing his own project with the blessing of the European Commission. Eventually, the German ambassador in Dakar asked Krupp to withdraw its project to avoid a diplomatic crisis.[126] President Senghor had made the project 'a political issue of prime importance. He does not want to lose face in this affair', the ambassador advised.[127] For the German government, the project became all the more important as it was the first time that a major German company had been involved in an EDF project. Senghor's direct appeal to Charles de Gaulle eventually led the French government to support the project officially. The president of Senegal was not above enlisting other supporters, if necessary: he told the French government he would seek funds from the USSR, as he had already done for other projects.[128] As the EDF rapporteur for the project, Ferrandi tried to block it and to prevent any strong coalition among member state representatives in the EDF Committee from being established; still, the project ended up being built. It had become a 'poisonous affair' (to use Ferrandi's term), as during a Committee meeting Ferrandi accused Mannesmann of having tried to bribe him.[129] The poisonous affair became 'a plot', to quote Mannesmann, as the contract concerning the EDF-funded part of the pipeline was eventually won by a French company, Pont-à-Mousson. Mannesmann accused Ferrandi and his good friend Pirzio Birolli, the EDF controller in Senegal, of having put pressure on the Senegalese civil servants in charge of managing the call for tenders.[130] Mannesmann staffers, for their part, continued to denounce Ferrandi's 'disloyal methods',[131] and to pressure the German Ministry of the Economy and the BDI into intervening against Ferrandi and his 'friends'.[132]

CONCLUSION

Opening up the colonial economic space of France was particularly difficult, even in the framework of the EEC, a new political entity fundamentally based on economic competition. French firms tried their best to retain their privileges in former African colonies. The constant German criticisms reported in this chapter shed light on the variety of strategies they used for that purpose. One of them used technical assistance: they could rely on former French colonial staffers still working as technicians or advisers in the new African states (through French cooperation agreements), or on private or semi-private French consultancy firms with whom they had close ties. These experts and consultancy firms would help the African states to devise projects and write calls for tenders in such a way as to favour French firms. French firms, largely supported by the French government, also relied on their personal ties with African political elites and indulged in neo-patrimonial practices (including bribery and corruption). Hence, the European Commission's attempts to impose the norms of fair competition and to control the EDF calls for tenders (by introducing technical controllers) remained limited. Indeed, the Commission could not interfere too much in the political business of its partners (which involved commercial business with French firms) lest it be accused of breaching their sovereignty. Eventually, competition was introduced as German firms adjusted to local practices and the Commission developed an ability to bypass its own rules in order to adapt to local political games.

As far as EDF funding was concerned, however, this competition never extended beyond the EEC's borders. Indeed, when it came to the question of opening EDF funding to third-country firms (other than EEC and associated states), France and Germany largely agreed that EDF funding had to be reserved for European firms. This was a clear extension of the principle of tied aid to the EEC. When, in 1963, influenced by the reflection of the OECD's Development Assistance Committee on tied aid, the Commission made the awkward decision to open the bids for tenders to firms of other countries without consulting the member states, it faced adamant opposition from the French and German firms and governments. Eventually international calls for tenders were not implemented.[133] The French government claimed it wanted to 'strictly monitor the possibility of resorting to US and Japanese firms', which 'constituted a serious threat' to European firms (including, obviously, French ones),[134] especially in light of the strategies the African elites used to secure funding. Even more striking (as Olivier Van den Bossche will show in his chapter) is the capacity of European firms to collaborate in order to influence EEC development policy.

NOTES

1. Paul Coste Floret, *Marchés coloniaux du monde*, 1952, p. 2965.
2. Léopold Senghor, *Marchés coloniaux du monde*, 1953, p. 124.
3. Véronique Dimier, *The Invention of a European Development Aid Bureaucracy: Recycling Empire* (Basingstoke, 2014).
4. This oral archive can be found at: https://www.youtube.com/watch?v=7dlJxpEMEs4.
5. Archives of the French Ministry of Foreign Affairs (Paris, série Affaires Economiques et Financières, sous-série, Service de la Coopération Economique)/720, intergovernmental conference for the Common Market and Euratom, 23 January 1957, meeting of the Heads of delegations, working paper written by the German delegation; note on the conference of the Ministers of Foreign Affairs, Brussels, concerning the Association of the overseas territories and countries with the Common Market, 25 January 1957.
6. If the EDF Committee did not approve a project, it was forwarded to the College of Commissioners for them to decide whether to approve it or not (on a qualified majority basis).
7. Dimier, *The invention of a European development aid bureaucracy.*
8. Archives of the French Ministry of Foreign Affairs, (Nantes) AFFM, 184 PO/1/296, letter Michel Debré, prime minister, to R. Dusseaux, MP of Seine Maritime, November 1961.
9. Ibid.
10. AFFM, 184 PO/1/528, letter Lagarde to Couve de Murville (French Minister of Foreign Affairs), 17 March 1965.

11. AFFM, 184 PO/1/528, note by the French Ministry of Foreign Affairs, 18 April 1965.
12. AFFM, 184 PO/1/528, note by the French Ministry of Foreign Affairs, about US aid in Senegal, 26 July 1965.
13. Ibid.
14. AFFM, 184 PO/1/520, letter Xavier Daufresne de la Chevalerie (ambassador in Senegal) to Michel Jobert, French minister of foreign affairs, 23 January 1974.
15. AFFM, 184 PO/1/520, telegram by the French embassy in Dakar, summary of a meeting among Japanese ambassadors in Africa in Addis Ababa, 2 September 1965.
16. AFFM, 184 PO/1/520, telegram by the French embassy in Dakar, 10 November 1984.
17. Ibid.
18. AFFM, 184 PO/1/520, telegram by the French embassy in Dakar, 29 December 1964.
19. AFFM, 184 PO/1/520, letter Lagarde, French ambassador in Dakar, to Couve de Murville, 26 July 1966; note by the French Ministry of Foreign Affairs, 25 November 1965.
20. AFFM, 184 PO/1/520, letter René Castets (Secretary of State in charge of Cooperation in the French Ministry of Foreign Affairs) to the head of the permanent mission of aid and cooperation in Dakar, 27 January 1966.
21. AFFM, 184 PO/1/520, letter Emmanuel de Margerie (chargé d'affaire in French embassy in Japan) to the French minister of foreign affairs, Maurice Schuman, 26 September 1969.
22. AFFM, 184 PO/1/520, letter Robert Mazeyrac (French ambassador in Mali) to Jean Sauvagnargues, French minister of foreign affairs, 3 June 1975.
23. AFFM, 184 PO/1/520, letter Morizot, chargé d'affaire in the French embassy in Dakar, to Louis de Guiringaut, French minister of foreign affairs, 8 December 1976.
24. AFFM, 184, PO/1/296, technical note from the French Ministry of Foreign Affairs to the Military Ministry (Direction Générale SSEC) 6 April 1960; letter from the Secrétaire d'Etat aux Relations avec les Etats de la Communauté (former French colonial Ministry) to the high representative of France in Dakar, 17 January 1961.
25. AFFM, 184, PO/1/750, letter Meadmore, chargé d'affaire in the French embassy in Dakar, to Schuman, French minister of foreign affairs, 3 June 1971.
26. See also: Abou Bamba, *African Miracle, African Mirage: Transnational Politics and the Paradox of Modernization in Ivory Coast* (Athens, OH, 2016); Abou Bamba, 'Triangulating a Modernization experiment: the

United States, France and the making of the Kossou project in Central Ivory Coast', *Journal of Modern European History*, 8 (2010), pp. 66–83; Monika Pohle Fraser, "'Not the needy but the speedy ones'": West German development aid and private investment in the Middle East, 1960–1967', in Helge O. Pharo, Monika Phole Fraser (eds.), *The Aid Rush: aid regimes in Northern Europe during the Cold War*, Vol 2 (Oslo, 2008), pp. 217–243.

27. AFFM, 184, PO/1/750, news report, French embassy in Senegal, Hubert Argot, 21 January 1970.

28. AFFM, PO/1/161, letter Raphael Leygues (French ambassador in Ivory Coast) to the director of Alstom, 21 August 1972.

29. Archives of the German Ministry of Foreign Affairs, Berlin (AGFM) B/20-200, 1214, letter from the German embassy in Senegal to the German Ministry of Foreign Affairs, 17 December 1965.

30. Quoted in: 'Le FED s'efforce de maintenir la concurrence entre les entreprises des Six dans les adjudications de marché', La correspondance européenne, quotidien d'information et de documentation sur l'Europe, 2 January 1967: archives of the EEC Delegation in the USA, archives of the EU Delegation in Washington (AEUD), 448/3.

31. AEUD European Commission, answer to the written question No. 308/1968, by Pedini (Italy), European Parliament.

32. Victoria Lickerts, *Légitimité et légitimation des pratiques et discours du monde des affaires français en Afrique depuis les années 1990*, Thèse, Science Politique, Université Paris Sorbonne, 2015.

33. German Federal Archives, archives of the German Ministry of Cooperation, Koblenz (AGMC), B. 213.1140, internal note by Rambow about the judicial advice of Professor Steindorff on the discrimination issue, 15 August 1966.

34. AGMC, B. 213.1140, letter and memorandum from the BDI to the German Ministry of Cooperation, 20 September 1966.

35. AGMC, B. 213.1137, note Kawanon on a conversation between Pfeiffer (representative of the BDI) and Hallstein (president of the Commission) and Hendus, DG VIII Director General, 21 October 1963. This note states that for the 1st EDF, 90% of the EDF money went to the construction sector (the rest to supply), and almost all projects contracts were granted to French firms (2% for German firms only).

36. Archives of the European Commission (AEC), 131/1983/491, draft of the new specifications for supplies and public works contracts financed by the EDF, observations by the Italian delegation, 21 September 1978. Article 8 of the proposal provided for 15% of the contracts to be reserved for firms from the ACP. This seemed 'excessive' to the Italian delegation, 'as these firms are often direct off-shoots of firms from the member

states'. See also: AGMC, 213.1137, internal note of a conversation between the German minister of the economy and Walter (a German consulting firm), 18 May 1963.

37. Archives Jacques Foccart, French National Archives, Paris, (AJF)/ Mauritania, note by Mialet to the French president of the Republic, 26 April 1962.

38. Archives of the SGCI (Secrétariat Général des Affaires Européennes), Paris, French National Archives (SGCI), 19880053, letter Bar (Société Commerciale des Potasses d'Alsace), to the ingénieur en chef (head engineer) of the direction des Industries Chimiques, 3 June 1966.

39. SGCI, 19880053, note by the Société Commerciale des Potasses d'Alsace, 26 April 1966.

40. AGMC, B. 213.1137, letter Strabag (a German firm) to Hendus, 15 August 1963 (report by Helmut Homann, Strabag, 9 May, attached.

41. AGMC, B. 213.1137, letter from the German minister of foreign affairs (Sachs) to the German minister of cooperation, 18 March 1963.

42. Emmanuel Conte, *La Formation du régime européen de migrations, de 1947 à 1992*, Thèse Histoire, Université Paris Sorbonne, 2014.

43. AGMC, B. 213. 1137, memorandum from the German Ministry of Foreign Affairs included in a letter from Harkort (German embassy in Brussels) to the various German Ministries, 6 March 1963.

44. AGMC, B. 213.1142, letter Hauptverband der Deutschen Bauindustrie to the German Ministry of Cooperation, 27 June 1967.

45. AGMC. B. 213.1137, letter Osswald Hessische, Minister für Wirtschaft und Verkehr (minister of the economy of the Hesse) to the Federal Minister of the Economy 27, May, 1963.

46. Lickerts, *Légitimité et légitimation*, p. 133.

47. Archives of the Court of Auditors, Luxembourg, Draft report of the Mission of the Court of Auditors of the EEC in Cameroon, from 23 April to 4 May 1979.

48. AJF/Congo Leopoldville, Garnier de Garet (chargé d'affaire in the French embassy) to the French Ministry of Cooperation, 27 July 1962

49. Fraser shows, however, that bribery was also common among German firms operating in the Middle East: Fraser, 'not the needy...', p. 230.

50. German Federal Archives, archives of the German Ministry of the Economy, Koblenz, (AGME), 750, letter Bollinger (Hauptverband der Deutschen Bauindustrie) to the Ministry of the Economy, 1 October 1981.

51. AGFM, B. 58.240 letter Janse, German Ministry of Foreign Affairs, to all the German embassies of African countries, 27 August 1964.

52. AGFM B, 58.457, letter Junges (German embassy in Ivory Coast) to the German Ministry of Foreign Affairs, 13 September 1967.

53. AGFM, B. 58.457, letter from the German embassy in Ivory Coast to Houphouët-Boigny, 12 March 1967.

54. AGFM B. 68. 635, telegram from the German embassy in Dakar, 16 March 1965.

55. AGMC, B. 213. 1142, memorandum of the Arbeitsgemeinschaft Entwicklungsländers (a working group including the BDI, and other representatives of the German banks and industries), included in a letter from Ehm (German Ministry of Cooperation) to the German Ministry of the Economy, 15 February 1967.

56. AGMC, B. 213.1137, letter Strabag (a German firm) to Hendus, 15 August 1963 (report by Helmut Homann, Strabag, 9 May, attached). This firm remarked that in 1960, the EDF had 160 contracts with consultancy firms. 150 were awarded to French firms, 4 to Germany. The sources of these figures are not specified.

57. AGMC, B. 213.1142, letter Ehm (German Ministry of Cooperation) to the German Ministry of the Economy, 15 February 1967. See also: AGMC, B. 213.1142, memorandum of the Arbeitsgemeinschaft Entwicklungsländers, 15 February 1967; AGMC, B. 213.1137, note Ehm, 8 November 1962; AGMC, B. 213.1140, letter and memorandum from the BDI to the Ministry of Cooperation, 20 September 1966. This kind of criticism is also noted by Fraser, 'not the needy...', p. 229.

58. AGMC, B. 213.1137, letter Deutsch Endoskop Gesselschaft, Sass Wolf and Co to Vialon (Secretary of State in the German Ministry of Cooperation), 11 April 1963.

59. Here in the sector of medical materials, the list of which was incomprehensible to non-French firms: AGMC, B. 213. 1137, letter Deutsch Endoskop Gesselschaft, Sass Wolf and Co to the Secretary of State in the German Ministry of Cooperation, 10 May 1963.

60. AGMC, B. 213.1142, Memorandum of the Arbeitsgemeinschaft Entwicklungsländers, 15 February 1967; see also: AGMC, 213.1137, note Ehm, 8 November 1962.

61. AGMC, B. 213. 1142, letter Bayer to DG VIII, 6 April 1967.

62. AGME, 750, letter Dr Fischer (Handelskammer Bremen) to Herr Korn (Deutschen Industrie und Handelstag), 14 September 1981.

63. AGME, 750, Ministry of the Economy, extract from an engineer report 'Speerspitze für des Auslandsbau', 1978.

64. AGMC, B. 213. 1142, note Jannsen (BDI) to the German minister of cooperation (Wischnewski), 30 October 1967.

65. AGME, 750, letter Dr Fischer (Handelskammer Bremen) to Herr Korn (Deutschen Industrie und Handelstag), 14 September 1981.

66. Communication of the Commission to the Council on the measures it took or intended to take in order to improve the conditions of competi-

tion concerning participation in the EDF bids, 29 November 1968, SEC (68) 3394 final.

67. AGME, 364, letter Metzger (Bundesverband des Deutschen Industrie) to Heiser (German minister of the economy), 8 July 1968.

68. AGMC, B. 213.1137, internal note on a conversation between the minister of the economy and Walter (a consulting firm), 18 May 1963.

69. AGME, 253, letter Afrika Verein to the German minister of the economy, 28 February 1968.

70. AGFM, B. 58. 457, letter from the German embassy in Ivory Coast to Houphouët-Boigny, 12 March 1967.

71. AGMC, B. 213.1137, letter Exportauschuss Bauwirtschaft (Commission of Exportation For the Construction Industry) to the German Ministry of Cooperation, 16 November 1962.

72. AGMC, B. 213. 1137, letter Deusche Endoskopbau Gesellschaft Sass Wolf and Co to Vialon (Secretary of State in the Ministry of Cooperation), 6 August 1963.

73. AGME, 750, letter Dr Schenk (Bfai, German Office of Foreign Trade) to Herr Walenby, 17 February 1981.

74. AGME, 750, letter Fischer (Handelskammer Bremen) to Herr Korn (Deutschen Industrie und Handelstag), 14 September 1981.

75. AGMC, B. 213.1142, letter Hauptverband der Deutschen Bauindustrie to the German Ministry of Cooperation, 27 June 1967.

76. AGMC, B. 213.1137, letter Deutsch Endoskop Gesselschaft, Sass Wolf and Co to Vialon (Secretary of State in the German Ministry of Cooperation), 11 April 1963; AGMC, B. 213. 1137, letter Deutsch Endoskop Gesselschaft, Sass Wolf and Co to the Secretary of State in the German Ministry of Cooperation, 10 May 1963.

77. AGMC, B. 213. 1137, memorandum from the German Ministry of Foreign Affairs included in a letter by Harkort (German embassy in Brussels) to the various German ministries 6 March 1963; AGMC. B. 213.1140, confidential note from the German Ministry of Cooperation (Sachs) to the German Ministry of Foreign Affairs, 30 September 1966.

78. AGME, 750, letter Fischer (Handelskammer Bremen) to Herr Korn (Deutschen Industrie und Handelstag), 14 September 1981.

79. AGMC, B. 213. 1137, letter Strabag (a German firm) to Hendus, Director General, DG VIII, 17 July 1962; report by Helmut Homann, representative of Strabag, 9 May 1962, attached.

80. AGMC, B. 213.1142, letter Hauptverband der Deutschen Bauindustrie to the German Ministry of Cooperation, 27 June 1967.

81. AGMC, B. 213. 1142, note by Jannsen (BDI) to the minister of cooperation (Wischnewski), 30 October 1967; AGMC, B. 213.1142, memoran-

dum of the Arbeitsgemeinschaft Entwicklungsländers, 15 February 1967; AGMC, B. 213.1137, note by Ehm, 8 November 1962. For example, German firms were required to ask the associated states for a transfer. This process was automatic for French firms.

82. AGMC, B. 213.1137, letter Strabag (a German firm) to Hendus, 15 August 1963 (report by Helmut Homann, Strabag, 9 May, attached).

83. AGMC, B. 213.137, memorandum of the German Foreign Ministry included in a letter by Harkort (German embassy in Brussels) to the various German Ministries 6 March 1963; B. 213.1137, remarks on the participation of German firms in the EDF (27 March 1963), included in a note by Ehm, 28 March 1963: a project was of interest if it was worth more than 8 to 10 million Deutschmarks.

84. AGMC, B. 213.1137, note by Westrick (Secretary of State in the Ministry of Cooperation) answering a question by a German MP as to why German firms were not awarded EDF projects (parliamentary session of 28 June 1962); AGMC, B. 213.1137, letter from the German Minister of Cooperation to the German Minister of the Economy, 18 May 1962.

85. AGMC, B. 213.1137, letter Deutsch Endoskop Gesselschaft, Sass Wolf and Co to Vialon (Secretary of State in the German Ministry of Cooperation), 11 April 1963.

86. AGMC, B. 213. 1137, letter Deutsch Endoskop Gesselschaft, Sass Wolf and Co to the Secretary of State in the German Ministry of Cooperation, 10 May 1963.

87. AGMC, B. 213-1142, Ehm to the German minister of the economy, 15 February 1967.

88. Dimier, *The invention of a European Development Aid Bureaucracy*, pp. 22–42.

89. When he retired he became president of the CIAN, a French association of firms with interests in Africa.

90. Dimier, *The invention of a European Development Aid Bureaucracy*, pp. 59–75.

91. Ibid., pp. 76–79.

92. Ibid.

93. AEUD, notes by the Director General of DG VIII on measures taken to increase information about EDF operations, 8 March 1960 and 17 May 1963.

94. SGCI, 19880053, note on a Franco-German meeting 5 January 1967, in Bonn.

95. AGMC, B. 213.1142, memorandum of the Arbeitsgemeinschaft Entwicklungsländers, 15 February 1967.

96. AEC, 25/1980/1041, draft project of a common contract law and specification for public work financed by the EDF, 1970.

97. AGME, B. 102. 1095, letter Jensen (BDI) to the German Ministry of the Economy, 4 September 1959.
98. AEUD, note by Cohen on Ferrandi's trip to The Hague, 28 February1964.
99. AGME, 750, letter Bollinger (Hauptverband der Deutschen Bauindustrie) to the Ministry of the Economy, 12 May 1981.
100. AGMC, B. 213.1142, letter from the German minister of cooperation to Jansen (BDI), 18 May 1967.
101. AGMC, B. 213. 1142, note Jannsen (BDI) to the German minister of cooperation (Wischnewski), 30 October 1967.
102. AGME, 750, letter Bollinger (Hauptverband der Deutschen Bauindustrie) to the Ministry of the Economy, 1 October 1981.
103. AGFM, B 58-, letter from the German embassy in the Ivory Coast to the German Ministry of Foreign Affairs, 18 November 1966.
104. AEC, 131/1983/491, draft of a new general specifications document, observations by the Italian delegation, 21 September 1978.
105. AGMC, B. 213. 457, memorandum of the German Ministry of Foreign Affairs included in a letter by Harkort to all German Ministries 6 March 1963.
106. AJF/Senegal, head of the French permanent mission of aid and cooperation to the Ministry of Cooperation, 28 May 1962.
107. See, for example, proceeding of the European Court of Justice 17/85, case 118/83, CMC *Cooperative Muratori e cimenti* and others vs the Commission. They brought an action primarily for a declaration annulling a Commission decision, the expected effect of which was to deprive the applicants of the awards of a contract for the construction of a hydroelectric dam in Ethiopia. (AEUD, 448/32); AJF/Senegal, letter from the head of the French permanent mission of aid and cooperation to the French Ministry of Cooperation, 29 June 1966. This letter referred to a case brought by Mercedes-Benz to the EEC court of justice to complain about the monopoly of a French firm (Berliet) in Senegal regarding an EEC-funded project.
108. AGMC, B. 213. 1142, note Jannsen (BDI) to the German minister of cooperation (Wischnewski), 30 October 1967. This note was written following a request from the German Ministry of Cooperation (on the participation of German firms in EDF bids) and after gathering many letters from German firms.
109. AGMC, B. 213.1137, letter Heise (German minister of the economy) to the German senator für Wirtschaft and Credit, 13 August 1963.
110. AFFM, 186, PO 1, note on the implementation of the second phase of the road works in Casamance, without date.
111. AGMC. B. 213. 1137, note by Harkort (German embassy in Brussels), 14 November 1962, included in a letter from Shell (German minister of

cooperation) to Beutler (president of the BDI), 29 January 1963; copy of a letter from the director general of DG VIII to Strabag, 2 August 1962.

112. AGME, 750, report on the visit of the German minister of the economy (Offergeld) to Niger, from 14 to 29 January 1981.

113. AGMC, B. 213.1142, letter Ehm to Moltrecht (German embassy in France), 14 July 1967; AGMC B. 213.1140, note Sonnenhol for the German Minister of Cooperation, referring to a discussion with Hendus, 27 October 1966.

114. AGME, 750, letter Bollinger (*Hauptverband der Deutschen Bauindustrie*) to Herr Görtemaker, 12 May, 1981.

115. *Official Journal of the European Communities*, 24 August 1981, S 161, pp. 3–7. Position for the 4th EDF on 31 December 1980. If we consider the works contracts only, changes are less significant, with Germany securing 5.58% of them, vs. 24.34% for France and 3.65% for the UK.

116. AJF/Madagascar, letter Mermet, head of the French permanent mission of aid and cooperation to the French Ministry of Cooperation, 30 December 1965.

117. Ibid.

118. AJF/Madagascar, letter Mermet to the French Ministry of Cooperation, 27 April 1965.

119. AGME, B102, 375751, letter Ehlermann (lawyer of the firm Gauff Consultants) to the EEC court of Justice, 3 December 1980; letter Kittel (German permanent representation in Brussels) to Meyer, 12 July 1979.

120. See Dimier, *The invention of a European Development Aid Bureaucracy*, p. 66; Martin Rempe, *Entwicklung im konflikt. Die EWG und des Senegal, 1957–1975* (Köln, 2012), pp. 180–199.

121. ASGCI, 19880053, note by DG VIII services, 7 July 1967.

122. AJF/Senegal, letter Paye, French ambassador in Senegal, to Triboulet, French Minister of Cooperation, 11 March 1964.

123. ASGCI, 19880053, note by Peltier, 23 November 1966; letter Boegner (SGCI) to the French Ministry of Foreign Affairs, 23 February 1966.

124. ASGCI, 19880053, note on the Mannesmann project, 23 February 1966.

125. AGFM, B. 68.636, note by the German Ministry of Foreign Affairs, 26 December 1966.

126. Ibid., German embassy in Dakar to the German Ministry of Foreign Affairs, 16 January1967.

127. Ibid., German ambassador to the German Ministry of Foreign Affairs, 16 December 1966.

128. AJF/Senegal, telegram Lagarde, French embassy in Senegal, 9 March 1965.

129. AGMF, B. 68. 636, note by Moltrecht on the Mannesmann Affair, 5 July 1967.

130. AGFM, AV 7. 313, letter Mannesmann Export GMDH to Steinlein, 30 March 1970. See also: memorandum Mannesmann sent to the German Ministry of Foreign Affairs, January 1970.

131. AGMF, AV 7. 313, Memorandum sent by Mannesmann to the German Ministry of Foreign Affairs, January 1970.

132. Ibid.

133. Dimier, *The invention of a European Development Aid Bureaucracy*, p. 64.

134. SGCI, 19880053, letter Mayoux (Deputy Secretary General, SGCI) to Boegner (SGCI), 23 April 1963.

References

Bamba, Abou, 'Triangulating a Modernization Experiment: The United States, France and the Making of the Kossou Project in Central Ivory Coast', *Journal of Modern European History*, 8 (2010), pp. 66–83.

Bamba, Abou, *African Miracle, African Mirage: Transnational Politics and the Paradox of Modernization in Ivory Coast* (Ohio University Press, Athens, OH, 2016).

Conte, Emmanuel, *La Formation du Régime européen de Migrations, de 1947 à 1992* (Thèse Histoire, Université Paris Sorbonne, 2014).

Dimier, Véronique, *The Invention of a European Development Aid Bureaucracy: Recycling Empire* (Palgrave Macmillan, Basingstoke, 2014).

Fraser, Monika Pohle, 'Not the Needy but the Speedy Ones: West German Development Aid and Private Investment in the Middle East, 1960–1967', in Helge O. Pharo and Monika Phole Fraser (eds.), *The Aid Rush: Aid Regimes in Northern Europe During the Cold War*, Vol. 2 (Oslo Academic Press, 2008), pp. 217–243.

Lickerts, Victoria, *Légitimité et légitimation des pratiques et discours du monde des affaires français en Afrique depuis les années 1990* (Thèse, Science Politique, Université Paris Sorbonne, 2015).

Rempe, Martin, *Entwicklung im konflikt. Die EWG und des Senegal, 1957–1975* (Böhlau, Köln, 2012).

CHAPTER 10

Displacing the French? Ivorian Development and the Question of Economic Decolonisation, 1946–1975

Abou B. Bamba

In the 1950s, 1960s, and 1970s—decades that many saw as heydays of decolonisation and developmentalism in the Global South—the authorities in Ivory Coast opted to implement an economic policy informed by both an open-door philosophy regarding foreign investment and the theory of comparative advantage. Exploiting the benefits of a peasant-led agricultural boom, they not only envisioned making cash cropping and agribusiness the cornerstones of Ivorian development, but also looked at a gradual industrialisation of the economy as the surest means of emancipation, modernisation, and postcolonial nation-building. Such choices inevitably turned the country into a giant construction site with a booming development industry that piqued the interests of more than one pundit.[1] While contemporary observers in the capitalist Global North praised and usually supported the government's options, critical social scientists raised concerns over the sustainability of the Ivorian model, especially its

A. B. Bamba (✉)
Gettysburg College in Pennsylvania, Gettysburg, PA, USA
e-mail: abamba@gettysburg.edu

© The Author(s) 2020
V. Dimier, S. Stockwell (eds.), *The Business of Development in Post-Colonial Africa*, Cambridge Imperial and Post-Colonial Studies Series, https://doi.org/10.1007/978-3-030-51106-7_10

outward-looking orientation and the persistence of poverty among the peasants who were the engine of its very development.[2]

The criticisms of the Ivorian intellectuals, if epistemologically incipient and mostly disseminated through in-house academic publications, were arguably the more pertinent in terms of laying bare the underbelly of the phenomenal growth of the Ivorian economy. Consider the case of Moustapha Diabaté, who defended in 1973 a dissertation in which he argued that the primary beneficiaries of the spectacular economic growth in Ivory Coast were the French expatriates. In contrast to the apologists who marvelled at the Ivorian post-independence drive towards modernity and dubbed it an 'economic miracle,' the economist only saw a 'dominated economy' and a system that deployed 'every tricks, including the confiscation of basic freedoms in order to satisfy international capitalists who [were] willing to invest in the domestic economy.'[3] While Diabaté denounced this situation as pernicious, it was instead historian Laurent Gbagbo who became the most vocal Ivorian critic of postcolonial development in Ivory Coast—indeed one of the earliest Ivorians to articulate the need to wean the country's economy from the dominance of French interests. Already in 1978 the scholar-activist had suggested that the 'question of decolonisation precisely puts into relief the problematic of independence, that is, the unblocking of economic growth in the periphery.'[4] Reflecting later more specifically on Ivoiro-French relations in the postcolonial era, he would declare that the Ivory Coast was the 'most successful example of France's neo-colonialism in Africa.'[5]

With hindsight, it appears that Gbagbo and his fellow Ivorian social scientists were fleshing out the ideas of Samir Amin and other dependency theorists. And ever since the voicing of their initial apprehensions, the general contours of their argument have proved to be on target, especially with regard to the nature and foundations of the Ivorian economy up to the late 1970s.[6] Yet there were wrinkles to the denunciations of these critics. For while it is undeniable that one of the key features of the Ivorian economy had been the supremacy of French business interests, such domination was never a given. Part of my point of departure in this chapter is to historicise this resilient hegemony even as I reveal the existence of an undercurrent of opposition and challenges to its continuance.

Evidently, there is room to argue that the peasant-led displacement of expatriate interests in Ivorian agriculture was one of the first signs of this history of resistance. Ironically, as this chapter shows, this home-grown opposition to French economic dominance paved the way for the expansion and diversification of French activities in other sectors of the economy in Ivory Coast.[7] More significantly, in an era marked by the retreat of colonial empires and (post)colonial modernisation, French firms were able to exploit the development ambitions and strategies of the Ivorian government to assume new interests and roles in the Ivorian economy. Put differently, it was the very success of the Ivorian economic nationalists in pushing the French out from cash cropping that dialectically resulted in the consolidation of the French presence in other sectors of the Ivorian economy. If the process began during the late colonial period, by the 1970s French companies had emerged as some of the most energetic players in the business of development in postcolonial Ivory Coast. To understand these dynamics fully, this chapter will not merely map out specific policies and strategies of development that the Ivorian government deployed. Rather, and more significantly, it will pay attention to certain historical and structural features of the Ivorian (indeed, the larger Francophone African) economy which worked in the interests of French firms in a politics of postcolonial development that was increasingly being internationalised.

French-Style Decolonisation and the Evanescence of the Displacement

In November 1973 the director of the French Aid and Cooperation Mission in Abidjan received an unusual letter: 'You must understand that the colonial era is over, and that the French must return to their country of origin!' the missive began, and then it added, as demanding as it was reproachful, 'Remove your technicians, and your teachers, because we need technicians from friendly countries, of Africa or Asia. You came to enrich yourselves in our country and to exploit us.' Turning more threatening, the anonymous correspondence whose author called himself/herself 'Corbeau Noir' (Black Crow) concluded: 'You must understand that the current Government does not represent the people of Ivory Coast, the revolution will break out one day, and the traitors of Africa will be punished. It is time, before you are murdered here, to leave quickly with your technicians.'[8] Although the French diplomats downplayed the significance of the angry correspondence, calling it an 'isolated act,' they nonetheless ruled that it was worth conducting 'discreet investigations to identify the author of the threats.'[9]

We do not know the conclusions of these inquiries, nor are we even certain that they were actually carried out. Yet it is clear that the letter 'was the tip of an iceberg of frustration with and hostility to the Ivorian model of development that relied so heavily on foreign human capital.'[10] In fact, by the time the communication was sent, not only had the French demographic presence in Ivory Coast gone up exponentially, but the proportion of French expatriates working in business and the private sector was statistically the highest.[11] In addition, French trading firms such as the Compagnie française d'Afrique Occidentale (CFAO), the Société commerciale de l'Ouest Africain (SCOA), and the Compagnie française de Côte d'Ivoire continued to dominate the wholesale and import-export sector of Ivorian trade.[12] Even more revealing of the tenacity and unrelenting power of French interests was the mushrooming of French firms to tap the market of development expertise in the wake of government-initiated modernisation projects.[13]

Some observers have suggested that the persistence of French business interests in the world of development in postcolonial Ivory Coast was all the more possible because the Ivorian president, Félix Houphouët-Boigny, was none other than one of the key architects of Françafrique—the close, if corrupting, Franco-African relations that maintained France's sphere of influence in postcolonial Africa.[14] Yet other historical fixtures equally explain the continued firmness of French power. Arguably, the first of these was the establishment of a development aid bureaucracy in 1946 to manage the flow of financial resources to France's colonies and dependencies. Indeed, realising that decolonisation and development had become irreversible forces in the post-war era and taking their inspiration from the experience of the British in colonial development as a way to placate anti-colonial criticism, decision-makers in Paris resolved to set up the Fonds d'investissement pour le développement économique et social (FIDES) and the Caisse centrale de la France d'Outre-Mer (CCFOM).[15] Ostensibly, the role of these institutions was to finance the modernisation of the overseas territories. Yet, as a keen observer underlined in 1966, the new French development system not only 'created a dependence on French aid,' since it was 'specifically not designed to promote the self-sufficiency of the different parts of the French Union,' but the implementation of aid-financed projects benefited French interests.[16] In fact, contemporaries were aware that in carrying out development projects the French aid bureaucracy made 'lavish use both of French private firms and of autonomous public or semi-public organisations.' This resulted in 'excessive' profits for French interests, especially for the private contracting firms that 'had very little competition, and a great deal of protection.'[17]

In writing to the head of the aid mission in the early 1970s, Corbeau Noir may have been lashing out at this rather debased situation whose origin is unmistakably traced to the late colonial period. As will become clearer later, a second historical institution that structured and gave an edge to French firms was the existence of the Franc CFA zone. This was also created in the immediate aftermath of the Second World War and slightly readjusted thereafter, and African participation in the economic zone was maintained as most of France's former colonies use a monetary arrangement that pegged their currency to the French franc. The initial establishment of the monetary zone provided France with 'currency facilities' together with markets and easy access to raw materials.[18] Guided by the principle of 'free movement of capital within the zone' and supported by such African leaders as Houphouët-Boigny, the renewal of the controversial monetary agreements with France after 1960 ensured that French interests dominated financial and economic activities in Francophone Africa, especially since French firms could conduct business in the Franc Zone without the need to use foreign exchange.[19] The Ivorian case sheds light on how these historical arrangements played out on the ground to give some crucial advantages to the French, especially in the business of late colonial and postcolonial development. A few examples will be mobilised to illustrate this point.

In a bustling post-war Ivory Coast, trade had reportedly emerged as the 'most important activity' in the territory.[20] This was all the more possible because the peasant-led cash crop revolution had opened new business opportunities. Anticipating the challenge of an Africanisation of export agriculture, many of the settlers had reinvested part of their surplus revenue into commodity trade, transport, or other urban-based services—a move similar to the 1920s when African and Lebanese entrepreneurs began to compete with the white planters who dominated the cash cropping industry.[21] By the mid-1950s, 'Europeans were no longer in direct competition with African primary producers but rather were engaged in complementary activities—notably processing and commercialization.'[22] This type of complementarity, albeit subsequently adjusted, would later become the linchpin of the interaction between the Ivorian leadership and foreign business investors. It was ultimately with this kind of economic arrangement that Ivory Coast achieved political independence and national statehood in 1960 within the larger context of the disintegration of the French empire in West Africa.[23]

In the framework of the execution of plans to modernise the overseas territories in the post-war years, it was conceivable that some former planters would set up their own construction or service companies to tap the booming sector of infrastructural development that came in the wake of the conjugated activities of the FIDES and the CCFOM.[24] While there were some colonists who were adamant in criticising bureaucrats in Paris for their opaque management of FIDES resources, it was the case that the modernisation projects that the FIDES initiated provided numerous business opportunities for French firms.[25] In fact, in the absence of major local companies to carry out large-scale public works (grands travaux), it was the metropolitan firms that benefited the most from the upsurge in building and construction opportunities, especially since bureaucrats in Paris were eager to promote French firms in the awarding of contracts. Illustrative of the boon that late colonial developmentalism offered to French firms were the cases of the Société française d'entreprises de dragages et de travaux publics, the Société nationale des travaux publics, and the Société de construction des batignoles—three firms that would be granted major contracts in the completion of the deep-sea harbour of Abidjan that FIDES money helped complete.[26]

In the housing and urban development sector, some local businesses that were in fact French firms equally saw new opportunities in the modernisation *élan* of the post-war era. For instance, the Compagnie des scieries africaines (SCAF), a long-standing wood and timber firm, diversified into prefabricated housing to offer a variety of heat-insulating bungalow units to the public.[27] Yet it was the metropolitan-backed firms that benefited the most from the boom in housing construction. Consider the examples of the Société immobilière d'habitation de Côte d'Ivoire (SIHCI), the Société d'urbanisme et de construction de la Côte d'Ivoire (SUCCI) and the Société d'équipement de la Côte d'Ivoire (SECI)—three semi-public companies largely financed by the CCFOM through their affiliation with France's Société centrale pour l'equipement du territoire (SCET). Set up in the 1950s in the context of the urban expansion of Abidjan, SIHCI, SUCCI, and SECI all went on to build housing projects to accommodate the needs of a city whose population was constantly on the rise.[28] Architects and construction impresarios as diverse as Henri Chomette, Pierre Dufau, Jean-Maurice Lafon, Daniel Badani, and Pierre

Roux-Dorlut also profited from the same urban boom, as their companies were awarded numerous contracts to survey or construct housing units and public buildings in Abidjan and other urban centres in post-war Ivory Coast.[29]

One of the key features of these contracts was the pervasiveness of informal common accord deals in the procurement procedures. For instance, the initial consulting work on the housing needs of the country that the government granted to Dufau and Lafon in 1957 was orchestrated without a formal bidding process. And when the time came to realise the various governmental buildings that were recommended, the French consultants surreptitiously brought on board metropolitan firms with whom they were familiar.[30] This type of clientelistic practice in the business of development would become a fixture in postcolonial modernisation writ large.[31]

From Triangulation to State-Led Industrial Development

While this transnational clientelism of sorts sanctioned the omnipresence of French interests in the development world in the case of Ivory Coast, the practice was not without challenges. The politics that informed the Ivorian bid for industrial development put this point into relief quite remarkably, especially because it demonstrates that actors and institutions beyond the Franco-Ivorian patrimonial world were potential competitors to whom the Ivorian development planners could appeal.

Until the 1950s, the industrial sector had remained the Cinderella of the Ivorian colonial economy. To be sure, this was one of the trade-offs of France's mercantilist policy (cf. pacte colonial) which did not encourage the setting up of industrial businesses in the colonies, except for the processing of a few agro-based products for export.[32] This situation was to change, however, after the Second World War, when, in the wake of the post-war modernisation drive, the colonial authorities attempted to jumpstart the manufacturing activities.[33] Taking their cue from the Vichy planners who had envisioned an industrialisation policy for the overseas territories, the officials authorised the state in 1945 to become directly involved in the industrial processing of palm oil through the scientific and technical works of the Institut de recherches pour les huiles et oléagineux.

In subsequent years, the government mobilised FIDES resources to seek participation in other industrial ventures, including the pulp industry.[34]

However, a state-controlled industrialisation of the economy was not to become the norm. In fact, even as the imperial bureaucrats planned the modernisation of the overseas territories, private interests had been active in protecting their access to the industrial opportunities that had resulted from the post-war boom and developmentalism. While they applauded the authorities for the infrastructural development that fed the post-war economic growth, imperial interests in the private sector vehemently challenged the priorities given to parastatals in FIDES contracts. They argued that for an effective and efficient development and exploitation of the territories the parastatal companies were not up to the task, especially since the public companies were likely to fail in the implementation of development initiatives. Historical conjunctures, at times, provided them with ammunition to support their position, as exemplified in the difficulties and ultimate demise of the government-run paper factory project.[35]

By the time of independence, then, French manufacturing firms and their trading counterparts as agents of modernisation remained key players in the politics of industrial development in Ivory Coast. Even for the casual observer, the exclusive French composition of the officers of the trade association of industrialists operating in the country provided an indication of this predicament in the waning years of colonialism.[36] Rather than embark on the nationalisation of foreign firms as the soundest form of decolonisation and nation-building, the postcolonial leaders of Ivory Coast opted to organise the activities of the existing industries while channelling the investment capacities of potential foreign industrialists into targeted areas of the economy that needed expansion. As he charted the direction of his country's manufacturing sector at independence, President Houphouët-Boigny articulated this strategy succinctly in 1965 during a speech before the 4th Congress of his party:

> In the aftermath of independence, the general tendency was to give in to nationalisation. We always listened respectfully to the reasons that others advanced to justify their actions in this regard. But we forcefully said that in Ivory Coast we did not have factories to nationalise but to set up, no land to redistribute but to develop, no business to collectivise but to organise.
>
> For us, it is a problem that is both economic and moral. In a country as young as ours, a country which covers three-fifths of the area of France, sparsely populated, where fertile land is not lacking, a country that com-

mends a certain potential wealth but lacks in capital and technicians, it would be an economic nonsense to launch in the nationalisation of I don't know what, and thus dry up the sources of goodwill necessary and even essential for our economic development.[37]

A seeming philosophy of colonial status quo thus guided the political economy of industrialisation and development in the Ivorian postcolony. Early in the aftermath of the amicable divorce from the French empire in 1960, the authorities in Abidjan disclosed that they did not plan on shelving the investment law of 1959. Rather, they were ready to reaffirm their policy of an open door to foreign investment, tax exemption and/or fiscal incentives for priority enterprises, and the free transfer of profits for companies. In the meantime, the economic planners groomed the country to become a key destination for foreign development assistance.[38] While the conjugated effects of these choices accelerated the industrialisation of the economy, they also entrenched the position of French businesses, capital, and technical know-how in the manufacturing sector. To be sure, this situation led several observers to characterise the Ivorian economy in terms of neo-colonialism.[39]

A series of studies commissioned by Ivory Coast's Ministry of Planning in the late 1960s confirmed this observation. In fact, the data generated by the investigation suggested that in 1971 there were more French firms in Ivory Coast's industrial sector (129 companies out of 183) than any other nationality. Statistically, they also provided the lion's share of the investment capital in the manufacturing sector. As a result, the French manufacturers pocketed about 72 percent of the entire revenue produced by the industries operating in Ivory Coast.[40]

That the Ivorian government underwrote this investigation shows that there was some awareness of the handicaps that the continued heavy reliance on French capital and expertise might pose to the drive towards industrialisation and nation-building. In fact, in the early 1970s, economic planners had noted that in addition to 'the risk of being poorly supported by the social body, especially by the young people in school,' the dependence resulted in substantial outflow of financial resources through 'large transfers of savings.'[41] For this reason, the authorities developed new strategies to mitigate the dominance of French interests, especially since the university graduates were incessantly calling for 'true' independence.[42] The first of these strategies was the courtship of non-French investment, including capital from American sources. Already in 1959, the Ivorian government had translated its investment code into English to maximise its dissemination among American and other Anglophone interests. In the post-independence era, these efforts at recruiting potential investors beyond France continued unabated through an intense economic diplomacy and various public relations campaigns in the United States.[43]

While the ultimate outcome of Ivorian efforts to tap American investment capital is hard to pin down, there are pointers that indicate there were some positive responses. For instance, during his visit to attend the first anniversary celebration of Ivorian independence in 1961, Robert Kennedy committed American participation in the establishment of an industrial development bank in the country.[44] The resulting Banque ivoirienne de développement industriel (BIDI), with the sponsorship of US financial institutions such as the Chase Manhattan Bank and Lazard Frères and the participation of the French Caisse centrale de coopération économique, became a reality in the landscape of Ivorian development in 1965.[45] By the late 1960s, other American companies such as Westinghouse, Pickands Mather & Co., Development and Resources Corporation, and International Systems & Controls Inc. had also all become involved in the country's industrial sector or associated development consultancy businesses.[46]

It is tempting to conclude that the willingness of the Ivorian leadership to court American investment capital was nothing but the mark of postcolonial naïveté, especially since the critical discourse of dependency theorists at the time was indexing American companies in Latin America as reproducing a colonial-type situation in the Global South.[47] In the neighbouring country of Ghana, Kwame Nkrumah—the nemesis of Houphouët-Boigny—had voiced similar arguments which he ultimately couched in a book that denounced the transnational activities of Anglo-American multinational corporations, calling them a mark of neo-colonialism.[48] In Ivory Coast itself, certain elements of the French expatriate community were appropriating dependency ideas, mobilising them to argue that Houphouët-Boigny's country was on its way to becoming an American neo-colony in Africa.[49]

These criticisms notwithstanding, one should not dismiss the strategy of the Ivorian authorities. Economic geographer Alain Dubresson has forcefully argued that in an early postcolonial context where Ivorian nationals were said to lack in substantial investment capital and the moneyed elite was unwilling to invest in the industrial sector, opening up the Ivorian manufacturing sector to transnational investment appeared as one option to displace the omnipresence of the French.[50] By triangulating development partnership and soliciting American investment, it is conceivable that the Ivorian economic planners were trying at least to mitigate the dominance of the French interests. There is evidence that this strategy of decolonisation bore some dividends, as demonstrated by an expansion of manoeuvring possibilities that opened to the Ivorian government as a result of the involvement of Westinghouse in Ivory Coast's energy sector in the early 1960s.[51] Even more revealing that the scheme of triangulation was shaking up established colonialist arrangements was the pressure that some French business interests began to feel after the initiation of the strategy, leading a number of them to accuse Houphouët-Boigny of beginning to shun French development partners to become the 'right-hand man of the Americans.'[52]

Triangulation was but one of the tools deployed to seek economic sovereignty in Ivory Coast. Another, and arguably the more likely to be successful, was the direct involvement of the state in the development of the manufacturing sector. Unlike in the agricultural business where the agency of African small-holders contributed to the displacement of French *colons*, manufacturing did not initially appeal to the Ivorians, not even to the group of affluent planters most of whom preferred to reinvest their surplus in real estate and other activities of the tertiary sector of the economy where profits were assumed to be guaranteed as fast.[53] Seemingly, this reality compelled the state to step in through holding larger shares in commercial banks and other financial institutions—enabled, as it were, by the availability of surplus funds from the marketing of Ivorian primary commodities. The strategic use of these surpluses not only facilitated the creation of the BIDI, but also turned out to be a windfall for the establishment of the government-run Société nationale de financement and the Fonds de garantie des crédits accordés aux entreprises ivoiriennes, both of which, in time, would become major conduits for Ivorian participation in numerous industrial ventures.[54]

Partly thanks to these institutions and the ever entrepreneurial commodity marketing board, the share of publicly-owned Ivorian interests in manufacturing grew progressively. In 1961, French interests controlled

92 percent of the total revenue of Ivory Coast's industrial production. By the early 1970s, however, the participation of French firms was down to 72 percent. In the realm of investment in industries, the trend was similar. If at independence French companies invested a combined share of 91 percent, by 1971 this had been brought down to 64 percent. At the same time, the share of the Ivorians in the overall industrial capital moved from virtually zero in the early 1960s to almost 15 percent in the late 1970s. From these data, then, it appears that the Ivorianisation of the manufacturing sector was becoming a reality in postcolonial Ivory Coast.[55]

However, one would be hard-pressed to argue that this process was ever a sign of economic decolonisation. Consider the case of the expansion of the textile industry during the modernisation drive of the 1960s. In collaboration with French interests, the postcolonial state prodded Ivorian farmers into increasing the cultivation of cotton to provide raw materials to the new textile factories.[56] To speed up the creation of import-substitution industries in the sector, sympathetic investment conditions were offered to would-be industrialists, including subsidies, market protection, tax exemption, or other reliefs on import of industrial equipment. These incentives, however, would only entrench the dominance of non-Ivorian interests over the sector. Thus in 1970, the Ivorian textile industry was still controlled by foreign-based corporations and trading houses such as CFAO and SCOA who had diversified their operations into manufacturing. Although the Ivorian government attempted to mitigate the situation by supplying share capital, it still remained the case that Ivorian participation in the various firms operating in textiles almost never went beyond 35 percent. At best then, as many contemporary observers noted at the time, the Ivorianisation of the textile industry was an incomplete scheme.[57]

The story of the expansion of the textile industry points to a larger articulation between business and postcolonial development in Ivory Coast: an initial top-down vision of modernisation of a particular sector of the economy. This is followed by a liberal policy to attract investment capital to realise the vision; ultimately the execution ends up with the triumph of foreign expertise and factors in actualising and delivering the goods of modernity. Arguably, the planning and implementation of the large-scale development projects of the 1960s and 1970s best epitomised this alignment of sorts.

LARGE-SCALE DEVELOPMENT AND THE TRIUMPH OF FOREIGN FIRMS

Even as the Ivorian government became involved in the business of industrial development through the establishment of import-substitution and import-reproduction manufacturing firms, economic planners in the country were increasingly aware of the dangers of enacting development solely in terms of sectoral growth. This would lead to a rethinking of development planning. Appropriating an emerging orthodoxy regarding the benefits of a development strategy evenly distributed across the various regions of a country, the authorities launched in 1962 a vast programme of surveys whose ultimate goal was to map the resources, potential, and developmental needs of each major region of Ivory Coast.[58] The initiation of these large-scale socio-demographic studies turned out to be a business opportunity for various French research firms, especially since France's Fonds d'aide et de coopération (FAC) co-financed the project. By the mid-1960s, the investigative task had been carved up and responsibility to undertake the studies was entrusted to various research groups, including the Société d'études mathématiques appliquées, the Société d'études pour le développement économique et social, the Bureau pour le développement de la production agricole, and the Office de la recherche scientifique et technique d'outre-mer (ORSTOM).[59]

In addition to creating opportunity for operational research for consulting firms, the regionalisation of development was a boon for many construction companies as well. This became evident during the implementation of the Kossou and the San Pedro development projects—the twin modernisation endeavours that came to epitomise the Ivorian bid for regional development. Whether it was for the creation of the brand new harbour of San Pedro to 'open up' the hinterland of southwestern Ivory Coast, the building of a completely new port city to demonstrate the power of modernity, or the construction of a dam to 'energise' the import-substitution industrialisation of the country as in the case of Kossou, there was always the need for infrastructural development that transnational companies readily exploited with the help of the economic diplomats of their home countries.[60]

The involvement of Kaiser Engineers in the damming of the Bandama River at Kossou highlighted this point. In fact, although the American company was not initially a key player in the technopolitics of Kossou, once it managed to get introduced to the development project through its alliance with Electricité de France, it not only out-manoeuvred the French partner, but also succeeded in bringing on board the American government. Subsequently, Impregilo—the Italian business associate with whom Kaiser Engineers had recently worked to build Ghana's Akosombo Dam—would join the venture, supported, as it were, by the Italian government.[61] Similarly, the initial expansion of the sugar industry as cornerstone of the modernisation of northern Ivory Coast resulted in the opening of business opportunities for US firms since the early stage of the Ivorian sugar programme was supported by American aid money.[62]

While remarkable, the American breakthrough in Kossou, San Pedro, and the sugar expansion schemes should certainly not overshadow the fact that the majority of the companies to become involved in the business of postcolonial development in Ivory Coast were French in origin. This caveat is all the more important because American-initiated projects almost always ended up with a heavy French sub-contracting of the actual development work. A number of reasons explain this situation. First, French firms in the world of development in the country had a long history of operation in the Global South, their initiation in development business dating back to the FIDES-run modernisation drive of the postwar years. The public-private networks developed during these times endured in the postcolonial era. The activities of the SCET, which began its Ivorian stint in the late 1950s and became a major player in the urban development efforts of postcolonial Ivory Coast, can be used to demonstrate this point.

Although the expansion of housing projects was initiated with the launching of FIDES, it was really after independence that the Ivorian leadership tackled the question of affordable accommodation for the many. Contextually, the economic boom that the country was witnessing had resulted in a rapid urbanisation of the population. To meet the challenges of this situation, SCET was awarded contracts to assist urban planners in producing the master plans of various cities, including Abidjan, Bouaké, Korhogo, and Daloa.[63] To address the dire shortage of housing, the postcolonial government took steps to reorganise the sector, particularly since it posited urban policy as a key instrument of nation-building. A Ministry of Construction and Town-Planning was established in 1961 to overhaul the coordination of programmes and policies related to urban development.[64] Given the inefficiency of the construction firms in delivering housing units, the authorities spearheaded the creation of the state-run Société de gestion financière de l'habitat in 1964 and, a year later, amalgamated

SIHCI and SUCCI into the Société ivoirienne de construction et gestion immobilière (SICOGI).[65] The French cooperation and aid apparatus was involved in this restructuring of Ivorian urban policy. It came as no surprise then that French firms carried out much of the construction consultancy and work. Not only did SCET hire out experts to SICOGI to run its bureaucracy, but it was French architects such as Badani, Roux-Dorlut, and Ducharme—all old-timers on the Ivorian construction scene—who came to dominate the housing construction boom that took place in the aftermath of decolonisation.[66]

Within the context of bilateral aid, the omnipresence of French firms in the procurement of development work in Ivory Coast speaks to the predicament of Franco-African cooperation and the phenomenon of tied aid.[67] However, research has demonstrated that the problem of aid-financed business that largely benefits the companies of the donor country is not restricted to France and its former colonies.[68] More intriguing is that even in a multilateral aid system such as the European Development Fund (EDF), French firms tended to have a larger share of the development contracts. Critiques of this situation were almost coeval with the beginning of the disbursement of EDF money. Some critics denounced the opacity in the attribution of aid-financed business contracts; others decried the favours that 'local' or 'resident firms' (i.e., disguised French companies) received.[69]

Although less discussed in the literature, it was arguably the membership of France's former possessions like Ivory Coast in the Franc Zone that gave the greatest boost to French firms in the business of postcolonial development. Bonnie Campbell has painstakingly demonstrated how this played out during the expansion of the textile industry in Ivory Coast. Indeed, during the euphoria of the Ivorian economic boom, the country's membership of the zone not only allowed a plethora of French firms to proliferate and fatten their margins of profit, but, as some contemporary analysts have rightly noted, Ivory Coast's participation in the monetary zone contributed to the increase of French residents who came to dominate the Ivorian economy through preferential hiring and business practices.[70]

This was bound to raise questions and apprehensions, both domestically and in the international arena. As early as 1961 American diplomats in Abidjan had criticised the omnipresence of French nationals in the Ivorian modernisation *élan* as the 'basic weakness' of the country's developmental endeavours.[71] In fact, some observers were alarmed that the

Ivorian leadership 'continued to allow Frenchmen to hold many of the key bureaucratic jobs, and to own much of the commerce and many of the best plantations.' To be sure, this led to 'rumblings from trade unions (who think too much money is going to the planters); students (who think too many jobs are going to Frenchmen); and native traders (who think too much commerce is handled by Frenchmen).'[72] By the end of the 1960s, there were renewed mass demonstrations led by an ever more radicalised youth that rejected the status quo over the involvement of the French in the procurement of aid-assisted development.[73] When such demonstrations re-emerged in the late 1970s, the Ivorian authorities were forced to recognise that their modernisation model was leading to a dead-end. Consequently, they began to seriously contemplate alternatives, lest a revolution snatch away their power and bring down the entire edifice of the patrimonial state they had so patiently built over the years.[74]

CONCLUSION

On the whole, the story of development as carried out in Ivory Coast from 1946 to the mid-1970s highlights the challenges of discarding foreign hegemony, a key feature of the Ivorian drive towards postcolonial modernity. While foreseeable for many critics of the so-called Ivorian miracle, this dogged resilience of a controversial mode of operation must have come as a surprise for some of the French historical actors who were quite concerned that Africanisation was out to overtake them. In fact, alarmed by the gradual displacement of their compatriots from the lucrative cash crop business in previous decades, many French planters, industrialists, bankers, and civil servants had been worried in the aftermath of the Ivorian declaration of independence in 1960 that their sojourn in the country was coming to a close.[75]

As this chapter has shown, however, these concerns proved largely misplaced because the clientelistic relationships fostered between the departing French and the Ivorian elite in the 1950s came to endure and even expand. Moreover, the launching of large-scale modernisation and nation-building projects in the postcolonial era opened new business opportunities that a growing number of French firms readily tapped. While the post-independence Ivorian state resorted to an ingenious politics of triangulation as a way to retake the initiative and presumably to get a fairer deal on development, the deep structures inherited from colonialism during the last years of imperial rule conspired to maintain a certain competitive edge for the French interests. By the late 1970s, both the industrial sector of the Ivorian economy and the market of development expertise and contracts were still dominated by French businesses.

In light of the evidence deployed in this study, there is ground to argue that the political economy of modernisation in Ivory Coast did not witness a dramatic transformation in the two decades that followed the independence of the country. This is particularly true when one pays attention to the systemic arrangement and actors of the business of postcolonial development. Whether it was supported by the FIDES, the FAC, or the EDF, French firms tended to receive the largest share of the aid-financed development work that catered to Ivory Coast. As the country began to feel the negative impacts of the oil shocks of the 1970s, it then made sense that the critics of the Ivorian model of development renewed their call for economic decolonisation, which in their eyes meant liberating the country from the grip of French interests.

NOTES

1. Bastiaan A. den Tuinder, *Ivory Coast: The Challenge of Success* (Baltimore, 1978); Elliot J. Berg, "Structural Transformation versus Gradualism: Recent Economic Development in Ghana and the Ivory Coast," in *Ghana & the Ivory Coast: Perspectives on Modernization*, ed. Philip Foster and Aristide R. Zolberg (Chicago and London, 1971), pp. 187–230; Thomas A. Johnson, "New Dam Brightens Economic Picture in Ivory Coast," *New York Times*, 25 November 1972, 41, 48; Marvine Howe, "Ivory Coast's Port Project: San Pedro Seen Aiding Growth in West," *New York Times*, 21 May 1972, F18; "San Pedro: New Ivory Atlantic Port," *New York Times*, 29 January 1971, 61; Drew Middleton, "Ivory Coast: A Success Story," *New York Times*, 25 April 1966, 45; "Business Opportunities in the Ivory Coast Republic," *New York Times*, 25 January 1965, 61; Ruth S. Knowles, "Enterprise & Diplomacy: Pan-Am Airways' Hotel Unit Helps Itself by Aiding Nations," *Wall Street Journal*, 14 April 1964, 18.
2. Neil B. Ridler, "Comparative Advantage as a Development Model: The Ivory Coast," *Journal of Modern African Studies* 23, 3 (Sept. 1985), pp. 407–417; Robert M. Hecht, "The Ivory Coast Economic 'Miracle': What Benefits for Peasant Farmers?" *Journal of Modern African Studies* 21, 1 (March 1983), pp. 25–53; P. Anyang Nyongo, "Liberal Models of Capitalist Development in Africa: Ivory Coast," *Africa Development* 3, 2 (April–June 1978), pp. 5–20; Samir Amin, *Le développement du capitalisme en Côte d'Ivoire* (Paris, 1967).

3. Moustapha Diabaté, "Le modèle ivoirien du développement," (Thèse d'Etat, Université René Descartes & Institut d'Ethnosociologie [Université d'Abidjan], 1973), pp. 313, 581, 665–671. See also Moustapha Diabaté, "Le modèle ivoirien du développement," *Annales de l'Université d'Abidjan*, ser. F (*Ethnosociologie*), 5 (1973), pp. 116–135.
4. Laurent Gbagbo, "La décolonisation: Essai de définition d'une problématique," *Annales de l'Université d'Abidjan*, sér. I (*Histoire*), 6 (1978), p. 71.
5. Laurent Gbagbo, *Côte d'Ivoire: Pour une alternative démocratique* (Paris, 1983), p. 170.
6. Abou B. Bamba, *African Miracle, African Mirage: Transnational Politics and the Paradox of Modernization in Ivory Coast* (Athens, OH, 2016).
7. John Rapley, *Ivoirien Capitalism: African Entrepreneurs in Côte d'Ivoire* (Boulder & London, 1993).
8. Corbeau noir [pseudonym] to Directeur de la Mission d'Aide et de Coopération, 13 Nov. 1973, Archives des Postes [AP]/Abidjan, Carton 53, Centre des Archives Diplomatiques (Nantes, France, hereafter CAD).
9. Memo: Lettre anonyme de menaces adressée au Chef de la Mission Permanente Française de Coopération en Côte d'Ivoire, 26 Nov. 1973, AP/Abidjan, Carton 53, CAD.
10. Abou B. Bamba, "Conspicuous, Yet Invisible: Migration, Whiteness, and the French Residents of Ivory Coast, 1950–1985," *Journal of Modern European History* 13, 4 (2015), pp. 549–565.
11. Consulat Général/Abidjan to Ministre des Affaires Etrangères, 15 February 1974, AP/Abidjan, Carton 37, CAD.
12. Catherine Boone, "Commerce in Côte d'Ivoire: Ivoirianisation without Ivoirian Traders," *Journal of Modern African Studies* 31, 1 (1993), pp. 75–76; Atsé Léon Bonnefonds, "La transformation du commerce de traite en Côte d'Ivoire," *Cahiers d'outre-mer* 84 (October–December 1968), pp. 395–413.
13. "Note sur les sociétés, cabinets et bureaux d'Etudes en Côte d'Ivoire," 6 February 1969, AP/Abidjan, Carton 55, CAD.
14. Maja Bovcon, "French Repatriates from Côte d'Ivoire and the Resilience of *Françafrique*," *Modern & Contemporary France* 17, 3 (Aug. 2009), pp. 283–299; François-Xavier Verschave, *La Françafrique: Le plus long scandale de la République* (Paris 1999). For the life and political career of Houphouët-Boigny, see Frédéric Grah Mel, *Félix Houphouët-Boigny*, 3 vols. (Abidjan & Paris, 2003–2010).
15. François Pacquement, *Histoire de l'Agence française de développement en Côte d'Ivoire* (Paris, 2015), pp. 44–50; Guia Migani, *La France et l'Afrique sub-saharienne, 1957–1963: Histoire d'une décolonisation entre idéaux eurafricains et politique de puissance* (Brussels, 2008), pp. 40–41; Teresa Hayter, *French Aid* (London, 1966), pp. 35–37.

16. Hayter, *French Aid*, p. 73.
17. Hayter, *French Aid*, p. 51.
18. Hayter, *French Aid*, pp. 79–84.
19. Thomas Noirot, "Les entreprises françaises en Afrique: Pillage contre trans-parence," *Outre-terre: Revue française de géopolitique* 33–34 (2012), pp. 539–540; Kako Nubukpo, "Politique monétaire et servitude volontaire: La gestion du Franc CFA par la BCEAO," *Politique Africaine*, 105, no. 1 (2007), pp. 70–84; Nicolas van de Walle, "The Decline of the Franc Zone: Monetary Politics in Francophone Africa," *African Affairs* 90, 360 (Jul. 1991), pp. 383–405; Guy Martin, "The Franc Zone, Underdevelopment and Dependency in Francophone Africa," *Third World Quarterly*, 8, no. 1 (Jan. 1986), pp. 205–235. For the post-independence negotiations for the maintenance of the Franc Zone, see El Gabsi "Une communauté financière africaine est née," *Jeune Afrique*, 25 June–1 July 1962, pp. 14–15; "Nouveaux accords monétaires," *Jeune Afrique*, 27 May–2 June 1962; "Les accords de coopération France-Entente ont été définitivement ratifiés hier par le parlement français," *Abidjan Matin*, 16 June 1961, p. 1; "'Je repars de Paris vivement réconforté' a dit le Président Houphouët-Boigny à la fin de sa visite," *Abidjan Matin*, 12 June 1961, p. 1.
20. Paul Humblot, "Les investissements en Côte d'Ivoire," *Marchés coloniaux*, 28 April 1951, 1153; G. M., "Un territoire en plein essor: La Côte d'Ivoire," *Bulletin du comité de l'Afrique française*, July-August 1954, pp. 213–214.
21. Chris Bierwirth, "The Initial Establishment of the Lebanese Community in Côte d'Ivoire, ca. 1925–1945," *International Journal of African Historical Studies*, 30, no. 2 (1997), pp. 325–348; Salma Kojok, "Migration, réseaux familiaux et stratégies commerciales: La trajectoire d'un immigré arabe dans la Côte d'Ivoire colonial," in *La Côte d'Ivoire: Regards croisés sur les relations entre la France et l'Afrique*, ed. Rémi Fabre and Alain Tirefort (Nantes, 1999), pp. 156–159; Hubert Fréchou, "Les plantations européennes en Côte d'Ivoire," *Cahiers d'Outre-mer*, 29 (Jan-Mar. 1955), pp. 1–32; André Köbben, "Le planteur noir," *Etudes Eburnéennes*, 5 (1956), pp. 7–189; Gabriel Rougerie, "Les pays Agni du Sud-est de la Côte d'Ivoire forestière," *Etudes Eburnéennes*, 6 (1957), pp. 7–211; Marguerite Dupire, "Les planteurs autochtones et étrangers en Basse-Côte d'Ivoire orientale," *Etudes Eburnéennes*, 7, (1960), pp. 7–237.
22. Lynn Krieger Mytelka, "Foreign Business and Economic Development," in *The Political Economy of the Ivory Coast*, ed. William Zartman & Christopher Delgado (New York, 1984), p. 150.
23. Bamba, *African Miracle, African Mirage*, pp. 38–39. For the larger context of the end of the French empire in West Africa, see Frederick Cooper, *Citizenship between Empire and Nation: Remaking France and French*

Africa, 1945–1960 (Princeton, 2014); Tony Chafer, *The End of Empire in French West Africa: France's Successful Decolonization?* (Oxford and New York, 2002).

24. For the activities of FIDES and CCFOM, see Pacquement, *Histoire de l'Agence française de développement*, pp. 48–51; Hayter, *French Aid*, pp. 37–42; Ambassade de France/USA, *French Africa: A Decade of Progress, 1948–1958* (New York, 1958).

25. "Note sur les investissements publics français en Côte d'Ivoire de 1948 à 1959," 14 September 1960, 1, AP/Abidjan, Carton 53, CAD; Raphaël Saller, "Le problème des investissements outre-mer a mis en lumière l'égoïsme métropolitain," *Marchés coloniaux*, 16 April 1949, p. 673; Catherine Hodeir, *Stratégies d'empire: Le grand patronat colonial face à la décolonisation* (Paris, 2003), pp. 222–225.

26. Gabriel Rougerie, *Le port d'Abidjan. Le problème des débouchés maritimes de la Côte d'Ivoire. Sa solution lagunaire* (Paris, 1951); Philip Clarke, "Abidjan Port: Boom Town of African Coast," *New York Herald Tribune*, 29 March 1951, pp. 6–7; Laurent Gbagbo, *Côte d'Ivoire: Economie et société à la veille de l'indépendance, 1940–1960* (Paris, 1982), p. 111. Such awarding of building contracts to the French firms happened in the context of competition from foreign companies and renewed calls for protectionism of French interests. For details, see André Schock to Chargé d'Affaire/Liberia, 18 July 1946, Carton 6, série: Afrique-Levant (AL) 1944–1952/sous-série: Afrique Occidentale Française (AOF), Archives du Ministère des Affaires Etrangères (Paris, France, hereafter AMAE); Chargé d'Affaire/Liberia to Ministre des Affaires Etrangères, 3 September 1946, Carton 6, AL/AOF, AMAE.

27. "Bungalow athermique SCAF: Tarification au 28 février 1954," nd, 4P 2696, 4AP-AOF, Archives Nationales du Sénégal (Dakar/Senegal).

28. Lucie Haguenauer-Caceres, "Construire à l'étranger: Le rôle de la SCET Coopération en Côte d'Ivoire de 1959 à 1976," *Histoire urbaine*, 23, no. 3 (2008), pp. 149–150; René Parenteau and François Charbonneau, "Abidjan: Une politique de l'habitat au service du plan," *Cahier de géographie du Québec*, 36, no. 99 (1992), pp. 419–420; Pacquement, *Histoire de l'Agence française de développement*, pp. 54–55.

29. Hugo Massire, "Le Palais présidentiel d'Abidjan: La logique de l'opulence," *In Situ: Revue des patrimoines*, 34 (2018), 10.4000/insitu.15837; Diala Touré, *Créations architecturales et artistiques en Afrique sub-saharienne, 1948–1995: Bureaux d'etudes Henri Chomette* (Paris, 2002), pp. 135–145; Alain Dubresson, *Villes et industries en Côte d'Ivoire: Pour une géographie de l'accumulation urbaine* (Paris, 1989), pp. 197–203; "L'habitat en Côte d'Ivoire," *Bulletin du comité de l'Afrique française*, November-December 1955, pp. 184–188.

30. Massire, "Palais présidentiel d'Abidjan."
31. Véronique Dimier, "Eurafrica and Its Business: The European Development Fund between the Member States, the European Commission and European Firms," *Journal of European Integration History*, 23, no. 2 (2018), pp. 187–210.
32. For an overview of the pacte colonial regime, see Mamadou Koulibaly, *Les servitudes du pacte colonial* (Abidjan, 2005); Jean Normand, *Le pacte colonial* (Paris, 1900), pp. 19–23; Horace Say, "Pacte colonial," in *Dictionnaire de l'économie politique*, vol. 2: *J-Z*, ed. Charles Coquelin & Gilbert Urbain Guillaumin (Paris, 1854), pp. 304–305.
33. Dubresson, *Villes et industries*, pp. 19–27; Amin, Amin, *Développement du capitalisme*, 120, pp. 186–192.
34. Jean Peter, "Les progrès de l'industrie en Côte d'Ivoire," *Bulletin du comité de l'Afrique française*, October 1952, pp. 12–13; "L'industrie de la pâte à papier en Côte d'Ivoire," *Bulletin du comité de l'Afrique française*, July 1952, p. 13; J. Péchoutre, "L'industrie de la cellulose et la valorisation de la forêt tropicale," *Marchés coloniaux*, 28 April 1951, pp. 1219–1220; P. Worms, "La contribution de l'I.R.H.O. au développement économique de la Côte d'Ivoire," *Marchés coloniaux*, 28 April 1951, pp. 1203–1205. On the Vichy government's vision of industrialisation in the colonies, see Jacques Marseille, *Empire colonial et capitalisme français: Histoire d'un divorce* (Paris, 1984), pp. 269–275.
35. Dubresson, *Villes et industries*, 37; Hodeir, *Stratégies d'empire*, pp. 221–224.
36. "Le nouveau bureau du syndicat des industriels de Côte d'Ivoire," *Abidjan-Matin*, 2 July 1959, p. 1.
37. *Le Président Félix Houphouët-Boigny et la nation ivoirienne* (Abidjan, 1975), pp. 189–190.
38. Washington to Paris, 24 August 1960, série: Amérique/sous-série: Etats-Unis, Carton 453, AMAE; Ministre des Affaires Etrangères to Secrétaire d'Etat aux relations avec les états de la Communauté, 16 December 1960, Amérique/Etats-Unis, Carton 453, AMAE; Abidjan to Secretary of State, 20 August 1960, 770M.5-MSP/8-2060, U.S. National Archives and Record Administration (College Park, MD, hereafter USNA); Côte d'Ivoire, *Les investissements privés dans la République de Côte d'Ivoire: Loi n° 59/134 du 3 septembre 1959 et modalités d'application* (Abidjan, 1959); "Le Président Houphouët-Boigny aux Américains: 'Aidez vos vrais amis,'" *Fraternité*, 27 November, 1959, p. 7. For an overview of the provision of foreign aid to Ivory Coast, see Paul Cacheux and Yves Cogoluegnes, "L'aide au développement de la Côte d'Ivoire," *Cahiers ivoiriens de Recherche économique et sociale* 5 (1975), pp. 46–60.
39. Raphaël-Leygues (Abidjan) to Ministre des Affaires Etrangères, 27 July 1965, Carton 1888, DAM/CI, AMAE; Brasseur (Abidjan) to Secrétariat

d'Etat aux Affaires Etrangères, 22 December 1961, Carton 1885, DAM/ CI, AMAE; "Depuis 4 ans, l'industrialisation de la Côte d'Ivoire se fait à un rythme remarquable," *Abidjan-Matin*, 23 February 1960, 4. For the views of contemporary observers, see Kevin Phillips, "Neocolonialism in West Africa," *Washington Post*, 19 August 1971, A21; "Ivory Coast's Economy Remains Under French at Leader's Wish," *New York Times*, 25 March 1962, p. 21.

40. Jean Chevassu and Alain Valette, *Les industriels de la Côte d'Ivoire: Qui et pourquoi?* (Abidjan, 1975), p. 5; Jean Chevassu and Alain Valette, "Le système de production industrielle de la Côte d'Ivoire: Types d'analyse et premiers résultats," February 1973, Fonds Documentaire, F A06244, Centre de Documentation de l'IRD (Bondy/France, hereafter CDIRD); Jean Chevassu, "Réflexions sur les problèmes d'analyse et de planification régionales et sur l'industrialisation en Côte d'Ivoire,"1972, Fonds Documentaire, F A022059, CDIRD.

41. République de Côte d'Ivoire, *Plan quinquennal de développement économique, social et culturel, 1971–1975* (Paris & Dakar, 1976), p. 28.

42. Frédéric Grah Mel, *Félix Houphouët*-Boigny, vol. 3: *La fin & la suite* (Abidjan & Paris, 2010), pp. 361–369.

43. "The Ivory Coast: Investment Made Easy," *New York Times*, 14 December 1969, F17; "The Ivory Coast: Africa's Economic Miracle," *New York Times*, 14 December 1969, p. 82; "The Ivory Coast: Africa's New Riviera," *New York Times*, 14 December 1969, E4; "Notification of Invitation to Bid," *Wall Street Journal*, 29 July 1968, p. 16; "The Republic of the Ivory Coast: As Economic Progress Continues in the Ivory Coast, Government Welcomes American Private Investments," *New York Times*, 26 January 1968, p. 67; "Submission for the Preparation of 7,050 Hectar[e]s Land in Ivory Coast," *Wall Street Journal*, 13 July 1967, p. 22; "Business Opportunities in the Ivory Coast Republic," *New York Times*, 25 January 1965, p. 61; "The Republic of the Ivory Coast: A Plan for Economic Growth … that Works!" *New York Times*, 20 January 1964, p. 79; "'Nous présentons toutes les garanties pour les investissements étrangers,' déclare le Président Houphouët aux milieux d'affaires américains," *Fraternité*, 25 May 1962, p. 9; "Le Président Houphouët explique la Côte d'Ivoire aux Américains," *Fraternité*, 25 May 1962, p. 3; "Le discours du Président de la République au déjeuner de la Westinghouse Electric Corporation," *Abidjan Matin*, 19 May 1962, p. 6; "Le discours du Président à l'Université Harvard," *Abidjan Matin*, 18 May 1962, p. 6; Côte d'Ivoire, *Private Investments in Ivory Coast: Investment Law/Act of 3 September 1959* (Abidjan: Ministère des finances, des affaires économiques et du plan, 1959).

44. "Aide américaine," 8 May 1962, Carton 45, AP/Abidjan, CAD; Abidjan to Secretary of State, 23 September 1961, 611M.43-MSP/12-761, USNA.

45. "Finance Company for the Ivory Coast," *London Times*, 17 February 1965, p. 20; Robert Badouin, "Les Banques de développement en Afrique noire francophone," *Revue Tiers Monde*, 21 (1965), pp. 265–271; Pacquement, *Histoire de l'Agence française de développement*, 96, pp. 100–101.

46. George S. Springsteen, "Memorandum for Major General Brent Scowcroft," 14 February 1974, National Security Files (NSF), Africa: Box 737, Ivory Coast (March 1969–March 1974), Nixon Presidential Library (Yorba Linda, CA/USA, hereafter Nixon Library); "International Systems' Unit Gets $63 Million West African Contract," *Wall Street Journal*, 23 May 1972, p. 40; "Pickands Mather Gets Rights to Seek Iron Ore in Part of Ivory Coast," *Wall Street Journal*, 26 December 1968, p. 5; "Côte d'Ivoire—Etats-Unis: a/s du voyage présidentiel aux Etats-Unis," 9 May 1962, Carton 45, AP/Abidjan, CAD.

47. On the dependency theorists, see Arturo Escobar, *Encountering Development: The Making and Unmaking of the Third World* (Princeton, 1995), pp. 80–81; Alvin Y. So, *Social Change and Development: Modernization, Dependency, and World-System Theories* (London, 1990), pp. 91–95.

48. Kwame Nkrumah, *Neo-Colonialism. The Last Stage of Imperialism* (London, 1965).

49. "Côte d'Ivoire: Journal-tract, *L'écho des comptoirs* provenant de France," 12 December 1973, AP/Abidjan, Carton 53, CAD; "La Côte d'Ivoire, province française d'Afrique, va-t-elle devenir une néo-colonie américaine?" *L'écho des comptoirs*, nd, 7–8, AP/Abidjan, Carton 53, CAD.

50. Dubresson, *Villes et industries*, pp. 42–47.

51. Bamba, *African Miracle, African Mirage*, pp. 97–99.

52. Ambassadeur de France (Abidjan) to [unidentified] correspondent, 25 June 1964, DAM/CI, Carton 1885, AMAE.

53. Marie-Claude Guerrini, "Le rôle du tertiaire supérieur dans la domination de l'économie ivoirienne," *Revue Tiers Monde* 16, 61 (1975), pp. 121–122; Dubresson, *Villes et industries*, 41, pp. 44–45.

54. Frédéric Grah Mel, *Félix Houphouët-Boigny*, vol. 2: *L'épreuve du pouvoir* (Abidjan & Paris, 2010), pp. 447–456; Frank Zingoua, "Le rôle de la Société nationale de financement (SONAFI) en Côte d'Ivoire," *Revue juridique et politique* 32, 1 (1978), pp. 451–456; Rapley, *Ivoirien Capitalism*, pp. 69–74; Chevassu and Valette, *Industriels de la Côte d'Ivoire*, 7, pp. 13–14.

55. Dubresson, *Villes et industries*, pp. 47, 61–62; Rapley, *Ivoirien Capitalism*, pp. 80–81; Chevassu and Valette, *Industriels de la Côte d'Ivoire*, 5.

56. Thomas J. Bassett, *The Peasant Cotton Revolution in West Africa: Côte d'Ivoire, 1880–1995* (Cambridge, 2001), pp. 103–145; Henrik S. Marcussen and Jens E. Torp, *Internationalization of Capitals: Prospects*

for the Third World (London & Uppsala, 1982), p. 106; Bonnie Campbell, "Neocolonialism, Economic Dependence and Political Change: A Case Study of Cotton and Textile Production in the Ivory Coast 1960 to 1970," *Review of African Political Economy*, 2, no. 2 (1975), pp. 42–45.

57. Campbell, "Neocolonialism," 48–53; Mytelka, "Foreign Business and Economic Development," pp. 163–67; Marcussen and Torp, *Internationalization of Capitals*, pp. 45–46, 101–110; Dubresson, *Villes et industries*, pp. 283–288.

58. Louise Barré, "Compter pour planifier: Dénombrement de la population et 'capitalisme d'Etat' en Côte d'Ivoire (1954–1967)," *Politique africaine*, 145, no. 1 (2017), pp. 109–128; Bamba, *African Miracle, African Mirage*, pp. 78–93. For the late-colonial origins of this type of survey known as *études régionales*, see "Enquêtes démographiques et socio-économiques," in *Sciences au sud: Dictionnaire de 50 années de recherche pour le développement*, ed. Marie Lise Sabrié (Paris, 1994), pp. 48–49.

59. Jean-Paul Duchemin, "La population de la Côte d'Ivoire en 1965: Essai d'évaluation pour l'établissement des cartes de l'Atlas de Côte d'Ivoire," *Cahiers ORSTOM*, sér. *Sciences Humaines*, 4, no. 3–4 (1967), pp. 65–71; 81–82; Gérard Ancey & Michel Pescay, *La planification à base régionale en Côte d'Ivoire: Le plan 1981–1985 et ses antécédents* (Paris, 1983).

60. Bourgeois, "Les opérations Kossou et San Pedro et les besoins de financement de la Côte d'Ivoire," 28 August 1969, AP/Abidjan, Carton 61, CAD; Thomas A. Johnson, "New Dam Brightens Economic Picture in Ivory Coast," *New York Times*, 25 November 1972, pp. 41, 48; Marvine Howe, "Ivory Coast's Port Project," *New York Times*, 21 May 1972, F18.

61. Logdigiani to Kaiser, 30 March 1968, Edgar F. Kaiser Papers, BANC MSS 85/61c, Carton 328/1b., Bancroft Library (University of California at Berkeley); "Bandama River Project: Status Report," August 1967, Edgar F. Kaiser Papers, BANC MSS 85/61c, Carton 328/1a., Bancroft Library; Earl G. Peacock to J. R. Conner et al., 10 August 1966, Edgar F. Kaiser Papers, BANC MSS 85/61c, Carton 328/1c., Bancroft Library; Earl G. Peacock, "Bandama Valley Development Program," 28 September 1966, Edgar F. Kaiser Papers, BANC MSS 85/61c, Carton 328/1c., Bancroft Library.

62. "Export-Import Bank Clears $ 48.5 Million for Ivory Coast," *Wall Street Journal*, 16 May 1972, p. 40; Nixon to Houphouët-Boigny, 21 November 1972, NSF, Africa: Box 737, Ivory Coast (March 1969–March 1974), Nixon Library; Kissinger to Nixon, 26 November 1972, NSF, Africa: Box 737, Ivory Coast (March 1969–March 1974), Nixon Library; Theodore Eliot to Kissinger, 27 November 1972, NSF, Africa: Box 737, Ivory Coast (March 1969–March 1974), Nixon Library; USAID, "Program and Project Data Related to Proposed Programs, FY 1965: Africa Region," 455, United States Agency for International Development Reference

Center (Washington, D.C.); Abidjan to Paris, 25 May 1964, DAM/CI, Carton 1888, AMAE.

63. Haguenauer-Caceres, "Construire à l'étranger," pp. 150–154.

64. Michael Cohen, *Urban Policy and Political Conflict in Africa: A Study of the Ivory Coast* (Chicago and London, 1974), pp. 29–30.

65. Haguenauer-Caceres, "Construire à l'étranger," pp. 155–156; Dubresson, *Villes et industries*, p. 447; Cohen, *Urban Policy and Political Conflict*, p. 32.

66. Pacquement, *Histoire de l'Agence française de développement*, pp. 94–95; Haguenauer-Caceres, "Construire à l'étranger," pp. 155–158; Dubresson, *Villes et industries*, pp. 446–448.

67. Verschave, *La Françafrique*, pp. 56–75.

68. For examples that shed light on the British or American aid-giving, see Oliver Morrissey, "The Commercialization of Aid: Business Interests and the UK Aid Budget 1978–1988," *Development Policy Review*, 8 (1990), pp. 301–322; Ranald S. May, "A Micro-economic Study of the Effects of Overseas Development Aid on British Companies, 1979–1983," *Development Policy Review*, 5 (1987), pp. 35–62; Aurelius Morgner, "The American Foreign Aid Program: Costs, Accomplishments, Alternatives?" *Review of Politics*, 29, no. 1 (January 1967), pp. 65–75.

69. Rolf O. Brenner, "EFD Favours Resident Construction Firms," *Intereconomics*, 2, no. 1 (1967), pp. 20–23; Dimier, "Eurafrica and Its Business," pp. 191–197.

70. Philippe Bonnet, "La minorité française en Côte d'Ivoire: Pouvoir économique et indépendance nationale," *L'Afrique et l'Asie modernes*, 118 (1978), pp. 38–40; Campbell, "Neocolonialism," pp. 46–47.

71. Abidjan to Secretary of State, 11 August 1961, 2, 5, 770M.5-MSP/8-1161, USNA.

72. Joseph Kraft to Ted Sorensen, 29 August 1961, National Security Files (NSF), Country/Ivory Coast, General 1/61–9/61, John F. Kennedy Presidential Library (Boston, MA/USA).

73. Justin Vieyra, "Quand le gouvernement organise la contestation," *Jeune Afrique*, 29 October—4 November 1969, p. 29; B. Diallo, "Côte d'Ivoire: Les chômeurs se fâchent," *Jeune Afrique*, 8–14 October 1969, p. 32; "A propos des 'remous sociaux': La Présidence communique," *Fraternité Matin*, 2 October 1969, p. 1.

74. "Interview: Une fois de plus, les 'prophètes de malheur' en sont pour leur frais," *Fraternité Matin*, 12 December 1978, pp. 10–11; Amin Maalouf, "Côte d'Ivoire: Le malaise," *Jeune Afrique*, 6 September 1978, pp. 23–25; Bureau politique [PDCI/RDA], "Non aux tracts! Tout citoyen dispose du dialogue pour s'exprimer," *Fraternité Matin*, 16 August 1978, p. 1.

75. Henry Rollet (Chargé d'Affaire/Abidjan) to Secrétaire d'Etat aux Affaires Etrangères, 18 August 1961, AP/Abidjan, Carton 37, CAD.

References

Amin, Samir, *Le développement du capitalisme en Côte d'Ivoire* (Editions Minuit, Paris, 1967).

Ancey, Gérard, and Michel Pescay, *La planification à base régionale en Côte d'Ivoire: Le plan 1981–1985 et ses antécédents* (Ministère [Français] des Relations extérieures—Coopération & Développement, Paris, 1983).

Badouin, Robert, 'Les Banques de développement en Afrique noire francophone', *Revue Tiers Monde*, 21 (1965), pp. 265–271.

Bamba, Abou B., *African Miracle, African Mirage: Transnational Politics and the Paradox of Modernization in Ivory Coast* (Ohio University Press, Athens, 2016).

Barré, Louise, 'Compter pour planifier: Dénombrement de la population et "capitalisme d'Etat" en Côte d'Ivoire (1954–1967)', *Politique africaine* 145, no. 1 (2017), pp. 109–128.

Bassett, Thomas, *The Peasant Cotton Revolution in West Africa: Côte d'Ivoire, 1880–1995* (Cambridge University Press, Cambridge, 2001).

Berg, Elliot J., 'Structural Transformation versus Gradualism: Recent Economic Development in Ghana and the Ivory Coast', in Philip Foster and Aristide R. Zolberg (eds.), *Ghana & the Ivory Coast: Perspectives on Modernization* (The University of Chicago Press, Chicago and London, 1971), pp. 187–230.

Bierwirth, Chris, 'The Initial Establishment of the Lebanese Community in Côte d'Ivoire, ca. 1925–1945', *International Journal of African Historical Studies* 30, no. 2 (1997), pp. 325–348.

Bonnet, Philippe, 'La minorité française en Côte d'Ivoire: Pouvoir économique et indépendance Nationale', *L'Afrique et l'Asie modernes*, 118 (1978), pp. 29–40.

Bonnefonds, Atsé Léon, 'La transformation du commerce de traite en Côte d'Ivoire', *Cahiers d'outre-mer*, 84 (October–December 1968), pp. 395–413.

Boone, Catherine, 'Commerce in Côte d'Ivoire: Ivoirianisation without Ivoirian Traders', *Journal of Modern African Studies*, 31, no. 1 (1993), pp. 67–92.

Bovcon, Maja, 'French Repatriates from Côte d'Ivoire and the Resilience of Françafrique', *Modern & Contemporary France*, 17, no. 3 (2009), pp. 283–299.

Brenner, Rolf O., 'EFD Favours Resident Construction Firms', *Intereconomics*, 2, no. 1 (1967), pp. 20–23.

Cacheux, Paul, and Yves Cogoluegnes, 'L'aide au développement de la Côte d'Ivoire', *Cahiers ivoiriens de Recherche économique et sociale*, 5 (1975), pp. 46–60.

Campbell, Bonnie, 'Neocolonialism, Economic Dependence and Political Change: A Case Study of Cotton and Textile Production in the Ivory Coast 1960 to 1970', *Review of African Political Economy*, 2, no. 2 (1975), pp. 36–53.

Chafer, Tony, *The End of Empire in French West Africa: France's Successful Decolonization?* (Berg, Oxford and New York, 2002).

Chevassu, Jean, and Alain Valette, *Les industriels de la Côte d'Ivoire: Qui et pour-quoi?* (ORSTOM/Ministère du Plan, Abidjan, 1975).

Cohen, Michael, *Urban Policy and Political Conflict in Africa: A Study of the Ivory Coast* (The University of Chicago Press, Chicago and London, 1974).

Cooper, Frederick, *Citizenship between Empire and Nation: Remaking France and French Africa, 1945–1960* (Princeton University Press, Princeton, 2014).

den Tuinder, Bastiaan A., *Ivory Coast: The Challenge of Success* (Johns Hopkins University Press, Baltimore, 1978).

Diabaté, Moustapha, 'Le modèle ivoirien du développement', *Annales de l'Université d'Abidjan*, sér. F (*Ethnosociologie*), 5 (1973a), pp. 116–135.

Diabaté, Moustapha, 'Le modèle ivoirien du développement' (Thèse d'Etat, Université René Descartes & Institut d'Ethnosociologie [Université d'Abidjan], 1973b).

Dimier, Véronique, 'Eurafrica and Its Business: The European Development Fund between the Member States, the European Commission and European Firms', *Journal of European Integration History*, 23, no. 2 (2018), pp. 187–210.

Dubresson, Alain, *Villes et industries en Côte d'Ivoire: Pour une géographie de l'accumulation Urbaine* (Karthala, Paris, 1989).

Duchemin, Jean-Paul, 'La population de la Côte d'Ivoire en 1965: Essai d'évaluation pour l'établissement des cartes de l'Atlas de Côte d'Ivoire', *Cahiers ORSTOM*, sér. *Sciences Humaines*, 4, no. 3–4 (1967), pp. 57–82.

Dupire, Marguerite, 'Les planteurs autochtones et étrangers en Basse-Côte d'Ivoire orientale', *Etudes Eburnéennes*, 7 (1960), pp. 7–237.

'Enquêtes démographiques et socio-économiques', in Marie Lise Sabrié (ed.), *Sciences au sud: Dictionnaire de 50 années de recherche pour le développement* (ORSTOM Editions, Paris, 1994), pp. 48–49.

Escobar, Arturo, *Encountering Development: The Making and Unmaking of the Third World* (Princeton University Press, Princeton, 1995).

Fréchou, Hubert, 'Les plantations européennes en Côte d'Ivoire', *Cahiers d'Outre-mer*, 29 (Jan.–Mar. 1955), pp. 1–32.

Gbagbo, Laurent, 'La décolonisation: Essai de définition d'une problématique', *Annales de l'Université d'Abidjan*, sér. I (*Histoire*), 6 (1978), pp. 53–87.

Gbagbo, Laurent, *Côte d'Ivoire: Economie et société à la veille de l'indépendance, 1940–1960* (L'Harmattan, Paris, 1982).

Gbagbo, Laurent, *Côte d'Ivoire: Pour une alternative démocratique* (L'Harmattan, Paris, 1983).

Grah Mel, Frédéric, *Félix Houphouët-Boigny*, 3 vols. (CERAP/Karthala/Larose, Abidjan and Paris, 2003–2010).

Guerrini, Marie-Claude, 'Le rôle du tertiaire supérieur dans la domination de l'économie Ivoirienne', *Revue Tiers Monde*, 16, no. 61 (1975), pp. 113–134.

Haguenauer-Caceres, Lucie, 'Construire à l'étranger: Le rôle de la SCET Coopération en Côte d'Ivoire de 1959 à 1976', *Histoire urbaine*, 23, no. 3 (2008), pp. 145–159.

Hayter, Teresa, *French Aid* (Overseas Development Institute, London, 1966).

Hecht, Robert M., 'The Ivory Coast Economic "Miracle": What Benefits for Peasant Farmers?', *Journal of Modern African Studies*, 21, no. 1 (March 1983), pp. 25–53.

Hodeir, Catherine, *Stratégies d'empire: Le grand patronat colonial face à la décolonisation* (Belin, Paris, 2003).

Köbben, André, 'Le planteur noir', *Etudes Eburnéennes* 5 (1956), pp. 7–189.

Kojok, Salma, 'Migration, réseaux familiaux et stratégies commerciales: La trajectoire d'un immigré arabe dans la Côte d'Ivoire colonial', in Rémi Fabre and Alain Tirefort (eds.), *La Côte d'Ivoire: Regards croisés sur les relations entre la France et l'Afrique* (Presses Académiques de l'Ouest and Ouest Editions, Nantes, 1999), pp. 151–164.

Koulibaly, Mamadou, *Les servitudes du pacte* colonial (CEDA/NEI, Abidjan, 2005).

Le Président Félix Houphouët-Boigny et la nation ivoirienne (Nouvelles Editions Africaines, Abidjan, 1975).

Marcussen, Henrik S., and Jens E. Torp, *Internationalization of Capitals: Prospects for the Third World* (Zed Press & Scandinavian Institute of African Studies, London and Uppsala, 1982).

Marseille, Jacques, *Empire colonial et capitalisme français: Histoire d'un divorce* (Albin Michel, Paris, 1984).

Martin, Guy, 'The Franc Zone, Underdevelopment and Dependency in Francophone Africa', *Third World Quarterly*, 8, no. 1 (Jan. 1986), pp. 205–235.

Massire, Hugo, 'Le Palais présidentiel d'Abidjan: La logique de l'opulence', *In Situ: Revue des patrimoines*, 34 (2018), https://doi.org/10.4000/insitu.15837.

May, Ranald S., 'A Micro-economic Study of the Effects of Overseas Development Aid on British Companies, 1979–1983', *Development Policy Review*, 5 (1987) pp. 35–62.

Migani, Guia, *La France et l'Afrique sub-saharienne, 1957–1963: Histoire d'une décolonisation entre idéaux eurafricains et politique de puissance* (Peter Lang, Brussels, 2008).

Morgner, Aurelius, 'The American Foreign Aid Program: Costs, Accomplishments, Alternatives?', *Review of Politics*, 29, no. 1 (Jan. 1967), pp. 65–75.

Morrissey, Oliver, 'The Commercialization of Aid: Business Interests and the UK Aid Budget 1978–1988', *Development Policy Review*, 8 (1990), pp. 301–322.

Mytelka, Lynn Krieger, 'Foreign Business and Economic Development', in William Zartman and Christopher Delgado (eds.), *The Political Economy of the Ivory Coast* (Praeger, New York, 1984), pp. 149–173.

Nkrumah, Kwame, *Neo-Colonialism. The Last Stage of Imperialism* (Thomas Nelson & Sons, Ltd., London, 1965).

Noirot, Thomas, 'Les entreprises françaises en Afrique: Pillage contre transparence', *Outre-terre: Revue française de géopolitique*, 33–34 (2012), pp. 537–546.

Normand, Jean, *Le pacte colonial* (Pedone, Paris, 1900).

Nubukpo, Kako, 'Politique monétaire et servitude volontaire: La gestion du Franc CFA par la BCEAO', *Politique Africaine*, 105, no. 1 (2007), pp. 70–84.

Nyongo, P. Anyang, 'Liberal Models of Capitalist Development in Africa: Ivory Coast', *Africa Development*, 3, no. 2 (Apr.–Jun. 1978), pp. 5–20.

Pacquement, François, *Histoire de l'Agence française de développement en Côte d'Ivoire* (Karthala, Paris, 2015).

Parenteau, René, and François Charbonneau. 'Abidjan: Une politique de l'habitat au service du Plan', *Cahier de géographie du Québec*, 36, no. 99 (1992), pp. 415–437.

Rapley, John, *Ivoirien Capitalism: African Entrepreneurs in Côte d'Ivoire* (Lynne Rienner Publishers, Boulder and London, 1993).

République de Côte d'Ivoire, *Plan quinquennal de développement économique, social et culturel, 1971–1975* (SAE, Paris and Dakar, 1976).

Ridler, Neil B., 'Comparative Advantage as a Development Model: The Ivory Coast', *Journal of Modern African Studies*, 23, no. 3 (Sept. 1985), pp. 407–417.

Rougerie, Gabriel, 'Les pays Agni du Sud-est de la Côte d'Ivoire forestière', *Etudes Eburnéennes*, 6 (1957), pp. 7–211.

Rougerie, Gabriel, *Le port d'Abidjan. Le problème des débouchés maritimes de la Côte d'Ivoire. Sa solution lagunaire* (Documentation Française, Paris, 1951).

Say, Horace, 'Pacte Colonial', in Charles Coquelin and Gilbert Urbain Guillaumin (eds.), *Dictionnaire de l'économie politique, vol. 2: J-Z* (Hachette, Paris, 1854), pp. 304–305.

So, Alvin Y., *Social Change and Development: Modernization, Dependency, and World-System Theories* (Sage Publications, London, 1990).

Touré, Diala, *Créations architecturales et artistiques en Afrique sub-saharienne, 1948–1995: Bureaux d'etudes Henri Chomette* (L'Harmattan, Paris, 2002).

van de Walle, Nicolas, 'The Decline of the Franc Zone: Monetary Politics in Francophone Africa', *African Affairs*, 90, no. 360 (Jul. 1991), pp. 383–405.

Verschave, François-Xavier, *La Françafrique: Le plus long scandale de la République* (Stock, Paris, 1999).

Zingoua, Frank, 'Le rôle de la Société nationale de financement (SONAFI) en Côte d'Ivoire', *Revue juridique et politique*, 32, no. 1 (1978), pp. 451–456.

Zolberg, Aristide, *One-Party Government in the Ivory Coast* (Princeton University Press, Princeton, 1964).

CHAPTER 11

European Private Sector and African Firms in EU-ACP Development Cooperation (1975–2000)

Olivier Van den Bossche

INTRODUCTION

In 1975, the cooperation framework between the EEC and the 46 countries of the African Caribbean and Pacific (ACP) Group under the Lomé Convention established the first Community policy to support local ACP companies under the name of 'industrial cooperation'. This policy was meant to enable ACP countries to catch up economically and to lead to a massive development of manufacturing in ACP countries. At that time 'developing' countries presented a common front after the wave of independence in the 1960s. They facilitated discussion of the New International Economic Order (NIEO), which aimed at establishing a better division of labour and a South-North economic catching-up.[1] The 'spirit of Lomé' referred to in this chapter is dependent on this particular context. Signed in 1975 in the capital of Togo, the Lomé Convention was presented as a

O. Van den Bossche (✉)
Université Paris 3, Sorbonne Nouvelle, Paris, France

© The Author(s) 2020
V. Dimier, S. Stockwell (eds.), *The Business of Development in Post-Colonial Africa*, Cambridge Imperial and Post-Colonial Studies Series, https://doi.org/10.1007/978-3-030-51106-7_11

'small-scale NIEO' with the aim of satisfying ACP countries that were keen to achieve rapid industrialisation.[2]

Beyond a discourse of solidarity and of a new global economic balance through industrial development, the EEC also tried to redeploy European industrial sectors that were losing growth and competitiveness in the 1970s in ACP countries.[3] For the EEC the challenge of industrial cooperation was thus two-fold: to secure access to raw materials in the ACP states, and to introduce European industrial sectors into the ACP states. For some directors at the European Commission, industrial cooperation was thus born out of economic necessity.[4]

In order to implement this new European policy, new cooperation instruments were created the same year. At the request of the ACP group, the Centre for the Development of Industry (CDI) was set up as a body specifically to deal with industrial development. The CDI was financed by the European Development Fund (EDF) and established to promote industrial projects for ACP firms in cooperation with European industrialists. Managed by the European Commission, the CDI was designed as an operational instrument with strong links to both European and ACP industrial circles. DG VIII, the European Commission's directorate-general in charge of cooperation with ACP development countries, and in particular some of its administrators (directors, heads of units and policy officers alike), were given considerable leeway and initiative in the implementation of programming industrial cooperation.[5]

In outlining this new policy, administrators of DG VIII acted as privileged interlocutors between European business circles and ACP firms, each party having different views on industrial cooperation. Consequently, while a common agreement was reached on pursuing industrial cooperation—and later, private sector development—in African countries (the main focus of the ACP group), the notion of beneficiaries itself (which private sector?) was never really clearly defined, leaving a certain vagueness about the aims of this policy. Schematically put, was it to promote the development of small African companies or larger European groups?

This chapter explores the extent to which the interests of European business networks operating in African markets influenced the definition of EEC-ACP cooperation policies by looking at the debates around industrial cooperation and the European companies' lobbying of the Commission. It draws on interviews with DG VIII officials,[6] and the Commission archives.[7] The first part of the chapter goes back to the establishment of industrial cooperation at DG VIII, announced as a priority development policy. The links between DG VIII administrators and European private sector representatives in the 1970s and 1980s are then analysed to trace their role in defining industrial cooperation—here major industrialists gathered in more or less institutionalised confederations or speaking in their own name. The goal is to estimate to what extent European private sector representatives, some of them already very present during colonisation, have succeeded in extending Brussels-developed approaches towards ACP countries—approaches consisting in serving European private interests. Meanwhile in the late 1980s some administrators at DG VIII's unit in charge of industrial cooperation tried to put in place an autonomous policy in strong favour of African firms. Towards the end of the 1980s, industrial cooperation was put aside in favour of other development policies known as 'private sector development', still with the participation of European firms. As a substitute to industrial cooperation and previous support to ACP companies, private sector development has become a policy consisting mainly of supporting macroeconomic reforms and has aimed to develop foreign investment and Europe-oriented export sectors in ACP countries.

INDUSTRIAL COOPERATION IN THE 1970S: ACCELERATING BUSINESS DEVELOPMENT IN ACP COUNTRIES

In 1975 the five-year cooperation framework known as Lomé Convention introduced a new part on 'industrial cooperation' among other innovative measures to speed up the development of ACP countries through trade and cooperation. None of the instruments in Title III of the Convention on 'industrial cooperation' were new. Some of them existed at a bilateral level, but their formulation into a European policy in 1975 was new. In this context, industrial cooperation was presented by the European Commission as the *par excellence* area in which the EEC-ACP partnership could best be exercised.[8] Industrial cooperation consisted of financial support from the EDF to production sectors covering industry, agriculture, tourism and mining.[9] It thus consisted in supporting the processing of raw materials and manufacturing of finished and semi-finished products. It also aimed at developing a network of small and medium-sized industrial enterprises (SMIs-SMEs) through cooperation measures such as support for the financing of firms, the creation of infrastructure and industrial parks, vocational training, and setting up specialised business credit structures. The development of small businesses was supposed to strengthen links with large companies, and in particular European ones. Industrial cooperation had a double objective: to develop ACP production sectors, while at the same time benefiting the European private sector, which would create joint ventures in ACP countries. The firms' nationality to be supported by the industrial cooperation policy, whether ACP or European, had not been specified in the texts and the words remain elusive. The Convention cautiously specified that it aimed at establishing industrial and commercial links between the EEC and the ACP countries, by means of various instruments, some of which are 'joint instruments'— that is, ACP-EU—created with Lomé.

In the 1970s, the European Investment Bank (EIB) was a second increasingly important instrument to serve industrial cooperation. The EIB had been financing investment projects in Europe since 1957 and in African countries since 1963. The Bank's lending to projects in the ACP countries remained limited in the 1970s in proportion to the amounts invested in Europe and other regions of the world,[10] but after industrialisation was given international priority in the 1960s, the number of projects increased. Between 1965 and 1975, only 36 industrial projects were financed by the Bank; from 1975 to 1990, over an equivalent period of time, the EIB invested in 183 projects worth several million ECU (European Currency Units) in industrial projects. The projects were large-scale and mostly involved public enterprises, not SMIs-SMEs, since the Bank is allowed to lend to states only. Cement factories, flour mills, nationalised mining companies, sugar factories, processing factories in the oil-seed industry, and other industrial plants in agro-industry and textiles were among the regular beneficiaries.[11] But there was a need to create a new, more flexible instrument to support SMIs-SMEs at a smaller scale.

A third important milestone in European-African industrial cooperation was the creation of the CDI. Established in 1975, this was operational by 1977. As a new joint EEC-ACP body based in Brussels, the CDI's main function was to facilitate contacts between European and ACP business owners. It also served as a consulting firm by carrying out feasibility studies of industrial projects. The CDI was conceived as the vehicle for the industrialisation of ACP states through its links with European businesses. European firms would be accompanied by the CDI and would be called on to invest capital, technology and know-how in industrial projects in the ACP countries by creating joint ventures. A bi-monthly bulletin, *Industrial Opportunities*, was published in the pages of the *Courier*, the official magazine of EEC-ACP cooperation, and offered requests from European businessmen in ACP countries in the form of classified ads. The premise of industrial cooperation was thus based on a call for intensifying EEC-ACP joint ventures to hasten industrial development in the ACP countries.

The CDI had a very diverse joint board of directors that was politically connected and directly linked to the business networks operating in ACP countries, on both the EEC and ACP sides. In order to facilitate the development of production sectors in the ACP countries, a joint EEC-ACP Committee on Industrial Cooperation was also established in the form of a high-level group (ambassadors and 'experts' from ACP and European business circles), under supervision of the ACP Committee of Ambassadors and the EEC's Committee of Permanent Representatives.

Because it was important to the EEC that the CDI be as close as possible to both private sectors, the Commission's DG VIII proposed that it be accompanied by an advisory board composed of both European and ACP industrialists. Depending on the date, around twenty businessmen mostly from Europe and from ACP countries advised the Committee on Industrial Cooperation and the CDI on EEC-ACP industrial policy.[12] The ACP and EEC sides were equivalent in numbers. ACP members of the board were mainly institutional actors, political representatives, and members of chambers of commerce or other business organisations: Lazare Soré (Burkina Faso) managed a large tyre factory and was a long-time member of the Burkina Faso Chamber of Commerce and Industry; a Congolese businessman and director of the prime minister's cabinet, Max Munga, headed ANIZA, an industrial association in Zaire; Roderick Rainford was a former Jamaican minister of industry. On the European side, members were entrepreneurs or representatives of employers' organisations, and almost all had lucrative activities in Africa. Being close to EEC-ACP cooperation institutions allowed them to keep an eye on industrial opportunities in ACP markets. Wilhelm A. de Jonge (Netherlands) sat on the board of directors of the Philips group; Jean-Paul Gardinier (France) represented firms in the agri-food industry and the French Conseil des investisseurs en Afrique noire (CIAN); Yves Salmon (France) worked for the metallurgical Pechiney group, then joined Brasseries du Cameroun and the construction firm Fougerolle in Africa; Michel Relecom (Belgium) ran breweries in Zaire; former minister Mario Pedini (Italy) was also president of Assafrica, the African business-oriented club of the Italian industrial confederation Confindustria.

The role of the European private sector in industrial cooperation was thus one of North-South transfer (of investments, know-how, technologies) to ACP markets. In the EEC's official discourse it was also meant to strengthen the means of official development assistance by injecting private investments into EEC-ACP cooperation. By drawing attention to the role of the European private sector in development assistance, the EEC bypassed the ACP public authority as unique entrepreneur of development. The European Commission's speech was clear on this: it presented European investors as a 'means of accelerated development for the industrialisation of ACP countries'.[13] In other words, ACP development would be achieved through EEC-ACP public development assistance complementary to European private sector investment. Yet the state was not entirely absent in the Commission's discourse: public policies had to be able to oversee private financial flows. And limits were set to the power of the European private sector, which could not have complete freedom of profit: the text reminded ACP states to clearly announce their development priorities so that EEC member states could encourage their national operators to invest in accordance with these choices.

EUROPEAN BUSINESS NETWORKS AROUND DG VIII IN THE 1970s

When industrial cooperation was developing, closeness to European business networks was of major importance for the administration in charge in DG VIII. The Commission's contacts with European industry and employers took place at several levels, alternating between the regular presence of pressure groups (or lobbies) and informal meetings with individual actors. The situation was not new. When he was appointed first commissioner for development in 1958, Robert Lemaignen was already a leading figure of the French business community in colonial Africa.[14] Although he quickly distanced himself from the French government,[15] he was originally chosen to defend the interests of French firms that were present in the colonies.[16]

European business interest in development policies continued in the 1970s. In 1973, when the United Kingdom entered the EEC, the largest investor groups of seven European member states came together under the informal and self-proclaimed 'Group of Seven', the name being a reference to the other political G7.[17] The Group of Seven brought together the main European investor associations: the Italian Assafrica; the British African business associations; the Dutch Africa Instituut; Germany's Afrika Verein; the Belgian-Luxembourg Chamber ACP; the Portuguese Association for Economic Development and Cooperation ELO; and the already mentioned French CIAN, later to be chaired by the EDF director Jacques Ferrandi after his retirement. In total the Group of Seven represented the interests of some 1200 European companies.[18] The Group of Seven was regularly present in Brussels: its members used to take part in Commission meetings on behalf of the group or individually, as representatives of employers' organisations.[19] Some members of the Group of Seven also sat on the CDI's advisory board.

Due to the discretionary nature of the visits, neither the Commission's archives nor the interviews make it possible to trace the content of the meetings between DG VIII officials and representatives of the Group of Seven. However, one can note that, in their own name or under the umbrella of their national organisation or the Group of Seven, major European business representatives maintained close formal links and had 'very constructive exchanges' with Commission officials, as a former director-general of DG VIII remembers,[20] or as also recalled by another director at DG VIII:

> the CIAN was the only structured French private sector group known [to the Commission]. In Germany, there was the *Afrika Verein*. They were together under the Group of Seven, and they often came to Brussels, yes. I went to conferences very often, I had been to Hamburg. I knew the secretary-general of the Group of Seven, he was German. We would talk about the same things. We had very constructive exchanges with the European private sector, with the industrialists gathered under the CIAN or the Group of Seven.[21]

Contacts were made now and then and between counterparts: chairmen of employer's organisations traditionally met with the commissioner or his chief of staff, while experts often met DG VIII administrators on their own initiative. This was the case, for example, with Jean-Paul Gardinier. Coming from a family of French entrepreneurs specialised in agribusiness, he had developed an important activity in Africa.[22] At the invitation of DG VIII, he wrote different articles to share his 'expert' views on industrial cooperation in the bimonthly journal of DG VIII, the EEC-ACP *Courier*.[23] Gardinier's presence in this privileged communication tool, the only regular and long-term publication with a wide audience in professional, academic and private circles, both in ACP countries and in Europe, suggests that the Commission valued the voice of European industrial investors.[24] The example of Gardinier illustrates the extent to which EEC-ACP cooperation networks were interconnected: he was also a member of the French investors' group CIAN, and he subsequently published further on industrial development in Africa.[25] In February 1977, he attended the public consultation meeting on the fertilisers sector at the United Nations Industrial Development Organisation in Vienna on behalf of his company, and became a member of the CDI's advisory board in 1980.[26] With other European industrialists, he attended meetings in Brussels in 1975 and 1976 with Commissioner Cheysson (1973–1981) for the French Centre français de promotion industrielle en Afrique (CEPIA), a structure he also chaired as vice-president.[27] The Commissioner met with seventeen European businessmen from industrial federations (Fédération des entreprises de Belgique, Conseil national du patronat français (CNPF), Confindustria and Verbond van nederlandse ondernemingen, among others) or companies (Unilever, among others), individually present in Brussels or in other confederations.[28] For observers in the Commission, the logic was simple:

> the few [European] industrialists present in Africa realised that there was money to be made. As they were few in number, they were always in Brussels. To share the cake […]. From the beginning, there was no room for [ACP] industry. Industrial cooperation was really a gift, but rather a European gift, rather a Franco-French gift, for the few French companies there.[29]

For European industrialists from the Group of Seven, coming to Brussels was

> not a way to bring in new companies, it was a way to protect their existing interests against other companies.[30]

There were—and still are—other institutionalised private sector networks in Brussels. One such network is the UNICE, the Union of Industrial and Employers' Confederations of Europe (renamed in 2007 Business Europe), a pressure group that acts both at Commission level and at member states level via the national organisations it represents.[31] UNICE represents above all large industrial employers, that is, only some of the European (and, until the EEC's enlargement to include the United Kingdom, in particular French) employers in the 1970s.[32] Through UNICE, French employers were also present in Brussels and able to intervene and defend market-oriented interests in the cooperation framework with African countries.[33]

Minutes of the meetings have kept track of the position of the European employers' confederations since 1975 on the issue of EEC industrial cooperation with African countries. A common 'European private sector' message emerged in the 1970s that supported the Commission's efforts in deepening industrial cooperation policy. Their common message also called on ACP states to improve guarantee conditions for their own investments in ACP countries. One meeting at the Commission in particular between DG VIII and UNICE's elected members in 1975 is illustrative of the extent to which European business circles had a strong voice in defining a (theoretically) joint ACP-EEC industrial cooperation policy. On 24 July 1975, Commissioner Cheysson set out the aims and tools of industrial cooperation as he saw it. The few European industrialists that were present responded that they commended the work of DG VIII: the paragraphs on industrial cooperation in the Lomé Convention were of direct interest to European businesses who felt that they were rightly taken into account. The industrialists stressed the need to ensure that the CDI (in preparation until 1977) became fully operational. They also suggested that the CDI should involve European private operators even more closely so that cooperation policies would not rely only on the activities of public authorities. The industrialists, including Jean-Paul Gardinier, also expressed their disappointment that the level of protection of foreign investments in Africa was insufficient in relation to the political and economic risks European businesses were running in African countries. They consequently asked DG VIII to reflect on the creation of a common 'guarantee system'.[34] Commissioner Cheysson insisted he was counting on the European private sector to co-define EEC-ACP policies and asked UNICE representatives to remain the Commission's 'natural interlocutor'.[35] Cheysson used his background as a former industrialist (he was head of the Compagnie des potasses du Congo until 1973) to ensure that the European private sector representatives supported and maintained a common language.[36] In the commissioner's discourse, the European private sector had to be a major actor in development; the role of public authorities had then already been limited to simply 'guide, protect and facilitate' European businesses in ACP countries for their development.[37] At another meeting the same year, Cheysson recommended to European industrialists that they meet directly, officially or unofficially, with those, among the ACP countries, that were at the time most favourable to industrialisation through European private investment: mainly Senegal, Côte d'Ivoire and Cameroon.[38]

Meetings with European employers gave DG VIII a role of facilitating contact between ACP authorities willing to industrialise and investors wishing to maintain or develop their activities in African countries. In 1975, industrial cooperation policy had to be defined and it took the shape mainly given to it by the dialogue between DG VIII and European industrialists. In January 1976 UNICE sent a note to the Community suggesting a list of European businessmen to sit on what would become the CDI's advisory board.[39] Indeed, after this proposal, the CDI's advisory board mostly included industrialists selected by UNICE. UNICE would later continue to support DG VIII's work in the field of industrial cooperation.[40]

In the 1970s, the employers' confederations expressed an interest in industrial cooperation with ACP States. European industrial sectors were directly concerned as the discussions dealt with a possible Community harmonisation of business conduct rules, investment protection measures and, in the long term, a relocalisation of the EEC's industrial sectors in the Southern countries. These are subjects on which European member states' confederations exceptionally agreed, in the event that the redeployment of European industries would take place in Africa, as suggested by the Commission in the 1970s.[41]

As an institutional go-between, DG VIII also addressed messages from European business groups directly to ACP states. One of the ways to transfer messages was through the EEC-ACP cooperation journal, the *Courier*, which was published every two months. Around 60,000 copies were circulated among economic and political circles interested in cooperation issues.[42] Since 1975, several issues of the magazine have featured the voice of the European private sector, and expressed the expectations of industrialists regarding the situation of their investments in ACP States. The contributors included the lobby Centre européen pour le développement industriel et la mise en valeur de l'outremer led by former French governor in Guinea Roland Pré, and founded by the presidents of the metallurgical firm Pechiney (Raoul de Vitry) and Fiat (M. Valletta);[43] the Federal Association of German Industry; the Dutch Federation of Employers' Organisations; the British company Bookers Ltd.; the International Merchant and Financial Corporation, exporter of industrial machinery;[44] Danish investors;[45] and investors from the Italian organ-isation Confindustria.[46] They had a common message that opposed the New International Economic Order debates: they criticised the major NIEO conferences in the 1960s and 1970s in Caracas, Lima, Geneva and Paris, which were to them 'unnecessary provocations' and failures.[47] They strongly recommended that developing countries maintain close economic ties with the North and broaden their cooperation with the EEC by welcoming its firms and its investments. In the articles, indus-trialists point to the inconvenient paradox faced by the businesses they represent: if companies are regarded with suspicion by public authorities, they are also deemed necessary as a source of capital. In the *Courier*, their articles argue at length for the need for African countries to welcome for-eign investments and to secure them by clearly announcing any change in advance of fiscal or political measures (i.e. expropriation, nationalisation, or international disputes). Taking opportunity of the *Courier* as a medium for dialogue, European business representatives also discussed their needs as far as their markets in African countries were concerned; industrial cooperation policy could not be for the sole benefit of ACP states. The Italian Confindustria and the Institute for the Reconstruction of Italian Industry (IRI) for example, speaking on behalf of the Italian oil company Ente Nazionale Idrocarburi (ENI), the automobile manufacturer Fiat and other particular factories, did not hide their need for direct access to raw material markets in ACP countries, and declared that they would rather develop processing chains to meet their own supply needs than support small and medium-sized enterprises in the ACP countries.[48]

Through industrial cooperation, development aid was only secondary to industrial benefit. In the early years of EEC-ACP industrial coopera-tion, their proximity to development cooperation was such that European private sector representatives expressed their views, in the form of good practices, on what they needed to see emerge in the ACP states. Their message to the officials of DG VIII was strongly in favour of private initia-tive at a time when African countries were increasingly turning to planned and state-directed economies. The few industrialists often present in Brussels called for Europe to affirm the principles of free enterprise in ACP countries and to encourage reducing barriers to private initiatives of any kind. French industrialist Jean-Paul Gardinier wrote such articles in the *Courier*[49] at a time when he was representing the CEPIA and the Société de promotion et de gestion industrielle,[50] and serving as a European expert on the CDI advisory committee. It was while wearing those many hats and in a personal capacity that he advocated the need to develop European private investment in Africa even when these investments were not oriented towards the national development plan desired by the ACP states. Such a message moved industrial cooperation away from its basic principle as stated by the Commission in 1975, namely respect for the sovereign political and economic choices of the ACP states. For the sake of simplification and in a rather paternalistic tone, Gardinier opposed the 'bad' ACP state and commended the 'good' ACP neighbour which would understand that foreign investors must be given a 'warm welcome', offering guarantees, security, confidence, infrastructure, energy and even—more prosaically—schools, hotels and neighbourhoods for expatriates. During the 1970s, although different private sectors (from different European countries) were at play, European businesses' representatives who had the opportunity to speak individually or collectively all agreed on the content of the messages to be sent to ACP states through industrial cooperation. Therefore one could see a common European private sector approach as far as EEC-ACP business interests were concerned.

THE EUROPEAN COMMISSION BETWEEN EUROPEAN AND AFRICAN BUSINESSES IN THE LATE 1980s

While European businesses had an influence on the Commission at the birth of EEC-ACP industrial cooperation, it would be wrong to assume that the Commission was working solely in their favour. DG VIII's B4 unit, the Commission's unit in charge of private sector actions in ACP countries, set up an autonomous action in favour of African SMIs-SMEs in the late 1980s. The team, made up of only three administrators in the late 1970s, aimed at formulating a particular approach to development directed towards local ACP firms. This approach would on the one hand move traditional ACP-EEC cooperation away from a too strong focus on ACP public sector projects, that is, projects implemented by ACP ministries or other public structures. On the other hand, the DG VIII team's approach aimed at autonomous and local private sector development, and not only that which would benefit European companies.

Meanwhile, thought of as an innovative and ambitious tool, industrial cooperation faced difficulties from the very beginning. The partnership with the European Investment Bank on industrial cooperation was gradually called into question, as staff at the Bank and the Commission increasingly struggled to reach agreements on lending for industrial enterprises.[51]

The Commission was in charge of coordinating the activities and therefore introduced banking instruments (venture capital, interest subsidies, credit lines) to encourage investments by the EIB, considered reluctant to lend in ACP countries. In addition, the CDI, designed in 1975 as the vehicle for industrialisation in the ACP countries, was given limited resources in view of the ambitious objectives assigned to it, and the multi-layer complexity of its political structure did not facilitate its operational character. From the very first years of its launch, the complex nature of the CDI—dependent on the European member states, the 46 and then 58 ACP states—appeared to be a limit to the development of the Centre's activities.

On a parallel level, some local private sector experiments were being carried out by officials in unit B4 at DG VIII (unofficially referred to as the 'private sector' team) at the Commission in the late 1980s. At the time, public industrial promotion agencies and industrial development banks in the ACP countries were gradually put aside in favour of other sectors because they were state organisations, and international donors were increasingly favouring a general withdrawal from the state in economic affairs—an aspect of the growing trend of neoliberalism in development policies. According to the then administrators of the B4 unit at DG VIII, new ways needed to be found to include local SMIs-SMEs as existing arrangements were not working. Many of the industrial zones that had been established at significant cost were little or badly used by SMEs. At the same time banks had been pushed by African governments to provide loans that were too large to companies that did not 'deserve' them (and were unable to repay 'and manage a correct business').[52]

Following structural adjustment programmes in sub-Saharan African countries in the late 1980s, former state-owned sectors became liberalised and private initiative was more and more promoted in public discourse. The Commission DG VIII's aligned progressively with neoliberalism, but the staff at unit B4—a Portuguese head of unit, his Italian deputy and a few policy officers—developed a deliberately 'restrictive' and protectionist approach to development.[53] Their approach was non-neoliberal in the sense that it was different from what would soon become the dominant model known as the 'Washington consensus' in the 1990s: the B4 team at DG VIII were in favour of giving local markets time to structure and of guaranteeing higher prices for producers, rather than advocating complete trade openness. Some of the civil servants of unit B4 had been working for DG VIII since 1970, and deliberately opposed the policies of the World Bank ('ultraliberal') or the European Investment Bank, which they considered too narrowly based on an overly simple logic of sheer economic profitability.[54]

The administrators of unit B4 were keen to support a policy specifically geared towards the development of SMIs-SMEs, rather than large African companies exporting to Europe, or European companies. Thus, these actors started to advocate measures to improve the situation of local businesses: economic measures (higher prices controlled by the state to provide farmers with more income, new services or infrastructure to create local and regulated markets) and changes in the financial system (to have more flexible financial institutions on credit and rates).[55] The B4 'private sector' unit developed this restrictive approach in an almost autonomous way, largely because its administrators were still personally committed to defending a traditional model of endogenous development inherited from a third-world context of the 1970s.[56] They belonged to a generation of traditional 'developers' at DG VIII. To them it was important to 'develop entrepreneurship' in African societies. SMEs were important, not only for their ability to create employment or strengthen a local economic fabric, but also because they would spread an entrepreneurial culture and skills.[57] As elsewhere, private sector development and entrepreneurship were becoming a top priority in Brussels: 'we need to change mentalities', the director of the CDI said in 1986.[58] They also aimed to create a 'development centred on man'[59] and to have a 'class of entrepreneurs' take root in Africa,[60] 'to produce entrepreneurs'[61] in a continent where the African entrepreneur was yet still to be seen and often considered 'non-existent'.[62]

At the end of the 1980s, DG VIII's unit B4 fostered, in its intermediary role between European investors and African countries, a Commission approach that focused on local development and employment. It thus detached from what could be interpreted as a former logic of serving European businesses' interests as primary objective. One particular programme in Mali, called 'Babougou N'Ci', is illustrative of the attempt of the unit's administrators to promote an alternative path for EEC-ACP cooperation. Launched in 1987, this programme aimed to develop a flourishing local private sector without connecting it to European businesses per se. The EDF provided Malian entrepreneurs with credit lines of 1.4 million ECU and 3.2 million ECU through an intermediary bank set up by DG VIII, bypassing the traditional channel of the EIB or the CDI.[63] The Commission tested this model by first offering direct support for

Malian companies in Segou. Officials at DG VIII believed that the region's Bambara people showed more 'cultural interest in business' and greater 'entrepreneurial capacity' than other African peoples.[64]

According to the Belgian project manager in Mali, the project in Mali represented a move away from a traditional orientation of European public subsidies to 'poorly-adapted industrialisation projects' that

> were always based on a sectoral approach, with 'white elephants' projects [whose cost of upkeep is not in line with how useful or valuable the item is], which never gave anything, [or] gave absurd things, paper mills in the middle of the bush or [...] all kinds of industrial development fantasies at forced march.[65]

Support to local entrepreneurship was thus conceived as a global project to create employment and growth and to respond to the consequences of structural adjustment plans in countries—here in Mali—where the state apparatus was asked to withdraw from prior prerogatives such as social services for the population. The project was considered by its administrators from unit B4 as paving a new way for European development aid, by focusing on African entrepreneurs and their SMEs, and not on the state as the traditional aid beneficiary. Concretely, the project offered young Malian graduates and unemployed people (who had bankable business projects) the opportunity to get a loan, repayable at lower rates than those usually charged by banks to create a private lucrative activity: crafts business, fish farming projects, new feed mills, or fish trade. The first innovation of the project, compared to usual DG VIII programmes, lay in the fact that the loan was not granted or managed by the European Bank. The EDF credit line (managed by the Commission) was made available directly to operators through a business support structure with branches in the capital of Mali and in the regions. The European project officer was administratively detached from the Ministry of Employment and Public Service in Mali. However, the choice of sending a project manager chosen by DG VIII rather than an authorising officer appointed by the Ministry allowed the Commission to free itself from the Malian public sector and hence to bypass the state.

The Mali experiment was quickly considered successful by the unit in charge at the Commission. After one year, about 1100 jobs had been officially created in more than 200 SMEs in the Ségou region alone, with investments redistributed to 1.2 billion CFA francs (1.8 million ECU).[66] After seven years, 4500 entrepreneurs had been identified, and 910 projects had been financed for 5.5 billion CFA francs (8.3 million ECU). Approximately 3600 direct jobs were said to have been created. Nearly 85% of the loans were repaid on time, and the teams in Mali were also seeing the beginning of savings: local private savings were gradually transformed into 'tontines' amounting to 1.3 billion CFA francs (2 million ECU).[67] The programme was replicated in other major cities in Mali: other branches were set up with increasing funding from the Commission,[68] in Bamako, Sikasso, Mopti, Kayes and Timbuktu. Attempts were made in Senegal, but a 'large-scale fraud' affair put an end to the experience there.[69] European financing to the projects in Mali stopped during the 1990s as the businesses were considered autonomous and because the Commission re-orientated funding from local development projects towards more large-scale and macroeconomic programmes.

A NEOLIBERAL VERSION OF BUSINESS SUPPORT IN THE 1990S—FOR ACP OR EUROPEAN COMPANIES?

Within DG VIII a larger-scale programme approach emerged from the 1990s onwards and can be illustrated within unit B4. According to an official working there at the time, 'there was a shift from a project approach to a more global economic policy approach with attention to budgetary framing',[70] involving larger objectives and sums of money. This change was in line with a more general evolution of European development policies increasingly aligned with the neoliberal paradigm of the Bretton Woods institutions. In addition, DG VIII had then already undergone a major generational change, with a new team of officials who kept close links to the World Bank.[71] After a renewal of industrial cooperation in Lomé II (1979–1984) and Lomé III (1985–1990), new priority was given to the private sector as a substitute for industrial cooperation under the Lomé IV Convention (1990–1995). But in the 1990s the approach was no longer the same as it used to be in 1975 (public industrial cooperation) nor as it had evolved during the 1980s (entailing loans and financial support to SMEs). In an article published in the *Courier*, the deputy head of unit B4 pointed out in 1991 that the Commission progressively intervened more and more at the macroeconomic level, providing grants and technical assistance in exchange for the adoption of national reforms to improve the fiscal and legal framework for business in ACP countries. The terminology 'private sector development', progressively used in lieu of the industrial cooperation of the 1980s, more and more resulted in macroeconomic reforms in ACP countries, and in less direct support to SMIs-SMEs. The very concept of private sector thus had become even more vague: was it still a question of favouring small African companies, or large European groups that had ties in ACP countries?

From 1990 onwards, with a view to defining more 'private sector development' programmes in African countries' national indicative programmes, the staff at unit B4 increased the number of missions to Africa at the request of European delegations or national authorising officers. One gets an impression of forced liberalisation: the team at B4 introduced private sector development programmes mainly in regimes that chose the path of liberalisation relatively late, after having rejected the market economy for a long time. This was, for example, the case for the Republic of Guinea under Sékou Touré before he changed his Marxist policy, for Ethiopia under Mengistu, Mozambique under Chissano, Tanzania, and the People's Republic of the Congo.

In the 1990s EEC-ACP programmes of private sector development in these poor countries increasingly corresponded to the dominant global paradigm. Unit B4 used this to its own advantage to get more attention, and thus more power, more projects and more funds. The team would strongly push private sector development projects but would not always take into account the local social and environmental dimensions. Projects were numerous and sometimes criticised by NGOs for the haste of their intervention—such as with projects to support teak industry, a rare wood, in the Caribbean:

for the teak industry sectors, we were told [by the NGOs], 'but you will destroy everything'. Okay, for one tree we would take fifty, but at least we would create market opportunities.[72]

Other examples abound: schemes to mass produce flowers in Ethiopia or Uganda, which were detrimental to the interests of local horticulturists;[73] support to fishermen on the shores of Lake Victoria in East Africa in the 1990s, where the introduction of the Nile perch in the 1960s had already caused major environmental and social damage.[74]

Private sector development projects increased in number in the late 1980s and in the early 1990s, whether financed by the European Commission (technical assistance, feasibility studies, on-lending of credit lines to local banks) or the EIB (venture capital investments, credit lines). In 1991 two thirds of the Bank's loans in ACP countries were directed towards private sector development projects,[75] and the EIB focused on supporting private companies, particularly in sub-Saharan Africa,[76] illustrating the extent to which private sector development had become relatively more important than industrial cooperation. The Bank's loans increased both in real and relative terms as credit lines to local banks that enabled companies to become self-financing. In 1992, 42% of the ACP activities of the Bank were granted to the ACP private sector. While only 30% of loans reached private companies between 1975 and 1987, the figures reached 84–90% in 1994.[77]

EIB loans in ACP countries (1989–1995)

Loans (M ECU)	1989	1990	1991	1992	1993	1994	1995
African countries	192,7	140	314,37	235,58	Unknown	Unknown	Unknown
Caribbean	44,43	5,2	56,10	5,8	Unknown	Unknown	Unknown
Pacific	21,3	2	11,4	0	Unknown	Unknown	Unknown
Total ACP	258,4	147,2	381,9	241	265	457	430
Total SMEs loans in ACP	46,2	65,2	59,98	101,22	50,3	163	71

Source: Annual reports of the ACP-EEC Council of ministers; eib.org

In line with the Commission's recommendations, it appears that the Bank tended to direct its investments mostly towards SMEs that would present clear export projects to Europe.[78] The reason for this choice was two-fold: when exporting, ACP operators would obtain currencies, precious tools against devalued local currencies,[79] and the Community countries would also secure access to raw materials and strengthen a policy of expanding into ACP markets.[80]

European business circles remained prominent around the Commission's DG VIII in order to guarantee their interests between and during the negotiations for the renewal of the various EU-ACP partnership agreements. During the 1990s DG VIII administrators increasingly harmonised the Community's development policies with the approaches of other international institutions, so that all would agree on ways to bring investment to Africa. On the eve of the new cooperation agreement, known as the 'Cotonou Agreement' and signed on June 23, 2000, some twenty-five years after the first Lomé Convention, DG VIII officials still liaise with the business community, yet less so with national representatives of industrial sectors than with larger multinationals that had interests in African markets and in the establishment of large free-trade areas.[81]

According to an official of the 'private sector' unit in 1998, contacts were made, for example, through organisations such as the French employers' organisation CNPF, but also with 'representatives of industries from Anglo-Saxon countries', with investment banks and development banks, 'which were also in the process of reorganising their investment system' towards Africa.[82] Contacts with the European business community were not only made out of sheer institutional courtesy, but also as a way of representing interests for some and of serving European employment for others. In the late 1990s, the involvement of private sector representatives was strong at an individual level, and some businessmen voluntarily worked closely with Commission officials to contribute to European policies, as reflected in the Community Strategy for Private Sector Development (1998).[83] For example, the lack of coherence of legal systems within the African continent kept the application of business law difficult, particularly for European companies wishing to establish themselves more firmly in Africa. At the end of the 1990s, a Commission head of unit worked with the CEO of a famous French hotel chain to create more interesting business environments in West Africa.[84] The Organisation pour l'harmonisation du droit des affaires en Afrique (OHADA), a system of business laws and implementing institutions, for one, was born this way, partly through the direct cooperation between European companies and Commission administrators, first in West Africa and then beyond:

OHADA's [future developments] were in part the result of [that hotel] group. The owner of [...] came to Brussels to ask for action on this. I still remember well, during the discussion, I asked that the [...] group co-finance OHADA, and the group brought in 4 million [ECU]. Which [...] was a tremendous boost for this small project. Many groups, especially in public construction, have been asked to support this project.[85]

There is no evidence of a European call to cooperate with ACP services in defining this Community strategy on private sector development. The reason, according to the officials of the unit in charge, lies in the undisputable absence of a structured African private sector,[86] and hence the necessary use of 'expertise' (or experience) of European companies that had been present on ACP markets for a long time. According to the newly-appointed head of the transformed 'private sector' unit in 1998, there were no private interlocutors for the Commission, particularly in Africa. In his words again, the entire private sector was a 'nightmare' to work with. The simplistic vision prevailed and justified the Commission setting aside the African private sector in the definition of programmes:

> Developing a private sector in Senegal or Côte d'Ivoire was a nightmare. Everything was very monopolised, difficult to break through, they were mafia structures, controlled by political authorities.[87]

After gradually replacing industrial cooperation with private sector development programmes in the 1990s and after formalising a Community strategy in 1998, the Commission transformed it into a constituent element of the EU-ACP relationship by 2000 and private sector development became a channel for the EU to push ACP liberalisation policies, and one of the three pillars of development policies in the Cotonou Agreement signed in 2000.[88] Cotonou has given the private sector an important and dual role in the EU-ACP relationship: on the one hand, it must play a leading role in developing ACP countries and in the fight against poverty, and on the other hand, it is called upon to be a new and full partner in the EU-ACP dialogue, alongside other non-state development actors.[89]

CONCLUSION

Established in 1975 to close the North-South industrial and economic gap, industrial cooperation was intended to promote the development of both small private and large public companies in ACP countries, to the co-benefit of European companies that were called upon to invest in ACP production sectors. To ensure the protection of their investments and access to raw materials, industrial groups from European countries developed strategies at a national and Community level, in particular in the form of the 'Group of Seven' and UNICE: this seems surprising in view of the conflicts described in Véronique Dimier's chapter over access to the EDF between German and French companies.

In the mid-1980s the Commission (pushed by the council of ministers) considered that industrial cooperation with ACP countries was not working well enough. The Commission gradually replaced it with reforms aimed at facilitating business frameworks in ACP countries and new support measures for private companies, in line with the principles of neoliberalism which developed in the late 1980s and extended also to the Commission's DG VIII.[90] At the end of the 1980s, the European private sector still exerted influence on DG VIII's decision-making, advocating the establishment of major sub-regional markets in the ACP countries and recognition of the role of international private investment in development, in line with the guidelines emerging from the EU-ACP Cotonou Partnership Agreement signed in 2000.

During the 1975–2000 timespan, the Commission acted as a go-between, defending more or less the interests of both European private companies and African companies, thanks to the administrators of the unit in charge of 'private sector' projects in ACP countries. Nevertheless, it appears that the private sector in question has never been clearly defined. Who was meant to benefit from industrial cooperation and then private sector development? Was it the European private sector as a source of investment for ACP countries, large public industrial firms in ACP countries, or local ACP small- and medium-sized (and micro-) enterprises? Since the 1990s, apart from a few projects such as Babougou N'Ci in Mali, European private sector development has consisted in improving the fiscal, legal and institutional context in the ACP countries in order to promote European investment, and not strictly speaking to promote a local economic and social development that would create direct employment. A post-colonial cooperation model in the 1970s serving European companies that were still present in former colonies, gave way in the 1990s to a situation of the Commission paving the way for other European and multinational companies in ACP 'colonies'.

Notes

1. The expression was coined in Algiers in 1973 by so-called developing countries, and officially used in UN General Assembly Resolution nr.3201 in December 1974. See Craig N. Murphy, *The Emergence of the NIEO Ideology* (Boulder, 1984).
2. Dieter Frisch, 'Eine neue Weltwirtschaftsordnung—aus der Sicht der EWG (March 11–13, 1977)', *Tutzinger Studien*, 1(1977), pp. 5–15. Dieter Frisch was then director of the studies department at DG VIII, and later became one of the Commission's prominent historic directors from 1982 to 1993.

3. ACP Secretariat Archives: file ACP/Ga.89/74 (Amb) res.doc. S/972/74 f(ACP25) (FIN 23), 'ACP Memorandum presented in Kingston', 23.07.1974.

4. Dieter Frisch, 'Eine neue Weltwirtschaftsordnung'.

5. To know more about the profile of key administrators for industrial cooperation at DG VIII such as Jean Durieux or André Huybrechts, see Olivier Van den Bossche, 'Lomé et la coopération industrielle CEE-ACP en 1975: entre Nouvel ordre économique international et poursuite des intérêts industriels européens', *Journal of European Integration History*, 25, no. 2 (2019), pp. 243–262.

6. All interviews have been anonymised. Some of this chapter's arguments can also be found in the PhD dissertation: Olivier Van den Bossche, 'Entreprendre pour le développement. A history of EU-ACP private sector development policies (1975–2000)', Doctorate in contemporary history, Paris III—Sorbonne Nouvelle, Paris, 2018.

7. Historical Archives of the European Union (HAEU) in Florence and Brussels, and ACP archives from the ACP Secretariat in Brussels.

8. HAEU, BAC 542/2004-2, 'Déclaration de la CEE du 28 avril 1976, Coopération industrielle, approche générale', p. 1.

9. Industrial cooperation amounts to 830 million ECU on December 31, 1979 for the development of production sectors (Annual report of the ACP-EEC Council of Ministers 1976–1980, p. 135). For an analysis of the first years, see: Guia Migani, 'The EEC and the Challenge of the ACP States' Industrialization, 1972–1975', in Christian Grabas, Alexander Nützenadel (eds.), *Industrial Policy in Europe after 1945: Wealth, Power and Economic Development in the Cold War* (New York, 2014), pp. 256–276.

10. The European Investment Bank's investment projects in ACP countries from 1975 to 1980 only represent 4,5% of all EIB global loans, that is, 546 million ECU out of the 12,580 billion ECU (http://www.eib.org/en/projects/loan/list/).

11. See Éric Bussière, Michel Dumoulin, Éric Willaert (eds.), *La banque de l'Union européenne. La BEI, 1958–2008* (Luxembourg, 2008).

12. The word 'businessmen' can be kept because only three women would sit on the advisory board from 1975 to 1988. Designated for a five-year mandate, there are sixteen advisory board members until 1984 and twenty-four in 1985. All subsequent information can be found in the annual reports of the ACP-EEC council of ministers and in the bi-monthly *Business opportunities* bulletin.

13. *The Courier*, 60 (1980), pp. 93–94.

14. Robert Lemaignen was vice-president of the economic commission of the organisation of the French employers' organisation CNPF, vice-president

of the International chamber of Commerce (1942–1958) and board member of the Compagnie de l'Afrique orientale et la Banque d'Afrique occidentale. He worked for the Société commerciale d'affrètements et de commission, the Société commerciale des ports de l'Afrique occidentale, and played an unofficial role in the Rome Treaty negotiations. See Guia Migani, 'The Commissioner Robert Lemaignen and the African States: the Origins of the European Development Policy (1958–1961)', *Historische Mitteilungen der Ranke-Gesellschaft*, vol. 18 (2005), pp. 150–161; Claude Malon, 'Le Havre colonial, de 1800 à 1960 (Lille, 2003), p. 305; Guia Migani, *La France et l'Afrique sub-saharienne, 1957–1963* (Bruxelles, 2008); J.-M. Palayret and A. Legendre, 'Interview with Jacques Ferrandi' (28 May 2004–29 May 2004). The European Commission 1973–1986. Memories of an institution Collection.

15. Véronique Dimier, *The Invention of a European Development Aid Bureaucracy: Recycling empire* (Basingstoke, 2014), pp. 19, 55.

16. Catherine Hodeir, *Stratégie d'Empire. Le grand patronat face à la décolonisation, 1945–1963* (Paris, 2003), pp. 72–73.

17. Following European enlargements, this lobby group becomes the Business Council Europe-Africa-Mediterranean in the 1990s and the European Business Council for Africa and the Mediterranean.

18. *Marchés tropicaux*, 18.11.1988, p. 3184.

19. *The Courier*, 74 (1982), 136 (1992).

20. Interview, 25 January 2018, Brussels.

21. Interview, 14 April 2017, Brussels.

22. Before or after Africa's independence waves (insufficient evidence).

23. *The Courier*, 60 (1980), pp. 91–92.

24. In 1978, about 57,000 copies were published every two months. In 1981, 78,500 copies were sent in European and ACP countries (ACP-CEE annual reports of technical and financial cooperation 1978 and 1981); interview, 14 April 2016, Brussels.

25. See for example Jean-Paul Gardinier, *Le pari industriel de l'Afrique* (Paris, 1977).

26. HAEU, BAC 542/2004–2, Mission report '1re réunion de consultation sur le secteur de l'engrais à Vienne dans le cadre de l'ONUDI du 17 au 21 février 1977—Annexe 1 liste de participants'.

27. CEPIA was created in 1972 by Paul Huvelin, president of the French employers' organisation CNPF (1966–1972), and aimed to create French-African joint ventures, just as the Centre for the Development of Industry would do three years later. Quoted by Jean-François Bayart, *La politique africaine de François Mitterrand: essai* (Paris, 1984); Abdoulaye Diarra, *La gauche française et l'Afrique subsaharienne. Colonisation, décolonisation, coopération, XIXe–XXe siècles* (Paris, 2014), p. 89.

28. HAEU, BAC 542/2004–2, Reports 'Meetings with Commissioner Cheysson, 24.07.1975 and 31.05.1976'.
29. Interview, 13 October 2017, Paris.
30. Interview, 25 January 2018, Brussels.
31. Lucia Segreto, 'L'UNICE et la construction européenne (1947–1959)', in Antonio Varsori, Guia Migani (eds.), *Europe in the International Arena during the 1970s. Entering a Different World* (Brussels, 2011), pp. 195–208.
32. Yohann Morival, 'La fabrique des légitimités européennes: les acteurs de la confédération patronale européenne depuis 1952', *Critique internationale*, 6 January 2017, pp. 33–51; Yohann Morival, 'Passage à Bruxelles et structuration nationale de l'intérêt européen au sein du CNPF', *Relations internationales*, 2 (2014), p. 97.
33. The French employers' organisation CNPF expressed preference for African countries over Arab oil-exporting countries. See Anne-Marie Mureau, *L'Europe communautaire dans la négociation Nord-Sud* (Paris, Genève, 1984), p. 66.
34. The Community Guarantee system had already been subject to debate in the 1960s, and was discussed again in the 1970s and in the 1990s, but European member states could not agree on a common position. When a European common position was later found and presented to the Council in the 1990s, ACP countries ultimately did not accept it.
35. HAEU, BAC 542/2004–2, 'Compte-rendu de réunion avec le commissaire Cheysson', 24 July 1975.
36. *Journal officiel*, 'Décret du 30 janvier 1970 portant nomination du président et d'un membre du directoire de l'Entreprise minière et chimique', Paris, 1970.
37. HAEU, BAC 542/2004–1, VIII/A/1—SEK(76)165—8/92/76 (DIAL5), 'Actions des pouvoirs publics et rôle des opérateurs dans la coopération industrielle', 1976.
38. HAEU, BAC 542/2004–1, 'Réunion avec le commissaire Cheysson', 25 April 1975.
39. HAEU, BAC 129/1983–614 (1975–1976), 'Note by Bernard Sassen, Secretary general of UNICE to the Council of the European Community', 15 January1976.
40. HAEU, BAC 16/2001–43, 'Prises de position de l'UNICE envoyées par courrier à la DG VIII du 10 octobre 1978 et du 6 décembre 1978', 1978.
41. Anne-Marie Mureau, *L'Europe communautaire dans la négociation Nord-Sud*, p. 87.
42. Annual report of ACP-CEE technical and financial cooperation, 1978.
43. *The Courier*, 33 (1975).
44. *The Courier*, 39 (1976).
45. *The Courier*, 45 (1977).

46. *The Courier*, 51 (1978), pp. 10–14.
47. Ibid.
48. Ibid. About IRI, see Gioacchino Fraenkel-Haeberle, 'IRI and ENI—Instruments of development policy', *Intereconomics*, vol. 2, no. 5 (1967), pp. 136–139.
49. *The Courier*, 60 (1980).
50. He would stay close to political and economic circles: 'A huis clos au patronat français—Côte d'Ivoire', *La Lettre du Continent*, 25 November 2004.
51. Problems of liquidity and devaluation in African States in the 1980s made it more it difficult for the EIB to grant loans to African States.
52. Paolo Logli, 'Nouvelles approches pour les projets PME: le rôle des organismes intermédiaires' (in *The Courier*, 129 (1991), pp. 6–8).
53. Interview, 16 May 2016, Brussels; Interview, 6 June 2016, Brussels; Interview, 19 January 2017, Brussels.
54. Ibid.
55. Paolo Logli, 'Nouvelles approches pour les projets PME: le rôle des organismes intermédiaires'.
56. Véronique Dimier, '"Adieu les artistes, here are the managers": les réformes managériales au sein de la DG Développement de la Commission européenne', *Sociologie du travail*, vol. 52, no. 2 (2010), pp. 234–254.
57. Ibid.
58. *The Courier*, 95 (1986), p. 21. See also the article written by Jean-Louis Clavier and Jacques Lassort in *The Courier* 115 (1989), pp. 58–60, or Lord Plumb MEP's intervention at a EEC-ACP plenary session that highlights the importance to promote private sector and calls for the creation of an 'enterprise culture' in African countries (*The Courier*, 150 (1995), p. 5).
59. *The Courier*, 141 (1993), p. 50, recalls a 'development centred on man, not on institutions'.
60. *The Courier*, 122 (1990), p. 32. The annual report of the ACP-EEC council of ministers in 1990 recalls the new strategy launched by the CDI that consists in 'favouring the emergence of a new category of entrepreneurs in ACP countries, composed of businessmen [...]' (p. 63, our translation).
61. An article talks about 'producing entrepreneurs in Mali' (*The Courier*, 146 (1994), pp. 86–87).
62. Article by Vishnu Persaud, director at the Commonwealth Secretariat in *The Courier*, 115 (1989), pp. 63–65.
63. *The Courier*, 122 (1990), pp. 22–23.
64. Interview, 6 June 2016, Brussels.
65. Interview, 22 December 2017, Brussels; confirmed by another interview, 19 January 2017, Brussels.

66. *The Courier*, 122 (1990), pp. 22–23.
67. *The Courier*, 146 (1994), pp. 85–87.
68. *The Courier*, 131 (1992). The article recalls a new 13 million ECU funding (*News round-up*, p. VI).
69. Interview, 22 December 2017, Brussels; confirmed by another interview, 14 April 2017, Brussels.
70. Interview, 25 January 2018, Brussels.
71. Olivier Van den Bossche, 'Entreprendre pour le développement', pp. 194–204. These pages go back to the different ways ideas evolve between DG VIII and World Bank administrators: civil servants' 'exchanges' between Washington and Brussels, regular working groups, co-publications, common missions and so forth.
72. Interview, 21 September 2016, Brussels.
73. Ibid. For this example, see also Mark Langan, 'Uganda's flower farms and private sector development', *Development and change*, 42, no. 5 (2011), pp. 1207–1239.
74. *The Courier*, 136 (1992), p. 45.
75. Annual report of the ACP-EEC Council of ministers, 1991.
76. See the Annual reports of the ACP-EEC Council of ministers, from 1990 to 1995.
77. Annual report of the ACP-EEC Council of ministers, 1994.
78. Annual reports of the ACP-EEC Council of ministers 1990–1991.
79. Article proposed by the EIB, 'Financing the SMEs', *The Courier*, 115 (1989), pp. 66–69.
80. See the arguments in the European Commission's document 'European Community Support for the Private Sector in ACP Countries', June 1997, p. 21.
81. See, for example, the words of a multinational cement company with activities in Africa, who legitimates a development path that would imply reinforcing already large international companies: 'For leaders struggling to provide a better way of life for their people, big business was just another threat to be resisted. Fortunately, that view is changing. Developing countries have begun to see global corporations as part of the solution to the challenge of achieving sustainable development. Leaders have learned that multinational businesses can help address some of their problems […]. Business can help start a cycle that feeds development' (Efthimios O. Vidalis, 'Warming up for businesses', *The Courier*, 164 (1997), pp. 72–74).
82. Interview, 21 December 2016, Brussels.
83. Communication from the Commission to the Council and the European Parliament—*A European Community Strategy for Private Sector Development in ACP Countries*, COM (1998) 667.

84. Unilever, Shell and the Accor group are quoted (interview, 18 November 2016, Brussels; interview, 19 January 2017, Brussels).
85. Interview, 18 November 2016, Brussels. After a French model, the system was translated and extended to Lusophone countries in Africa.
86. Contrary to the private sector in Caribbean countries, for example, where private operators were supposedly more present.
87. Interview, 18 November 2016, Brussels.
88. In Cotonou (2000), growth is based on private sector development (1st pillar), social policies (2nd pillar) and regional integration (3rd pillar).
89. Articles 1, 2, 6, 10, 19, 20, 21, 22, 64 and Chap. 7 'Investment and private sector development support' in the partnership agreement (Cotonou) signed on 23 June 2000.
90. See Olivier Van den Bossche, 'Le développement du secteur privé en Afrique subsaharienne: le transfert d'une norme entre l'Europe et les pays ACP (1985–1990)', *Critique internationale*, 85, no. 4 (2019), pp. 125–143.

References

Bayart, Jean-François, *La politique africaine de François Mitterrand: essai* (Karthala, Paris, 1984).

Bussière, Eric, Michel Dumoulin, and Eric Willaert (eds.), *La banque de l'Union européenne. La BEI, 1958–2008* (Banque européenne d'investissement, Imp. Centrale, Luxembourg, 2008).

Diarra, Abdoulaye, *La gauche française et l'Afrique subsaharienne. Colonisation, décolonisation, coopération, XIXᵉ–XXᵉ siècles* (Karthala, Paris, 2014).

Dimier, Véronique, '"Adieu les artistes, here are the Managers": les réformes managériales au sein de la DG Développement de la Commission européenne', *Sociologie du travail*, 52, no. 2 (2010), pp. 234–254.

Dimier, Véronique, *The Invention of a European Development Aid Bureaucracy: Recycling Empire* (Palgrave Macmillan, Basingstoke, 2014).

Grabas, Christian, and Alexander Nützenadel (eds.), *Industrial Policy in Europe after 1945: Wealth, Power and Economic Development in the Cold War* (Palgrave Macmillan, New York, 2014).

Langan, Mark, 'Uganda's Flower Farms and Private Sector Development', *Development and Change*, 42, no. 5 (2011), pp. 1207–1239.

Migani, Guia, 'The Commissioner Robert Lemaignen and the African States: The Origins of the European Development Policy (1958–1961)', *Historische Mitteilungen der Ranke-Gesellschaft*, 18 (2005), pp. 150–161.

Migani, Guia, *La France et l'Afrique Sub-saharienne, 1957–1963* (P.I.E.-P. Lang, Bruxelles, 2008).

Morival, Yohann, 'La fabrique des légitimités européennes: les acteurs de la confédération patronale européenne depuis 1952', *Critique internationale*, 74, no. 1 (2017), pp. 33–51.

Morival, Yohann, 'Passage à Bruxelles et structuration nationale de l'intérêt européen au sein du CNPF', *Relations internationales*, 2 (2014), p. 97.

Mureau, Anne-Marie, *L'Europe communautaire dans la négociation Nord-Sud* (PUF, Institut universitaire de hautes études internationales, Paris, Genève, 1984).

Murphy, Craig N., *The Emergence of the NIEO Ideology* (Westview Press, Boulder, 1984).

Segreto, Lucia, 'L'UNICE et la construction européenne (1947–1959)', in Antonio Varsori, Guia Migani (dir.), *Europe in the International Arena During the 1970s. Entering a Different World* (PIE-Peter Lang, Bruxelles, 2011), pp. 195–208.

CHAPTER 12

Afterword

Véronique Dimier and Sarah Stockwell

> For every franc that goes to Zaïre, two francs are returned to Belgium. And that is a conservative estimate. One could probably demonstrate quite easily that for each franc leaving Belgium, three are returned.[1]

This remark by the Belgian economist Baudoin Piret reflects the critical climate of opinion increasingly common in the 1970s concerning external aid, including—as Abou Bamba shows in this volume—among an emergent African intellectual elite. That development aid can be a lucrative business emerges clearly from this volume. A larger question which has not been discussed here is whether development aid is principally driven by commercial considerations reflecting the interests of the donors and a small African elite among the recipients, or whether it indeed reflects genuinely altruistic developmental ambitions. Nor can there be any simple answer to this question. As shown by several scholars, the dynamics behind

V. Dimier (✉)
Université Libre de Bruxelles, Bruxelles, Belgium
e-mail: vdimier@ulb.ac.be

S. Stockwell
King's College London, London, UK
e-mail: sarah.stockwell@kcl.ac.uk

© The Author(s) 2020
V. Dimier, S. Stockwell (eds.), *The Business of Development in Post-Colonial Africa*, Cambridge Imperial and Post-Colonial Studies Series, https://doi.org/10.1007/978-3-030-51106-7_12

development aid varied according to time, the donor countries or agencies, their institutions and domestic politics, their values, and their economic, strategic, and geo-political interests.[2] In his reflections on Zaire, Piret concluded that aid was no more than the continuation of colonial domination and the interests behind it. This book focuses on precisely these continuities in development discourse, actors, and practice between the colonial and post-colonial eras, and how these bore upon the private-sector corporations that had interests in Africa.

Collectively, the contributions to this volume highlight the ways in which development discourse was instrumentalised by both expatriate firms and the old colonial powers. For the former, employing the rhetoric of development could be a means of maintaining their existing privileges in the changing context of African decolonisation and/or of exploiting new opportunities that arose in independent African states. Musso, Minton, Bamba, and Strick all show how firms used the language of development, both in relation to the colonial powers as Strick shows in the case of the Société générale de Belgique, and to cultivate good relations with the newly independent elite. They might try to frame, and sometimes succeeded in framing, development programmes. In these respects the chapters build on, and complement, a small body of existing literature discussed in the introduction that pioneered analysis of the ways in which business deployed development idioms and objectives to further its own interests. Cullen, Dilley, and Van den Bossche similarly explore the ways in which the development agendas of both the departing colonial powers and post-colonial African governments resonated with, and were adopted by, the private sector, but in this case at the level of business associations like the East African Association (Cullen), the Group of 7 (Van den Bossche), and the Federation of Commonwealth Chambers of Commerce (Dilley). In their accounts, two authors, Minton and Dilley, highlight the prominence of the concept of 'partnership' in business discourse and explore how the meanings attached to 'partnership' shifted with the changing political context. Minton's discussion of Shell-BP also reveals that it could be difficult for expatriate firms if their activities became too closely linked to the development ambitions of new states. In Nigeria, 'black gold hype' (the expectations surrounding the role that oil could play in Nigerian economic development) led to sometimes inflated ideas of what Shell-BP could achieve in the country among politicians at both a federal and regional level which had to be carefully managed.

For the former European colonial powers too, development pro-grammes were also a means of maintaining influence. While this was sought for a variety of reasons, including geopolitical, the ex-imperial states hoped that aid would benefit the private sector in their own countries.

Several chapters explore this theme of 'development as business' through analysis of various European development institutions. Pacquement and Stockwell focus on the Caisse centrale de coopération économique and the Commonwealth Development Corporation (CDC) respectively. Both bodies were originally established as vehicles for colonial development, designed to assist the metropolitan economies as much as the colonial ones, as the French and British sought to navigate their way through the political and financial aftermath of the Second World War. Both survived into the post-colonial era. Dimier concentrates on the European Development Fund (EDF) set up by the EEC on the eve of African decolonisation, and Van den Bossche on the Centre for the Development of Industry (CDI), formed specifically to deal with indus-trial development and financed by the EDF. The CDC, Proparco, a sub-sidiary created by the Caisse, and the CDI aimed specifically at assisting the development of the private sector in Africa.

However, whether CDC, the Caisse, and the CDI served as instru-ments also to assist British, French, and Belgian firms respectively is a mat-ter of debate. Stockwell shows that in the 1960s and 1970s British officials hoped that CDC would promote British trade and industry, but that this was a secondary rather than a primary goal and, in so far as British firms were privileged over other private-sector partners in CDC's projects, this was in some cases indirectly rather than deliberately. In contrast, Dimier shows that the EDF, although a European rather than a French body, proved particularly in its early years to be a very effective instrument for the promotion of French business, notably in the face of German competi-tion. At the same time, both Stockwell and Dimier show that as far as both CDC and the EDF were concerned, aid also contributed to opening for-mer French and British colonial space to other firms, whether (as in the EDF's case) those of other member states or of other foreign origin.

Bamba and Minton use country or sector case studies similarly to address the theme of 'development as business'. As Dimier has shown for the EDF, they also demonstrate that European states sought to advance the interests of their own national companies against potential competi-tors, including Americans in the case of the Ivory Coast (Bamba) and

Italians in the case of Algeria (Musso). As far as Bamba's analysis of the Ivorian case is concerned, there is no doubt: French aid evidently favoured French firms at the expense of local, African ones.

The balance of advantage did not all lie in one direction: African elites became masters in using this rivalry between donors to obtain funding and to perpetuate their clientelistic systems. As Bamba, Dimier, Minton, and Musso all show, development business could be instrumentalised by this elite to gain political support and enhance their own authority. Yet paradoxically, Minton and Bamba also demonstrate that the strategy pursued by independent African governments in Nigeria and the Ivory Coast to increase their political and economic autonomy eventually led to an increased rather than reduced reliance on French and British firms. For example, Minton reveals that when the British government proved unwilling to provide all the aid sought by the independent Nigerian government the latter turned instead to Shell-BP, thereby increasing the influence of the oil company. Clearly, African ambitions to build national economies based on local (African) firms and banks met with many obstacles. As variously discussed by Pacquement, Bamba, and Minton, these included the absence of an African professional class; an overdependence on former colonial powers for credit and technical assistance; and the predominance on the ground of firms from the colonial era that had long-established links to local elites.

Van den Bossche extends the analysis of these themes to the 1990s. At this point the neo-liberal approach followed by the World Bank and other donors, with its new focus on 'encouraging the private sector', blurred even further the line between the goals of promoting the private sector in developing countries on the one hand, and, on the other, advancing the interests of European firms. Was this a new attempt by development agencies to favour small African businesses, or a new strategy to facilitate investment from multinational corporations? There are grounds for concluding that the neo-liberal turn of the EDF in the 1990s is encouraging investment by multinational corporations, whose nationality is more and more unclear. We might suggest that if a decolonisation of old colonial interests eventually occurred, it saw a new set of expatriate firms benefit: multinationals. Was this a new colonial turn or simply the extension of a new kind of capitalism?

If bringing together in one volume historical analyses of different European countries and different sectors reveals common themes and experiences, it also indicates some differences. While further research is needed before we can reach firm conclusions, some variations in the extent to which each country prioritised the interests of the private sector emerge. France appears as quite an effective champion of French business. The evidence that emerges in the British case is more mixed, although several instruments of British aid policy were specifically intended to promote British exports, and, more generally, there was a presumption that bilateral aid should assist British trade and industry.[3]

The extent to which the experiences of firms operating in different sectors diverged is more readily apparent. Development programmes dovetailed with the interests of firms in some sectors more than in others. As Bamba shows, firms working in construction were notable beneficiaries of post-colonial investment in prestige infrastructure and building projects. Because European oil firms had the capital and the expertise new states needed, oil companies also enjoyed particular advantages in their dealings with post-colonial governments. Oil companies were also more likely than those in almost any other sector to command the support of their home governments. Nonetheless, as Musso argues, the fixed nature of the asset—oil—and the international community's dependence on it meant that the balance of advantage was far from lying all in one direction. Rather, Algerian elites were able to play off foreign firms against one another and, ultimately, assert their own national interests. A distinction can also be drawn between businesses that manufactured goods for export to Africa and the old-style mercantile firms that had dominated African external trade in the colonial era. Some of the former became involved in new manufacturing enterprises in African states, capitalising on the willingness of new regimes to shelter infant industries behind protective tariff regimes. Like mining and oil companies, these firms had the capital and expertise new states needed. Some of the old mercantile firms also began diversifying into manufacturing, as they sought to protect their established market shares, but they did not necessarily have the same expertise as European manufacturing firms. As others have shown, this strategy met with mixed success.[4]

As this reminds us, post-colonial Africa was by no means uniformly regarded as a land of opportunity. Indeed, in the post-war era it was precisely because of the difficulties of attracting private-sector investment to Africa that state initiatives were perceived as necessary. CDC, for example, was intended to engage in projects where the private sector was unlikely or willing to do so. As Stockwell discusses, it was the lack of sufficient British private-sector capital that led the British government in the late colonial period also to welcome American investment in British colonies. Pacquement reminds us that in the 1950s Africa was still considered a 'continent with limited economic prospects'. Moreover, in the later 1960s and 1970s investors faced new uncertainties and challenges in Africa. This was a consequence of the political instability of many post-colonial African states, and of regime change that brought governments to power that were more willing to compel the transfer of management and ownership of foreign enterprises to local hands.[5]

The significance to business decision-making of this environment emerges especially clearly in Dilley's chapter. Dilley shows that an attempt by the Federation of Commonwealth Chambers of Commerce to pivot towards Africa ultimately failed as it ran counter to the interests of the established members of the Federation located in Britain as well as the older, white, Commonwealth countries. As he comments, the Federation's embrace of development as it oriented towards Africa lacked 'economic rationale'. This was powerfully illustrated by the lack of interest among non-African chambers in attending two gatherings which the Federation planned to hold in Lagos and Nairobi: neither offered sufficient opportunities for business networking to make attendance worthwhile. Despite this, the choice of these two locations was no coincidence: in the 1960s Nigeria and Kenya appeared to offer some of the best opportunities for foreign business. In her chapter, Cullen notes that in Kenya, despite an initial nervousness among British firms around the time of independence, expatriate businesses recovered some confidence. The market potential of small, less developed African states was much less, and they were correspondingly less attractive to the foreign private sector. The uneven appeal to foreign investors in different sectors helped give rise, as Dilley observes, to 'enclave economies'.

Inevitably, this volume raises as many questions as it answers. How far some of the insights gained from studies of French, British, Italian, and Belgian firms also apply in the case of Portugal, the other key European colonial power in Africa, must await further study. One question that deserves further investigation is whether, within the neo-patrimonial state emerging in most African countries after 1960, European firms were clients or patrons. What is certain is that they participated in a system which encouraged corruption, as Dimier shows in the case of the Mannesmann affair. Further analysis is needed to show how businesses built their networks and to what extent—as recently discussed by Fantini and

Puddu—they may have contributed in the long term to the consolidation of neo-patrimonial and authoritarian states.[6] With the exception of Van den Bossche's chapter, our analysis has also focused on the early post-colonial period of state-led development. It would be worth seeing how private actors involved in development businesses became more diversified over the years, especially in the 1990s with the advent of result-oriented approaches, the discourse on good governance, and collaboration with 'civil society'. Consultancy firms, audits, and NGOs saw their role enhanced with evaluation processes and the multiplicity of funding opportunities. To some extent, they enlarged the number of competing interests in the world of development business.[7] These issues await more scholarly analysis. Yet we hope that this volume illustrates the value to be gleaned from bringing together business and development, two subjects that have more typically been discussed in separate historiographies, stimulating further research and discussion.

NOTES

1. Baudoin Piret, 'Le sous-développement du Zaïre vu à travers la balance des paiements Belgique-Zaïre', *Contradictions*, 15–16 (1978, p. 189. Quoted in Guy Vanthemsche, *Belgium and the Congo, 1885–1980* (Cambridge, 2012), p. 259.
2. On this debate see: Thorsten B. Olesen, Helge Pharo, and Kristian Paaskesen, 'Conclusion: aid norms, foreign Policy and the domestic context', in Thorsten B. Olesen, Helge Pharo, and Kristian Paaskesen (eds.), *Saints and sinners. Official development aid and its dynamics in a historical and comparative perspective* (Akademica Forlag, 2013), pp. 329–365; Olav Stokke, 'The changing international and conceptual environments of development cooperation', in Paul Hoebink and Olav Stokke (eds.), *Perspectives on European Development Cooperation. Policy and performance of individual donor countries and the EU* (Abingdon, 2005), pp. 38–41; C. Lancaster, *Foreign aid. Diplomacy, development, domestic politics* (Chicago, 2006).
3. Oliver Morrissey's argument is relevant here. He argues that even in the 1980s when aid policy was more commercial, British business was unable to exert much influence over policy, and did not benefit as much from support from the British government as foreign companies did from theirs: 'Commercialization of British Aid: Business Interests and the UK Aid Budget 1978–1988', *Development Policy Review*, 8, no. 3 (1990), pp. 301–322, esp. 319.

4. David Fieldhouse, *Merchant Capital and Economic Decolonization. The United Africa Company 1929–1989* (Oxford, 1994).
5. Albeit as Chibuike U. Uche has shown for Nigeria, British companies with the support of their government sought to frustrate such measures: 'British Government, British Businesses, and the Indigenization Exercises in Post-Independence Nigeria', *Business History Review*, 86, no. 4 (2012), pp. 745–771; Nicholas J. White, 'Imperial Business Interests, Decolonization, and Post-Colonial Diversification' in Martin Thomas and Andrew S. Thompson (eds.), *The Oxford Handbook of the Ends of Empire* (Oxford, 2018), pp. 639–660, esp. 649.
6. Emanuele Fantini and Luca Puddu, 'Ethiopia and the international aid: development between high modernism and exceptional measures', in Tobias Hagmann, Filip Reyntjens (eds.), *Aid and authoritarianism in Africa. Development without Democracy* (London, 2016), pp. 91–108.
7. Philippe Lavigne-Delville, *Aide international et société civile au Niger* (Karthala, 2016).

References

Fantini, Emanuele, and Luca Puddu, 'Ethiopia and the International Aid: Development between High Modernism and Exceptional Measures', in Tobias Hagmann and Filip Reyntjens (eds.), *Aid and Authoritarianism in Africa. Development Without Democracy* (Zed books, London, 2016), pp. 91–108.

Fieldhouse, David K., *Merchant Capital and Economic Decolonization. The United Africa Company 1929–1989* (Oxford University Press, Oxford, 1994).

Lancaster, Carol, *Foreign Aid. Diplomacy, Development, Domestic Politics* (University of Chicago Press, Chicago, 2006).

Lavigne-Delville, Philippe, *Aide international et société civile au Niger* (Kathala, 2016).

Morrissey, Oliver, 'Commercialization of British Aid: Business Interests and the UK Aid Budget 1978–1988', *Development Policy Review*, 8, no. 3 (1990), pp. 301–322.

Olesen, Thorsten B., Helge Pharo, and Kristian Paaskesen, 'Conclusion: Aid Norms, Foreign Policy and the Domestic Context', in Thorsten B. Olesen, Helge Pharo, and Paaskesen Kristian (eds.), *Saints and Sinners. Official Development Aid and its Dynamics in a Historical and Comparative Perspective* (Akademica Forlag, Trondheim, 2013), pp. 329–365.

Stokke, Olav, 'The Changing International and Conceptual Environments of Development Cooperation', in Paul Hoebink and Stokke Olav (eds.), *Perspectives on European Development Cooperation. Policy and Performance of Individual Donor Countries and the EU* (Routledge, Abingdon, 2005), pp. 38–41.

Uche, Chibuike U., 'British Government, British Businesses, and the Indigenization Exercises in Post-Independence Nigeria', *Business History Review*, 86, no. 4 (2012), pp. 745–771.

Vanthemsche, Guy, *Belgium and the Congo, 1885–1980* (Cambridge University Press, Cambridge, 2012).

White, Nicholas J., 'Imperial Business Interests, Decolonization, and Post-Colonial Diversification', in Martin Thomas and Andrew S. Thompson (eds.), *The Oxford Handbook of the Ends of Empire* (Oxford University Press, Oxford, 2018), pp. 639–660.

Index[1]

A

AAMS, *see* Associated African and
    Malagasy States
Abelinga, 104
Accra, 45, 46, 77
ACP, *see* African Caribbean Pacific
    Group of States
ACP-EEC Council of Ministers,
    324n12, 326, 329n60
ACF—FAC, *see* Aid and
    Cooperation Fund
Adatig, 190–192, 206n41
AFD, *see* Agence Française de
    Développement
African Caribbean Pacific Group of
    States (ACP), 253, 261,
    267n36, 305–325
    Committee of Ambassadors,
      309
    cooperation with EU (*see* EU-ACP
      development cooperation)

African Chamber of
    Commerce, 45
Africanisation, 71, 81–83, 87,
    88, 213–216
    on the cheap, 221
    of customers, 218
    of executives, 220
    of ownership, 223–228
    of personnel, 219–223
Africanising banking,
    213–229
Afrika instituut, 311
Afrika Verein, 248, 254, 311
Agence Française de Développement
    (AFD), 14, 213, 214
Aggressive foreign policy,
    136
Aid and Cooperation Fund (ACF—
    FAC), 219, 224
Aiton, Sir A. J., 40–41
Algemene Bank Nederland, 80

---

[1] Note: Page numbers followed by 'n' refer to notes.

Milton Keynes UK
Ingram Content Group UK Ltd.
UKHW040154181024
449646UK00001B/1